THROUGH THE PRIESTLY MINISTRY
THE GIFT OF SALVATION

Through the
Priestly Ministry
the
Gift of Salvation

VOLUME 2

Messages of John Paul II
to Bishops, Priests and Deacons

Compiled and indexed by
the Daughters of St. Paul

ST. PAUL EDITIONS

Addresses reprinted with permission from *L'Osservatore Romano*, English Edition.

Library of Congress Cataloging in Publication Data

John Paul II, Pope, 1920-
Through the Priestly Ministry, the Gift of Salvation

Includes index.
1. Catholic Church—Doctrinal works—Catholic authors—
Addresses, essays, lectures.
I. Daughters of St. Paul. II. Title.
BX1755.J648   282   82-19528
                            AACR2

ISBN 0-8198-7341-1 cloth
     0-8198-7325-X paper

Printed in the U.S.A. by the Daughters of St. Paul
50 St. Paul's Ave., Boston, MA 02130

The Daughters of St. Paul are an international congregation of religious women serving the Church with the communications media.

CONTENTS

Catechesis, a Fundamental Task of the Church's Mission

The following are excerpts from a letter dated May 1, 1980, sent by the Holy Father to the Church in Hungary on the importance of catechesis in the Church's mission.

To Cardinal László Lékai, Archbishop of Esztergom, to the archbishops, bishops, the clergy, men and women religious and all the faithful of Hungary.

1. In December 1978, just a few weeks after my election to the supreme pontificate, I sent you a letter which brought you my greeting and my apostolic blessing as well as my fervid good wishes for you, Catholics, and for the whole noble Hungarian people. In the document I also recalled the particular historical and affective bonds that unite me with you, I exalted the great figure of St. Stephen, the father of your country and an apostle of Christ and of the Catholic Faith, and I expressed the hope that the Catholic Church, which had such an important part in the history of your nation, might continue also in the future to illuminate the spiritual face of Hungary.

2. At the beginning of April last year I received Cardinal László Lékai, surrounded by various prelates and by a group of priests and faithful gathered in Rome to celebrate the fourth centenary of the Hungarian College—united from the first years with the Germanic College—and the 50th anniversary of the erection of the Hungarian Ecclesiastical Institute: two institutions which have formed holy and learned priests, who not infrequently rose to high responsibilities in the Church.

Addressing those present, I stated among other things that I had learned with deep satisfaction that bishops and clergy are dedicating themselves, with special and increased commitment, to the formation of youth. I am now happy to see that, in addition to the Hungarian Ecclesiastical Institute, also the Hungarian College has resumed its activity with the presence of two seminarians sent to Rome to complete their ecclesiastical formation.

3. I also wish to recall that, during this first period of my pontificate, I have had the possibility to receive in private audience various prelates of yours and also groups of Hungarian pilgrims at the general audiences. I wish to express here, too, my joy at these meetings and the consolation they gave me.

4. I now feel it my duty to speak to you about a subject of prime importance for the life and development of the Catholic Church everywhere, and therefore also in Hungary, a subject that is particularly close to my heart: the catechesis of the faithful and especially of boys and girls and young people.

The Church has always considered catechesis one of her fundamental duties, which sprang from the final command of the risen Lord: to make disciples of all the nations, and teach them to observe everything that He had commanded. The Church, in her almost bimillenary life, has constantly dedicated her energies to this purpose.

Recalling merely the times nearest to us, I must say that the Popes gave an eminent place to catechesis in their pastoral solicitude. Paul VI served the catechism of the Church in an exemplary way with his preaching, his authoritative interpretation of the Second Vatican Ecumenical Council, which he considered the great catechism of modern times, and with his own life. Among the various documents he approved or issued, I wish to recall the Apostolic Exhortation *Evangelii nuntiandi* of December 8, 1975; and it was Paul VI who decided that catechesis, especially that addressed to children and to the young, should be the theme of the Fourth General Assembly of the Synod of Bishops, celebrated during the month of October 1977, in which I myself had the chance and the joy of participating.

This Synod worked in an exceptional atmosphere of hope and it saw with gratitude, in catechetical renewal a precious gift of the Holy Spirit to the modern Church, a gift to which Christian communities respond with generosity and dedication everywhere.

It was in the same atmosphere of faith and hope that on October 16, 1979, I addressed to bishops, to the clergy and to the faithful of the whole Church, my Apostolic Exhortation *Catechesi tradendae.*

In this document I took up again, substantially, the considerations which Pope Paul VI had prepared, utilizing the documentation left by the Synod, and which the unforgettable Pope John Paul I, a catechist par excellence, was about to publish when he was unexpectedly called to the Father's house.

5. It is not my intention to repeat what I wrote in my recent Exhortation; I recall here some points of special interest for the Church in Hungary, while I invite and exhort you to meditate on all the teaching contained in this document of mine.

In catechesis it is Christ, the Word Incarnate and the Son of God, that is taught, and everything else that is taught is in reference to Him. Only Christ is our Teacher; everyone else teaches to the extent to which he is His spokesman, permitting Christ to teach through his mouth.

Catechetical action is an absolutely fundamental task of the mission of the Church. The Church must dedicate her best energies to catechesis. This is an attitude of faith, and God will not fail to respond.

Catechesis, being first of all a way that must make possible a vital meeting with the Person of Christ by means of faith, comprises especially teaching of the doctrine of Christ, in order to initiate listeners—children, the young and adults—to the Christian life and to its enrichment. While it is true that to be Christians means saying "yes" to Jesus Christ, it should be remembered that this "yes" has two levels: it consists in abandonment to the Word of God, relying on it; but it also means, in a second phase, endeavoring to get to know better the deep meaning of this Word. Catechesis is necessary both for the maturing of the Christians' faith, and for their witness in the world.

The task of catechesis concerns the bishops in the first place. The Second Vatican Ecumenical Council already recalled this serious duty (CD 14) and the Fathers of the Fourth General Assembly of the Synod laid great stress on it. The bishops are the very first persons responsible for catechesis; you, dear brothers in the episcopate, are catechists par excellence. The commitment of promoting an active and efficacious catechesis must not take second place to any other concern. Your main role will be that of arousing and maintaining in your churches a real passion for catechesis, a passion that is incarnated in an adequate and efficient organization. If catechesis is carried out well in the local churches, all the rest will be done more easily.

As for you, *priests,* this is a field in which you are the direct collaborators of your bishops. You are "educators in faith" (PO 6). The Church expects of you that you will neglect no effort with regard to a well-structured and orderly catechetical work. All believers have the right to catechesis, all pastors have the duty to provide for it. Never, for lack of zeal, let the faithful remain without catechesis.

At the end of this letter of mine, I exhort you to turn your hearts to Him who is the main inspirer of all cate- chetical work, and of those who carry it out: the Holy Spirit. Catechesis, which is growth in faith and the matura- tion of the Christian life towards fullness, is a work that only He can bring forth and nourish in the Church. There- fore when the Church, and every member of it, carries out the mission of engaging in catechesis, she must be fully aware of acting as a living and docile instrument of the Holy Spirit. It should also be said that the desire to under- stand better the action of the Spirit and abandon ourselves more to Him, cannot but lead to a catechetical revival.

I willingly invoke on the catechizing Church in Hungary the Spirit of the Father and of the Son, and I beg Him to renew catechetical dynamism in it.

May the Virgin of Pentecost—"living catechism," "mother and model of catechists"—obtain all this for you through her most valuable intercession.

"May the Centenary of Evangelization Give a New Impulse to Your Faith"

On May 2, 1980, after the official welcoming ceremonies at N'djili airport, the Holy Father drove in a motorcade to Kinshasa Cathedral of "Notre Dame du Zaire." There he was awaited by about one thousand five hundred priests, religious and seminarians. After an address of homage by Cardinal Malula, John Paul II spoke as follows:

Blessed be Jesus Christ!

May God our Father and Jesus Christ our Lord grant you grace and peace!

May the Holy Spirit be your joy!

1. Dear brothers and sisters in Christ,

Your Archbishop, dear Cardinal Joseph Malula, has just now welcomed me on behalf of you all, bishops, priests, men and women religious, seminarians and laity of the archdiocese of Kinshasa and other Catholic communities of Zaire. I thank him heartily. He recalled the vitality of the Church in Zaire, a vitality that the Church of Rome knows and appreciates. And I, Bishop of Rome, had a great desire to come to you.

I come as servant of Jesus Christ, the invisible Head of the Church. I come as the Successor of the Apostle Peter, to whom Jesus said: "Strengthen your brothers"; then, three times: "Feed my lambs...tend my sheep" (Jn. 21:15-17), that is, the whole flock of my disciples. By the will of God, in spite of my unworthiness, I have inherited in my turn this task, which is that of the Pope, that is of the Father, that of the Vicar of Christ on earth, who presides over the unity in faith and charity.

CENTENARY CELEBRATION

2. In the very first place, I thank God with you for all that He has carried out in Zaire in a hundred years. Today I come to celebrate with you the centenary of evangelization, to look with you at the way traveled, a way that has known difficulties and sorrows, joys and hopes. A way of grace! The centenary enables us to assess better, in a way, the blessings of the Lord and the merits of your predecessors. And, supported by this Christian history, to start off again with new impetus.

Just a century ago, in fact, some missionaries, burning with love for Christ and for you, came to share with you the faith they had themselves received; they wished, right from the beginning, to implant the Church, set up a local Church with the Africans. The harvest was a large one. Your fathers accepted the Word of God with generosity and enthusiasm. Today the tree of the Church is firmly rooted in this country; its branches spread all over the country. Faith has become the lot of a considerable number of citizens of Zaire. From your Zairean families have come bishops, priests, sisters, catechists, committed lay people, who guide or support your communities. The Gospel has left its mark in life and in morals. God be praised! And blessed be all those who made this Church flourish, those who came from far away and those who were born in this country! Blessed be they who lead it today!

NEW STAGE OPENS

3. Dear friends, you have lived a first great stage, an irreversible stage. *A new stage* is open to you, a no less exalting one, even if it necessarily involves new trials, and perhaps temptations to discouragement. It is the stage of

perseverance, that in which it is necessary to pursue the *strengthening of faith*, the conversion, in depth, of souls and ways of life, so that they will correspond better and better to your sublime Christian vocation; not to mention evangelization which you must yourselves continue in sectors or environments where the Gospel is still unknown. As St. Peter wrote to the first generations of converts in the Diaspora, I say to you: "Gird up your minds...as he who called you is holy, be holy yourselves in all your conduct" (1 Pt. 1:13-16). The task of being a Christian never ends.

In this way the Church that is in Zaire will reach its full Christian and African maturity.

TO ENCOURAGE YOU

4. I know that *your bishops*—who are your pastors and your fathers—guide you clear-sightedly and courageously along these ways of the kingdom of God, as the exhortations, letters or appeals that they have addressed to you personally or collegially bear witness. I come to strengthen and encourage the ministry of these bishops who are my brothers. But at the same time, I come to encourage all Christian men and women of Kinshasa and Zaire.

I am happy that my first meeting, in this cathedral, is with the priests, men and women religious and seminarians. You have a very special place in the building up of the Church. Your ordination, your religious consecration, your call to the priesthood, are priceless graces. Give thanks to the Lord! Serve Him in joy, simplicity and purity of heart. You are destined, more than the other disciples of Christ, to be the salt that gives flavor, and the light that shines; I desired to have a long talk with priests, then with sisters, in the course of the coming days. But this very evening, I greet you with all my affection. My first word is a word of comfort, in the note of thanksgiving that is fitting for a centenary.

Priests, be happy to be ministers of Christ, proclaimers of His Word and dispensers of His mysteries: *"Imitamini quod tractatis,"* "Practice what you preach." Be educators to faith, men of prayer; have the zeal and humility of servants; live your complete consecration to the kingdom of God of which your celibacy is the sign.

THAT ALL MAY BE ONE

5. I must recommend to you all that the Apostle St. Paul expressed in all his letters, he who visited so many of the first Christian communities. It is the recommendation that inspired the last prayer of Jesus after the Last Supper: *"that they may all be one."* Yes, banish all division; live in the unity which pleases God and which is your strength, around your priests. And may the priests be united in their presbyterium around their bishops. Offer a kind welcome and real collaboration to one another, Zairean men and women, and to the foreigners who have come to share your life. The Church is a family from which no one is excluded.

Receiving your witness, I will bring you in my turn that of *the Church which is in Rome,* and that of *the universal Church* which has its center in Rome. It is one family. No community lives withdrawn within itself: it is connected with the great Church, the one Church. Your Church has been grafted onto the great tree of the Church, whence, for a hundred years, it has drawn its sap, which now enables it to give its fruits to her and to become a missionary to others itself. Your Church will have to deepen its local, African dimension, without ever forgetting its universal dimension. I know how fervently attached you are to the Pope. So I say to you: through him, remain united with the whole Church.

Now, I call upon you to turn, with me, your eyes and your hearts to the Virgin Mary.

ACT OF CONSECRATION

6. Allow me, in fact, in this year in which you are giving thanks to God for the centenary of evangelization and the baptism of your country, to refer to the tradition that we find at the beginning of this century, at the beginning of evangelization in the land of Africa.

The missionaries who came to proclaim the Gospel began their missionary service with an act of consecration to the Mother of Christ.

They addressed her as follows:

"Here we are, among those who are our brothers and our sisters, and whom your Son, O Virgin Mary, loved to the end. Out of love, He offered His life for them on the cross; out of love, He remains in the Eucharist to be the nourishment of souls; out of love, He founded the Church to be the unshakable community in which salvation is found. All this is still unknown to these brothers and these sisters among whom we arrive; they do not know yet the Good News of the Gospel. But we believe deeply that their hearts and their consciences are prepared to accept the Gospel of salvation thanks to the sacrifice of Christ, and also to your motherly intercession and mediation.

"We believe that, when Christ, from the cross, gave you every man as your son, in the person of His disciple, St. John, you also accepted as sons and daughters these brothers and these sisters to whom His holy Church sends us now, as missionaries.

"Help us to carry out the missionary mandate of your Son in this land; help us to carry out here the salvific mission of the Gospel and of the Church. We consecrate to you all those whom the Spirit of Jesus Christ wishes to illuminate with the light of faith and in whom He wishes to light the fire of His love. We consecrate to you their families, their tribes, the communities and societies they form, their work, their joys and their sufferings, their villages and their cities. We consecrate everything, we consecrate everyone to you. Accept them in this eternal love, whose first servant you were, and deign to guide, however unworthy it may be, the apostolic service that we are beginning."

FAITH AND TRUST

7. Today, a hundred years have passed since these beginnings. At the moment when the Church, in this country of Zaire, thanks God in the Holy Trinity for the waters of holy Baptism that gave salvation to so many of its sons and daughters, permit me, O Mother of Christ and Mother of the Church, permit me, Pope John Paul II, who has the privilege of taking part in this jubilee, to recall and at the same time renew this missionary consecration which took place in this land at the beginning of its evangelization.

To consecrate itself to Christ through you!

To consecrate itself to you for Christ!

Permit me also, O Mother of divine Grace, while expressing my thanks for all the light that the Church has received and for all the fruit she has yielded in this country of Zaire in the course of this century, to entrust this Church to you again, to place it in your hands again for the years and the centuries to come, to the end of time!

And at the same time, I entrust to you also the whole nation, which is living its own independent life today. I do so in the same spirit of faith and with the same trust as the first missionaries, and I do so at the same time with all the greater joy since the act of consecration and abandonment that I make now, is made with me at the same time by all the pastors of this Church and also by the whole People of God: this People of God that wishes to assume and continue with its pastors, in love and apostolic courage, the work of the construction of the Body of Christ and the approach of the kingdom of God on this earth.

Accept, O Mother, this act of trust of ours. Open hearts and give strength to souls to listen to the word of life and do what your Son constantly orders and urges us.

May grace and peace, justice and love be the lot of this people; giving thanks for the centenary of its faith and its baptism, may it look confidently towards its temporal and eternal future! Amen!

Bring the Authentic Gospel to the African Cultures

After the Mass for the family on May 3, 1980, John Paul II blessed the foundation stone of the Kinshasa Faculty of Theology. He then went to the nunciature and continued on foot to the interdiocesan center where he met the Zairean bishops to whom he gave the following address.

Beloved brothers in Christ,

1. What a joy for me to meet you all together! What a comfort! A century ago, it could be said that real evangelization was just beginning; and now today the Christian faith is implanted nearly everywhere in this country; the ecclesiastical hierarchy is organized; sons of this country — *ex hominibus assumpti*—have taken over the guidance of the Church, in union with the Church in Rome. The springing up of your Christian communities, the vitality of this People of God, is a miracle of grace which renews in our time what it did at the time of the Apostles Peter and Paul.

There have been stages, dates which no one can forget:

—the ordination of the first Zairean priest, Stefano Kaoze (1917);

—the consecration of the first Zairean bishop, Most Rev. Pierre Kimbondo (1956);

—the establishment of the hierarchy in Zaire (1959);

—the call of the first Zairean bishop to enter the Sacred College of Cardinals, Cardinal Joseph Malula (1969).

I have come to thank God with you, to celebrate the centenary of evangelization!

I have come to recognize with you the apostolic toil, patient and sagacious, of the many missionaries, bishops, priests, men and women religious. They loved you to the extent of dedicating their lives to initiating your fathers to the Gospel, a Gospel which they themselves had received through grace, and they had enough confidence in your forebears to consider them, too, capable of setting up a local Church, and to prepare its pastors. I have come to recognize the good work that you yourselves have undertaken, following them, or with them, to the extent to which they still offer you an indispensable service today. I have come to tell you of my respect, my esteem, my affection, for your persons, for your episcopal body, for the Church that gathers in your country. And I have come to strengthen your holy ministry, as Jesus asked Peter to do.

EVANGELIZATION CONTINUES

2. The aim of this ministry is still evangelization. It is the same for all countries, for old Christian communities as for the young Churches. For evangelization consists of stages and ever deeper levels, and it is a work to be resumed constantly. Certainly, about half of your fellow-citizens have joined the Church through Baptism; others are preparing to do so. But there is still a wide field of apostolate, in order that the light of the Gospel may also shine in the eyes of the others. Above all, it is necessary to bring about the penetration in depth of this Gospel in minds, in morals, in the daily faith and charity of persons, families and communities, and perseverance must be ensured. It was the problem that the Apostle Paul met with, in the communities he visited, and the Apostle John, in the communities that he sustained with his letters, to the third generation of Christians (cf. Rv. 1-3), or again my Predecessor, St. Clement of Rome. It was the problem known, too, to the courageous bishops of my nation, such as St. Stanislaus.

DOCUMENTS ON FAITH

3. In this connection, I have noticed the zeal, courage and cohesion that you have shown, to enlighten and guide your Christian people, when circumstances demanded it. For you have not been spared trials! For example, you drew up and published documents on faith in Jesus Christ in 1974, then "on the present situation." In 1977, you stimulated your faithful, "all jointly liable and responsible," to overcome discouragement and immorality. In the same year, you exhorted your priests, and men and women religious, to conversion. You even called your fellow-countrymen as a whole to bring about "the recovery of the nation." These acts of the episcopal conference, without counting those of bishops in their dioceses, show your sense of pastoral responsibility.

I hope with you that these appeals, together with the assiduous reading of the Word of God, will be taken up again, meditated upon and above all put into practice, in their consequences and with perseverance, by those whose consciences you wished to form or awaken. For, you know as I do, this education to faith calls not only for clear texts, but for closeness, a pedagogy which exploits this teaching, which convinces and sustains, with a patience and love inseparable from pastoral authority, thanks to priests and educators who themselves set an example. I wanted, with these simple words, to express to you appreciation and encouragement for your work of evangelization.

IMPORTANT ASPECTS

4. One of the aspects of this evangelization is the *inculturation* of the Gospel, the *Africanization* of the Church. Several people have told me that you set great store by it, and rightly so. That is part of the indispensable efforts to incarnate the message of Christ. The Gospel, certainly, is not identified with cultures, and transcends them all. But the kingdom that the Gospel proclaims is lived by men deeply tied to a culture; the construction of the

kingdom cannot dispense with borrowing elements of human cultures (cf. EN 20). Indeed, evangelization must help the latter to bring forth out of their own living tradition original expressions of Christian life, celebration and thought (cf. CT 53). You wish to be at once fully Christains and fully Africans. The Holy Spirit asks us to believe, in fact, that the leaven of the Gospel, in its authenticity, has the power to bring forth Christians in the different cultures, with all the riches of their heritage, purified and transfigured.

In this connection, the Second Vatican Council had expressed very well some principles which always throw light on the way to follow in this field: "The Church... fosters and takes to herself, insofar as they are good, the abilities, the resources and customs of peoples. In so taking them to herself, she purifies, strengthens and elevates them....

"In virtue of this catholicity, each part contributes its own gifts to other parts and to the whole Church, so that the whole and each of the parts are strengthened by the common sharing of all things and by the common effort to attain to fullness in unity....

"The Chair of Peter...presides over the whole assembly of charity, and protects their legitimate variety while at the same time taking care that these differences do not hinder unity, but rather contribute to it" (LG 13).

Africanization covers wide and deep fields, which have not yet been sufficiently explored, whether it is a question of the language to present the Christian message in a way that will reach the spirit and the heart of Zaireans, of catechesis, theological reflection, the most suitable expression in liturgy or sacred art, or community forms of Christian life.

WISDOM AND ALSO TIME

5. It is up to you, bishops, to promote and harmonize the advance in this field, after mature reflection, in con-

certed action among yourselves, in union also with the universal Church and with the Holy See. Inculturation, for the people as a whole, cannot be, moreover, but the fruit of gradual maturity in faith. For you are convinced as I am that this work, for which I am anxious to express to you all my confidence, requires a great deal of theological lucidity, spiritual discernment, wisdom and prudence, and also time.

Allow me to recall, among other examples, the experience of my own country. In Poland, a deep union has been established between the ways of thinking and living that characterize the nation and Catholicism; this impregnation took centuries. Here, taking into consideration a different situation, it should be possible for Christianity to unite with what is deepest in the Zairean soul for an original culture, at the same time African and Christian.

As regards faith and theology, everyone sees that important problems are at stake: the content of faith, the search for its best expression, the connection between theology and faith, the unity of faith. My venerated Predecessor Paul VI had referred to this matter at the end of the 1974 Synod (cf. AAS 66 [1974], pp. 636-637). And he had himself recalled certain rules to the delegates of SCEAM in September 1975:

"a) When it is a question of the Christian faith, it is necessary to abide by the 'identical, essential, constitutional heritage of Christ's own doctrine, professed by authentic tradition and authorized by the one, true Church';

"b) it is important to carry out a thorough investigation of the cultural traditions of the various populations, and of the philosophical ideas that underlie them, in order to detect elements that are not in contradiction with the Christian religion and the contributions that can enrich theological reflection" (AAS 67 [1975], p. 572).

Last year, in the exhortation on catechesis, I myself drew attention to the fact that the evangelical message cannot be isolated purely and simply from the biblical culture in which it took its place to begin with, nor even, without serious loss, from the cultures in which it was expressed throughout the centuries; and that on the other hand the power of the Gospel transforms and regenerates everywhere (cf. CT 53).

In the field of *catechesis*, presentations better suited to the African soul can and must be made, while at the same time taking into account the more and more frequent cultural exchanges with the rest of the world. Care must be taken simply that the work is carried out in a team and controlled by the episcopate, so that the expression may be correct and the whole doctrine may be presented.

In the field of sacred arts and the *liturgy*, a whole enrichment is possible (cf. SC 37-38), provided the meaning of the Christian rite is always preserved and that the universal, catholic element of the Church is clearly seen ("the substantial unity of the Roman rite"), in union with other local Churches and in agreement with the Holy See.

In the *ethical* field, all the resources of the African soul, which are, as it were, toothing stones of Christianity, must be highlighted. Paul VI had already recalled them in his message to Africa on October 29, 1967, and you know them better than anyone, as regards the spiritual view of life, the sense of the family and children, of community life, etc. As in all civilizations, there are other less favorable aspects.

Anyhow, as you recalled so well, there is always a conversion to be effected, in regard to the Person of Christ, the only Savior, and His teaching, such as the Church transmits it to us: it is then that the liberation, the purification, the transfiguration, the elevation that He came to bring and that He realized in His Paschal Mystery of death and resurrection takes place. It is necessary to consider both the Incarnation of Christ and His redemption. You yourselves made a point of specifying that recourse to authenticity does not permit "opposing the principles of Christian morality to those of traditional morality" (Letter of February 27, 1977). In a way, the Gospel satisfies human aspirations to the full, but by challenging man's depths in order to make him open to the call of grace and in particular to a more trusting approach to God, to a widened, universal human authenticity; it does not turn the African man away from his duty of conversion. In short, it is a question of becoming authentic Christians, authentically African.

MARRIAGE PROBLEMS

6. In this work of inculturation and the pursuit of indigenousness, already well begun, as in the work of evangelization as a whole, many particular questions will arise on the way, concerning such and such a custom—I am thinking in particular of the difficult problems of marriage—such and such a religious act, such and such a method. Difficult questions, the attempt to solve which is entrusted to your pastoral responsibility, to you bishops, in dialogue with Rome: you cannot abandon it—it calls in the first place for *perfect cohesion among you.* Each Church has its problems, but everywhere—I am not afraid of repeating, as I said to the Polish bishops—"It is this unity which is the source of spiritual strength." This solidarity applies to all fields: research, great pastoral decisions, and also mutual esteem, whatever your origin may be, without forgetting mutual support, in the exemplary life which is asked of you and which may call for brotherly admonitions.

TRUSTING COMMUNION

7. It will not have escaped your notice either to what extent *solidarity with the universal Church* in things that must be common, and in particular *trusting communion with the Holy See,* are necessary for the Catholic authenticity of the Church in Zaire, for its strength and for its harmonious advance. But they are also necessary for the vitality of the universal Church, to which you will bring the testimony of your pastoral solicitude and the contribu-

tion of your evangelizing zeal, on important points for the whole Church. These are the requirements, or rather, the grace of our catholicity (cf. LG 13, quoted above). God be praised for allowing His Church this vital exchange and this communion between all the members of the same Body, the Body of Christ! The Holy See will not release you from any responsibility; on the contrary, it will drive home to you your responsibility, and it will help you to find the solutions most in keeping with your vocation. Personally, I am sure that your concerns will meet with understanding there.

CONCRETE PROBLEMS

8. Now, I would like to say a word also about some concrete pastoral problems: I recall them to show the share I take in your responsibility.

I have spoken of your unity among bishops, of your collegial co-responsibility which has stood the test of experience in particularly difficult moments. I also encourage you to stimulate as much as you can, in each of your dioceses, the unity of the living forces of evangelization, and in the first place of your priests. Some of them are Zaireans and it is very lucky for the future of your Church. Many others, secular and often religious priests, have come as "missionaries" or have stayed to help you, while they are aware that they must, as opportunities arise, yield the first place to indigenous pastors. You all recognize that their service was essential for the evangelization the centenary of which we are celebrating, and that it remains important and indispensable today, in view of the large number of the faithful and the complexity of apostolic needs. They remain among you, the expression of the universality and of necessary exchanges among Churches. Let them all, Zaireans or not, form only one presbyterium around you! Let everything be done to smooth and multiply the ways of mutual esteem, brotherhood and collaboration! Let everything be banished that would be the cause of suffering or exclusion, on both sides! Let everyone be penetrated with sentiments of humility and mutual service! For Christ! For the witness of the Church! Let everyone be able to say: "See how they love one another!" For the advance of evangelization! Progress has already been made. I am sure that you will do everything to create this atmosphere.

Furthermore, you have called all your priests and sisters several times to great dignity of life. I have noted a passage that you quoted in its poetic form: "You yourselves, be the first to reform. Be clad in virtues, not silk. Be chaste in body, simple in conscience. Both by night and by day, apply yourselves to study. Keep a humble dignity for the people and combine sweetness with earnestness" (Exhortation of June 10, 1977). Yes, the radical love that consecrated souls have dedicated to the Lord, for Himself and for a more available service for all their brothers and the proclamation of the world to come, with the discipline of life it demands, must shine forth like light, be like salt, maintain "within the People of God the indispensable 'tonus' which helps it to raise the human dough" *(ibid.)*. In particular, priests, religious men—and also sisters—must have strong convictions about the positive and essential values of chastity in celibacy, and be very vigilant in their behavior in order to be faithful without any ambiguity to this commitment that they have undertaken—for the Lord and for the Church—and which is essential, in Africa as elsewhere, as witness and to carry along the Christian people in the laborious march towards holiness. All that is possible with the grace of God, and particularly by taking to heart the spiritual means and the multiple needs which call for pastoral zeal. Priests are certainly in great need of your brotherly help, your closeness, your personal example, your affection.

PRIESTLY VOCATIONS

9. The holiness and zeal of your priests will also greatly facilitate the awakening of priestly vocations, and I

think I am touching here on one of your major concerns. How will the Church in Zaire face the future if it does not have more of its own priests, secular or religious? We must pray and get people to pray for that. We must "call" to the Lord's service, make families and young people understand the beauty of this service. But the problem is also that of the formation of these seminarians or novices: may they always be able to benefit from the presence, the dialogue and the example of spiritual directors, expert in the guidance of souls.

I believe, moreover, that many religious *vocations* have flourished among you, in the framework either of the missionary congregations, or now of institutes born on your soil. May they, thanks to a thorough formation, thanks to their dedication to apostolic works, thanks to their transparent witness, write a new page in the life of sisters in the Church! I do not forget the one who has left such a luminous trail that there has been talk of her beatification, Sister Anwarite.

ROLE OF CATECHISTS

10. I rejoice, too, at everything that has been done in this country to endow the Church with *lay catechists* and leaders of little communities, who are the mainsprings of evangelization, in constant and direct contact with families, children, and the different categories of the People of God. It is certainly necessary to promote all this deployment of the indispensable action of the laity, in close communion with the pastors. I will have the opportunity to deal with this subject at greater length in the course of my journey.

As regards *family life*, I spoke about it at length this morning. How to make the young and married couples progress towards the full realization of God's plan for spouses and parents, in spite of the difficulties that certainly exist, but relying at the same time on the resources of the African soul, on the centuries-old experience of the

Church and on grace—that is a pastoral aim of prime importance. It will be a blessing for the Church and an outstanding step forward for the country.

One thing that parents, pastors and all workers of evangelization must take to heart is *the religious education of children*, whatever the position of schools may be and particularly because of the present position: family initiation to the Gospel, continued by a systematic catechesis, as I set forth, following upon the Synod of Bishops, in the Exhortation *Catechesi tradendae*.

FOR THE COMMON GOOD

11. I am also thinking of the whole participation that the Church brings to the development of the country, not only by forming the conscience of citizens to the sense of loyalty, gratuitous service, work well done, brotherhood —which is directly her role—but by providing *on many planes* for the multiple needs of the populations, which are often aggravated by trials: on the plane of schools, medical care, means of subsistence, etc. Making good what is lacking in this way is a duty imposed by charity on the Church —*caritas urget nos*—which the sense of the common good of your country makes you accept as natural.

LOVE OF COUNTRY

12. You love this country deeply. I understand these feelings. You know the love I bear for the land in which I have my roots. The unity of a country is forged, furthermore, through trials and efforts in which Christians have their share, especially when they form a considerable part of the nation. Your service of God includes this love of your country. It contributes to the good of the country, just as the civil power is ordained to this on its own plane. But it is distinguished from the latter, and, while respecting its competence and responsibility, it must be able to exercise itself in full freedom, in its sphere which is the education to faith, the formation of consciences, religious

practice, the life of Christian communities, and the defense of the human person, of his freedoms and his rights, and of his dignity. I know that this has been your concern. And I hope that the result will be a peace beneficial to all.

RESEARCH AND TEACHING

13. A last point: to help the Christian elite to cope according to faith with the problems that a rapid evolution and the contact with other civilizations, other systems of thought, will not fail to raise, it is essential, on the theological plane, that research and teaching should be promoted in your country in the right way, that is, by combining with deep-rootedness in the tradition of the whole Church, which has given your community its sap, the reflection required by your African roots and the new problems that arise. This is to say, that I form fervent good wishes for your theology faculty at Kinshasa, for its high intellectual level, its ecclesial faithfulness and its influence in your country and beyond.

DIALOGUE TO CONTINUE

14. I will stop here today. But it is a dialogue that will always have to be continued with the Successor of Peter, with the authorities of the Holy See, and with other local Churches, which have only one concern: to enable the impetus of your Church to continue on its way under the best conditions, "quite openly and unhindered" (Acts 28:31). And I hope that this impetus will be of advantage not only to yourselves, but that it will be more and more *missionary*. "You are your own missionaries," Paul VI said at Kampala eleven years ago. It is partly realized. But I add: Aim at being missionaries in your turn, not only in this country where the Gospel is still awaited, but outside, and in particular in other African countries. A Church that gives, even from its limited resources, will be blessed by the Lord, for one can always find someone poorer than oneself.

The Holy Spirit has made you pastors of your people at this important hour of the Christian history of Zaire. May He strengthen the faith and charity of all those entrusted to you! And may Mary, the Mother of the Church, intercede for you all. Be assured of my prayers, as I count on yours. With my affectionate apostolic blessing.

"Keep United in the Faith"

On May 3, 1980, after his address to the Zairean bishops, the Holy Father subsequently met a group of visiting bishops from various African countries, who had come to the Interdiocesan Center at Kinshasa to meet him. He spoke to them briefly as follows.

I now add a word for bishops who have come from other African countries.

Beloved brothers in Christ, this meeting with you gives me great joy. I long to get to know, too, each of your countries, each of your Churches, on the spot. I would have liked to widen the circle of my visits. Perhaps you are some of those who invited me insistently? It did not seem possible this time to go beyond the program which was fixed for converging and well-pondered reasons. I deeply regret it, all the more so in that your Christian communities are very fervently and spontaneously attached to the Pope, and deserved particular encouragement, either because of their vitality, or because of their trials. I regret it also for my own sake, for I would have appreciated this new witness. But I consider myself bound by each of these invitations, which I will try to honor with the help of God in due time. In the meantime, tell your confreres, your priests, your men and women religious, your laity, that the Pope loves them and blesses them with great affection.

I know that Africa is far from being uniform, that the peoples and races are different, the traditions special, and also the implantation of the Catholic Church is varied. It sometimes happens that you find yourselves in the situation of the little flock which must preserve its Christian identity and at the same time bear witness to it.

However, a part of the pastoral problems that I have tackled with your confrères of Zaire apply also to you: the continuation of evangelization, the deepening of the Christian spirit, Africanization, the solidarity of the bishops with one another, with the other local Churches and with the Holy See, the dignity of the life of priests and religious, your presence in their life, the question of vocations, family problems, human advancement, etc. A magnificent role is entrusted to you all, with the grace of God: to contribute to build up a civilization in which God has His place and in which man is consequently respected. If it were necessary to leave an order to all members of your Churches, I would say: Keep united.

Thank you for your visit! May the peace of Christ be with you all!

Loving Presence of Christ in the Ministry of the Community

On May 4, 1980, the Holy Father's first engagement was the ordination of eight bishops: four for Zaire, two for Burundi, one for the Sudan and one for Djibouti. The ordination ceremony took place, in the presence of an estimated one and a half million people, at an altar erected in front of the People's Palace. The following is the text of the Pope's homily during the Mass at which he was assisted by Cardinals Agnelo Rossi and Joseph Malula.

Dear brothers in Christ,

On this day of great joy, on this solemn occasion, I address first of all you who are going to receive the grace of the episcopate: "No longer do I call you servants,...but I have called you friends" (Jn. 15:15). That is what Christ says to the Apostles, that is what He says to you.

LIKE THE APOSTLES

1. For a long time already, you have been closely associated with Christ's life. Your faith developed on this African soil, in your family or in your Christian community, and it yielded its fruits. Then you followed Christ who beckoned to you to dedicate yourselves entirely to His mission. You received the ministerial priesthood of priests in order to be dispensers of the mysteries of God. You endeavored to exercise it with wisdom and courage.

Now you have been chosen to "feed the flock of which the Holy Spirit has made you guardians," as St. Paul said to the elders of Ephesus, bishops to preside over it in the name and in the place of God, and to walk at its head. You receive, as St. Ignatius of Antioch said, "the ministry of the community." For this purpose, like the Apostles, you are enriched by Christ with a special outpouring of the Holy Spirit which will make your ministry fruitful (cf. prayer of the anointing of bishops). You are invested with the fullness of the priesthood, a sacrament which impresses its sacred character upon you; thus, in an eminent and visible way, you will hold the place of Christ Himself, Doctor, Priest and Pastor (cf. LG 20-21). Give thanks to the Lord! And sing: Alleluia!

It is a great joy and an honor for the communities in which you have your roots or which receive you as pastors, for Zaire, Burundi, the Sudan, Djibouti, and also for the religious communities that formed you. You have been "chosen from among men...appointed to act on behalf of men in relation to God" (Heb. 5:1). When young Churches see their sons assume the work of evangelization and become bishops of their brothers, it is a particularly eloquent sign of the maturity and autonomy of these Churches! On this day, let us take care not to forget also the merits of all the pioneers who have prepared, remotely or closely, these new leaders, and in particular the missionary priests and bishops. For them, too, let us give thanks to the Lord!

OVER FIFTY ZAIREAN BISHOPS

2. It is the risen Christ, glorified by the hand of God and put by His Father in possession of the promised Holy Spirit (cf. Acts 2:33), this Christ whom we contemplate with particular joy in this paschal time—it is He who acts through our ministry. For He is the Beginning; He is the Head of the Body which is the Church (cf. Col. 1:18). In the Holy Spirit, Christ continues His work through those whom He has established as pastors and who constantly transmit this spiritual gift through the laying on of hands. They are the "vineshoots through which the apostolic seed is transmitted" (cf. LG 20, quoting Tertullian). Thus the line of the episcopate continues unbroken from the origins. So you enter the episcopal college which succeeds the college of the Apostles. You will work beside your elders, with your elders.

Over fifty Zaireans have already been aggregated to the episcopal body since the first episcopal ordination in 1956, and the situation is similar in the other countries represented here. You will work in communion with your brothers scattered all over the universe, who form only one whole in Christ, united around the Bishop of Rome, Peter's Successor. You will be all the more attached to this indispensable communion because you are ordained by the one to whom the Holy Spirit has entrusted, as to Peter, the task of presiding over unity. Yes, give thanks to the Lord! And sing: Alleluia!

TO PREACH AND SANCTIFY

3. You receive a great grace to exercise a demanding pastoral task. You know its three aspects which are usually designated as "teaching of doctrine, ministry of sacred worship and holding of office in government" (LG 20). The conciliar Constitution *Lumen gentium* (nos. 18-27) and the Decree *Christus Dominus* (nos. 11-19) remain the charter of your ministry on which you must often meditate.

You are responsible in the first place for the preaching of the Gospel, the book of which will be laid on your head during the consecrating prayer, and then placed in your hands. Here, in Africa, the first thing asked of ecclesiastics is: Give us the Word of God. Yes, it is a marvelous thing to see the thirst of your fellow-countrymen for the Gospel: they know, they feel, that it is a message of life.

To do so, you will not be alone. Your priests, your deacons, your women and men religious, your catechists, your lay people are also very meritorious, daily and tenacious evangelizers, very close to the people, and sometimes even pioneers, in places or environments where the Gospel has not yet fully penetrated. Your role will be to sustain their zeal, harmonize their apostolate, see to it that the proclamation, preaching and catechesis are faithful to the authentic meaning of the Gospel and to the whole doctrine, dogmatic and ethical, that the Church has set forth in the course of these twenty centuries on the basis of the Gospel.

You will have to try at the same time to see to it that the message really reaches hearts and transforms behavior, using a language adapted to your African faithful. As the liturgy will tell you: In season and out of season, "preach the word of God yourselves with great patience and with a care to instruct." You are essentially witnesses to the divine and Catholic truth.

You receive the charge of *sanctifying* the People of God. In this sense, you are fathers and you transmit Christ's life through the sacraments, which you celebrate or entrust to your priests for regular, worthy and fruitful celebration. You will have to prepare your faithful for these sacraments, and encourage them to live by them perseveringly. Your prayer will constantly accompany your people along the ways to holiness. You will contribute to preparing, with the grace of the Lord, a Church without a spot or a wrinkle, which proclaims the new Jerusalem, of which Revelation speaks to us, "prepared as a bride adorned for her husband" (Rv. 21:2).

SPECIAL AUTHORITY

4. Finally, you receive the *pastoral government* of a diocese, or you take part in it as auxiliary bishop. Christ gives you authority to exhort, to distribute ministries and services according to needs and capacities, to see to it that they are carried out, to reprove mercifully, if need be, those who go astray, to watch over the whole flock and defend it, as St. Paul said (cf. Acts 20:29-31), and to arouse an increasingly missionary spirit. In all things seek the communion and the building up of the Body of Christ.

You rightly bear on your head the emblem of the leader and in your hand the shepherd's crook. Remember that your authority, according to Jesus, is that of the Good Shepherd, who knows His sheep and is very attentive to each one; that of the Father who reveals Himself through His spirit of love and dedication; that of the steward, ready to give an account to his Master; that of the "minister," who is in the midst of his people "as he who serves" and is ready to give his life. The Church has always urged the head of the Christian community to care particularly for the poor, the weak, those who are suffering, and the underprivileged of every kind. She asks you to give special support to your companions in service, the priests and the deacons: They are brothers, sons and friends for you (cf. CD 16).

The strict administration which is entrusted to you requires of you, together with authority, the prudence and wisdom of "elders"; the spirit of fairness and peace; faithfulness to the Church, of which your ring is the symbol; exemplary purity of doctrine and life. It is a question, in a word, of leading ecclesiastics, religious and laity to the holiness of our Lord; of leading them to live the new commandment of brotherly love, which Jesus left us as His testament (Jn. 13:34). That is why the recent Council reminds all bishops of the fundamental duty of "giving an example of sanctity in charity, humility and simplicity of life" (cf. CD 15). St. Peter wrote to the "elders": "Tend the flock of God that is your charge...being examples to the flock" (1 Pt. 5:2-3).

ACCORDING TO GOD'S LAW

5. In this way you will provide for the good of souls, for their salvation. In this way you will continue the building of the Church already so well implanted in the heart of Africa and particularly in each of your countries. In this way you will contribute a precious share to the vitality of the universal Church, bearing with me and with the bishops as a whole the solicitude for all the Churches.

Moreover, by forming consciences according to the law of God and by educating them to responsibilities and to communion in the Church, you will contribute to form honest and courageous citizens whom the country needs, enemies of corruption, lies and injustice; architects of concord and of brotherly love without frontiers, concerned about harmonious development, especially of the poorest categories. By doing so, you exercise your mission which is of the spiritual and moral order: It enables you to speak out on ethical aspects of society, whenever the fundamental rights of persons, fundamental freedoms and the common good require it. All that in respect of the civil authorities which, on the political plane, and in the pursuit of means to promote the common good, have their specific spheres of competence and responsibilities. In this way you will prepare in depth social progress, the welfare and peace of your dear country, and you will merit the esteem of your fellow-citizens. You are here the pioneers of the Gospel and of the Church, and at the same time the pioneers of the history of your people.

SUBMITTING TO CHRIST

6. Beloved brothers, this ideal must not overwhelm you. On the contrary, it must attract you, and serve you as a springboard and hope. Certainly, we all have this treas-

ure in earthen vessels (cf. 2 Cor. 4:7), including the one who is speaking to you, to whom the name of "Holiness" is given. A great deal of humility is necessary to bear this name! But by humbly submitting your whole person to Christ, who calls you to represent Him, you are sure of His grace, His strength, His peace. Like St. Paul, "I commend you to God and to the word of his grace" (Acts 20:32). May God be glorified in you!

WELCOME TO NEIGHBORS

7. And now, I turn more directly towards all those who surround you with their sympathy and their prayer. Dear brothers and sisters of Kinshasa, Zaire, Burundi, the Sudan and Djibouti, welcome with joy our brothers who become your fathers and pastors. Have for them the respect, affection and obedience that you owe to the ministers of Christ who is Truth, Life and the Way. Listen to their testimony, for they come to you as the first witnesses of the Gospel. Their message is the message of Jesus Christ. Open your souls to the blessings of Christ, to the life of Christ which they bring you. Follow them along the ways they trace out for you, in order that your conduct may be worthy of the disciples of Christ. Pray for them. With them, you are going to build the Church in Africa; you are going to develop Christian communities, in close communion with the universal Church whose sap you have received and continue to receive, in a trusting relationship with Peter's See, the principle of unity, but with the vigor and the spiritual and moral riches that the Gospel will have caused to spring from your African souls.

By the Providence of God, this great hour touches also English-speaking Africa, and in particular the Sudan. In the person of the new auxiliary bishop of Juba, I greet the entire archdiocese and all the sons and daughters of the Church in that land: Grace and peace to all of you in Jesus Christ, the Son of God, in Jesus Christ, the Good

Shepherd who, through the ministry of bishops, continues the pastoral care of His entire Church. May the love of the Savior be in your hearts today and always!

And you, dear friends who do not share the Christian faith but wished to accompany Catholics at this liturgical celebration, I thank you and I invite you, too, to welcome these new bishops as religious leaders and defenders of man and as peacemakers.

Now we prepare for the Rite of Ordination. Like the Apostle Paul beside the elders of Ephesus to whom he had just made his pressing recommendations, we are going to pray. Blessed be the Lord who prolongs in this way His work among us! May all the Apostles intercede for us! May the Virgin Mary, the Mother of the Savior, the Mother of the Church, the Queen of Apostles, intercede for us! We dedicate to her these new servants of the Church. Let us give thanks to the Lord, in faith, charity and hope! Amen. Alleluia!

The Christian Vocation of Africans Is Nourished by Your Ministry

After his meeting with the university students on May 4, 1980, the Holy Father then met the priests and men religious in the Sacred Heart Church beside the nunciature. After an enthusiastic welcome from them, he spoke to them as follows.

Dear brother priests,

1. I have deeply desired this meeting with you. Priests, as you know, have a special place in my heart and my prayer. It is natural: with you, I am a priest. He who has

been constituted Pastor of the whole flock has his eyes fixed first on those who share his pastorate—which is the pastorate of Christ—on those who bear every day "the weight and heat of the day." And your mission is so important for the Church!

Last year, for Holy Thursday, I made a point of addressing a special letter to all priests in the world, through their bishops. In the name of the whole Church, I expressed to you my feelings of gratitude and trust. I reminded you of your priestly identity, in relation to Christ the Priest, the Good Shepherd: I set your ministry in its place in the Church. I also showed the meaning of the requirements attached to your priestly state. I hope that you have read this letter, and that you will reread it. I cannot take up again here all its themes, not even briefly. I shall rather give some thoughts as an extension of it. I was anxious particularly to speak personally to you, priests in Africa, priests in Zaire. It is one of my first meetings on African soil, a very special meeting with my brother priests.

PRIESTS FROM AFRICA

2. Beyond your persons, I am thinking of all the priests of the African continent, of those who came from far away for the beginnings of evangelization and who continue to bring their precious and indispensable help. I hardly dare say "missionaries," for you must all be missionaries. I am thinking also—and quite particularly in this talk—of the priests who have come from African peoples: They already constitute an answer rich in consoling promises. They are the most convincing proof of the maturity that your young Churches have acquired; they are already, and they are called more and more, to be their animators. They are particularly numerous in this country. It is a great grace for which we thank God, in this centenary of evangelization. It is also a great responsibility.

TO BE A PRIEST

3. Among so many thoughts that crowd in on me at this moment, which will I choose as the subject of this meeting? It seems to me that the best beginning is given to us by the Apostle Paul, when he exhorts his disciple Timothy to rekindle the gift of God that is within him through the laying on of his hands (cf. 2 Tm. 1:6), and to draw, from renewed awareness of this grace, the courage to continue generously along the way undertaken, because "God did not give us a spirit of timidity but a spirit of power and love and self-control" *(ibid.,* 1:7).

Our meditation today must begin then by recalling the fundamental features of the priesthood. To be a priest means being a mediator between God and men, in the Mediator par excellence who is Christ.

Jesus was able to carry out His mission thanks to His complete union with the Father, because He was one only with Him. In His condition as a pilgrim along the ways of our earth *(viator)*, He was already in possession of the end *(comprehensor)* to which He was to lead others. In order to be able to continue Christ's mission effectively, the priest must also, in a way, have already arrived at the destination to which he wishes to lead others: he does so through assiduous contemplation of the mystery of God, nourished by study of the Scripture, a study which blossoms in prayer. Faithfulness to the moments and means of personal prayer, the more official prayer of the hours, but also the worthy and generous accomplishment of the sacred acts of the ministry, help to sanctify the priest and lead him to an experience of the mysterious and fascinating presence of the living God, enabling him to act forcefully on the human environment around him.

THE PRIEST AS MEDIATOR

4. Christ exercised His office as Mediator mainly by offering up His life in the sacrifice of the cross, accepted out of obedience to the Father. The cross remains the

"necessary" way for the meeting with God. It is a way on which the priest first and foremost must embark courageously. As I recalled in my recent letter on the Eucharist, is he not called to renew *"in persona Christi,"* in the Eucharistic Celebration, the sacrifice of the cross? According to the fine expression of the African Augustine of Hippo, Christ on Calvary was "priest and sacrifice, and therefore priest because he was sacrifice" *(Confessions, X, 43, 69).* The priest who, in the radical poverty of obedience to God, to the Church, to his bishop, has been able to make his life a pure offering to offer, in union with Christ to the heavenly Father, will experience in his ministry the victorious power of the grace of Christ who died and rose again.

As Mediator, the Lord Jesus was, in all the dimensions of His Being, the Man for God and for brothers. Likewise the priest; that is the reason why he is asked to dedicate his whole life to God and to the Church, in the depths of his being, his faculties, his feelings. The priest who, in the choice of celibacy, renounces human love in order to be open completely to love of God, becomes free to give himself to men through a gift that does not exclude anyone, but embraces them all in the flow of charity, which comes from God (cf. Rom. 5:5) and leads to God. Celibacy, by linking the priest with God, sets him free for all the work required by the care of souls.

AFRICAN AND CHRISTIAN

5. Here we have sketched in a few strokes the essential character of the priest, such as it has been handed down to us by the venerable tradition of the Church. It has a permanent value, yesterday, today, tomorrow. It is not a question of ignoring the new problems raised by the modern world, and also by the African context, for it is important to prepare priests who are at once fully African and truly Christian. The questions raised by the culture in which the priestly ministry is integrated call for mature

reflection. But in any case it is in the light of the fundamental theology that I have recalled that they must be tackled and solved.

IMPORTANT MINISTRY
OF RECONCILIATION

6. It is not necessary for me now to dwell on the different functions of the priest. You have meditated upon, and you must often take up again, the texts of the Second Vatican Council, the constitution *Lumen gentium* (no. 28) and the whole decree *Presbyterorum ordinis.*

The proclamation of the Gospel, of the whole Gospel, to every category of Christians and also to non-Christians, must have an important place in your life. The faithful are entitled to this. Under this ministry of the Word of God there fall particularly *catechesis*, which must be able to reach the heart and the mind of your fellow countrymen, and the *formation of catechists*, religious and lay. Be educators to the Faith and the Christian life according to the Church, in the personal, family and professional fields.

The worthy celebration of the sacraments, the dispensation of the mysteries of God, is equally central in your lives as priests. In this field, take assiduous care to prepare the faithful to receive them, so that, for example, the sacraments of Baptism, Penance, the Eucharist, marriage, may bear all the fruit. For Christ exercises the power of His redeeming action in the sacraments. He does so particularly in the Eucharist and in the sacrament of Penance.

The Apostle Paul said: "God...gave us the ministry of reconciliation" (2 Cor. 5:18). The People of God are called to a continual conversion, to an ever-renewed reconciliation with God in Christ. This reconciliation is carried out in the sacrament of Penance, and it is there that you exercise, par excellence, your ministry of reconciliation.

Yes, the Pope knows your difficulties: you have so many pastoral tasks to carry out, and time is always lacking. But each Christian has a right, yes, a right, to a personal meeting with the crucified, forgiving Christ. As I said in my first encyclical, "it is evident that this is also a right on Christ's part with regard to every human being redeemed by Him" (RH 20). That is why I beg you, always consider this ministry of reconciliation in the sacrament of Penance as one of the most important of your tasks.

Finally, the "spiritual power" that has been given to you (cf. PO 6), has been given to construct the Church, to lead it like the Lord, the Good Shepherd, with humble and disinterested devotion, always welcoming, ready to assume the different ministries and services that are necessary and complementary in the unity of the presbyterium, with a great concern for collaboration among you, priests, and with your bishops. The Christian people must be carried along to unity on seeing the brotherly love and cohesion that you manifest. Your authority in the exercise of your functions is bound up with your faithfulness to the Church which entrusted them to you. Leave political responsibilities to those who are charged with them: you have another part, a magnificent part—you are "leaders" for another reason and in another way, participating in the priesthood of Christ, as His ministers. Your field of interventions, and it is a vast one, is that of Faith and morals, where people expect you to preach at the same time with courageous words and with the example of your life.

DEVELOPING THE ROLE
OF THE LAITY

7. Every member of the Church has an irreplaceable role. Yours consists also in helping all those who belong to your communities to carry out theirs—religious, sisters and laity. In particular you must develop the role of the laity: It must never be forgotten, in fact, that Baptism and Confirmation confer a specific responsibility in the Church. I deeply approve, therefore, of your concern to bring forth collaborators, to train them for their respon-

sibilities. Yes, you must know how to address them, tirelessly—direct, concrete and precise appeals. You must form them by making them become aware of the hidden riches they bear within them. Finally, you must really be able to collaborate, without monopolizing all the tasks, with all the initiatives or all the decisions, when it is a question of what is in their sphere of competence and responsibility. It is in this way that living communities are formed, which really represent an image of the primitive Church, in which we see appear, around the Apostle, the names of those many helpers, men and women, whom Saint Paul greets as his "fellow workers in Christ Jesus" (Rom. 16:3).

HOPE IN THE RISEN CHRIST

8. In all this pastoral work, the inevitable difficulties must not affect our confidence. *"Scimus Christum surrexisse a mortuis vere."* The presence of the risen Christ is the certain foundation of a hope "that does not disappoint us" (Rom. 5:5). That is why the priest must be, always and everywhere, *a man of hope.* It is true that the world is racked by deep tensions, which very often give rise to difficulties the immediate solution of which is beyond us. Under these circumstances, and at all times, the priest must be able to offer his brothers, by word and example, convincing reasons for hope. He can do so because his certainties are not based on human opinions, but on the solid rock of the Word of God.

THE PRIEST MUST BE A MAN OF DISCERNMENT

9. Sustained by it, the priest must show himself to be *a man of discernment and a true teacher of the Faith.*

Yes, he must be a man of discernment, especially in our age. For, as we all know, if the modern world has made great progress in the field of knowledge and human advancement, it is also steeped in a large number of ideologies and pseudo-values which, through a fallacious language, too often succeed in luring and deceiving a number of our contemporaries. Not only is it necessary not to succumb to them, this is only too evident, but the task of pastors is also to form the Christian judgment of the faithful (cf. 1 Tm. 5:21; 1 Jn. 4:1), in order that they, too, may be capable of resisting the deceptive fascination of these new "idols."

In this way, the priest will reveal himself also as a true teacher of the Faith. He will lead Christians to become mature in their Faith, by communicating to them an ever deeper knowledge of the Gospel message—"not their own wisdom but the Word of God" (PO 4)—and helping them to judge by its light the circumstances of life. Thus, thanks to your persevering efforts, today, in Africa, Catholics will be able to discover the answers which, in full faithfulness to the immutable values of Tradition, will also be able to satisfy adequately the needs and challenges of the present.

FOSTERING VOCATIONS

10. I have recalled the role of all the faithful in the Church. But, at the end of this talk, I draw your attention to the primary duty you have with regard to vocations. The meaning of every Christian vocation depends so closely on that of the priestly vocation that, in communities where the latter disappears, the very authenticity of Christian life is affected. Work tirelessly, therefore, dear brothers, to make the whole People of God understand the importance of vocations; pray and get people to pray for that. Take care that Christ's call is presented well to the young; help those that the Lord calls to the priesthood or to the religious life to discern the signs of their vocation; support them throughout their formation. You are certainly convinced that the future of the Church will depend on holy priests, because the priesthood belongs to the structure of the Church such as the Lord willed it. Finally, dear brothers, do you not think that the Lord will use in

the first place the example of our own life, generous and radiant, to bring forth other vocations?

FAITH IN THE PRIESTHOOD

11. Beloved brothers, have faith in your priesthood. It is the priesthood of always, because it is a participation in the eternal priesthood of Christ, who "is the same yesterday and today and forever" (Heb. 13:8; cf. Rv. 1:17ff.). Yes, if the demands of the priesthood are very great, and if I have not hesitated, however, to speak to you about them, it is because they are simply the consequence of the closeness of the Lord, of the confidence He shows in His priests. "No longer do I call you servants,...but I have called you friends" (Jn. 15:15). May this song of the day of our ordination remain for each of you, as for me, a permanent source of joy and trust. It is this joy that I call upon you to renew today. May the Virgin Mary always sustain you on the way, and may she introduce you more and more every day to intimacy with the Lord! With my affectionate apostolic blessing.

Certainty of the Faith— a Support of Daily Trials

After the official welcome by the president of the republic at Brazzaville on May 5, 1980, John Paul II drove in an open car to the Cathedral of the Sacred Heart where there were assembled to meet him all the bishops of the People's Republic of the Congo, and also of the Central African Republic and of the Republic of Chad. Also present were very many priests, men and women religious, and many of the laity. After the Pope's address which is published below, the Holy Father visited the tomb of Cardinal Emile Biayenda who was assassinated during the night between March 22-23, 1971. At the tomb, His Holiness knelt in prayer for a few minutes.

Dear brothers in the episcopate, and you who have dedicated your lives to the Lord, and you faithful of the Church in the Congo.

1. Receive the fatherly and affectionate greeting of the Vicar of Christ, who has come to see you as a pilgrim of the Gospel, to say to you like the Apostle Paul: (I am) "thankful for your partnership in the gospel from the first day until now. And I am sure that he who began a good work in you will bring it to completion at the day of Jesus Christ.... For God is my witness, how I yearn for you all with the affection of Christ Jesus" (Phil. 1:5-6, 8).

I wanted to express to you personally this constant solicitude which I feel for you, so great was my desire to see you, to encourage you all and to bless you. You yourselves wished to be able to give the Pope, in the course of his journey in Africa, the testimony of your Faith and your faithfulness to the Church. Answering your invitation with joy, I am aware that we are living a very special moment, on both sides, and that the Lord asks us to make it fruitful. Beyond the human and spiritual joy of this meeting among brothers in Jesus Christ, it is the very presence of Christ that seizes us in this venerable place, the first episcopal see of the Congo. Let us turn our gaze together in a prayer of thanksgiving and supplication towards Him who was sent into the world "so that we might live through him" (1 Jn. 4:9).

THE CHURCH IN AFRICA
REACHES MATURITY

2. A prayer of thanksgiving for everything He has already realized in you and with you, all of you whom He called to go and bear fruit. Was it not as a result of your persevering efforts that the seed sown by the first missionaries had such a large yield? That the formation of catechists, undertaken systematically, offers a remarkable tool for evangelization today? I know, moreover, that a number of young people are available to cooperate in the religious instruction of school children, and to transmit to them their own reasons for hope. I know too that everywhere, in parishes as in distant stations, people are not afraid of difficulties, and are working courageously to pro-

claim the Good News. That is, it seems to me, a proof, as it were, of maturity. The disciples of Jesus will drink His cup (cf. Mk. 10:39). They were chosen for that reason. He made them acquainted with that, too, and that is why He now calls them His friends (cf. Jn. 15:15). When I see all these courageous Christians here in Africa, I cannot help thinking that, nowadays, Christ has many friends in Africa, and that the Church in Africa has the maturity to face up to all vexations and all trials.

Courage, loyalty, enthusiasm about possessing a treasure, and the desire to share it, such are the qualities of the apostle, and you have to cultivate them. In the eyes of men this treasure is intangible; it cannot but be mysterious. But you know yourselves, and, in a way, you are living these words, such profound ones, that the Scriptures put in Peter's mouth: "I have no silver and gold, but I give you what I have; in the name of Jesus Christ of Nazareth, walk" (Acts 3:16).

In the history of the Congo faithful witnesses have already arisen, faithful to their God, faithful to the Gospel message, faithful to the universal Church and to the teaching of the Pope. I want to give thanks also for all of them, and especially for the example left by dear and venerated Cardinal Emile Biayenda. His tragic death made you mourn a father. I myself mourned a beloved brother. I come to mourn him and pray here, on his tomb, in your midst, with you, certain that if Christ wanted him beside Him, it was because his place was ready in eternity (cf. Jn. 14:2-3), and because in this way he can intercede even better for you and for his country. In this sense, his pastoral ministry is continuing in your service. The Lord be thanked for having given us this pastor, this son of the Congolese nation and of the Church, Cardinal Biayenda!

PRAYER FOR CATHOLICS IN THE CONGO

3. And now, Lord, I beseech You for my brothers and sisters, the Catholics of the Congo. I entrust them to You,

since You have permitted me to visit them in their country. I commend to You their faith, young but now full of vitality, that it may grow, that it may be pure and beautiful, and communicative, that it may continue to express itself and to be freely proclaimed, for eternal life is that they know the only true God and Jesus Christ, whom He sent (cf. Jn. 17:3). I entrust them also to Your holy Mother, the Blessed Virgin Mary, Mother of the Church and our Mother. May she take them under her motherly protection and watch over them in their difficulties! May she teach them to stand at the foot of Your cross and to gather around her while waiting for Your coming, at the end of time!

With them, I pray to You for their unity, which has its source in You, and without which their testimony would be weakened: unity of the episcopal body, unity in the clergy and in the dioceses, capacity of collaborating beyond all ethnical or social differences, unity also with Peter's See and the Church as a whole. You cannot close Your ears to this prayer, You who gave Yourself up to gather the children of God.

Listen further to the invocation we address to You on this day for the sanctification of priests, men and women religious, and all those who, in the various formation centers, are preparing to consecrate their lives to You. Answering Your call, may they be able to renounce for You things of this world, and all pursuit of material or human glory, and be available for the urgent needs of the Church in some mission that will be entrusted to them (cf. AG 20). Rejoicing in their total gift, rejoicing in their celibacy, may they experience more and more deeply, they for whom the Eucharist marks the peak point of all their days, what it means to offer one's life as a sacrifice for the salvation of men.

THE SACRIFICES OF MISSIONARIES

In Your goodness, I know that You will remember particularly the sacrifice of missionaries, who, out of love for You, left their country of origin, their families, everything they had, to come and live in the midst of their Congolese brothers, to love this people, become theirs, and to serve them. Reward such generosity, Lord! Let it be recognized, let it bring forth other vocations, let it awaken a real missionary spirit in everyone.

Surround with Your benevolence also and particularly Your humble servants, the bishops, to whom You have entrusted these local Churches. I am beside them, this morning, to strengthen them in Your name. They are there, the three pastors of the Congo, and most of their confreres of the neighboring episcopal conferences with whom they usually meet under the presidency, today, of Archbishop N'Dayen of Banguli. There are even some bishops from other nearby countries. They have brought their pastoral concerns and all the intentions with which their communities have charged them. Yes, as You asked of Peter and his Successors, I wish to bring them the calm strength and the certainty of Your help in their daily toil, which is so meritorious. And I wish to assure those who have not been able to join us of my brotherly and spiritual closeness, to take a part of their burden on my shoulders, while some of them are suffering so cruelly from the sufferings of their people. Dear confreres of Chad, I am thinking of you in the first place, and of the flock entrusted to you. May God help you to dress wounds and to cure hearts! May He give you peace!

BE PIOUS AND
YOU WILL UNDERSTAND

4. Brothers and sisters, I cannot continue any longer. So many thoughts fill my mind about which I would have liked to talk to you. It seemed to me that, limited by the program, the Pope could at least dedicate this meeting to a common prayer, inviting you implicitly in this way to do the same on every occasion, so that you will really proclaim what you have contemplated of the Word of Life (cf.

1 Jn. 1:1). That is what is expected of God's ministers. All the rest can be given by others. If you wish to be zealous, be pious in the first place, and you will understand everything. Live in union with God. He will help you to bear human tribulations, because you will learn to connect them with the cross, with redemption. But, more than that, He will come within you and make His dwelling there.

Pray for me, too, my beloved in the Lord. Have I your promise? I promise you on my part that this new tie that has just been established with this part of Africa will have a concrete expression, at the memory of your faces, your persons, those who benefit from your pastoral care or whom you represent here in some way. To all, my blessing and very fervent wishes. And may God bless your country, too, and all the surrounding nations.

We Are the People Redeemed by the Precious Blood of Christ

After the official welcome at Nairobi Airport, on May 6, 1980, the Holy Father drove across the city in an open car to the Cathedral of the Holy Family for his meeting with the Church of Nairobi and of all Kenya. Among those present in the Cathedral there was also Cardinal Laurean Rugambwa, Archbishop of Dar-es-Salaam in neighboring Tanzania. After an address of welcome by Cardinal Maurice Otunga, the Holy Father spoke. The following are excerpts.

Your Eminence, zealous pastor of this
beloved Church of Nairobi,
Venerable brothers in the episcopate,
Sons and daughters of Kenya,
My brothers and sisters in Christ,

1. My first desire in this House of God is to express the Church's praise for the Father of our Lord Jesus Christ,

who has gathered us together in His Son, sending forth His Holy Spirit into our midst. In the words of the Apostle Peter: "Blessed be the God and Father of our Lord Jesus Christ! By his great mercy we have been born anew to a living hope through the resurrection of Jesus Christ from the dead..." (1 Pt. 1:3).

2. Today in this cathedral dedicated to the Holy Family—to Jesus, Mary and Joseph—all of us realize that together we make up the Body of Christ—together we are the Church. We are a living Church, a spiritual house made up of living stones—all of us live in Christ. We are one with all our brothers and sisters here in Kenya and throughout the world; we are one in the communion of saints, one with the living and the dead—our families, our ancestors, those who brought to us the Word of God and whose memory is enshrined forever in our hearts.

Today, in particular, we are a communion of faith and love, confessing Jesus Christ as the Son of God, the Lord of history, the Redeemer of man and the Savior of the whole world. We are one united community, living in the mystery of the Church, the life of the crucified and risen Christ, and therefore His praise is in our hearts and on our lips. It finds expression in our Easter *Alleluia*. We are, as it were, the extended Holy Family, called to build and enlarge the edifice of justice and peace and the civilization of love.

3. Because of this we are challenged to live a life worthy of our calling as members of Christ's Body and as brothers and sisters of Christ in accord with our Christian dignity and duty to walk humbly and peacefully together along the path of life. Jesus Himself exhorts us to be, by our lives, the salt of the earth and the light of the world. With Him I say to you: "Let your light so shine before men, that they may see your good works and give glory to your Father who is in heaven" (Mt. 5:16).

4. Each one of us has a unique place in the communion of the one universal Church throughout Africa and the whole world.... You, my brothers in the priesthood,

yours is a mission of proclaiming salvation, of building up the Church by the Eucharistic Sacrifice; yours is a vocation of special companionship with Christ, offering your lives in celibacy in order to be like Jesus, the Good Shepherd, in the midst of your people—the people of Kenya.

And finally, my dear brother bishops, in union with the whole episcopal college that is united with the Successor of Peter, you are called to exercise the pastoral leadership of the whole flock in the name of Jesus Christ, "the chief Shepherd" (1 Pt. 5:4); yours is therefore a role of special servanthood. You are the appointed guardians of the unity that we are living and experiencing today, because you are the guardians of God's Word upon which all unity is based. And, in a particular way, dear Cardinal Otunga, by reason of your eminent position, you are yourself a visible link with the See of Rome, and a special sign of Catholic unity within your local Church. I am deeply grateful for your fidelity and for your devoted collaboration.

5. And so let us all, as one redeemed people, one Body of Christ, one Church, stand firm together in the faith of our Lord Jesus Christ, acknowledging Him as "God from God, Light from Light, true God from true God." With St. Peter, let us say to Jesus: "You are the Christ, the Son of the living God" (Mt. 16:16). And again: "You have the words of eternal life" (Jn. 6:68).

And on my part, as the Successor of Peter, I have come to you today to repeat Christ's words of eternal life, to proclaim His message of salvation and hope, and to offer all of you His peace:

"Peace to all of you who are in Christ" (1 Pt. 5:14).

Two Dynamic Aspects
of the Life of Christ

On May 7, 1980, the Holy Father met the visiting bishops from the countries bordering on Kenya. Among them was Cardinal Laurean Rugambwa, Archbishop of Dar-es-Salaam. To them His Holiness delivered the following address.

My dear brothers in the episcopate,

1. It is a great pleasure for me to greet you here today. You have come as visitors to Kenya to show your solidarity with your brother bishops and with their people. Since this is an extraordinary ecclesial celebration for them, you have wished to be close to them in the joy of the Faith. In coming, you have brought with you not only the fellowship of your own local Churches, but a special manifestation of Catholic unity. And because you are members of the universal College of Bishops, united with the Successor of Peter, you bear collective pastoral responsibility for the good of the whole Church and for her pastoral activities throughout the world. Hence, with an awareness of the deep reality of the episcopate you have gathered in prayerful and fraternal solidarity.

2. Our being together today evokes, quite naturally, a consideration of our common ministry, our shared responsibility and our common likeness to Jesus Christ, the Incarnate Word and the High Priest of the New Testament.

In Jesus Christ, the Son of God, we find a fundamental insight into our deepest Christian identity. In Jesus Christ, the Good Shepherd, we have a full perception—in simplicity and profundity—of all pastoral ministry in the Church of God. In Jesus Christ, the Suffering Servant, we discern the complete meaning of a sacrificial life. In Jesus Christ, the risen Lord, we comprehend the final goal of the Paschal Mystery—to which all our preaching and catechesis are directed.

3. All I wish to do in these moments with you is to direct my thoughts and yours to Jesus Christ—to Him who

is *Unigenitus Dei Filius*, but who has become *Primogenitus in multis fratribus* (Rom. 8:29). This Son of God, this Son of Mary, this Priest and Victim of redemption explains us to ourselves and declares the meaning of our ministry today and always: "Jesus Christ is the same yesterday, and today, and for ever" (Heb. 13:8).

As He called His Apostles, so He has also called us: to be His companions, to remain in His love, and to proclaim His Gospel. And in our full pastoral role as successors of the Apostles we are called to communicate Christ to our people. Sharing in His sonship by divine adoption, we are instruments of grace for others, as we lead our people to the fullness of His life revealed in the mystery of the Church, the Body of Christ.

4. Our identity and our mission, as well as the term of our mission, are all linked to Christ in His sonship; we are conformed to Him. Because of this likeness to Christ, we have great joy and comfort in living two dynamic aspects of Christ's life. With Christ we are conscious of loving the Father; His words pervade our consciousness and our daily activity as bishops: "I love the Father" (Jn. 14:30). At the same time each of us in Christ can say: "The Father loves me," precisely because Jesus has said: "The Father loves the Son" (Jn. 3:35). This awareness of being in Christ, of loving His Father and being loved by Him, is a source of pastoral strength. It confirms the meaning of our lives. It is a reason for thanksgiving to the Father and for endless praise of Jesus Christ.

Dear brother bishops: In the months and years ahead, may it bring us gladness to recall that in Kenya we manifested our episcopal unity together by praising Jesus Christ, the eternal Son of God. To Him be glory for ever, with the Father, in the unity of the Holy Spirit. Amen.

Episcopal Ministry at the Service of Life

The Holy Father's final engagement on May 7, 1980, was a meeting with the Kenyan bishops in the Nunciature at Nairobi. John Paul II spoke to them as follows.

Venerable and dear brothers in our Lord Jesus Christ,

1. Today during this Easter season it is a cause of deep joy and a source of pastoral strength for us to assemble in Nairobi, to gather together in the name of Jesus who said: "I am the resurrection and the life" (Jn. 11:25).

We are extremely conscious that our ministry in Africa and our service to the universal Church is placed under the sign of the risen Christ. For, together with all our brother bishops throughout the world, we are successors of the body of Apostles that was chosen to witness to the resurrection. The knowledge that "with great power the apostles gave their testimony to the resurrection of the Lord Jesus" (Acts 4:33) truly strengthens us and uplifts us, because we know that we have received the inheritance of the Apostolic College. For us bishops this is an hour of trust in the risen Lord, an hour of Easter joy, an hour of great hope for the future of Africa.

AMECEA'S INSTITUTE

2. On this occasion my thoughts go to all the bishops of Africa, and I note with deep satisfaction that the members of the episcopal conference of Kenya are resolutely engaged in many programs of collaboration and joint action with their fellow bishops from the AMECEA countries of Tanzania, Uganda, Zambia, Malawi, the Sudan and Ethiopia. In the abundant strength that comes from charity and mutual support, your ministry is sustained and enriched. Be assured of my admiration and esteem for the unity that you express in diversity and in fraternal collaboration, and for your concerted efforts on behalf of the evangelization of those countries that have so much in common.

An initiative worthy of particular mention is AMECEA's Pastoral Institute at Eldoret. This institute offers special opportunities to reflect on the Church's mission to guard and teach ever more effectively the Word of God. The Holy Spirit Himself is directing the Church in Africa to scrutinize "the signs of the times" in the light of the sacred deposit of God's Word as it is proclaimed by the Magisterium. It is only on this sound basis that true answers can be found to the real problems that touch people's lives. It is in judging according to this sacred norm that the bishops will exercise their personal responsibility to evaluate what pastoral activities and solutions are valid for Africa today.

MINISTRY OF SERVICE

3. Venerable brothers, the episcopal ministry is a ministry at the service of life, bringing the power of the resurrection to your people, so that they may "walk in newness of life" (Rom. 6:4), so that they may be ever more aware of the Christian life to which they are called by virtue of their Baptism, and so that in their daily lives—in the setting of Africa—they may have fellowship with the Father and His Son Jesus Christ in the unity of the Holy Spirit. And because this fellowship is fully achieved only in heaven, your ministry likewise involves a clear proclamation of eternal life.

PASTORS OF THE FLOCK

4. As Successor of Peter in the See of Rome and as your brother in the College of Bishops, I have come to Africa to encourage you in your efforts as pastors of the flock; in the efforts of each of you to offer to Christ a local Church in which unity reigns between the bishop and the priests, the religious and the laity; in your efforts to enlighten communities with the Gospel and make them vibrant with the life of Christ; in your efforts to bring the dynamic power of the resurrection into human life and by it to transform and elevate all levels of society.

I have come to confirm you in your total acceptance of God's holy Word as it is authentically proclaimed by the Catholic Church at all times and in all places. I wish to support you in the conviction, so splendidly expressed by the bishops of Kenya in their Pastoral Letter of April 27, 1979, that fidelity to the teachings of Christ and the Magisterium of His Church is truly in the interests of the people. By following your clear insights of faith, you showed yourselves true pastors of the flock, exercising real spiritual leadership when you declared: "We, your bishops, would do a disservice to the people if we did not expect of them the goodness and the fidelity that they are capable of by the grace of God" (Pastoral Letter, p. 10). Your greatest contribution to your people and to all Africa is indeed the gift of God's Word, the acceptance of which is the basis for all community and the condition for all progress.

RESPECT FAMILY VALUES

5. As the *Servus Servorum Dei* I have come to uphold with you the priorities of your ministry. In the first place, I offer my support for your pastoral efforts on behalf of the family—the African family. The great African tradition is faithful to so many family values, and to life itself, which takes its origin in the family. A profound respect for the family and for the good of children is a distinctive gift of Africa to the world. It is in the family that each generation learns to absorb these values and to transmit them. And the whole Church appreciates everything you do to preserve this heritage of your people, to purify it and uplift it in the sacramental fullness of Christ's new and original teaching. Hence we see the great value of presenting the Christian family in its relationship to the Most Holy Trinity, and of maintaining the Christian ideal in its evangelical purity. It is the divine law proclaimed by Christ that gives rise to the Christian ideal of monogamous marriage, which in turn is the basis for the Christian fam-

ily. Only a week before he died, my Predecessor, John Paul I, spoke to a group of bishops in these words, which I consider very relevant here today in Africa: "Let us never grow tired of proclaiming the family as a community of love: Conjugal love unites the couple and is procreative of new life; it mirrors the divine love, is communicated, and in the words of *Gaudium et spes* is actually a sharing in the covenant of love of Christ and His Church" (*AAS* 70 [1978], p. 766).

Be assured of my solidarity with you in this great task involving the diligent preparation of the young for marriage, the repeated proclamation of the unity and indissolubility of marriage, and the renewed invitation to the faithful to accept and foster with faith and love the Catholic celebration of the sacrament of marriage. Success in a pastoral program of this nature requires patience and perseverance and a strong conviction that Christ has come to "make all things new" (Rv. 21:5).

HUMANAE VITAE ENCYCLICAL

Know also that in all your efforts to build up strong united families, in which human love reflects divine love and in which the education of children is embraced with a true sense of mission, you have the support of the universal Church. With the love and sensitivity of pastors, you have well illustrated the great principle that any pastoral approach that does not rest on the doctrinal foundation of the Word of God is illusory. Hence with true pastoral charity you have faced various problems affecting human life and repeated the Church's teaching at the true service of man. You have clearly insisted, for example, on the most fundamental human right: the right to life from the moment of conception; you have effectively reiterated the Church's position on abortion, sterilization and contraception. Your faithful upholding of the Church's teaching contained in the encyclical *Humanae vitae* has been the expression of your pastoral concern and your profound attachment to the integral values of the human person.

Every effort to make society sensitive to the importance of the family is a great service to humanity. When the full dignity of parents and children is realized and is expressed in prayer, a new power for good is unleashed throughout the Church and the world. John Paul I expressed this eloquently when he said: "The holiness of the Christian family is indeed a most apt means for producing the serene renewal of the Church which the Council so eagerly desired. Through family prayer, the *ecclesia domestica* becomes an effective reality and leads to the transformation of the world" (*ibid.*, p. 767). Upon you, brethren, rest the hope and trust of the universal Church for the defense and promotion of the African family, both parents and children. The Holy Spirit of truth, who has implanted so many values in the hearts of the African people, will never cease to assist you as pastors in bringing the teaching of Jesus ever more effectively into the lives of your brothers and sisters. We need never be afraid to preach the fullness of His message in all its evangelical purity, for, as I stated on another occasion: "Let us never fear that the challenge is too great for our people: they were redeemed by the precious blood of Christ; they are His people. Through the Holy Spirit, Jesus Christ vindicates to Himself the final responsibility for the acceptance of His word and for the growth of His Church. It is He, Jesus Christ, who will continue to give the grace to His people to meet the requirements of His word, despite all difficulties, despite all weaknesses. And it is up to us to continue to proclaim the message of salvation in its entirety and purity, with patience, compassion and the conviction that what is impossible with man is possible with God" (*AAS* 71, [1979], pp. 1424f.).

CATECHESIS—A PRIORITY

6. Another great priority of your ministry is catechesis: developing the initial faith of your people and bringing them to the fullness of Christian life. I am close to

you, in praise and encouragement, in every undertaking of yours to communicate Christ, to make His Gospel incarnate in the lives and culture of your people. In union with the universal Church, and in openness to the patrimony of her long history, you are striving to lead your people in the reality of their daily lives to look to Christ for light and strength. The aim of your local Churches is to have the faithful living through, with and in Christ. Your efforts, in which you rightfully endeavor to associate the whole community—and in a special way the catechists—must have constant reference to Christ, to His divine Person, His Spirit, and His Gospel.

The "acculturation" or "inculturation" which you rightly promote will truly be a reflection of the Incarnation of the Word, when a culture, transformed and regenerated by the Gospel, brings forth from its own living tradition original expressions of Christian life, celebration and thought (cf. CT 53). By respecting, preserving and fostering the particular values and riches of your people's cultural heritage, you will be in a position to lead them to a better understanding of the mystery of Christ, which is to be lived in the noble, concrete and daily experiences of African life. There is no question of adulterating the Word of God, or of emptying the cross of its power (cf. 1 Cor. 1:17), but rather of bringing Christ into the very center of African life and of lifting up all African life to Christ. Thus, not only is Christianity relevant to Africa, but Christ, in the members of His Body, is Himself African.

PROPER FORMATION

7. Again, with good reason, you attribute great pastoral importance to the proper formation of priests and religious, as well as to fostering these vocations in the Church. This attitude is an expression of your deep understanding of the needs of the Body of Christ.

Since the beginning of my pontificate I have striven to point out the importance of religious consecration in the

Church and the value of religious life as it affects the whole community of the faithful. Religious have the task of showing forth the holiness of the whole Body of Christ and of bearing witness to a new and eternal life acquired by the redemption of Christ (cf. LG 44). At the same time they are called to many different apostolates in the Church. Their service in the Gospel is very necessary for the life of the Church. Missionary religious in Kenya have labored with great fidelity in the cause of the Gospel; only the Lord Jesus can adequately thank them and reward them for what has been accomplished for the implantation of the Church. Their mission now goes on side by side with their Kenyan fellow religious, who have heard the call of Christ and are working generously for the cause of the Gospel. The future of evangelization in this land will continue to owe much to the men and women religious, both autochthonous and from abroad.

I have likewise sought to draw attention to the essential nature, role and function of the priesthood in its unchanging relationship to the Eucharist, which is the summit of all evangelization (cf. PO 5).

In particular I wish to confirm the vital importance for the Christian people of having their priests properly trained in the Word of God, in the knowledge and love of Jesus Christ and His cross. In the divine plan, the transmission of the life-giving Gospel of Christ is linked with the preparation of the priests of this generation. To provide this proper seminary training is one of our greatest responsibilities as bishops of the Church of God; it can be one of our most effective contributions to the evangelization of the world.

UNITY AND COOPERATION

8. An important element that affects every community in the Church is the unity and cooperation between bishops and priests. By reason of his ordination, the priest is "a co-worker with the order of Bishop," and to live out

the truth of this vocation he is called to collaborate with the bishop and to pray for him. To explain the unity of the priests with the bishop, St. Ignatius of Antioch compared it to the relationship between the strings and the lute (Letter to the Ephesians IV).

On the part of the bishop this relationship requires that he should be close to his priests as a brother and father and friend. As such he must love them and encourage them, not only in their pastoral activities, but in their lives of personal consecration. The bishop is called to strengthen his priests in faith and to urge them to look constantly to Christ, the Good Shepherd, in order that they may realize ever more their priestly identity and dignity.

The Church renews her debt of gratitude to all the missionary and *Fidei Donum* priests who are laboring in the cause of Christ's Gospel. Their generosity is an expression of the power of Christ's grace, and their ministry is a great proof of Catholic unity.

9. In the building up of the Church, I am aware of your sustained work to build small Christian communities in which the Word of God is the guideline of action and in which the Eucharist is the true center of life. The whole community of the faithful benefits from these initiatives that make it possible for people to recognize the Church in her concrete expression and human dimension as a visible sacrament of God's universal love and saving grace. It is certainly the will of Jesus Christ that the love of Christians should be manifested in such a way that individual communities exemplify the universal norm: "By this will all men know that you are my disciples, if you have love for one another" (Jn. 13:35). In your pastoral zeal you know the wise criteria laid down by Paul VI and which remains a sure guide for the effectiveness of these communities (cf. EN 58). At this time I would just stress the great power which those communities have to fulfill an active ecclesial role in the evangelization of Africa. May they go forward

with you, their pastors, and with the priests, to communicate "the unsearchable riches of Christ" (Eph. 3:8).

10. Before concluding my words to you today, my dear brethren in Christ Jesus, I wish to emphasize once more the great need for holiness in our lives. To exercise fruitfully our role as pastors of God's people, we must know Christ and love Him. In a word, we are called to friendship with the Lord, just as the Apostles were. Like Jesus we are the object of the Father's love, and the Holy Spirit is alive in our hearts. The effectiveness of everything we do depends on our union with Jesus, on our holiness of life. There is no other way to be a worthy bishop, a good shepherd of the flock. There is no pastoral leadership without prayer, for only in prayer is union with Jesus maintained. Only by being like Jesus, Son of Mary, who is the Mother of us all, can we fulfill our mission to the Church.

May Mary, Queen of Apostles, sustain you in holiness and love, in prayer and pastoral charity, and help you to bring Jesus to all your people, to all Kenya, to all Africa.

Praised be Jesus Christ, "the chief Shepherd" (1 Pt. 5:4) of God's people, "the Bishop and Shepherd of our souls" (1 Pt. 2:25).

Evangelization Is the Duty of Each of You

After the official welcome at Accra Airport on May 8, 1980, the Holy Father drove in an open car to Accra Cathedral which was packed with priests, men and women religious, seminarians, and numerous groups of the laity. The following is an excerpt of his address.

Venerable and dear brothers in the episcopate,
Beloved brothers and sisters in Christ,

After His ascension into heaven, our Lord Jesus Christ sent the Holy Spirit upon His Apostles and into His

Church. The Holy Spirit was Jesus' first gift to those who believe. Jesus Himself had foretold the coming of the Spirit of Truth when He said: "...He will bear witness to me and you also are witnesses" (Jn. 15:26-27).

And today in Accra, in this cathedral dedicated to the Holy Spirit, we have assembled to celebrate this mystery, this great reality of the Holy Spirit's presence in the Church—the presence of the Holy Spirit who continues to bear witness to Jesus and who stirs up new witnesses among the faithful in every generation. We rejoice to know that the Holy Spirit is with us still, that He unites the Church in her communion and in her ministry (cf. LG 4). We rejoice that through the power of the Holy Spirit the great lifegiving message of the death and resurrection of Jesus has been passed on down the centuries, and that it has been brought to Ghana.

After the efforts at evangelization that had been made in previous centuries, two generous priests, Father Moreau and Father Murat, succeeded a hundred years ago in establishing the Catholic Church in this land. We praise the grace of God that brought them to the people of Ghana on that Pentecost Tuesday in 1880. And we bless the memory of all the missionaries who came subsequently, in order to bear witness to Christ through the power of His Holy Spirit. The seed of God's Word, planted on Ghanaian soil, has taken root; it has grown into a large tree and has brought forth fruits of holiness for the glory of the most Holy Trinity.

In spite of difficulties and the vicissitudes of history, the Gospel has been freely offered and freely accepted. The kingdom of God has been preached, and over and over again evangelization has reached its dynamic summit in the "clear proclamation that in Jesus Christ, the Son of God made man, who died and rose from the dead, salvation is offered to all men as a gift of God's grace and mercy" (EN 27).

The genuine charity of Christ was the motivation for one missionary congregation after another in sending its members to serve Ghana and her people, and the same genuine charity of Christ was the authentic means that bore such effective witness to the Gospel. Priests, sisters and brothers came on a mission of salvation and service. Each fulfilled his or her role. All of them together, through the power of the Holy Spirit, built up the Church by word and deed, by prayer and sacrifice. At a later date lay mission helpers came too, bearing witness to the universal missionary nature of the Church. And all of these laborers for the Gospel have served valiantly—and with God's help they will continue to work generously, side-by-side with their Ghanaian brothers and sisters, in the harvest of the Church.

But the same Holy Spirit who sustained dedicated missionaries also raised up new followers for Christ, vivifying the local Church and calling its members in turn to share the great task of evangelization. In the strength of the Paschal Mystery, people accepted the Word of God; they believed and were baptized; they were nurtured on the Eucharist and came to maturity in Christian living. Entire Christian communities accepted the challenge to "walk in newness of life" (Rom. 6:4) and to embrace the challenge of the beatitudes in their fullness. The missionary contact that had begun with human affability and kindness led finally to the full flowering of parishes, which became "the prime mover and the pre-eminent place for catechesis" and "a major point of reference for the Christian people" (CT 67).

From the midst of these parishes and other Christian communities there came forth those generous young people who would heed God's call to the priesthood and religious life and thus, together with the laity, fulfill their distinctive role in the one Church of God, as "a chosen race, a royal priesthood, a holy nation, God's own people" (1 Pt. 1:9).

In due time, Ghanaian bishops were appointed to the pastoral leadership of the People of God. With gratitude for what had already been achieved in the work of evangelization, they entered into the continuity of apostolic succession. The fact that all the bishops of this country are now native Ghanaians is an eloquent testimony to the success of the work of the missionaries and to the solid implantation of the Church in this land. For this we give special thanks to God on the occasion of the celebration of this centenary.

The one Body of Christ was likewise to perceive its common task, its essential mission, its deepest identity, which was later so accurately expressed by Paul VI in this way: "Evangelizing is, in fact, the grace and vocation proper to the Church" (EN 14). Above all, the spread of the Gospel was to be linked with the witness of love, in accordance with Christ's words: "This is my commandment: that you love one another as I have loved you" (Jn. 15:12). In the observance of this commandment all Christian societies find their secure basis. And the love to which all Christians are called is itself the ladder by which every generation ascends to God and to eternal life.

You, my brother priests, at the service of your brothers and sisters of the laity—all of whom are called to holiness of life, all of whom are witnesses for the kingdom of God—you have the particular mission of proclaiming the Gospel in its fullest enactment, which is the celebration of the Eucharist, wherein the work of redemption is renewed. In a special way you participate in the mission of Jesus for the benefit of the whole Body of Christ; you share deeply in the burning desire of His soul: "I must proclaim the Good News of the Kingdom...for I was sent for this purpose" (Lk. 4:43). It is because of this that you have offered your lives in celibacy and pastoral charity, to stay close to your people, to lead them in the path of salvation, building up the Church in faith and love, and in the unity and peace of Christ.

Original Expressions of Faith Deriving from Different Cultures

On May 9, 1980, after the awarding of the John XXIII International Peace Prize, John Paul II received the homage of the King of the Ashanti, Otombuo Opoku Ware II Asantehene, and of his entire court. Later he went to the minor seminary of Kumasi, where he met the bishops of Ghana and delivered the following address.

Venerable and dear brothers in our Lord Jesus Christ,

1. My coming among you today is intimately linked to Christ and His Gospel. I have come to share with you and the whole Catholic Church in Ghana the joy of your centenary celebrations. Together we praise the grace of God that initiated and sustained the full process of evangelization in your midst: missionaries were sent to preach the Word of God to your ancestors; these people heard the message of salvation; they believed and called upon Him in whom they put their faith, confessing with their lips that Jesus is Lord and believing in their hearts that God raised Him from the dead (cf. Rom. 10:9). Through the sacraments your people came to share in the death and resurrection of Christ and were grafted into the vital organic unity of the Church. Generous missionary congregations realized the need for workers in the vineyard of the Lord, and conversions were made through divine grace. In 1935, the first two Ghanaian priests were ordained, and in 1950, the hierarchy was established. And today there are two metropolitan sees and seven dioceses. The Church is thus fully implanted in Ghana, but her mission is not yet complete. By reason of their full membership in the Body of Christ, Ghanaian Catholics are called to be workers for evangelization in a Church that is, by her nature, missionary in her totality (cf. AG 35). Only in accepting their own responsibility for the spread of the Gospel do the Catholic people fulfill the vocation to which they are called.

SPIRIT OF CATHOLIC UNITY

2. This great ecclesial reality of an evangelized and evangelizing Church in Ghana, which explains the depth of our joy today, is celebrated in a spirit of Catholic unity. It is a unity that belongs to your individual local Churches: priests, religious and laity united with the bishop, who presides in love and service, and who is called to be an example to everyone in humility and holiness of life. This Catholic unity is further manifested in the solidarity of the sons and daughters of this country with the missionaries, who continue to give their fraternal service—deeply appreciated and very necessary—for the benefit of each local Church, under the direction of an autochthonous pastor.

The unity of this centenary celebration is likewise the unity of all the bishops of this country with the entire college of bishops united with the Successor of Peter, and intent on proclaiming the one Gospel of Christ and ensuring the enactment of Catholic unity in the Eucharistic Sacrifice, which is at one and the same time the expression of the worship of an individual community and of the universal Church. This is a special motive of joy for me as I celebrate with you your centenary celebrations. I wish to assure you of my gratitude for everything you have done, as pastors of local Churches, to preserve unity, you who likewise share responsibility for the Church throughout the world. Your fidelity and zeal are themselves an effective contribution to the spread of the kingdom.

INCULTURATION OF THE GOSPEL

3. Be assured that all your efforts to proclaim the Gospel directly and indirectly are a great credit to the Church. On my part I am close to you in all the joys and disappointments, the challenges and hopes of your ministry of the word, and in your sacramental ministry. I am close to you in all your concrete pastoral initiatives, in everything that brings the message of salvation into the lives of the people. A reflection on the essential and con-

stitutional patrimony of the Catholic Faith, which is identical for all people of all places and times, is a great help to the pastors of the Church as they ponder the requirements of the "inculturation" of the Gospel in the life of the people. You are familiar with what Paul VI called "the task of assimilating the essence of the Gospel message and of transposing it, without the slightest betrayal of its essential truth, into the language that these particular people understand" (EN 63). He singled out as subject to certain adaptations the areas of liturgical expression, catechesis, theological formulation, secondary ecclesial structures, and ministries. As local pastors you are eminently fitted for this work, because you are sons of the people to whom you are sent with the message of faith; in addition, in your episcopal ordination you have received the same "governing Spirit" who was communicated to Jesus and by Him to His Apostles for the building up of His Church. This work is of God; it is an activity of the living Body of Christ; it is a requirement of the Church as a truly universal means of salvation.

And so with serenity and confidence and with profound openness towards the universal Church, the bishops must carry on the task of inculturation of the Gospel for the good of each people, precisely so that Christ may be communicated to every man, woman and child. In this process, cultures themselves must be uplifted, transformed and permeated by Christ's original message of divine truth, without harming what is noble in them. Hence, worthy African traditions are to be preserved. Moreover, in accordance with the full truth of the Gospels and in harmony with the Magisterium of the Church, living and dynamic African Christian traditions are to be consolidated.

As you pursue this work in close union with the Apostolic See and the entire Church, you are strengthened in knowing that the responsibility for this activity is shared also by your brother bishops throughout the world. This is an important consequence of the doctrine of collegiality, in which every bishop shares responsibility for the rest of the Church; by the same token, his own Church, in which by divine right he exercises ordinary jurisdiction, is also the object of a common episcopal responsibility in the two dimensions of making the Gospel incarnate in the local Church: 1) preserving unaltered the content of the Catholic Faith and maintaining ecclesial unity throughout the world; and 2) bringing forth from cultures original expressions of Christian life, celebration and thought, whereby the Gospel is brought into the heart of peoples and their cultures.

Venerable brothers, your people are called to the highest ideals and to the most lofty virtues. In this saving power Christ is present in the humanity of Africa, or as I have already said during my visit to this continent: "Christ, in the members of His Body, is Himself African."

FOSTER VOCATIONS

4. There are many individual aspects of your apostolate that are worthy of special mention and support. Of particular importance for the future of your local Churches is every effort that is made to foster vocations to the priesthood and religious life. The faithful are called to share responsibility for this dimension of the Church; they exercise this responsibility by esteem and respect for these vocations and by helping to create the sound spiritual atmosphere of Christian families and other communities in which a vocation can develop and can persevere. Vigilance is needed on the part of priests to detect the signs of a vocation. Above all, the effectiveness of all these human efforts is linked to the prayer of the Church and to the witness of priests and religious.

When your people see priests and religious living a life of authentic celibacy in intimacy with Christ, when they perceive the human fulfillment that comes from the total giving of oneself in the service of the Gospel, when they observe the joy that comes from bearing witness to Christ

—then the priesthood and the religious life are attractive vocations for youth, who will then more easily hear Christ's personal invitation to them: Come, follow me!

Another dimension that I would like to stress in this regard is the missionary dimension of your Church with regard to the needs of sister Churches on the African continent and beyond. I understand your concern about the need of your own Christian communities to be guided by priests chosen by God from among their own people. But the Church is missionary by nature. And let us always remember that God will never fail to bless those who give with generosity. The promotion of missionary vocations —either in the framework of the *Fidei donum* formula or through membership in international missionary societies —will, in its turn, incite the local community to greater confidence in God's grace and to a deeper awareness of faith. It will open hearts to God's love.

WOMEN IN THE CHURCH

5. I know that you are committed to the advancement of the role of women in the Church and in society. It is an expression of this same concern to promote women's vocations to the religious life. African women have willingly been bearers of life and guardians of family values. Similarly, the consecration of women in radical self-giving to the Lord in chastity, obedience, and poverty constitutes an important way of bringing to your local Churches the life of Christ and an awareness of a larger human community and a divine communion. This requires, of course, that they be carefully formed, theologically and spiritually, so that they can assume their rightful place as workers for evangelization, exemplifying the true meaning of religious life in an African context, and thus enriching the whole Church.

YOUR SPECIAL MISSION

6. In the beautiful celebration in the stadium and by honoring the catechists, I have already expressed my

esteem for them, as well as my thoughts on the value of this institution for the Church—its value for the future as for the past. I shall not expand this point further except to repeat the words I addressed to the bishops in my apostolic exhortation: "Dearly beloved brothers, you have here a special mission within your Churches: you are beyond all others the ones primarily responsible for catechesis.... You can be sure that if catechesis is done well in your local Churches, everything else will be easier to do" (CT 63).

MEDIA OPPORTUNITIES

7. In this context I would draw attention to a special aspect of the apostolate: the question of the media. All over the world the communications media offer special opportunities for the spread of the Gospel and for the useful presentation of information from the viewpoint of charity and truth. Ghana and all Africa are no exception. Through your interest and collaboration may the mass media truly perform their providential role at the service of humanity. For the Church these are splendid instruments to preach the message of Christ, as from the housetops (cf. Mt. 10:27). Be assured of my admiration for your efforts to utilize these means as often as possible. In this regard, you deserve great praise for setting up *The Standard*, which I pray will ever assist you in the task of evangelization.

WORK OF DEVELOPMENT

8. Linked with evangelization is the work of development, which must continue to go on in Africa. In imitation of Christ, who was sensitive to the uplifting of humanity in all its aspects, the Church works for the total well-being of man. The laity have a distinctive part to play in the area of development; they have also been given a special charism in order to bring the presence of the serving Christ into all areas of human affairs. The human being asking to be uplifted from poverty and want is the same person in need of redemption and eternal life. Likewise, the

entire Church must serve development by offering to the world her total vision of man, and by proclaiming ceaselessly the preeminence of spiritual values (cf. *Address to the United Nations*, October 2, 1979, no. 14). Providence has endowed your people with an innate understanding of this fact. Only by being sensitive to every need can the Church continue to render her many services, but one of her most effective contributions to progress will be to point out that the goal of personal development is found only in a transcendent humanism, which is attained by union with Christ (cf. PP 16).

LEAD BY EXAMPLE

9. There are many other aspects to our pastoral ministry and we cannot now speak about all of them. But as bishops, let us call our people constantly to conversion of life, and by our example let us lead the way. The importance of the sacraments of Penance or Reconciliation and of the Eucharist cannot be overemphasized. In both of these we are the ministers of God's mercy and His love. At the same time, as bishops we are called to bear a consistent witness to Christ, the High Priest and Pontiff of salvation, by being signs of holiness in His Church. A difficult task? Yes, brothers. But this is our vocation, and the Holy Spirit is upon us. Moreover, the effectiveness of our pastoral ministry depends on our holiness of life. Let us not be afraid, for the Mother of Jesus is with us. She is in our midst today and always. And we are strong through her prayers and safe in her care. *Regina Caeli, laetare, alleluia!*

Through Our Ministry, the Gift of Salvation

After his meeting with the bishops of Ghana on May 9, 1980, the Holy Father then met, in the seminary chapel, the visiting bishops from the neighboring countries. Among these was Cardinal Ignatius Dominic Ekandem, Archbishop of Ikot Ekpene (Nigeria). The Pope addressed them as follows.

My dear brother bishops,

1. It is a joy for me to be with you today. You have come from your respective dioceses, and I from Rome, and all of us have assembled here in the name of our Lord Jesus Christ. We truly feel His presence in our midst. Indeed, we have come to Ghana to celebrate His Gospel, to celebrate the centenary of the implantation of His Church in this region. Our thoughts are turned, therefore, to the great reality of evangelization. This is very natural for us, since we are the successors of the Twelve and, like them, are called to be servants of the Gospel, proclaiming Jesus Christ and His message of Redemption.

Our ministry makes many demands on us. The effective preaching of the Gospel, which is "the power of God for salvation to everyone who has faith" (Rom. 1:16), requires our constant effort in going out to the People of God with a deep understanding of their culture, their pastoral needs and the pressures put upon them by the modern world. Evangelization requires farsighted planning on our part, the utilization of the proper means and the full collaboration of the local Churches. But I wish to limit myself today to a brief consideration on the content of evangelization, on what Paul VI called its "foundation and center" and what he described as being "a clear proclamation that in Jesus Christ, the Son of God made man, who died and rose from the dead, salvation is offered to all men as a gift of God's grace and mercy" (EN 38).

2. As bishops we must reflect not only on our duty, but also on the immense privilege it is to bring this fundamental message of salvation to the people. This is the

nature of our divine mission, this explains our human fulfillment: to proclaim salvation in Jesus Christ. What a wonderful ministry it is to preach a Gospel of redemption in Jesus, to explain to our people how they have been chosen by God the Father to live in Christ Jesus, how the Father "rescued us from the power of darkness and brought us into the Kingdom of his beloved Son. Through him we have redemption, the forgiveness of our sins" (Col. 1:14).

3. Christ's gift of salvation gives rise to our sacramental ministry and to all our efforts to build up the communion of the Church, a redeemed community living the new life of Christ. Because our message is the message of salvation, it is also a constant invitation to our people to respond to God's gift, to live a life worthy of the calling that they have received (cf. Eph. 4:1). The message of salvation brings with it an invitation to our people to praise God for His goodness, to rejoice in His gift, to forgive others just as they themselves have been forgiven, and to love others just as they themselves have been loved.

God gives this great gift of salvation through His Church, through our ministry. In accordance with God's will, let us go forward in our evangelizing activities, announcing with perseverance the Good News of salvation, and proclaiming explicitly: "It is in Christ and through his blood that we have been redeemed and our sins forgiven, so immeasurably generous is God's favor to us." This proclamation is fundamental to all our moral doctrine, to our social teaching, to our pastoral concern for the poor. It is the basis of our pastoral ministry to the needy, the suffering and those in prison. It is fundamental to everything we do, to our whole episcopal ministry.

Dear brothers: Praised be Jesus Christ, who has called us to proclaim His salvation and who sustains us by His love. May He keep us strong in joy, persevering in prayer together with His Mother Mary, and united to the end.

Praised be Jesus Christ.

Meaning of Vocations in the Divine Plan

After the Mass in Ouagadougou on May 10, 1980, the Holy Father then met the bishops of Upper Volta led by Cardinal Paul Zoungrana, Archbishop of Ouagadougou, and by the President of the Episcopal Conference of Upper Volta and of Niger, His Excellency Dieudonné Yougbare, Bishop of Koupêla. His Holiness addressed them as follows.

Dear brothers in the episcopate,

1. In the course of this journey of mine in your African land, I never tire of expressing my joy at meeting, too rapidly alas, those men and women who are the Church in your countries, the kingdom of God which takes root and grows among you.

This joy becomes even greater when I meet the bishops, the spiritual leaders of the new people, my brothers in the episcopate. I am particularly happy, as I said, to return in this way dear Cardinal Zoungrana's visit, who was the first African Cardinal who came to see me in Krakow. We have just time, dear brothers, to recall some thoughts which are close to my heart and yours.

The first one is our unity in collegiality. You live it among yourselves; we live it together, linking the Church which is in Upper Volta with the life and evangelical concerns of the universal Church. Collegiality is a structural element of the Church, a way of government of the episcopate, to which our age, following an important teaching of the Second Vatican Council, rightly attaches particular importance. The fact of putting it into practice well, as you certainly experience every day, is a great support for our pastoral action, and also a great hope for the growth of its effectiveness. But it is on spiritual and theological reasons, in the first place, that we must build our episcopal collaboration, the source of our ministry being the Person of the Lord.

2. I encourage you, therefore, to continue to work to found your unity and that of your presbyterium really in

Christ. The presbyterium consists of different elements; try to ensure that its diversity may always be a source of mutual enrichment, not of division or rivalry. For this purpose remain yourselves very close to your priests, very much present in their difficult life. Your words and your example will be able to direct more and more towards the service of the People of God the minds and the wills of those who have generously dedicated themselves to this mission.

Your dioceses, too, are varied, with different apostolic forces. Together you must face up to the common tasks and the sectors in greatest need. This spirit of solidarity must also extend outside your frontiers, particularly in the framework of the regional episcopal conference of West Africa, of which Your Eminence is president, and even in the framework of the SCEAM, for the whole of Africa and Madagascar. You have to become your own missionaries to an ever increasing extent.

3. That brings me to share with you two concerns of prime importance for evangelization and for the Christian fervor of your Church of Upper Volta. I wish to speak of your concern for vocations, and also for an apostolate based on the specifically African sense of the family.

In addition to the "missionaries," the incomparable service of whom, always so precious as a testimony of the universal Church, is recognized by everyone, you have the joy of having numerous priests, men and women religious, and seminarians of Upper Volta, as well as large numbers of catechists. The mission of the Church would require even more. It is an important part of your ministry to see to the awakening and guidance of priestly and religious vocations, through a thorough formation, which has stood the test of experience in the Church, and which is well integrated in the African reality. We must never tire of explaining the deep meaning of this vocation in God's plan. To offer oneself to follow Christ in all availability, in the exclusive service of His kingdom, to dedicate one's strength and love to Him in celibacy, is a grace that the Church, and therefore the African Churches, cannot lack today.

By these priests or religious, Christians will be helped to make progress in personal awareness of their own vocation. Among them, the catechists, whom I am anxious to encourage through you, set a magnificent example of a Christian lay vocation put in the service of the Church's mission. Paul VI had made a point of decorating, five years ago, the centenarian Simon Zerbo, the first catechist of Upper Volta and a pioneer of faith in your country.

4. For this mission you have been making, for several years, a pastoral effort aimed at showing that the Church is really the family of God, in which each one has his place, in which each one is understood and loved. In this way, I hope together with you, your Christian communities will benefit from a deep element of structuralization, which will also constitute a concrete testimony of the Gospel, and even an appeal to non-Christians. In this conception of the family, stress is also laid on the connection between a fundamental reality and the Gospel revelation and one of the moral values characteristic of the civilization of your people.

5. There are many other questions which could be considered. I have just dealt with the very serious one of the drought in Sahel, which must bring forth a more real, more concerted and more persevering solidarity in the whole world. I am also thinking of the fact that many of your fellow countrymen are followers of Islam. The two principal religious communities, Catholic and Muslim, must therefore continue their efforts to esteem one another, respecting on both sides what religious freedom, rightly understood, requires, and to collaborate when it is a question of meeting the human needs of the populations and their common good.

6. With you, dear brothers, I am full of hope, in spite of the difficulties, and I know your deep attachment to the Holy See and the universal Church. The Lord did not prom-

ise us a life and a ministry free of trials. He simply assured us that He had overcome the forces of evil at work in man. That is why we must always keep in mind the words He spoke on sending the Apostles on their mission after His resurrection: "Do not be afraid.... I am with you always, to the close of the age." How better could I express my encouragement to you? The efforts you make incessantly in the Lord's service will yield their fruit. May the Lord bless each of you, and all those in your hearts, priests, men and women religious and the faithful, one and all of your dioceses!

The World Needs
Gospel Witnesses

On May 11, 1980, the Holy Father's second engagement was at the Church of Notre Dame de Treichville, where he met a large gathering of priests, men and women religious, and the laity. He spoke to them as follows:

Dear brothers and sisters in Christ,

Your magnificent gathering enables me, once more, to measure the vitality of the Church in the Ivory Coast. Thank you for having come in such large numbers and so eager to advance along the ways of the kingdom of God and to help others to approach it!

I address the same pressing and trusting encouragement to all: Be what you must be, before the Lord who has called you, and in the eyes of the world which needs your evangelical witness! And be so in the vocation which belongs specifically to each one. It is a question of faithfulness to the Lord, of loyalty to yourselves, of respect for others, of ecclesial solidarity.

You have given a great deal to the Church and your country. Give them even more.

TO PRIESTS

To you, dear sons who have received the incomparable grace of priestly ordination, I express in the first place my deep happiness to know that you live in unity among yourselves, whether you are sons of the people of the Ivory Coast or have come from other countries, and in trusting collaboration with your bishops. May the cry of Christ's heart, "May they be one," always resound in your own heart! The credibility of the Gospel and the effectiveness of apostolic work depend largely on the unity of the pastors, called to form one presbyterium, whatever the post and the responsibilities of each one may be.

At this moment, so moving for me and for you, I would like above all to strengthen in you an absolutely essential conviction: Christ has made you His own (cf. Phil. 3:12-14) and has specially conformed you to Himself through the priestly character, to serve the Church and the men of today by dedicating all your physical and spiritual strength to them. The mystery of the priesthood is not determined by sociological analyses, wherever they may come from. It is in the Church, with the leaders of the Church, that it is possible to study deeply and live this gift of the Lord Jesus. I beg you: have faith in your priesthood!

I hasten to add another encouragement, which is also of essential importance. May Christ be, as it were, the breath of your daily life! Your everyday faithfulness and your radiating influence call for this. Develop even more your brotherhood among priests, in your parish teams, your meetings for apostolic reflection and concerted action, and even more so in your times of prayer and retreat. These two dimensions, with the Lord and among yourselves, will be the bulwark of your priestly celibacy and the guarantee of its fruitfulness. Live this evangelical renunciation of fatherhood in the flesh in the constant perspective of the spiritual fatherhood which fills the hearts of priests completely dedicated to their people. Live these requirements and these joys in the spirit of apostles of all times.

Unceasingly Proclaim
the Word of Salvation

After his meeting with the various groups in the church of Notre Dame de Treichville, on May 11, 1980, the Holy Father then went to the Catholic Institute for West Africa (I.C.A.O.) where he met the visiting bishops from the neighboring countries and addressed them as follows.

Dear brothers in the episcopate,

Great is my joy to meet you here, in this Catholic Institute for West Africa, which bears high witness to the effective collaboration of the episcopates of the whole region.

Too rapid, like all my visits, alas, my short stay here gives me, however, and will leave with me, an extremely comforting impression. Serious work, I know, is being carried out here. I earnestly encourage all the bishops on whom this institute depends to continue to be full of solicitude in order to ensure it fresh adherents, so that its future may be as fruitful as the present permits us to hope.

In a moment I am going to bless the first stone of the building that will house the Secretariat of the Regional Episcopal Conference of French-speaking West Africa. That, too, is a new symbol of your will to work together, for the sake of efficiency, and to bear witness better to the spirit of unity that animates you.

To you all, dear brothers, who have in many cases undertaken a long journey to come and greet me during my journey in Africa, in the Ivory Coast, my thanks for your presence. Thank you for the warm hospitality given me in these pastoral visits. My joy is great, I repeat, at seeing myself welcomed in this way and surrounded by so many bishops in order to manifest together the unity of the Church. Receive all my fervent and brotherly encouragement for the apostolic work you courageously assume. For the service of God, we must bear the weight of the day and the heat! So continue unceasingly to proclaim the word of salvation, this Gospel which was solemnly entrusted to us at our episcopal ordination!

Take my warm and deep encouragement also to all your dioceses, to everyone: to the priests whom I love so much, to men and women religious, to all the faithful, and particularly to those who are unhappy, to the sick, to those who are suffering. Take the Pope's affection and blessing to them all.

The Immense Field of Evangelization

Shortly after noon on May 11, 1980, John Paul II met the Ivory Coast bishops in the Nunciature and addressed them as follows.

Beloved brothers in the episcopate,

Since last night, we have been meeting in the midst of your people. Now, we have at our disposal some time which will be rather a family talk. We are a family party!

I do not forget that your nine dioceses are rather different as regards the implantation of the Church. I will speak of the situation as a whole.

1. In the first place, I rejoice with you in the vitality of the Church in the Ivory Coast, and I give thanks to God for it. There have certainly been favorable exterior conditions: peace, the hospitable and tolerant character of the inhabitants, an innate religious sense as is often found in Africa. But we owe it above all to remarkable men of faith, to the zeal of the pioneers that the missionaries were, to numerous and persevering initiatives on their part. We owe it today to you yourselves, dear brothers, whose courageous and far-seeing dedication I know. You have created an excellent atmosphere of collaboration between the African clergy and the numerous foreign priests and religious who, thank God, continue their mutual aid. You

are also trying to make your laity become aware of their responsibilities on the apostolic and material plane. While continuing in your concern for a really worthy liturgy and Christian life, you do not omit to cope with the many pastoral problems that arise.

SOME PASTORAL PROBLEMS

2. I take the liberty of stressing some of these problems, not to provide solutions which are the object of your reflection and concerted action, but to manifest to you the interest I take in your episcopal ministry.

I am thinking, for example, of the large towns of Abidjan and Bouaké, where a considerable number of newcomers have arrived from the country and also immigrants from neighboring countries: how to make the Church present in these new districts and these new environments? There are poor people of all kinds, the uprooted, the humble people to whom we owe a special presence and solicitude, like Christ. There is also an elite, the executives, who need a deeper Christian reflection at the level of their culture and their responsibilities, in the first place in order not to remain on the fringe of the Church, and also to take part in a more harmonious development of the country. For there is a social justice to be promoted, with regard to privileges of fortunes or power, too great inequalities, temptations of excessive enrichment, sometimes of corruption, as you yourselves say. The Church must help leaders not to transpose to your country certain Western patterns of life which tend to establish persons and families in materialism, individualism and practical atheism, and to abandon the underprivileged.

You are also concerned about the multitude of the young and of students. In the framework of parishes and schools, they merit a specialized apostolate and particularly a catechesis for which the help of their elders would certainly be welcome. You have done a great deal for

Catholic schools, in a country which should not have known the nasty whiffs of Western laicism, and you are right. The stake of student youth is a very great one; if only we could put at their disposal the chaplains they would need!

Catechists remain the indispensable collaborators of evangelization, and you are rightly concerned to give them an initial and continuous formation, suited to the needs of the various communities and the various environments. I have often spoken about this in the course of my journey. It is also necessary to train educators, priests, sisters and lay people who will engage in more thorough religious studies, taking their African culture into account. Evangelization will greatly benefit from their qualified service on the theological and apostolic plane. I know the excellent work that is being carried out here by the Catholic Institute of West Africa, which I have just visited. It is also a blessing for you.

The family apostolate is particularly important; I am aware of the difficult problems it raises. I spoke about them in Kinshasa. It is up to you, to you bishops, to solve them in concerted action, maintaining the conviction that, on the basis of the Gospel, according to the centuries-old experience of the Church expressed by the universal Magisterium and thanks to a patient formation of future spouses, it is possible for African couples to live, with particular intensity, the mystery of the covenant, of which God's covenant with His people—the covenant of Jesus Christ with His Church—remains the source and the symbol. Deep and lasting blessings will spring from these Christian families, for the faith of the young and vocations as well.

Your Catholic communities must also establish adequate relations with other Christian communities, with the Muslims and with other religious groups. But, above all, you have still an immense field of evangelization before you: those who remain available for the proclamation of the Gospel, in the villages and towns. There is a specifically missionary apostolate to be carried out here.

DEFINE PASTORAL PLANS TOGETHER

3. All that has its value, its importance, and it is very difficult for me to indicate to you priorities in these sectors of the apostolate. However, I think that you must, without neglecting anything, define pastoral plans together in order that efforts may converge on what is essential, in precise directions, and stick to them with perseverance.

On my part, I would like just to confirm your convictions on some fundamental attitudes.

In the first place with regard to your episcopal ministry. You know its requirements better than anyone. St. Paul warned us that to be ministers of Christ, with our eyes fixed on the Gospel, is to expose ourselves to misunderstanding and tribulations. As one of your proverbs says: "The tree by the side of the path receives blows from all those who pass." But I wish you also great spiritual consolations. Remain spiritual leaders who are at the same time Fathers for their people, in the manner of Christ who serves. Be free with regard to all secular power, while recognizing its sphere of competence and its specific responsibility. Continue to call forth wide collaboration on the part of your priests and your laity, to examine problems, and associate them with your decisions. Above all, maintain close union and real collaboration with one another, as also with the bishops of West Africa. Oh yes, live closely united in unfailing solidarity among yourselves and with the Holy See; this is your strength.

I lay stress especially on your priests, your born collaborators, whether they were born in the Ivory Coast or have come from afar. They form the same presbyterium, the same family. They are sometimes scattered, in a difficult apostolate. They need particularly to feel your support, your closeness, your friendly presence, your appreciation of their work, your encouragement for a worthy and generous priestly life. And that will also stimulate vocations.

For I greatly encourage the care you dedicate to bringing forth priestly and religious vocations, to providing young and older seminarians with a formation that gives them a taste for the Gospel, a solid faith, and the desire to meet Christ's call and serve the Church in a disinterested way, with regard to all the needs of the Christian communities and also of evangelization. Paul VI had said in Uganda in 1969: "You are your own missionaries." It is more and more necessary for you. The step has already taken place at the level of the episcopate; it must be prepared at the level of priests, even if, as I hope, you will still have at your disposal for a long time to come priests put at your service by other Churches or religious congregations. Finally, I will go even further along this "missionary" way: it is your entire Church that must become the missionary — priests, sisters, and laity, and the communities themselves —through the welcome, the witness and explicit proclamation, among those who still do not know the Gospel, in this country and in others.

4. These attitudes, as well as the different pastoral works to be promoted, must not make us lose sight of what is essential, dear brothers: the presence of Christ among us, acting with us and through us, to the extent to which we refer to Him our lives, our cares, our hopes, in constant prayer. Help all your collaborators to keep kindled within them this flame of spiritual life, this love of God without which we would be only clanging cymbals. Precisely at the moment when your Ivory Coast society is in rapid economic and cultural expansion, with all the opportunities but also the temptations to materialism, which this involves, it is a question of ensuring to this civilization a soul. Only spiritual beings will be able to bear it along in a deeply Christian direction which is at the same time deeply African. May our Lady open our hearts to the Spirit of her Son! Receive my affectionate blessing.

The Infallibility of the Church Is Christ's Gift

On May 15, 1980, John Paul II sent the German episcopal conference the following letter with regard to questions discussed and referred to as the case of Prof. Hans Küng.

To the venerable brothers
of the German episcopal conference,
Venerable and dear brothers in the episcopate,

1. The ample documentation which you have published with regard to certain theological affirmations of Prof. Hans Küng bears witness with what care and good will you endeavored to clarify this important and difficult problem. Also the latest publications, both the pastoral letter read in the Churches on January 13, 1980, and the detailed *Erklärung* published at the same time, are an expression of your responsibility as pastors and teachers, in keeping with the nature of your office and your episcopal mission.

In expectation of the approaching feast of Pentecost, I wish to strengthen you in your task as pastors in the spirit of divine love and truth, and to thank you for all the efforts you have made, over the years, with regard to this problem, in collaboration with the Holy See, in particular with the Sacred Congregation for the Doctrine of the Faith. The tasks of the latter—always essential for the life of the Church—seem particularly difficult and full of responsibility today. The Motu proprio *Integre servandae*, which already during the Second Vatican Council specified more precisely the sphere and the procedure of the Congregation for the Doctrine of the Faith, stresses the necessity of collaboration with the episcopate. This is quite in harmony with the *principle of collegiality*, reaffirmed by the Council itself. This collaboration was carried out in a particularly intense way in the case in question. There are many reasons why the Church of our time must show herself to be more than ever a Church of conscious and effective collegiality among bishops and pastors. In such a Church there can take place even more fully what St. Irenaeus said about the Roman See of Peter, indicating it as the center of the ecclesial community which must gather and unite the individual local Churches and all the faithful (cf. *Adversus haereses:* PG 7, 848).

In the same way the Church of today must be—more than ever before—the Church of *a real dialogue,* such as indicated by Paul VI in his fundamental encyclical *Ecclesiam suam* at the beginning of his pontificate. The exchange which dialogue implies must lead to meeting in truth and justice. In dialogue the Church tries to understand man better and thereby also her own mission. She brings him the knowledge and truth revealed to her in faith. Therefore, it does not contradict the essence of this dialogue that the Church should not be merely the one that seeks and receives, but also the one that gives, on the basis of a certainty which in such a conversation grows even more and is deepened, but can never be taken away. On the contrary, it would be contrary to the essence of dialogue if the Church were to suspend her own conviction and renounce the knowledge that has already been given to her. Furthermore, the dialogue that bishops carry out with a theologian who teaches the Faith of the Church in the name of the Church and charged by her to do so, has a particular character. It is based on different premises from those of the dialogue which takes place with men of different convictions in the common search for a ground of agreement. Here it is a question above all of clarifying whether the person who teaches by order of the Church actually corresponds, and wishes to correspond, to this order.

With regard to the teaching authorization of Prof. Küng, it was a question above all of asking the following questions: Does a theologian who no longer accepts completely the doctrine of the Church still have the right to teach in the name of the Church and on the basis of a special mission received from her? Can he himself still wish to do so, if some dogmas of the Church are contrary to his personal convictions? And under these circumstances can the Church—in this case her competent authority—continue to oblige him to do so?

The decision of the Congregation for the Doctrine of the Faith, taken in common agreement with the German episcopal conference, is the result of the honest and responsible answer to the above questions. At the root of these questions and the way of answering them, there is a fundamental right of the human person, that is, the right to truth, whose protection and defense was at issue. Certainly, Prof. Küng has declared insistently that he wishes to be and remain a Catholic theologian. In his works, however, he shows clearly that he does not consider some authentic doctrines of the Church as definitive and binding for himself and for his theology and consequently, on the basis of his personal convictions, he is no longer in a position to carry out the mission which he had received from the bishop on behalf of the Church.

The Catholic theologian, like every scientist, has the right to free analysis and research in his own field, naturally in the way that corresponds to the very nature of Catholic theology. But when it is a question of communicating, orally or in writing, the results of his researches and reflections, it is necessary to respect in a special way the principle formulated by the first Synod of Bishops in the year 1967 with the expression, *paedagogia fidei*.

It may be fitting and correct to set forth the rights of the theologian, but it is also necessary at the same time to take into due consideration his special responsibilities. Nor must *the right and the duty of the Magisterium* to decide whether or not something corresponds to the Church's doctrine of faith and morality be forgotten. The testing, approval or rejection of a doctrine belongs to the prophetic mission of the Church.

PRESERVING FIDELITY
TO CHRIST AND THE GOSPEL

2. Some questions and aspects connected with the discussion about Prof. Küng are of a fundamental kind and of more general significance for the present period of the post-conciliar renewal. I would like, therefore, to deal with them somewhat more thoroughly.

In the generation to which we belong, the Church has made an enormous effort to understand better her nature and the mission entrusted to her by Christ with regard to man and the world, especially the modern world. She did so by means of the historic service of the Second Vatican Council. We believe that Christ was present in the assembly of bishops, that He operated in them by means of the Holy Spirit, promised to His disciples on the eve of His passion when He spoke of the "Spirit of truth" who would teach them every truth and would remind them of everything they had heard from Christ Himself (cf. Jn. 14:17-28). From the work of the Council there arose the *program of the inner renewal of the Church*, a wide and at the same time courageous program, based on deep awareness of the true mission of the Church, which is by its very nature missionary.

Even if the post-conciliar period is not free from difficulties (as has been the case now and then in the history of the Church), we believe, nonetheless, that Christ is present in it, the same Christ who sometimes let the Apostles, too, experience storms on the lake which seemed to be leading them to shipwreck. After the night's fishing when they had caught nothing, He transformed this failure into an unexpected abundant draught, when they cast their nets on the Lord's word (cf. Lk. 5:4-5). If the Church wishes to do justice to her mission at this stage of her history, which is unquestionably a difficult and decisive one, she can do so only by listening to the Word of God, that is, by obeying the "word of the Spirit," as it has reached the Church by means of Tradition and, directly, through the Magisterium of the last Council.

In order that this work, which is difficult and "humanly" very arduous, can be carried out, special faithfulness to Christ and His Gospel is necessary, because He alone is "the way." Therefore, only by *preserving fidelity* to the established signs and by continuing perseveringly along the way that the Church has followed for two thousand years, can we be sure that we shall be sustained by that *power from above* which Christ Himself promised the Apostles and the Church as proof of His presence "to the close of the age" (Mt. 28:20).

If there is something essential and fundamental in the present stage of service of the Church, it is the particular orientation of souls and hearts to the fullness of the mystery of Christ, the Redeemer of man and of the world and, at the same time, faithfulness to that image of the nature and mission of the Church as it is presented, after so many historical experiences, by the Second Vatican Council. According to the express doctrine of the Council, "every renewal of the Church essentially consists in an increase of fidelity to her own calling" (UR 6). Any attempt to replace the image of the Church, as derived from the nature and mission of the Church herself, with another one, would inevitably take us away from the sources of light and the power of the Spirit, which we need so much precisely today. We must not labor under illusions, as if another—more "laicized"—model of the Church could meet more adequately the requirements of a greater presence of the Church in the world and of greater comprehension for the problems of man. That can be done only by a Church that is deeply rooted in Christ, in the sources of her faith, hope and charity.

The Church must also be very humble and at the same time certain that she remains in the same truth, in the same doctrine of faith and morality, which she received from Christ, who has provided her, in this sphere, with the gift of a specific "infallibility." Vatican II inherited from Vatican I the doctrine of Tradition in this connection, confirmed it and presented it in a wider context, namely, in the context of the mission of the Church, which, thanks to participation in the prophetic mission of Christ, has itself a prophetic character. In this connection and closely linked with the "sense of the faith" in which all the faithful participate, that *"infallibility" has the character of a gift and a service.*

If anyone understands it in a different way, he moves away from the authentic vision of the Faith and detaches the Church, in actual fact, even if perhaps unconsciously, from the One who "loved" her as her Bridegroom and gave Himself for her. When Christ endowed the Church with everything indispensable to carry out the mission entrusted to her, could He have withheld from her that gift of certainty about the truth professed and proclaimed? Could He have withheld this gift above all from those who, after Peter and the Apostles, inherit as pastors and teachers a special responsibility towards the community of the faithful? Precisely because man is fallible, Christ could not—if He wished to preserve the Church in the truth—leave her pastors and bishops and above all Peter and his Successors without that gift by means of which He guarantees infallibility in the teaching of the truths of Faith and the principles of morality.

So we profess infallibility, which is a gift entrusted by Christ to the Church. We cannot fail to profess it, if we believe in the love with which Christ loved His Church and loves her incessantly.

We believe in the infallibility of the Church not in consideration of any man, but of Christ Himself. We are convinced, indeed, that also for the one who participates in a special way in the infallibility of the Church, that infallibility is essentially and exclusively a condition of the service which he must discharge in this Church. "Power," in fact, cannot be understood and exercised anywhere, much less in the Church, but as service. The example of the Master is decisive in this regard.

We must be deeply concerned, on the other hand, when *faith in this gift of Christ is questioned in the*

Church. In this case there would be cut simultaneously the roots from which there springs the certainty of the truth professed and proclaimed in the Church. Although the truth about the infallibility of the Church may indeed seem a less central truth with a lower position in the hierarchy of the truths revealed by God and professed by the Church, it is, however, in a way, the key to that certainty with which the Faith is professed and proclaimed, as well as to the life and behavior of the faithful. For if this essential foundation is shaken or destroyed, even the most elementary truths of our Faith begin at once to disintegrate.

It is a question, therefore, of an important problem in the present post-conciliar period. If the Church is to undertake the work of renewal, she must have a special certainty in the Faith, which, while it is renewed in accordance with the doctrine of the Second Vatican Council, remains in the same truth which she received from Christ. Only in this way can she be sure that Christ is present in her bark and steering it firmly through even the most threatening storms.

THE CHURCH CANNOT RENOUNCE
THE TRUTHS SHE PROCLAIMS

3. Anyone who takes part in the history of our century and is aware of the different trials that the Church is going through within herself during these first post-conciliar years, knows about these storms. The Church, which has to face them, must not be affected with uncertainty in the Faith and by relativism in truth and morality. Only a Church *deeply consolidated in the Faith* can be *a Church of authentic dialogue.* For dialogue requires, indeed, a special maturity in the truth professed and proclaimed. Only this maturity, that is, certainty in the Faith, is able to resist the radical negations of our time, even when they use the various means of propaganda and pressure. Only a mature faith can be an effective advocate of true religious freedom, freedom of conscience and all human rights.

The program of the Second Vatican Council is a courageous one. Therefore, it requires in its implementation special confidence in the Spirit who spoke (cf. Rv. 2:7) and an equally fundamental confidence in the power of Christ. This dedication and confidence must be, corresponding to our time, as great as those of the Apostles, who, after the ascension of Jesus, "with one accord devoted themselves to prayer...together with Mary" in the Upper Room of Jerusalem (Acts 1:14).

This confidence in the power of Christ certainly calls also for ecumenical effort for the unity of Christians, which was started by the Second Vatican Council, provided we understand it as it was presented by the conciliar decree *Unitatis redintegratio.* It is significant that this document does not speak of a "compromise" but of meeting in a still more mature fullness of Christian truth: "The manner and order in which Catholic belief is expressed should in no way become an obstacle to dialogue with our brethren. It is, of course, essential that the doctrine be clearly presented in its entirety. Nothing is so foreign to the spirit of ecumenism as a false irenicism which harms the purity of Catholic doctrine and obscures its genuine and certain meaning" (no. 11; cf. no. 4).

So, from the ecumenical point of view of the union of Christians, it cannot be demanded that the Church should renounce certain truths that she proclaims. This would be contrary to the way that the Council indicated. If the Council itself, to reach this purpose, emphasizes that the Catholic Faith must be expressed more deeply and more precisely, it also indicates thereby the task of the theologian. Very significant is that passage of the decree *Unitatis redintegratio* in which, dealing directly with the Catholic theologian, it stresses that "Catholic theologians...searching together with separated brethren into the divine mysteries," should do so "with love for the truth" (no. 11). I have already referred above to the hierarchy," or order of the truths of Catholic doctrine, of which theologians must be aware, especially "when comparing doctrines with one another." The Council refers to this hierarchy "since they (i.e., the truths) vary in their relation to the foundation of the Christian faith" *(ibid.)*.

In this way ecumenism, this great heritage of the Council, can become an increasingly mature reality, but only on the way of a great commitment of the Church, inspired by the certainty of the Faith and by confidence in the power of Christ, by which pioneers in this work have been characterized from the start.

LOVING OUR BROTHER

4. Venerable and dear brothers of the German episcopal conference!

We can love Christ only when we love our brothers: one and all of them. Therefore this letter also, which I am writing to you in connection with the recent events regarding Prof. Hans Küng, is determined by love of this brother of ours.

To him, I would like to repeat once more what has already been expressed on another occasion: We continue to hope that it may be possible to arrive at such a meeting in the truth proclaimed and professed by the Church, and that he can again be called a "Catholic theologian." This title necessarily presupposes the true Faith of the Church and readiness to serve her mission in the way that has been clearly defined and put into practice in the course of the centuries.

Love demands that we should seek the meeting in truth with every man. Therefore, we do not cease to ask God for such a meeting particularly with that man, our brother, who as a Catholic theologian, as he would like to be and remain, must share special responsibility with us for the truth professed and proclaimed by the Church. Such a prayer is, in a certain sense, the fundamental word of love for man, our neighbor; for through it we find him in God Himself, who as the only Source of love is at the same time, in the Holy Spirit, the light of our hearts and our consciences. It is also the first and deepest expression of that concern for the Church in which everyone and particularly her pastors must participate.

In this communion of prayer and common pastoral solicitude I implore for you, for the imminent feast of Pentecost, the abundance of the gifts of the divine Spirit, and I greet you in the love of Christ with my special apostolic blessing.

From the Vatican, May 15, the feast of Christ's ascension, in the year 1980, the second of my pontificate.

Special Responsibility of Bishops Regarding Culture and the Gospel

Pope John Paul received, on May 20, 1980, the bishops of Japan present in Rome on their ad limina *visit. After an address of homage by Cardinal Joseph Satowaki the Holy Father delivered the following address.*

Dear brothers in our Lord Jesus Christ,

Your presence here today near the tomb of the Apostle Peter evokes many thoughts in our hearts.

1. This is a special moment of ecclesial unity, as we celebrate our oneness in Jesus Christ and in His Church. You come as pastors of the Church in Japan, bringing with you the hopes and joys, the challenges and problems of your Catholic people. At the same time, this is a moment when the Church in Rome respectfully greets in your persons the entire Japanese people, of whom you are illustrious and noble sons. All of you remember with what faithful attention, with what great love Paul VI welcomed Japanese visitors and pilgrims during all the years of his pontificate. Individuals and groups, Christians and non-Christians, religious leaders and representatives of various walks of life came to see him week after week, month after month. For all of them he had a gesture of cordial

greeting or a word of esteem and friendship. I too have had the honor of receiving many visits from your fellow countrymen, and I wish to attest publicly how much their presence is appreciated at the Vatican.

2. This *ad limina* visit, venerable brothers, is also a celebration of faith: the faith of the whole Church in Japan—the faith of which you, in union with the Successor of Peter, are guardians and authentic teachers. On my part today I wish to render homage to this faith, which through missionary effort was implanted by God as His gift in the hearts of the faithful. This gift of faith was generously accepted and genuinely lived. It became the object of the witnessing of Paul Miki and his martyr companions, who went to their death proclaiming the names of Jesus and Mary, and who by their martyrdom confirmed the Faith as an everlasting heritage in Japan. By the grace of God and the help of His Blessed Mother, this Catholic Faith was, moreover, preserved throughout generations by the Japanese laity who maintained by the instinct of faith their unbreakable attachment to the See of Peter.

And today this faith is still expressed in action, nurtured by prayer and offered freely to all who may wish to embrace the Gospel. Through their faith, manifested by fraternal love and by the consistency of their lives, the Christian people of Japan are called to give witness to Jesus Christ in their families, in their neighborhoods, and in all the milieux in which they live; they are called to communicate Jesus Christ to anyone who may wish to know Him or embrace His message of salvation and life.

3. Our own episcopal ministry of faith: a ministry that presupposes faith and is at the service of faith—a faith to be lived and communicated. Everything we do is aimed at proclaiming the mystery of faith, and at helping our people to live deeply their vocation of faith.

4. Precisely by reason of the central dimension of faith we see the great value that prayer has in the Church: faith is kept alive and is fortified by prayer. By prayer, hearts are opened to the promptings of the Holy Spirit and

to the message and action of Christ's Church. Hence, we know that fidelity to prayer is an essential element of the Church's life. In this regard Japan has been blessed with contemplative vocations, with religious who carry on Christ's loving praise of His Father. And in this contemplative aspect of the Church's life in Japan is there not an excellent element of dialogue with your non-Christian brethren, who in their own ancient traditions have given a place of prominence to contemplation? Is not the desire to be united with God in purity of heart one of those elements in which the teaching of our Savior Jesus Christ is so naturally inculturated into the lives of so many of your people?

5. It is a great credit to Japan how generations of Christians, steeped in their own culture, have been able to contribute by their activities to the uplifting of society. The relatively small Christian community in your land has served well in the fields of social assistance, science and education. Through schools and universities the Christian message has come into contact with the venerable traditions of your people. Zealous Christians who have realized the need to bring the Gospel values into their native culture have begun by giving the upright witness of their own lives. In the midst of their community, when Christians show their capacity for understanding and acceptance, when they share the life and destiny of their brothers and sisters and show solidarity with all that is good and noble, and at the same time give expression to their faith in higher values and to their hope in a life yet to be unfolded in God —then they are fulfilling a task of initial evangelization with regard to culture, a task consistent with their vocation and the obligations that flow therefrom (cf. EN 21).

What a lofty role it is for the bishops of the Church to sustain all the members of the community in their common efforts on behalf of the Gospel, encouraging them to be able to explain the hope that is theirs (cf. 1 Pt. 3:15). In God's Providence the primary witness of life must be coupled with an explicit proclamation of the name, the teaching, the life, the promises, the kingdom and the mystery of Christ (cf. EN 22). The encounter between the Gospel and culture can take place only on the condition that the Church faithfully proclaims and lives the Gospel. Here, too, the bishops are called to exercise a special responsibility.

6. On this occasion, dear brothers in Christ, it is my hope to encourage you to stand fast in your ministry of faith. The universal Church has been deeply enriched by the contribution of the Church in Japan. The *pusillus grex* has been a credit to the grace of Christ the Savior, and it continues to give praise to His Father. The future is in the hands of Jesus. It is He, Jesus, who is the Lord of history; it is He who definitively decides the destiny of His Church in each generation. In the preparation of the Easter candle on Holy Saturday we proclaim: "All time belongs to him and all ages; to him be glory and power through every age." Our response to the will of the Lord Jesus for His Church is one of absolute trust coupled with diligent labor, knowing that He will ask us for an accounting.

7. Our ministry of faith has its origin in Jesus Christ and leads to Him and through Him to the Father. Despite all obstacles and difficulties we must constantly call our people to the holiness of life that is found in Christ alone: *Tu solus sanctus.* In a particular way the Christian family of Japan should be the object of our pastoral care. In this "domestic Church" the catechesis of children must be effectively begun, and the evangelization of society must take place at its root. The great love of God for His people and Christ's faithful covenant with His Church must be evident in the family as a community of love and life. I exhort you, brethren, to make every effort to create in families those healthy conditions of Christian living that favor vocations to the priesthood and religious life. Keep constantly before the young the full challenge of Christ's love and truth, including His invitation to take up the cross and follow Him.

8. The fraternal unity that springs from faith in Jesus Christ must be lived by the entire Church, but in an exemplary way it should be evident in the life of the presbyterium of each diocese. Our ministry of faith requires that we be closely united with our priests, and they with us, in proclaiming Jesus Christ the Savior of the world and in living His message of redemptive love. All the forces of the Gospel must indeed unite to give credible witness to the fellowship that is ours with the Father and the Son and the Holy Spirit.

In concluding, I ask you all to carry back to Japan, to all your beloved priests, religious, seminarians and laity, the expression of my own pastoral love in the heart of Jesus Christ. In the words of St. Paul: "Greetings to those who love us in the faith. Grace be with you all" (Ti. 3:15).

The Life of Christ Continues in the Church Today

The Holy Father received in audience on May 23, 1980, the bishops of Malaysia, Singapore and Brunei, present in Rome for their ad limina *visit, and addressed them as follows.*

My dear brother bishops,

1. With deep fraternal affection in Christ Jesus, I welcome you today to the Vatican. Your presence here as pastors of the Church spread throughout Malaysia, Singapore and Brunei gives us the opportunity to express our unity in Christ and in the hierarchy of His Church. This is likewise a joyful occasion for reflecting briefly on the mystery of the Church as it is lived in your lands and by your people.

In this reflection, which we make through the grace of the Holy Spirit, we find encouragement in our pastoral ministry and strength for our lives. Our apostolic mission of evangelization is linked with complicated problems affecting people's daily lives, their human dignity and their eternal salvation. Although there are no facile solutions to the issues that confront us, meditating on the mystery of the Church lightens our burdens and gives us a heightened sense of our ecclesial mission. In turn, we are able more effectively to sustain our brethren in their Christian vocation, thereby fulfilling our pastoral mandate: *Pascite qui est in vobis gregem Dei* (1 Pt. 5:2).

2. Of paramount importance in the mystery of the Church is the fact that Christ is alive in His people. His life goes on in the communities of the faithful throughout the world, in all those who by faith and Baptism have received justification in His name. The life of Christ continues in the Church today, in all those brothers and sisters of the Lord whom you have been sent to serve. Even what is so basic to the person of Christ—His divine filiation—is lived in the Church through the grace of divine adoption (cf. Gal. 4:5; Eph. 1:5).

And because the faithful are configured to Christ the Son of God, they are able, through the Holy Spirit, to express Christ's sentiments to the Father. Hence, Christ's prayer goes on in each generation; His continuing praise of His Father is a reality in His Church.

Yes, Christ is living in His members, and He therefore wills to suffer in them, permitting them to fill up what is lacking in His sufferings for the sake of His Body, the Church (cf. Col. 1:24). This mystery has entered into the consciousness of Christians, who realize that they should rejoice to share Christ's sufferings (cf. 1 Pt. 4:13), and that, when they are tried for His sake, it is better to suffer for doing what is right, rather than for what is wrong (cf. 1 Pt. 3:17).

And in His Church—once again in accordance with the plan of the Father—Christ grows in wisdom, age and grace (cf. Lk. 2:52), as His members, through His word and the action of His sacraments, come to full maturity in Him (cf. Eph. 4:13).

In Christ's Body, His zeal is perpetuated; and His Church is aflame with the desire of His heart: "I must proclaim the good news of the kingdom" (Lk. 4:43). The sick are visited; healing is offered to the brokenhearted, and the poor have the Gospel preached to them. The catechesis of the kingdom goes on in the young and old.

And because Christ is living, His love above all is kept alive in the Church. Jesus continues to love His Father, and the Father continues to love His Son in all those whom the Son has taken to Himself as brothers and sisters. And the mystery of a love received from the Father and given back to the Father is the legacy of all Christ's disciples: "By this all men will know that you are my disciples, if you have love for one another" (Jn. 13:35).

3. This mystery of Christ living in the Church is enacted in every community. It is a mystery that goes on from generation to generation, and it became part of your people's lives through missionary activity that God's grace made fruitful. This universal design of Christ enacted in every community throughout the world creates a bond of unity between all communities, giving them an essential unity—a unity in living the life of Christ. Each individual Church, provided it remains anchored in this unity, is able to translate the treasure of faith into the concrete life of every day, where it has its own aspirations, riches, limitations, and ways of praying, loving and looking at life and the world (cf. EN 63). As the local Church endeavors to assimilate the truth ever more, it is constantly challenged to preserve unaltered the content of the apostolic faith which the Lord entrusted to the Apostles. This task is, above all, the responsibility of the bishops to be exercised in union with the Successor of Peter and all the bishops of the Catholic Church.

4. At every juncture of the Church's life, the Holy Spirit is present because He has been sent by Christ to dwell in the Church, and to keep it alive. In a word, the Holy Spirit perpetuates the life of Christ in the Church. The dignity of Christian life and the value of Christian

conduct are linked to the reality of Christ living for ever in His Church. And it is in the context of this reality that we are sent to minister as bishops.

The means at our disposal—the only means that could possibly be commensurate with the supernatural goals which are the aims of the Church's activities—are the instruments of faith. In the words of St. Paul, they are "the armor of God" and "the sword of the Spirit, which is the word of God" (Eph. 6:13, 17). As bishops we are called to give our people the Word of God, to expound to them the whole mystery of Christ (cf. CD 12), after the example of the Apostle who did not hesitate to announce "God's design in its entirety" (Acts 20:27).

5. Dear brethren, the realization that our ministry is totally dedicated to the life of Christ in His members—which is perpetuated through the proclamation of the Word, especially in the sacramental renewal of the death of Christ—gives us deep joy and trust. Christ is with us today and always, and He tells us and all our people: "Fear not, I am the first and the last, and the living one; I died, and behold I am alive for evermore" (Rv. 1:17-18).

6. Yes, beloved brothers, Christ is alive in Malaysia, in Singapore and in Brunei—in all Asia. He is alive forevermore in your parishes, in all your communities, in your dioceses. And may you find strength and hope in realizing that everything you do as bishops is directed to perpetuating the life of Jesus Christ in His Church.

7. And now I would ask you to take my special greetings to your priests and religious, and to speak with them of their important role in the living Body of Christ. I would ask you to encourage the seminarians in their vocation, and to do everything possible to promote vocations to the priesthood. Please tell the catechists how much the Church depends on their generous cooperation and on their holiness of life. And may all the Christian families be repeatedly reminded just how intimately they are linked with the mystery of Christ's life in the Church.

And may the Mother of the living Christ, the Star of evangelization, be always near you to light your path and to bring all your beloved people to the fullness of life in Jesus Christ our saving God.

Awareness in Local Churches of the Mystery of Catholic Unity

On May 26, 1980, Pope John Paul received in audience a group of bishops from Indonesia on their ad limina visit. After an address of homage by the President of the Indonesian Episcopal Conference, Most Rev. F. X. Sudartanto Hadisumarta, Bishop of Malang, the Pope addressed them as follows.

Venerable and dear brothers in the episcopate,

1. In the name of Jesus Christ, the Good Shepherd, you and I share, in different ways, a common pastoral responsibility for the People of God in Indonesia. This common pastoral responsibility is willed by Christ and is incumbent on us inasmuch as we are bishops of the Catholic Church, successors of the Apostles and members of the episcopal college.

It is this common pastoral responsibility that gathers us together today in the service of the Church, for we are eager to see the light of Christ shine on the face of the Church. We are eager to see the Church, as the sacrament of salvation, penetrate ever more deeply into the fabric of Indonesian society and play a part in the different aspects of the life of your people. I know with what laudable patriotism you have supported the *Pancasila* or Five Basic Principles of Indonesia's State philosophy, and how you have endeavored to show the love of Christ to all your brethren without any distinction whatsoever. Like my Predecessor, Paul VI, who went personally to Indonesia to confirm the faith of the pastors and people, and to encourage all of you in hope and perseverance, I too declare my ecclesial solidarity with you in your ministry, as you build up the community of faith and consolidate your people in their Christian vocation.

2. As we assemble here today we draw strength from our Catholic unity, of which our pastoral role is one aspect in the mystery of Christ's Church. It is this Catholic unity that clarifies our pastoral role in its various dimensions; it gives us insights into the deepest truths of our apostolic activities.

Your local Churches are individual expressions of the one redeemed People of God, delivered from the dominion of darkness and transferred to the kingdom of His beloved Son, in whom we have redemption, and the forgiveness of our sins (cf. Col. 1:13-14). The people of whom you are the pastors are called to live the new life of Christ, giving expression to it in their customs and culture, and faithfully manifesting its original character in their daily existence. In this way they are able to enrich the whole Body of Christ by their unique contribution.

In effect, it is the one, holy, catholic and apostolic Church that subsists in your individual Churches. And it is the one, holy, catholic and apostolic Faith that is the great inheritance of your people, and that all of us as bishops are charged to proclaim "in season and out of season" (2 Tm. 4:2). As Successor of Peter, I shall be called to give a special accounting "in the presence of God and of Christ Jesus who is the Judge of the living and the dead" (2 Tm. 4:1) for the manner in which I respond to the charge, laid upon me by Christ, to be the guarantor of the purity of the Faith of the whole Church and to fulfill worthily the role of the Roman Pontiff as "the perpetual and visible source and foundation of the unity of the bishops and of the multitude of the faithful" (LG 23).

3. The ecclesial communion that we share and foster brings us immense consolation and joy in our ministry as bishops of the Catholic Church. We are aware of being, together with our faithful, the one Church of Jesus Christ, united in Him and living by His Holy Spirit.

Our communion is first of all a communion of faith. It is the apostolic Faith that unites us, an apostolic Faith that the Spirit of truth assists the Magisterium in transmitting intact and pure from one generation to the next. In this regard, as bishops, we must constantly commit ourselves anew to the full profession of the Catholic Faith, which transcends by far the insights of our human wisdom and theological reasoning. Only the Spirit of truth, the Spirit of Jesus, can sufficiently guarantee our faith, and this He does through the Magisterium which we are called to accept and in turn to proclaim to others.

Ours is also a communion of love—a love that has its origin and pattern in the most Holy Trinity. We have been the object of God's love, and this love unites us all together in the community of the Church. Among the tasks of a bishop, how important it is for him to reflect the love of Jesus the Good Shepherd on a personal basis. At every moment of our lives as pastors, there is someone who needs our love, someone who deserves our love. Our priests, in particular, have a special title to this love. They are our friends, our brothers and our sons in Jesus Christ. For the entire flock our love is manifested in understanding and in generous, persevering service of their needs—especially their need for the Word of God in all its purity and power.

Our communion is a communion of prayer, in which we all draw strength from the whole praying Body of Christ. The activity of prayer is very much a part of the life of the Church, uniting us with the living and the dead in the communion of saints. The saints of God are our intercessors. In particular, the Mother of Jesus, who is the Mother of the whole Body, intercedes for all who have received life in her Son. Legions of faithful Christians fulfill an ecclesial role of inestimable value by praying for the Church and her mission. We count on all these prayers, and are especially grateful for the contribution of the sick and the suffering.

Our communion involves the solidarity of the universal Church. The local Churches are all concerned for each other, since it is the one Catholic Church that subsists in all of them. Our hierarchical communion is an expression of the bonds of a single episcopal college that unites us in proclaiming the Gospel of Christ. By collegiality the pastors of the Church in Indonesia bring their solidarity to the whole Church and all the other pastors of the Church bring their solidarity to the local Churches in Indonesia. In all of this, the Holy See endeavors to exercise a role of service in coordinating activities and services beneficial to all. Above all, the Holy See is committed to the service of unity and truth, in charity. In accordance with the will of the Lord, the Successor of Peter strives to remain the servant of all.

In living this communion of faith and love, of prayer and solidarity, let us do everything, beloved brethren, to point the awareness of the local Churches to the great mystery of Catholic unity. From this Catholic unity your people have received so much; to it they bring their own distinctive contribution, which is the incarnation of the Gospel in their lives and culture.

4. Venerable brothers, let us always hold up to our people a supernatural message of hope, founded on salvation in Jesus Christ, the Son of God, and communicated through His Church. It is Jesus Christ who beckons us to come to Him in His Church, and through Him to the Father, in the Holy Spirit. It is Christ who urges us to lead our people forward along the path of faith. It is Christ who invites us to open ourselves with all our limitations and our sins to His immense mercy. In the hope of mercy we present ourselves before "Christ Jesus our hope" (1 Tm. 1:1). In hope we consecrate to Him our being and all our ministry. To Him we must direct our local Churches; we must speak about Him to our priests, religious and laity; we must proclaim His Person and His promises, His kingdom and His coming. This hope gives great encouragement to our ministry and to our lives; it sustains us and urges us on. In the words of St. Paul: "For to this end we toil and

strive, because we have our hope set on the living God, who is the Savior of all men, especially of those who believe" (1 Tm. 4:10).

Dear brethren: In the love of Christ, in the communion of His Church, in the shared responsibility of our pastoral mission I embrace all the faithful of your local Churches. I also send my greetings to the civil authorities and to all your fellow-citizens, to all who make up the one family of your vast country. May God bless Indonesia and your own ministry at the service of the Gospel of our Lord Jesus Christ.

The Episcopal Conference Should Assume Autonomously Its Own Responsibilities

On May 29, 1980, the Holy Father delivered the following address to the Seventeenth General Assembly of the Italian Bishops in the Synod Hall.

Reverend and dear bishops of Italy!

1. I am very glad to be in your midst again, a brother among brothers, in the course of this Seventeenth General Assembly of the Italian Episcopal Conference. It is true that the imminence of my pilgrimage to Paris and Lisieux, and the commitments of these days, allow me to stop only once among you, unlike last year. But let the intensity of affection make up for the shortage of time! Meanwhile, I express to you all my joy and the consolation I feel on meeting you on this very special occasion of the annual activity of your conference, an activity which is planned and carried out on a collegial basis. I tell you of my spiritual participation in the preparation and course of this assembly, and the interest with which I shall read, on my return from France, the final results of these days of study.

In particular, I am close to you in prayer: if, as Clement of Alexandria expressed in a marvelous way, "the

Church has only one breath around the altar" *(Strom.* VII, 6), we continually find ourselves united again, breathing together in the Eucharistic Celebration of every day: *"quoniam unus panis, unum corpus, multi sumus, omnes qui de uno pane participamus"* (1 Cor. 10:17). It is a very special moment, an experience of communion, that of this evening, which allows us to experience more thoroughly the reality of donation and service of our episcopate on behalf of the Church of God which is in Italy, and which the Holy Spirit has given you and me the destiny of governing and sanctifying.

GREAT RESPONSIBILITY

2. "We are the bishops of this Church," I said to you last year on May 18, in the homily of the concelebration in the Sistine Chapel *(Insegnamenti,* 2, 1979, p. 1126). Yes, brothers, we are the bishops of the Church in Italy; we have received from God this enormous, exalting responsibility: you, who have been aggregated to the successors of the Apostolic College to be the spiritual guides, the teachers, the *"sacerdotes"* of that Italian people, to whom you belong by destiny of birth, by mental outlook and education, by human and ecclesial culture, and from whom you have been drawn to carry out your mission; and I who, though coming from another nation, have become, by inscrutable divine disposition, Bishop of Rome, Peter's Successor in the Roman See, receiving in this way that primacy, precisely in virtue of which I have the mandate of Vicar of Christ and Pastor of the universal Church, without forgetting for that reason the very particular concerns, the bonds and the commitments which the care of my diocese of Rome requires.

Bishops of the Church in Italy, you and I. To us, therefore, there has been entrusted directly from God the pastoral care of a people, whose civil and religious history, known to everyone, has always been inseparably intertwined and linked with that of the Holy See, in unique relations that distinguish it from the historical vicissitudes of any other country; a people, above all, whose religious soul, whose deep Catholic mold, has inspired and left its mark, unquestionably, on the manifestations of everyday life, the forms of piety, family and civil society, the springing up of charitable institutions, as well as the highest expressions of religious architecture, figurative art and also literature.

I have still before my eyes, and I will keep them engraved for ever in my heart, the spectacles of authentic faith, recollected liturgical piety, sincere human warmheartedness, which, from the beginnings of my Pontificate, the Italian people have offered me at those meetings, very rich in fervor and joy, which I have had up to now—and it has been a great grace!—in various Italian cities and sanctuaries: Assisi, Montecassino, Canale d'Agordo and Belluno, Treviso, Nettuno, Loreto and Ancona, Pomezia, Pompeii and Naples, Norcia, Turin, are so many images of a Church, a people, institutions, individual persons, which all speak to me of the goodness and faith of the Italian people and, better than any verbal definition, bear witness with extraordinary effectiveness to the religious *animus* of your faithful. Nor can I pass over the fact that a large number of the participants in the weekly Wednesday audiences come from Italian dioceses—from your dioceses, as well as other crowded pilgrimages, which I receive in the course of the year, facilitated, it is true, by geographical vicinity as compared with other nations, but still so indicative of the conviction of Catholic Faith which pulsates in the populations of the various Italian regions. And what should I say of the now customary meetings with the parishes of my diocese, here in Rome?

The fact of coming from another country, the religious traditions of which are so much alive, although in such a different situation of history, culture and psychological character, makes me discover more and more every day, and appreciate with all the greater emotion the riches, old and new, of Christian life in this country chosen by the ineffable ways of God to give hospitality at its center to Peter's See, to guard the relics of the Apostles, to spread the liberating Word of the Gospel in the world.

All this must instill, in you and in me, feelings of gratitude to God, renewed every day, for having considered us worthy, in spite of our limitations, to be constituted pastors in the midst of this people. All this must inspire us with great confidence, deep joy, growing encouragement to continue our mission without hesitation, seeking ever new openings, new possibilities, new ways of action. This should, therefore, arouse resolutions of commitment that are never weary or remiss in tackling our task, which is a task of strengthening the faith in a moment of transition and crisis. It should give us ever greater clarity of views and better organic unity of pastoral plans in order to respond to our vocation, which is "in a resplendent and visible manner, (to) take the place of Christ Himself, teacher, shepherd and priest, and act as His representatives *(in eius persona),*" as the Second Vatican Council said (cf. LG 21). Let us not be afraid! The Lord is with us to give us courage, and, with St. Paul, we can say: *"Omnia possum in eo qui me confortat"* (Phil. 4:13). The undeniable, magnificent ecclesial reality in which and for which we work instills such hope, especially for the future.

3. In the perspective of our ministry, set concretely in its historical situation, I would like to propose to your attention, revered brothers in the episcopate, some points which seem to me more significant and important for the accomplishment of your apostolate in the needs of the present moment, in fact, in the general framework of the life of the Italian Church.

In the first place the problem of a just and rightly understood autonomy of the episcopal conference, for the decision and implementation of its own pastoral tasks. This is a problem characteristic of Italy, since it may seem that the particular ties, by which it was and is connected with the Pontificate and with the Apostolic See, may have overshadowed, and sometimes still do, the episcopal conference itself. So to dispel the misunderstanding which, perhaps, may be explained historically, but which would distort fundamentally the aforesaid relations, it must, aware of its own activity and its own autonomy, succeed in reviving fully the collegial tradition, which has existed in the Church from the most remote antiquity. Moreover, the Second Vatican Council stressed with new vigor that the episcopal conferences, seen in the collegiality existing in the "catholicity of the undivided Church,...are in a position to contribute in many and fruitful ways to the concrete realization of the collegiate spirit" (LG 23).

You, therefore, are responsible—and you must be so in an increasingly conscious and penetrating way—for the Church which is in Italy: independently of the fact whether the Pope is of Italian origin or not—though taking into account, evidently, that he is Bishop of Rome and Primate of Italy. The episcopal conference must proceed in an increasingly organic and confident way to assume its own responsibilities, in order to turn to account all the forces present in the ecclesial community in Italy, for the whole nation, in which the conference itself must exist and work, be and act.

The picture that Italy offers is that of a country essentially Catholic in its underlying stratum, but which, on the surface, has had to face up to the attacks from the opposite fronts of laicism and materialism—according to the lines I analyzed in my address to the city of Turin—which have inflicted serious damages on the spiritual life of the nation. Consider the desacralization in progress, with dreadful repercussions on the plane of family life and public and private morality, and with the spread of reprehensible models of behavior, which have made a deep impact on the forms of individual and social life. It is not necessary, now, to analyze thoroughly the phenomenon (abortion, drugs, pornography, juvenile delinquency, permissiveness in all its forms of persuasion, veiled and concealed, etc.).

But it raises for the pastoral life horizons never explored before and dramatic questions which cannot be postponed.

In this undeniable clash of radically opposite positions—holiness of Catholic traditions which must face up to secularization—the Italian episcopal conference has the duty to assume all its own responsibilities autonomously, in order to stimulate the affirmation of healthy values, which constitute the genuine honor of the Italian people, and to check the dangers that try to corrode them from within. This requires a unity of action and programs with regard to the overall apostolate, which, in opportune stages and adapted to the requirements of the individual local Churches, can carry on, with joy and decision, the *opus ministerii* to which you have been called. Unity among bishops is not only the first guarantee for the success of your own activity, but is also a source of courage, optimism and confidence.

AWARE OF THE TIMES

4. The cohesion of forces within legitimate and fruitful autonomy should guarantee, within the nation in which the episcopal conference operates, that prestige, that impact, that credibility which are necessary for the effectiveness of pastoral action on behalf of the people. This is the second aspect which, it seems to me, deserves particular attention here. That is, it is necessary to bear always in mind that the bishops are a legitimate and qualified representation of the Italian people; they are a social force, which has a responsibility in the life of the whole nation.

The Church does not live uprooted from the conditions in which she finds herself; she is not an abstraction; she is not a symbol. The Pastoral Constitution *Gaudium et spes* stressed, right from the beginning, that "at all times the Church carries the responsibility of reading the signs of the time and of interpreting them in the light of the

Gospel.... In language intelligible to every generation, she should be able to answer the ever recurring questions which men ask about the meaning of this present life and of the life to come, and how one is related to the other. We must be aware of and understand the aspirations, the yearnings, and the other dramatic features of the world in which we live" (no. 4).

This means that, in a Catholic country like Italy, which is, sometimes, immersed and threatened by a hostile atmosphere, as a result of which the Church runs the risk of finding herself with an inferiority complex and of enduring also, in a certain way, conditions of injustice and discrimination, the bishops must make their presence felt, at all levels, in the context of Italian life, be really the active and conscious animators of the forces they represent, constitute their center of cohesion, the banner of identity, the point of reference.

LIKE A GREAT BLOOD DONOR

The Church, in her bishops, in her priests, in her more generous lay people, should be able to see what concrete possibilities she has for the good of the community and, aware of her own strength, find ever new fields in which to launch herself in order to live up to Christ's mandate: *"vos estis sal terrae,...vos estis lux mundi"* (Mt. 5:13f.). In her millenary history, the Church has never been short of ideas to plan and put into operation works required by the times, having recourse to her own immense potential of energies, dedicated to God and to souls. She has always been, as it were, a great "blood donor," continually providing new energies and initiatives, in a world that has always awaited her presence urgently, and in all fields. If, today, the state has taken over certain tasks in spheres which, in another period, were almost exclusively the concern of the Church, there is certainly no lack even today—and experience clearly proves it—of scope for charity and generous impetus to reach places where other forces do not arrive. In the pluralistic society of today, those who are able to undertake, with commitment and continuity, greater responsibilities for brothers, have a greater sphere of action. All the more should this apply to the Church!

The latter, moreover, while she acts with initiatives of her own, cannot refuse, before the faithful and the whole of society, to express when necessary her own evaluation of problems of an ethical nature, which have an impact on the direction of personal and community life.

It is necessary, therefore, to go forward, fearlessly, proposing to our communities the programmatic points of a Christian and Catholic view of earthly life, according to the Gospel, and of action consistent with it, providing for the most urgent needs which that requires from us pastors.

RESPONSIBILITY OF CATECHESIS

5. One of the primary responsibilities of the present moment is that of catechesis. This has always been a fundamental duty of the Church, and it is so particularly today, since, for various reasons, serious shortcomings can be noted in the religious and moral formation of the laity, especially of those committed at the professional and social level.

At the same time there is, however, a reawakening, fostered and promoted by the Italian episcopal conference, which in these years has proceeded with a serious work of study and catechetical programming, also with the publication of suitable new texts. These are, on the national scale, the fruits of the attention that the episcopate of the universal Church has given to the problem, especially in the specific treatment devoted to the subject of catechesis in the third and fourth general assembly of the *Synodus Episcoporum.*

But it is necessary to proceed, with tireless solicitude, to the implementation of what, together with the office of sanctifying and feeding the People of God, is our specific mission: the teaching of sound doctrine. How relevant

Paul's words remain today: *"Praedica verbum, insta opportune, importune, argue, obsecra, increpa in omni patientia et doctrina. Erit enim tempus, cum sanam doctrinam non sustinebunt, sed ad sua desideria coacervabunt sibi magistros prurientes auribus.... Tu vero vigila, in omnibus labora, opus fac evangelistae"* (2 Tm. 4:2-5). Our episcopal ordination lays on us the special obligation of proclaiming, with the whole commitment of our lives, that Gospel which was once placed on our heads. This should remind us that we are consecrated, to our last breath, to its proclamation, in order that our faithful may live by it and let themselves be guided by its light in all their ways of behavior, general and specific, in their personal, family, professional and social life.

In my Apostolic Exhortation *Catechesi tradendae*, stressing the primacy of this evangelizing work, and wishing to all those responsible the "courage, hope, enthusiasm" necessary for it, I addressed in particular my brother bishops, and I took the liberty of reminding them that "the concern to foster active and effective catechesis yields to no other care whatever in any way. This concern will lead you to transmit personally to your faithful the doctrine of life. But it should also lead you to take on in your diocese, in accordance with the plans of the episcopal conference to which you belong, the chief management of catechesis, while at the same time surrounding yourselves with competent and trustworthy assistants. Your principal role will be to bring about and maintain in your churches a real passion for catechesis, a passion embodied in a pertinent and effective organization, putting into operation the necessary personnel, means and equipment, and also financial resources. You can be sure that if catechesis is done well in your local Churches, everything else will be easier to do" (62-63; *AAS* 71, 1979, pp. 1328f.).

In this field, too, let the Italian episcopate be exemplarily committed, continuing those traditions of teaching, of organic and widespread catechesis, which have been at the origin of the spiritual blossoming of your dioceses, and which must continue, and even increase. Diocesan life must, in fact, be equal to present-day problems, and to the situation of crisis and doubt, which confronts Catholics with the duty of deepening their own faith more and more, and of giving an account for it, with ardor of conviction and force of persuasion, before a world which still has a great nostalgia for the things of God!

EVANGELIZATION OF THE FAMILY

6. A word, now, on the principal subject of the general assembly, chosen in preparation for the forthcoming Synod of Bishops: the extremely important and urgent theme of the "role of the Christian family in the modern world." If I recalled to you the special responsibility of catechesis, it was precisely because it finds in the family the first test, the principal destination, and the most propitious ground. Moreover, I have seen with pleasure that, among the parts into which the background document of this meeting of yours is subdivided, there is precisely "the primary task of evangelization," as well as those of the present-day social and cultural situation with regard to the family, and of the tasks of human and social advancement, due to it. By giving a special place, in the sphere of the family, to the theme of evangelization, you have hit the mark, and you have shown in this way that the magisterial mission of the Church must particularly address families, and all their members, in order that they, in turn, may be able to respond in full awareness and maturity of formation to that participation in Christ's prophetic office, which the Second Vatican Council proposed as a specific definition of the tasks of the Catholic laity in its Christian witness (LG 35; AA 2).

Paul VI highlighted, in unforgettable terms, this specific characteristic of the family, which consists in evangelizing action. The family, my Predecessor wrote in the Apostolic Exhortation *Evangelii nuntiandi*, "at different moments in the Church's history has well deserved the beautiful name of 'domestic Church,' accorded to it by the Second Vatican Council. This means that there should be found in every Christian family the various aspects of the entire Church. Furthermore, the family, like the Church, ought to be a place where the Gospel is transmitted and from which the Gospel radiates.

"In a family which is conscious of this mission, all the members evangelize and are evangelized. The parents not only communicate the Gospel to their children, but from their children they can themselves receive the same Gospel as deeply lived by them.

"And such a family becomes the evangelizer of many other families, and of the neighborhood of which it forms part" (71; AAS 68, 1976, pp. 60f.). Continuing along this clear line of thought, I myself confirmed this great and beautiful truth, in the document already quoted; and I added that "family catechesis therefore precedes, accompanies and enriches all other forms of catechesis" (CT 68, AAS 71, 1979, p. 1334).

AN ENVIRONMENT OF FAITH

7. It can be said, therefore, that the family, understood as a privileged place of catechesis, can offer to your discussions and your work the focalizing center, as it were, in order that the treatment and general discussion may have their interior and logical unity. Actually, in a correct perception of the tasks of the family community, understood as an "environment of faith"—where the parents exercise, with the help of the sacramental grace of marriage and in their function as witnesses of Christ already assumed in the sacrament of Confirmation, their most important duty—the presence and continuity of the greatest values, on the human and Christian plane, are assured: the upbringing of the children; their constant "challenging" to a consistent lifestyle, by example and instruction, the guarantee and defense of a moral wholesomeness, which, from the family sphere, becomes a

common and general good of the whole of society; reaction against the seeds of ideological and moral disintegration, of which the present-day permissive environment becomes the fatal carrier among adolescents and young people; readiness to welcome life and to become apostles of love for life.

From these simple references the necessity becomes clear of giving again to the family, as a whole, that primary attention which is due to it in the framework of pastoral care. An apostolate of the family is urgent!

Perhaps, and for laudable reasons, there has sometimes been an excessive fragmentation, and too many sectorial divisions have been created in the overall apostolate, focusing attention on age, social classes, various fields, which are certainly deserving of care, but which have caused the care due to the family in its globality to be lost sight of—or at least reduced in due interest. The consequence was a dispersion of energies, and perhaps the results were not proportionate to the effort made; and the nucleus of family unity, which is to be considered sacred in all its components, as the pages of the Old and New Testament Revelation testify, has suffered thereby with results that are beginning to be felt.

Consider, for example, the apostolate of the married couple, in the framework of the difficulties it meets with today both owing to the impact of anti-Christian ideologies, of hedonism, of escapism, and also owing to the limits set by the consumer society and the economic situation, with very serious personal and social consequences (individualism, flight from responsibilities, limitation of births, affective instability, difficulty in assuming an institutional bond).

Consider again, to give another example, the enormous human potential—of wisdom, experience, support, help—represented by the old, who today, unfortunately, are set aside by the inexorable law of productivity, but whom the Church cannot and must not forget in her daily action.

Every diocese must consider thoroughly all the problems connected with family life, always bearing in mind, as the Second Vatican Council said, that "the family is the place where different generations come together and help one another to grow wiser and harmonize the rights of individuals with other demands of social life; as such it constitutes the basis of society" (GS 52). And this reality calls for first-rate pastoral care.

Still viewing the evangelizing function of the family, I cannot forget also the action of promoting vocations, which must be at the basis of your pastoral efforts. Only, indeed, by the joint action of the Church and the family can those favorable conditions arise as a result of which Christ's voice calling for dedication to Him and to souls may be more easily accepted by the young.

8. The young! I lack time to speak of the various plans to which your attention is addressed in these days. But I cannot fail to devote at least a word precisely to the problem of youth, which calls for the most assiduous and generous care from you pastors. Think of them! Certainly, the other ages must certainly not be forgotten, in the whole framework of careful and motivated pastoral work. But it is the young who must attract attention before anyone else, also because the generations reach maturity more and more rapidly, and there is the risk of arriving perennially late if all efforts are not directed to the global formation of the youthful ranks which incessantly appear upon the human and ecclesial scene, and wish to take their place of presence and responsibility there.

Care for them with your best priests; do not let the social groups, in which they love to organize themselves, be a flash in the pan which at once disappears, dispersing precious energies, far less that they should develop outside the Church or, God forbid, in opposition to her. While respecting legitimate pluralistic forms of social groupings, of spirituality and apostolate, be able to channel in the right way the extraordinary energies of the youth of today, which can still look to the Church as the authentic form of life where there is the guarantee, by coming into contact with Christ, of exerting oneself generously for "something worthwhile."

I recommend to each of you the apostolate of youth, as the most precious point of your ministry.

ALWAYS CLOSE TO YOU

9. Revered and dear brother bishops of Italy!

Leaving to your reflection the points I have taken the liberty of setting forth to you simply in this informal talk, I am very happy to testify to you again my deep esteem, and to express to you once more all my encouragement for the delicate and worrisome work to which you have been sent by the Holy Spirit.

I am close to you in difficulties, and above all in apostolic work. We are all together engaged in the sanctification, in the teaching, in the guidance of the People of God. Our weak human forces could do nothing without the help, without the presence of Christ. He is our model, our stimulus, our strength. Just as He spent Himself even unto death for mankind, so let us—chosen by Him without any merit of our own—like Peter, like Paul, like Andrew, like all the Apostles, follow Him, with them and like them, to our last gasp, to carry out the Father's work: *"Me oportet operari opera Eius, qui misit me, donec dies est"* (Jn. 9:4). Yes, beloved brothers, let us work as long as we have strength, as long as it is day!

The Blessed Virgin, Mother of the Church, Queen of the Apostles, is beside us, as she was in the days of Pentecost, strengthening the courage and joy in the hearts of those men who were preparing to evangelize the world, in accordance with Christ's order. She will not abandon any of us. And with my eyes fixed on that Upper Room, from which the Apostles set out, I commend you one by one to her, and, with so much affection, I bless you all, together with your beloved dioceses.

The World Has Ever Greater Need of Your Ministry

After the Mass outside Notre Dame on May 30, 1980, the Holy Father met the Parisian clergy inside the Cathedral and addressed them as follows.

Dear brother priests,

1. It is a very great joy for me to address you already this evening—and in the first place—you priests and deacons of Paris and the Parisian region, and through you all the priests and deacons of France. For you, I am a bishop; with you, I am a priest. You are my brothers, by virtue of the sacrament of Holy Orders. The letter that I addressed to you last year for Holy Thursday told you already of my special esteem, affection and confidence. The day after tomorrow, I will have a long meeting with your bishops, who are my brothers in a special way; it is in union with them that I speak to you. But in my eyes, in the eyes of the Council, you are inseparable from the bishops, and I will think of you when I talk to them. Deep communion unites priests and bishops, based on the sacrament and the ministry. Dear friends, may you understand the love that I bear you in Christ Jesus! If Christ asks me, as He did the Apostle Peter, to "strengthen my brethren," it is certainly you in the first place who must benefit from it.

2. To walk with joy and hope in our priestly life, we must go back to the sources. It is not the world that fixes our role, our status, our identity. It is Christ Jesus; it is the Church. It is Christ Jesus who chose us as His friends, so that we may bear fruit; who made us His ministers: We take part in the task of the one Mediator, Christ. It is the Church, the Body of Christ, which, for two thousand years, has shown the indispensable place that bishops, priests and deacons have within her.

And you, priests of France, you have the fortune to be the heirs of a multitude of priests who remain examples for the whole Church, and who are for me myself a constant source of meditation. To speak only of the nearest period, I am thinking of St. Francis de Sales, St. Vincent de Paul, St. John Eudes, of the masters of the French School, of Saint Louis-Mary Grignon de Montfort, St. John-Mary Vianney, and the missionaries of the nineteenth and twentieth centuries whose work I admired in Africa. The spirituality of all these pastors bears the mark of their time, but the interior dynamism is the same and the characteristic of each one enriches the global witness of the priesthood which we have to live. How much I would have liked to go as a pilgrim to Ars, if that had been possible! The Curé of Ars remains, in fact, for all countries, a peerless model both of the accomplishment of the ministry, and of the holiness of the minister, dedicated to prayer and penitence for the conversion of souls.

Many studies and exhortations have also marked the way of the lives of priests of your country: I am thinking, for example, of the admirable letter of Cardinal Suhard: "The priest in the city." The Second Vatican Council took up again all the doctrine of the priesthood in the Constitution *Lumen gentium* (no. 28) and in the Decree *Presbyterorum ordinis,* which had the merit of envisaging the consecration of priests in the perspective of their apostolic mission, within the People of God, and as a participation in the priesthood and in the bishop's mission. These texts are extended by many others, in particular those of Paul VI, of the Synod, and my own letter.

Those are the testimonies, those are the documents which mark out the way of the priesthood for us. This evening, in this distinguished place which is, as it were, an Upper Room, I present to you, dear friends, merely some essential recommendations.

3. In the first place, have faith in your priesthood. Oh, I am not unaware of everything that could discourage and perhaps shake certain priests today. Many analyses and testimonies stress these real difficulties which I keep well in mind—in particular the small number of ordinations —even if I do not take time to enumerate them this eve-

ning. Yet, I say to you: be happy and proud of being priests. All the baptized form a priestly people, that is, they have to offer God the spiritual sacrifice of their whole life, animated with a loving faith, uniting it with Christ's unique Sacrifice. Happy Council that reminded us of this! But precisely for this reason, we have received a ministerial priesthood to make the laity aware of their priesthood and permit them to exercise it. We have been configured to Christ the Priest to be able to act on behalf of Christ the Head in person (cf. PO 2). We have been taken from among men, and we ourselves remain poor servants, but our mission as priests of the New Testament is sublime and indispensable. It is that of Christ, the one Mediator and Sanctifier, to such an extent that it calls for the total consecration of our life and our being.

Never can the Church resign herself to lacking priests, holy priests. The more the People of God reaches its maturity, and the more Christian families and Christian laity assume their role in their multiple apostolic commitments, the more they need priests who are fully priests, precisely for the vitality of their Christian life. In another direction, the more the world is dechristianized or lacks maturity in faith, the more it, too, needs priests who are completely dedicated to bearing witness to the fullness of Christ's mystery. That is the assurance that must sustain our own priestly zeal, that is the perspective that must urge us to encourage with all our strength, through prayer, witness, appeal and training, the vocations of priests and deacons.

4. I add: apostles of Christ Jesus by the will of God (cf. beginning of all St. Paul's letters), preserve the apostolic, missionary concern, which is so deep among most French priests. Many of them—that is particularly striking in the last thirty-five years—have been haunted by the desire to proclaim the Gospel at the heart of the world, at the heart of the life of our contemporaries, in all environments, whether it is a question of intellectuals, workers, or even of the "fourth world," and also to those who are often

far from the Church, who even seemed to be separated by
a wall from the Church. They did so by means of new
approaches of every kind, ingenious and courageous initiatives, even going to the extent of sharing the work and
living conditions of workers in the perspective of the mission, in any case nearly always with poor means. Many of
them—chaplains, for example—are constantly active to
meet the spiritual needs of a dechristianized, secularized
world, often agitated by new cultural questionings. This
pastoral concern, thought out and executed in union with
your bishops, is to your honor: may it be continued and
continually purified. Such is the Pope's wish. How is it
possible to be a priest without sharing the zeal of the Good
Shepherd? The Good Shepherd is concerned about those
who are far from the flock through lack of faith or religious practice (cf. PO 6). With all the more reason, he is
concerned about the whole flock of the faithful to be
gathered and fed, as the daily pastoral ministry of so many
parish priests and their assistants bears witness.

5. In this pastoral and missionary perspective, may
your ministry always be that of the apostle of Jesus Christ,
the priest of Jesus Christ. Never lose sight of the purpose
for which you are ordained: to cause men to advance in
divine life (cf. ibid., no. 2). The Second Vatican Council
asks you not to remain alien to the life of men and at the
same time to be "witnesses and dispensers of a life other
than that of this earth" (cf. ibid., no. 3).

Thus, you are ministers of God's word, to evangelize
and train evangelizers, to awaken, teach and nourish
faith—the faith of the Church—to invite men to conversion and holiness (cf. ibid., no. 4). You are associated with
Christ's work of sanctification, to teach Christians to make
the offering of their lives, at every moment, and especially
in the Eucharist which "appears as the source and the summit of all preaching of the Gospel" (ibid., no. 5). And
there, dear brother priests, we must always safeguard,
with extreme care, a celebration of the Eucharist which is
really worthy of this sacred mystery, as I recalled recently

in my letter on this subject. Our attitude in this celebration must really make the faithful enter into this holy action which puts them in relationship with Christ, the Holy One of God. The Church has entrusted this mystery to us and it is she who tells us how to celebrate. You also teach Christians to imbue their whole life with the spirit of prayer, you prepare them for the sacraments; I am thinking especially of the sacrament of Penance or Reconciliation, which is of essential importance for the way of conversion of the Christian people. You are educators in the faith, instructors of consciences, guides of souls, to enable every Christian to develop his personal vocation according to the Gospel, in sincere and active charity, to read in events what God expects of him, to take his full place in the community of Christians which you must gather together and lead and which must be missionary (cf. *ibid.*, no. 6), and also to assume his temporal responsibilities in the human community in a manner in conformity with the Christian faith. Catechumens, the baptized, the confirmed, married couples, men and women religious, individually or in association, rely on your specific assistance to become themselves what they ought to be.

In short, all your strength is dedicated to the spiritual growth of the Body of Christ, whatever may be the precise ministry or missionary presence entrusted to you. This is your lot, which is the source of very great joy and also of very great sacrifices. You are close to all men and to all their problems "as priests." You preserve your priestly identity which enables you to carry out the service of Christ for which you were ordained. Your priestly personality must be a sign and an indication for others; in this sense your priestly life cannot tolerate being laicized.

6. Clearly placed with regard to the laity, your priesthood is linked with that of your bishop. You take part, according to your rank, in the episcopal ministry through the sacrament of Holy Orders and the canonical mission. This is the foundation of your responsible and voluntary obedience to your bishop, your wise and trust-

ful cooperation with him. He is the father of the presbyterium. You cannot construct the Church of God outside him. It is he who establishes the unity of pastoral responsibility, as the Pope establishes the unity in the universal Church. Reciprocally, it is with you, thanks to you, that the bishop exercises his triple function which the Council developed at length (cf. LG 25-28). There is a fruitful communion there, which is not just in the field of practical coordination, but which is part of the mystery of the Church and which is emphasized particularly in the Priests' Council.

7. This unity with your bishops, dear friends, is inseparable from the unity you have to live among priests. All Christ's disciples have received the commandment of mutual love; for you, the Council goes so far as to speak of sacramental brotherhood: you participate in the same priesthood of Christ (cf. PO 8). Unity must be in truth: you establish the safe foundations of unity by being courageous witnesses to the truth taught by the Church in order that Christians may not be swept away by any wind of doctrine, and by carrying out all the acts of your ministry in conformity with the norms that the Church has specified, without which there would be scandal and division.

There must be unity in apostolic work, in which you are called to accept different and complementary tasks in mutual esteem and collaboration. Unity is no less necessary on the plane of brotherly love: no one must judge his brother, suspecting him *a priori* of being unfaithful, able only to criticize him, even slandering him, for which Jesus reproached the Pharisees. It is on the basis of our priestly charity that we bear witness to and build up the Church. All the more so in that we have the duty, as the Council says, of leading all the laity to unity in love and to ensuring that no one feels a stranger in the community of Christians (cf. PO 9). In a world that is often divided, in which options are unilateral and abrupt, and methods too exclusive, priests have the noble vocation of being architects of rapprochement and unity.

8. All that, dear brothers, is connected with the experience we have of Jesus Christ, that is, holiness. Our holiness is an essential contribution to make fruitful the ministry we are carrying out (cf. PO 12). We are the living instruments of Christ the eternal Priest. For this purpose, we are endowed with special grace, in order to aim, for the benefit of the People of God, at the perfection of Him whom we represent. It is above all the various acts of our ministry which ordain us by themselves to this holiness: to transmit what we have contemplated, imitate what we carry out, offer ourselves entirely at Mass, lend our voice to the Church in the prayer of the hours, join in the pastoral charity of Christ... (cf. *ibid.*, nos. 12-14).

Our celibacy manifests on its part that we are entirely consecrated to the work to which the Lord has called us. The priest, seized by Christ, becomes "the man for others," completely available for the kingdom, his heart undivided, capable of accepting fatherhood in Christ. Our attachment to the Person of Jesus Christ must, therefore, be strengthened in every way, by meditation on the Word, by prayer in relation to our ministry, and in the first place by the Holy Sacrifice which we celebrate every day (cf. my letter of Holy Thursday, no. 10), and it must take the means that the Church has always advised its priests to take. We must continually find again with joy the intuition of the first call that came to us from God: "Come, follow me."

9. Dear friends, I invite you to hope. I know that you bear "the burden of the day and the heat," with great merit. A list could be made of interior and exterior difficulties, subjects of anxiety, especially in this time of unbelief. No one has spoken better than the Apostle Paul of the tribulations of the apostolic ministry (cf. 2 Cor. 4:5), but also of its hopes.

First and foremost, then, it is a question of faith. Do we not believe that Christ has sanctified and sent us? Do we not believe that He dwells with us, even if we bear this treasure in fragile vessels and ourselves need His mercy, whose ministers we are for others? Do we not believe that He acts through us, at least if we do His work, and that He will cause to grow what we have laboriously sown according to His Spirit? And do we not believe that He will also grant the gift of priestly vocation to all those who will have to work with us and take over from us, especially if we ourselves are able to revive the gift we received with the laying on of hands? May God increase our faith!

Let us also extend our hope to the whole of the Church: certain members are suffering, others are in straits in many ways, others are living a real springtime. Christ must often repeat to us: "Why are you afraid, O men of little faith?" (Mt. 8:26) Christ will not abandon those who have devoted themselves to Him, those who devote themselves to Him every day.

10. This cathedral is dedicated to *Notre Dame*. Next year, I will go to the Massabielle grotto at Lourdes, and I rejoice at this. Your country has many shrines where your faithful like to pray to the Blessed Virgin, their Mother. We priests must be the first to invoke her as our Mother. She is the Mother of the priesthood that we have received from Christ. Entrust your ministry to her; I beg you, entrust your lives to her. May she accompany you, like the first disciples, from the first joyful meeting at Cana, which makes you think of the dawn of your priesthood, to the sacrifice of the cross, which necessarily marks our lives, to Pentecost in the more and more penetrating expectation of the Holy Spirit whose bride she has been since the Incarnation. We will end our meeting with an Ave Maria.

Regretfully, I must leave you, for today. But priests are always close to my heart and my prayer. In the Lord's name, I am going to bless you: bless each of you, bless the priests you represent, bless especially those who are going through a trial, physical or moral, solitude or temptation,

in order that God may give His peace to everyone. May
Christ be your joy! In the name of the Father, the Son and
the Holy Spirit! Amen!

Discernment Between Renewal and Modern Secularization

*On June 1, 1980, John Paul II traveled by helicopter to the Seminary of
Issy les Moulineaux. After meeting a Jewish delegation, he went to the
seminary chapel where he met the French bishops, who were meeting in
extraordinary plenary assembly, and addressed them as follows.*

1. God be praised for having given us time for quite a
long meeting in the framework of this short visit! I attach
great importance to this meeting, for reasons of "collegiality." We know that collegiality has a twofold character:
It is "effective," but it is also "affective." And that is deeply
in conformity with its origin around Christ in the communion of the "Twelve."

We are living, therefore, an important moment of our
episcopal communion, the bishops of France around the
Bishop of Rome who, this time, is their guest, whereas he
has received them on various occasions other times—for
example, in the course of the *ad limina* visits, especially in
1977 when Paul VI surveyed with you a large number of
questions, in a way that is still very valid today. We must
thank God that Vatican II undertook, confirmed and
renewed the doctrine on the collegiality of the episcopate,
as the living and authentic expression of the college which,
by the institution of Christ, the Apostles constituted with
Peter as their head.

We give thanks to God also for our being able, along
this way, to carry out our mission better: to bear witness

to the Gospel, and to serve the Church and also the modern world, to which we have been sent together with the whole Church.

I thank you heartily for having invited me, for having finalized, with great care, the details of this pastoral visit, for having carried out so many preparations, for having explained to the Christian people the meaning of my coming, for having shown eagerness and openness which are such important attitudes for our mission as pastors and teachers of the Faith. I pay tribute especially to Cardinal Marty who receives us in the seminary of his province; to Cardinal Etchegaray, President of the Episcopal Conference; to Cardinal Renard, the Primate of the Gauls; to Cardinal Gouyon and to Cardinal Guyot; but it would be necessary for me to name each bishop, and that is not possible. I have had the honor to meet and collaborate with a certain number of you in the past: first of all in the sessions of the Council, of course, but also in the various synods, at the Council of the Episcopal Conferences of Europe, or on other occasions, of which I preserve a happy memory. That enables us to work easily together, even if I now come with a special responsibility.

ESCHATOLOGICAL YET FULLY HISTORICAL

2. The mission of the Church, which is continually realized in the eschatological perspective, is at the same time fully historical. That is connected with the duty of reading "the signs of the times," which was so deeply considered by Vatican II. With great perspicacity, the Council also defined what the mission of the Church is in the present stage of history. Our common task remains, therefore, the acceptance and implementation of Vatican II, according to its authentic content. Doing so, we are guided by faith: it is our main and fundamental reason for acting. We believe that Christ, through the Holy Spirit, was with the conciliar Fathers, that the Council contains, in its

Magisterium, what the Spirit "says to the Church," and that He says it at the same time in full harmony with Tradition and according to the requirements dictated by the "signs of the times." This faith is based on Christ's promise: "I am with you always, to the close of the age" (Mt. 28:20). On this faith is founded also our conviction that we must "implement the Council" such as it is, and not as some people would like to see and understand it.

There is nothing surprising about the fact that, in this "post-conciliar" stage, there have also developed, quite intensely, certain interpretations of Vatican II which do not correspond to its authentic Magisterium. It is a question here of two well-known trends: "progressivism" and "integralism." The first is always eager to adapt even the content of faith, Christian ethics, the liturgy, ecclesial organization, to changes of mentalities, and to the demands of the "world," without sufficiently taking into account not only the general feeling of the faithful, who are bewildered, but also the essentials of the faith, already defined, the roots of the Church, her centuries-old experience, the norms necessary for her faithfulness, her unity, her universality. They are obsessed about "advancing," but towards what "progress," when all is said and done? The others—pointing out these abuses which we are, of course, the first to condemn and correct—adopt an intransient attitude, shutting themselves up in a given period of the Church, at a given stage of theological formulation of liturgical expression which they make an absolute, without sufficiently penetrating its underlying meaning, without considering the totality of history and its legitimate development, fearing new questions, without admitting, in a word, that the Spirit of God is at work in the Church today, with her pastors united with the Successor of Peter.

SIMILAR SITUATIONS

These facts are not surprising if we think of similar phenomena in the history of the Church. But it is all the more necessary to concentrate all forces on the correct, that is, authentic interpretation of the conciliar Magisterium, as the indispensable foundation of the further self-realization of the Church, for which this Magisterium is the source of correct inspirations and orientations. The two extreme trends which I have pointed out foster not only an opposition, but a regrettable and harmful division, as if they stirred up each other to the extent of creating uneasiness for everyone, even scandal, and of expending in this mutual suspicion and criticism so many energies which would be so useful for real renewal. It is to be hoped that both parties, which do not lack generosity or faith, will learn humbly, with their pastors, to overcome this opposition between brothers, to accept the authentic interpretation of the Council—for that is the fundamental question—and to face up together to the mission of the Church, in the diversity of their pastoral sensitivity.

Certainly, the vast majority of Christians in your country are ready to manifest their faithfulness and their readiness to follow the Church; they do not share these extreme and unauthorized positions, but a certain number hesitate between the two or are troubled by them; and the problem is also that they run the risk of becoming indifferent and of straying from the Faith. The time makes it necessary for you to be more than ever the architects of unity, watching over the fundamental questions which are at stake and at the same time the psychological difficulties which prevent ecclesial life in truth and in charity.

MODERN MAN TEMPTED TO DENY GOD

3. I now come to another fundamental question: Why is a particular concentration on man necessary, in the present stage of the mission of the Church? I developed that in the Encyclical *Redemptor hominis*, trying to highlight the fact that this anthropological emphasis has a deep and strong Christological root.

The causes vary. There are visible and perceptible causes, according to the multiple variations which depend, for example, on the environment, the country, the nation, history and culture. There certainly exists, therefore, a specific set of causes which are characteristic of the "French" reality of the Church in the modern world. You are in the best position to know them and understand them. If I take the liberty of tackling this subject, I do so with the conviction that the problem—in view of the present state of civilization on the one hand and the threats which weigh on humanity on the other hand—has a dimension that is at once fundamental and universal. In this universal and at the same time local dimension, the Church must consequently face up to the common problems of man as an integral part of her evangelical mission.

Not only is the Gospel message addressed to man, but it is a great messianic message about man: It is the revelation to man of the complete truth about himself and about his vocation in Christ (cf. GS).

Proclaiming this message, we are at the center of the implementation of Vatican II. The application of this message is imposed on us, moreover, by the overall situation of man in the modern world. I would not like to repeat what has already been said in *Gaudium et spes* and in *Redemptor hominis*, to which reference must always be made. However, it is perhaps not an exaggeration to say, in this place and in this framework, that we are living in a stage of particular temptation for man.

We know different stages of this temptation, beginning with the first one, in chapter three of Genesis, up to the highly significant temptations which Christ Himself underwent. They are, as it were, a synthesis of all the temptations that arise from the three forms of lust. The present-day temptation, however, goes further (it could almost be said that it is a "meta-temptation"); it goes "beyond" everything that, in the course of history, has constituted the subject of the temptation of man, and it manifests at the same time, it could be said, the very substance of all temptations. Modern man undergoes the temptation of denying God in the name of his own humanity.

It is a temptation that is particularly deep and particularly threatening from the anthropological point of view, if it is considered that man has no meaning himself unless as the image and likeness of God.

MATURE FAITH ANIMATED BY LOVE

4. As pastors of the Church sent to the man of our time, we must be clearly aware of this temptation, in its multiple aspects, not for the purpose of "judging man," but to love him even more: "to love" always means in the first place "to understand."

Together with this attitude which we would call a passive one, we must have, equally deeply, a positive attitude, I mean awareness of the fact that historical man is very deeply inscribed in the mystery of Christ, awareness of the anthropological capacity of this mystery, of "the breadth and length and height and depth," according to St. Paul's expression (Eph. 3:18).

We must then be particularly ready for dialogue. But first of all its main meaning and its fundamental conditions must be defined.

According to the thought of Paul VI, and it can also be said of the Council, "dialogue" certainly means openness, the capacity of understanding another down to his very roots: his history, the path he has traversed, the inspirations that animate him. It *does not mean* either indifferentism, or in any way "the art of confusing essential concepts"; now unfortunately this art is very often recognized as equivalent to the attitude of "dialogue." Nor does it mean "veiling" the truth of one's convictions, of one's "credo."

Certainly, the Council requires from the Church in our age a faith open to dialogue in the different circles of interlocutors of whom Paul VI spoke; it also requires that her faith should be capable of recognizing all the seeds of truth wherever they may be. But, for this very reason, it requires from the Church a very mature faith, a faith highly conscious of its own truth, and at the same time very deeply animated by love.

All that is important by reason of our mission as pastors of the Church and as preachers of the Gospel.

The fact must also be taken into consideration that these modern forms of the temptation of man taking man as an absolute also reach the community of the Church, also become forms of her temptation, and endeavor in this way to turn her aside from the self-realization to which she was called by the Spirit of Truth, precisely by the Council of our century.

On the one hand, we find ourselves up against the threat of "systematic" atheization, "enforced" in a way in the name of man's progress; but on the other hand there is here another threat, within the Church: It consists of wishing, in many ways, "to conform to the world" in its present "advanced" aspect.

We know how much this desire is radically distinguished from what Christ taught. It is enough to recall the Gospel comparison of the leaven and that of the salt of the earth, to warn the Apostles against conformity with the world.

Nevertheless, there is no lack of pioneers or "prophets" of this direction of "progress" in the Church.

GREAT TASK TO PRESERVE THE DEPOSIT OF FAITH

5. This shows the vastness of the task of pastors as regards "discernment," between what is a real "renewal" and what is a cover for the trends of modern "secularization" and "laicization," or else the tendency towards "compromise" with a system without knowing, perhaps, all its premises.

It also shows how great is the task of pastors to "preserve the deposit," to remain faithful to the mystery of

Christ inscribed in the whole of man's history, and also to remain faithful to this marvelous "supernatural sense of faith" of the whole People of God, which is generally not the object of publicity in the mass media, but which is expressed in the depth of hearts and consciences with the authentic language of the Spirit. Our doctrinal and pastoral ministry must remain particularly in the service of this "sensus fidelium," as the Constitution Lumen gentium (no. 12) recalled.

At a time when people talk so much of "prophetic charism"—not always using this concept in accordance with its exact meaning—it is necessary to renew deeply and reconstruct the awareness of prophetic charism linked with the episcopal ministry of the teachers of faith and "guides of the flock," who incarnate in life, according to an adequate analogy, Christ's words about the "Good Shepherd."

The Good Shepherd is concerned about pasturage, about feeding His sheep. Here, I am thinking particularly of the theological publications, which are spread very quickly far and wide, and in many environments, and of which the essential parts are popularized in reviews. It is they which, according to their qualities, their depth, their sense of the Church, educate and deepen faith, or on the contrary shake it or dissolve it through their partiality or their methods. French publications have often had, and still have, an international readership, even among the young Churches. Your prophetic charism makes it a duty for you to watch particularly over their doctrinal faithfulness, and their ecclesial quality.

EFFORTS OF THE CHURCH IN FRANCE

6. The fundamental question that we must ask ourselves, we bishops on whom there weighs a special responsibility as regards the truth of the Gospel and the mission of the Church, is that of the credibility of this mission and of our service. In this field, we are sometimes

questioned and judged severely; did not one of you write: "Our age will have been harsh with regard to the bishops"? Then, too, we are ready to judge ourselves severely, and to judge severely the religious situation of the country and the results of our apostolate. The Church in France has not been free from such judgments: It is enough to recall the famous book of Abbé Godin: "France, pays de mission?" (France, a mission country?), or else the well-known statement: "The Church has lost the working class."

These judgments sometimes call for a perspicacious moderation to be observed. It is also necessary to think for the long term, for that is essential for our mission. But it cannot be denied that the Church in France has undertaken, and is undertaking, great efforts in order "to reach those who are far away," especially in the de-christianized working class and rural environments.

These efforts must preserve fully an evangelical, apostolic and pastoral character. It is not possible to succumb to "the challenges of politics." Nor can we accept many resolutions which claim to be only "just." We cannot let ourselves be shut up in overall views which are in reality one-sided. It is true that social mechanisms, and also their political and economic characteristic, seem to confirm these overall views and certain painful facts: "mission country," "loss of the working class." It seems, however, that we must be ready not only for "self-criticism," but also for "criticism" of the mechanisms themselves. The Church must be ready to defend the rights of the workers, in every economic and political system.

Above all, the very great contribution of the Church and of French Catholicism in the missionary field of the Church, for example, or the field of Christian culture, cannot be forgotten. It cannot be accepted that these chapters should be closed! What is more, it cannot be accepted that, in these fields, the Church in France should change the quality of its contribution and the orientation it had taken, which merits complete credibility.

It would, of course, be necessary to consider here a whole series of elementary tasks within the Church in France itself, for example, catechesis, the apostolate of the family, the work of vocations, seminaries, Catholic education, theology. All that in a great synthesis of this "credibility" which is so necessary for the Church in France, as everywhere, and for the common good of the universal Church.

DISCOVER THE SENSE OF SELF-SACRIFICE

7. Your responsibility extends in fact—as among other episcopates, but in a different way—beyond "your" Church, beyond France. This is something you must accept, and you cannot shake it off. There again, a really universal view of the Church and of the world is necessary, and a particularly precise one, I would say "without an error." You cannot act only according to circumstances that presented themselves to you in the past and that are still offered to you. You must have a precise and exact "plan of solidarity" with regard to those who have a special right to rely on your solidarity and expect it from you. You must have your eyes wide open to the West and to the East, to the North and to the South. You must bear witness to your solidarity with those who are suffering from hunger and injustice, owing to the heritage of colonialism or the defective distribution of material goods. But you must also be very sensitive to all the harm that is being done to the human spirit: to conscience, religious convictions, etc. Do not forget that the future of the Gospel and of the Church is being worked out, perhaps, particularly where men sometimes undergo, for their faith and for the consequences of faith, sacrifices worthy of the early Christians. You cannot remain silent about that before your society and your Church. In this field a particular *solidarity of witness and common prayer* is necessary!

That is a sure way of strengthening the credibility of the Church in your country, and it must not be abandoned. You have your place, in fact, in a system of communicating vessels, even if, in this system, you are unquestionably a particularly venerable, particularly important and influential element. That creates a great many duties! The way to the future of the Church in France—the way perhaps to the great conversion, the need of which is felt by bishops, priests and faithful—passes through the acceptance of these duties!

But in the face of denials which concern many people, in the face of despair which, following upon the numerous vicissitudes of history, seems to form the spiritual face of modern society, do you not still have the same powerful structure of the Gospel and of holiness, which is a special heritage of the Church in France?

Does not Christianity belong immanently to the "genius of your nation"?

Is not France still "the eldest daughter of the Church"?

Vatican Council II— the Guide in Your Ecclesial Activities

The Holy Father received in audience on the morning of June 7, 1980, a group of bishops from Indonesia, present in Rome on their ad limina visit. After an address of homage by the Archbishop of Ende, Most Rev. Donatus Djagom, the Pope delivered the following address.

Venerable and dear brothers in our Lord Jesus Christ,

1. I am very grateful for your visit today—grateful for the greetings you bring me from your local Churches, grateful for your own fraternal love in Christ Jesus, grateful for the ecclesial communion we celebrate together in Catholic unity. This ecclesial communion—this Catholic unity—was the theme of my address to your brother bishops from Indonesia who were here less than two weeks ago. It is likewise the basis for this *ad limina* visit and for every *ad limina* visit to Rome.

2. Precisely because of this ecclesial communion, I personally, as Successor of Peter, experience deeply the need to make every effort to understand as fully as possible the problems of your local Churches and to assist in solving these problems in accordance with the will of Christ for His Church. The issues you have presented to me affect the well-being of your people. Some of them raise questions that touch the Catholic Faith and Catholic life in general. All of them represent pastoral concerns that in differing ways are the object of your responsibility and mine, matters to be examined with the assistance of the Holy Spirit, in the light of the perennial value of God's Word upheld by the Magisterium of the Church, and in the context of ecclesial communion.

3. Some of these issues, and other questions too, necessitate a thorough examination, which in turn requires time and a confident exchange of viewpoints between the bishops of Indonesia and the Apostolic See. In every discussion of pastoral needs, primacy must be given to the Word of God as the basis for truly effective solutions. The authentic interpretation of the Word of God and its applications to life have been made by the Church over the centuries, and this interpretation and these applications form part of the patrimony of Catholic life today.

In this generation, the Second Vatican Council—an eminently pastoral Ecumenical Council—has reiterated teachings and established norms that will continue to direct all our pastoral efforts and all our ecclesial activities.

4. On my part, I shall do everything in my power to promote the good of your people and of the universal Church. With God's help I hope to fulfill my role, which is to confirm you in your ministry of preaching "the unsearchable riches of Christ" (Eph. 3:8), of proclaiming salvation in Jesus Christ as the great gift of God's love, and of building up the Church day after day, year after year. In particular, my role as Successor of Peter is directed to the

strengthening of my brother bishops in the Catholic Faith, which they profess and teach, and which is the foundation of all pastoral endeavors and of all Christian living.

5. It was in the perspective of faith and the Word of God that John XXIII interpreted "the signs of the times." Before the Second Vatican Council would enter into a consideration of the many issues facing it, Pope John wanted to insist on the pastoral nature of the event. But he knew that a pastoral Council—in order to be genuinely effective, in order to reflect truly the pastoral love of the Good Shepherd—would have to have a strong doctrinal basis. For this reason, in his address at the opening of the Council, he stated: "The greatest concern of the Ecumenical Council is this: that the sacred deposit of Christian doctrine should be more effectively guarded and taught" (Address of October 11, 1962). This ever more effective guarding and teaching of the Word of God would take into account the manner of presentation of doctrine, and indeed the whole question of the incarnation of the Word of God in local cultures, but it would also mean the transmission of the pure and entire doctrine which, throughout the centuries, had become, in its perennial validity, the common patrimony of everyone.

6. In this spirit, the Council itself later on would emphasize the bishop's role of announcing the full truth of the Gospel and proclaiming "the whole mystery of Christ" (CD 12). Hence, as we deal with the many pastoral problems that face our Christian people—some of which are linked to their baptismal election, others to the particular circumstances of their lives—we are constantly challenged to bear witness to the fullness of the Catholic Faith. The Holy Spirit who assists us to read the signs of the times is the same Holy Spirit who came upon the Apostles, the same Holy Spirit who has assisted the Magisterium throughout the ages and has provided for the needs of the Church in every century, and who has produced fruits of justice and holiness in abundance in the hearts of the faithful.

In moral questions as in doctrinal issues we must continue to proclaim the Church's teaching "in season and out of season" (2 Tm. 4:2). Hence we urge our people to admit only one measure of Christian love: to love one another as Christ has loved us (cf. Jn. 13:34); we charge them to bear constant witness to Christ's justice and His truth.

7. In our ministry at the service of life we are called to testify to the fullness of the truth we hold, so that all may know the stand of the Catholic Church on the utter inviolability of human life from the moment of conception. Hence we proclaim with deep conviction that any willful destruction of human life by procured abortion, for any reason whatsoever, is not in accord with God's commandment, that it is entirely outside the competence of any individual or group, and that it cannot redound to their human progress.

8. In the question of the Church's teaching on *the regulation of birth,* we are called to profess in union with the whole Church the exigent but uplifting teaching recorded in the Encyclical *Humanae vitae,* which my Predecessor, Paul VI, put forth "by virtue of the mandate entrusted to us by Christ" *(AAS* 60, 1968, p. 485). Particularly in this regard we must be conscious of the fact that God's wisdom supersedes human calculations, and His grace is powerful in people's lives. It is important for us to realize the direct influence of Christ on the members of His Body in all realms of moral challenges. On the occasion of the *ad limina* visit of another group of bishops, I made reference to this principle, which has many applications, saying: "Let us never fear that the challenge is too great for our people: they were redeemed by the precious blood of Christ; they are His people. Through the Holy Spirit, Jesus Christ vindicates to Himself the final responsibility for the acceptance of His word and for the growth of His Church. It is He, Jesus Christ, who will continue to give the grace to His people to meet the requirements of His word, despite all difficulties, despite all weaknesses. And it is up to us to continue to proclaim the message of salvation in its

entirety and purity, with patience, compassion and the conviction that what is impossible with man is possible with God. We ourselves are only part of one generation in salvation history, but 'Jesus Christ is the same yesterday, today, and for ever' (Heb. 13:8). He is indeed able to sustain us as we recognize the strength of His grace, the power of His word and the efficacy of His merits" (*AAS* 71, 1979, pp. 1424f.).

9. Christ's grace does not eliminate the need for compassionate understanding and increased pastoral effort on our part, but it does point to the fact that, in the last analysis, everything depends on Christ. It is Christ's word we preach; it is His Church we construct day after day, according to His criterion. Jesus Christ has built His Church on the foundation of the Apostles and prophets (cf. Eph. 2:20), and in a special way on Peter (cf. Mt. 16:18). But *it remains His Church*, the Church of Christ: "...and on this rock I will build *my* Church." Our people are ours only because they are, above all, His. Jesus Christ is the Good Shepherd, the author of our Faith, the hope of the world.

It is important for us to reflect on the mystery of the headship of Christ over His Church. Through His Holy Spirit, Jesus Christ gives grace and strength to His people and He invites all of them to follow Him. At times, beginning with Peter, Christ calls His people to be led, as He Himself explains, where they do not wish to go (cf. Jn. 21:18).

10. Venerable brothers: my recent pastoral visits confirm something that we have all experienced. Our people are constantly turning to us with the expectation and the plea: proclaim to us the Word of God; *speak to us about Christ*. Their request is an echo of the request spoken of by St. John and made to the Apostle Philip: "We wish to see Jesus" (Jn. 12:21). Truly the world entreats us to speak about Christ. It is He who will shape the new heavens and the new earth. It is He who by His word of truth fashions and controls the destinies of our people.

With renewed pastoral love and zeal, let us proclaim His saving word to the world. Relying on the assistance of Mary, Mother of the Incarnate Word, let us together commend our people and our ministry to Him who alone has "the words of eternal life" (Jn. 6:68).

With these sentiments I send my greetings back to all the members of your local Churches, and especially to all the Christian families. I offer my encouragement and gratitude to the priests and religious and to all who collaborate with you in the cause of the Gospel. To the sick and suffering goes my special blessing, and to everyone the expression of my love in our Lord and Savior Jesus Christ.

The Priesthood in the Church: a Social Sacrament

On June 15, 1980, the Holy Father conferred the Order of Priesthood on forty-five deacons from various nations in Europe, America, and Oceania. At the solemn Eucharistic celebration in the Vatican Basilica, after the presentation of the candidates by Cardinal William W. Baum, Prefect of the Sacred Congregation for Catholic Education, the Pope delivered the following message to the Ordinandi.

1. Beloved in Christ!

You must find yourselves again. You must find again the rightful grandeur of the moment you are living, in the light of the words of Christ, which you listened to in today's Gospel.

Christ addresses His prayer to the Father. He prays aloud, before the twelve chosen by Him. He prays in the Upper Room on Holy Thursday, after having instituted the Sacrament of the New and Eternal Covenant. This prayer is commonly called the "priestly prayer." It runs as follows:

"I have manifested your name to the men whom you gave me out of the world; yours they were, and you gave them to me.... I do not pray that you should take them out of the world, but that you should keep them from the evil one" (Jn. 17:6, 15).

"Sanctify them in the truth; your word is truth. As you sent me into the world, so I have sent them into the world. And for their sake I consecrate myself, that they also may be consecrated in truth" (Jn. 17:17-19).

2. Listen to these words, you who are to receive priestly ordination at this moment, because they refer to you. They speak of you. They come directly from the heart of Christ, who revealed Himself to His disciples as the Priest of the New and Eternal Covenant...and they refer to you. And they speak of you. They say who you are—who you must become—who you must be. Listen carefully to these words and inscribe them deeply into your hearts, because they must constitute the foundation of your priestly identity throughout your whole lives.

3. So, first of all:

—You are "chosen from the world and given to Christ."

Shortly, that will take place definitively. You will be "chosen from among men" (as the Letter to the Hebrews 5:1 says), "taken from the world" and "given to Christ." By whom? By the Father! Not by men, even though "among men" and certainly also thanks to various men: your parents, your peers, your educators...in particular, perhaps, thanks to other priests: many, or only a certain one, through whom the divine will was revealed to you....

But finally, always and exclusively: by the Father. Today the Father gives you to Christ—just as He gave Him those first twelve, who were together with Him at the hour of the Last Supper. So "He chooses you"—you, too—"and gives you to Christ." That is to take place in just a moment at the very heart of the Church, by means of my priestly service.

4. In the Liturgy of the Word there was read the description of the vocation of a prophet, the call of Jeremiah—in order that you may remember once more

how your own call took place, in what way God revealed Himself to each of you with His grace, how He called each of you....

The prophet defended himself, excused himself, was afraid. Many of you, too, perhaps, have felt the same. In the priestly vocation there is always a mystery which confronts the human heart—an attractive mystery which, at the same time, is not easy: *fascinosum et tremendum.* Man must feel afraid, so that the power of the call may subsequently be manifested all the more, and that the fact may be highlighted all the more clearly that it is the Lord who calls, and that the one who is called will operate not because of his own will, nor because of his own strength, but only because of the will and the strength of God Himself. "One does not take the honor upon himself, but he is called by God," as the Letter to the Hebrews affirms (5:4) in its classical text on the priesthood.

5. In this way, therefore, it is necessary to keep a deep sense of the right proportions, at this moment and for one's whole life. It is necessary to remain humble: "We have this treasure in earthen vessels, to show that the transcendent power belongs to God and not to us" (2 Cor. 4:7). Yes! It is necessary to remain humble. Humility, too, is the source of true zeal. Zeal, in fact, is nothing but deep gratitude for the gift, which is expressed in one's whole life and in one's own behavior. So be fervent! Do not be hesitant in zeal! Let the inner truth of your ministerial priesthood radiate over others, in particular the young, so that they, too, may follow in your footsteps. The Church, through those whom she ordains priests, constantly calls new candidates along the way to the priestly ministry. Your ordination is accompanied by my prayer and, at the same time, by the prayer of the whole Church for priestly vocations.

6. "I do not pray that you should take them out of the world, but that you should keep them from the evil one" (Jn. 17:15). Yes! You are "chosen among men," "given to Christ" by the Father, to be in the world, at the heart of the masses. You are "appointed to act on behalf of man"

(Heb. 5:1). The priesthood is the sacrament in which the Church expresses herself as the society of the People of God. It is the "social" sacrament. Priests must "summon" the single communities of the People of God round themselves but not for themselves! For Christ! "For what we preach is not ourselves, but Jesus Christ as Lord, with ourselves as your servants for Jesus' sake" (2 Cor. 4:5).

Therefore, you must be faithful. The priesthood of Christ Himself must shine through you. Christ, the Good Shepherd, must be manifested in you. He must speak, through you, His and only His will.

Here is what the Apostle says further: "We have renounced disgraceful, underhanded ways; we refuse to practice cunning or to tamper with God's Word, but by the open statement of the truth we would commend ourselves to every man's conscience in the sight of God" (2 Cor. 4:2). Yes! Every man will have the right to judge you by the truth of your words and your works, in the name of that "sense of the faith," which is given to the whole People of God as the fruit of their participation in Jesus Christ's prophetic mission.

7. Therefore, I return once more to those splendid words of Paul in today's second reading—and therefore the warmest wishes that I form for you today, that the whole Church forms for you together with me, your Bishop, are the following: May God, who ordered light to shine out of darkness, shine in your hearts, in order to make knowledge of the divine glory, resplendent on Christ's face, shine forth (cf. 2 Cor. 4:6). This is the first wish.

And the second one is that you, clothed in this ministry by the mercy that has been bestowed on you, may never lose heart (cf. 2 Cor. 4:1).

Christ is with you. His Mother is your Mother. The saints, whose intercession we invoke today, are with you. The Church is with you. If you were to waver at any moment, remember that in the Body of Christ there are the powerful forces of the Spirit, capable of raising every man and of sustaining him along the way of his vocation, along the way to which God Himself called him.

8. These are the thoughts that have sprung from meditation on the Word of God, which the Church offers you at this solemn moment. And now enter! May the words of Christ's priestly prayer be accomplished in each of you: the words He spoke in the Upper Room, on the threshold of His Paschal Mystery. Let these words be fulfilled: Father, "as you sent me into the world, so I have sent them into the world. And for their sake I consecrate myself, that they also may be consecrated in truth" (Jn. 17:18-19). Amen.

Courage and Faithfulness of the Church in Vietnam

On June 17, 1980, the Holy Father received in audience a group of bishops from Vietnam on their visit ad limina Apostolorum. *The group consisted of thirteen Prelates, led by Cardinal Joseph-Mary Trinh van-Can, Archbishop of Hanoi, who addressed devoted words of homage to the Pope.*

John Paul II then delivered the following address.

Today is for me a day of great joy. I am deeply happy, in fact, to be able to receive in this dwelling a large group of bishops from Vietnam. You come mainly from the north of your country, but also from the center and south. To dear and zealous Cardinal Joseph-Mary Trinh van-Can, Archbishop of Hanoi, to valiant Archbishop Philip Nguyen-Kim-Dien of Hué, and to all of you, Pastors of the Christian people that is in Vietnam, I wish the most brotherly and affectionate welcome. It has been a long time since such a large number of bishops has come to bear witness to the faithfulness and attachment of the Catholics of Vietnam to Peter's Successor. Some of you are making your first visit to Rome, and, for many of you, it is the first meeting with him whose office is not so much "to preside as to serve" (St. Leo the Great, *Sermo* 5, 5, S.C. 200).

I would have many things to tell you on this important occasion of the visit *ad limina Apostolorum.* You come to venerate the tombs of the Apostles Peter and Paul, who confessed the Faith here to the point of martyrdom. You come to visit the Successor of Peter today. You come to see Peter.

In this way you take your place in turn in a procession which goes back to the origins of the Church. It was the Apostle Paul who made the first journey to meet Peter: "I went up to Jerusalem to visit Cephas, and remained with him fifteen days." It is in this spirit that Christians and their pastors make the pilgrimage to Rome to "see Peter."

You come to see Peter because he is, above all, the witness and the guardian of apostolic faith. It was because he confessed faith in Jesus, the Messiah, the Son of the living God, that he was able to hear Jesus Himself say: "You are Peter, and on this rock I will build my church" (Mt. 16:18). But Peter also strengthens the faith of his brothers in Christ: "I have prayed for you that your faith may not fail; and when you have turned again, strengthen your brethren" (Lk. 22:32).

Such is the ministry of service and authority which is Peter's and which strengthens you today in the office you have received from the Lord. For the bishops are the Doctors of faith: "By virtue of the Holy Spirit who has been given to them, bishops have been constituted true and authentic teachers of the Faith and have been made pontiffs and pastors" (CD 2). That is your first mission. You will carry it out by proclaiming the Gospel of Christ to men as well as possible.

To do so, it is necessary for the bishop to visit the members of his diocese regularly, in the service of faith. In this way you strengthen in the Faith those who are entrusted to your pastoral solicitude.

In the months preceding this visit, you were able to meet with all the bishops, according to their ecclesiastical provinces, and then all together in the episcopal conference of the country. In this way you were able to pray together. You exchanged pastoral experiences; you prepared for this meeting. Meetings of bishops are the sign of collegiality, which was rightly emphasized by the Second Vatican Council, and a concrete way of exercising it. It is my deep hope that it will be possible to hold these assemblies regularly.

My thought turns to your priests, "your helpers and advisers" (PO 7). They must have a very special place in your hearts. The Lord alone knows their difficulties and their merits. They are poor and work in conditions that are sometimes precarious. May they benefit more and more from the affection of Christian communities and may they meet with the understanding and esteem of everyone! Convey to them my deepest encouragement.

But priests are few in number and often old. To find workers for the harvest to replace them is indispensable; it is urgent. The work of the Church depends on it. The Catholic communities of Vietnam have given so many proofs of courage, generosity, and unequaled faithfulness to Christ and to His Church that they have aroused and still arouse the admiration of the whole world. That highlights even more the right they have—as religious freedom, moreover, fundamentally demands—to have their priests, all the priests that are necessary to maintain their faith and allow them to benefit from the acts of their priestly ministry that are indispensable for their Christian life, according to the requirements of their conscience. It is necessary, therefore, that candidates—who are numerous —receive intellectual and spiritual formation in seminaries according to the understanding of the Church. In this sense I rejoice at the good news you bring me of the reopening of Hanoi Seminary. I hope further that priests will always be dedicated to their spiritual ministry, without mingling with their own religious mission initiatives in other fields, which are foreign to the Church. Are not their religious zeal, their spirit of sacrifice in the service of ecclesial communities, already precisely a contribution to the good of their own country?

Your people has lived through long years of wars and devastations. It still experiences a great many difficulties. Catholics in Vietnam are bent, I know, on taking their part in the task of reconstruction. There is no need to recall the constant attention and solicitude of the Holy See in this connection. Catholic organizations of different countries will continue also in the future to make a generous contribution, to bring aid in the case of calamities, as well as in the work of economic and social development which is undertaken.

I take this very special opportunity to say that I appreciated the fact that the authorities of your country facilitated your visit. When the occasion arises, I am always happy, together with my collaborators, to have with them contacts which cannot but be useful for the good of Vietnam and also that of the whole Church.

Your dear Cardinal, taking possession of his title last year, said that the Church in Vietnam has always found in Mary "the powerful hand of a mother." I entrust to her protection your ecclesial mission and that of all the Christians of your country. On the return from my pilgrimage to Lisieux, allow me also to invoke the little Carmelite, St. Thérèse of the Child Jesus, whom many ties connect with Vietnam. Her Carmelite Order is at the origin of Carmelite life among you and, if her health had made it possible, she would willingly have gone to your country. May the hundred and seventeen blessed Vietnamese martyrs, who illustrate the intrepid fidelity of your people in faith, accompany you along the ways, sometimes difficult, that are yours!

At the end of this meeting, I address my fatherly apostolic blessing to all those whose pastoral care is in your hands: priests, men and women religious, catechists, parents, adolescents and children, with my warm wishes for courage, joy, and peace in Christ.

Fruitful Testimony
of an Interior Freedom

On June 26, 1980, the Holy Father concelebrated in the Vatican Basilica the solemn Papal Mass for the soul of Cardinal Sergio Pignedoli, who died on Sunday, June 15. Thirty-one Cardinals, including the Dean of the Sacred College, Cardinal Carlo Confalonieri, concelebrated with the Pope.

During the Liturgy of the Word, the Holy Father delivered the following homily.

Revered confreres of the Sacred College, and all of you beloved sons who are listening to me!

I desired this recollected concelebration within Saint Peter's Basilica to remember and pray, ten days after his premature and unexpected death, for the soul of our beloved brother, Cardinal Sergio Pignedoli. He withdrew from us silently, almost on tiptoe, in accordance with his delicate and discreet style, leaving in all of us a wave of deep and sincere regret.

1. Why has the Lord taken him away from us so unexpectedly? And why has this impression of painful amazement remained? I shall not try to answer the first of these two questions because it would lead us to try to probe—and it would be a fruitless attempt—into the mysterious, but always merciful and providential plans of the Lord, in whom we firmly believe as the giver and arbiter of human life for each of the days, many or few, which it is given to us to live on this earth. "For you, O Lord"—I shall repeat with the author of the Book of Wisdom—"have power over life and death; you lead men down to the gates of Hades and back again" (Wis. 16:13; cf. 1 Sm. 2:6).

2. To the second question, on the other hand, which is of a historical or anthropological type, it is possible and even easy to find a reply, by recalling, even if rapidly, the person and, I would say, the features of him who has left us. The fact is that, whenever a man dies who has worked well in the course of his life, the feeling of deep grief is natural and widespread.

All that took place at once at the beginning of last week, when the news arrived from Reggio Emilia that Cardinal Pignedoli had died. All that continues, as a precise sensation common to us all, also this afternoon, because before our minds or, better, within our hearts, there appears the image of our beloved brother. Could we really forget the human dynamism, that is, the rich sensitivity, the extraordinary capacity for relationships and the special attention he always revealed with regard to other men, in the multiplicity of contacts and meetings which he had, and in the very variety of the tasks entrusted to him? Rather than mention the assumption of growing responsibilities—from the youthful years of his priesthood, spent with the students of the Catholic University of the Sacred Heart, until the years of maturity passed as Secretary of the Sacred Congregation for the Evangelization of Peoples, and to the more recent period in which he was President of the Secretariat for non-Christians—it is right and opportune to highlight this outstanding quality of his, which in him was both natural and acquired, that is, it was not only a gift of his personality, but also a ripe fruit of his priestly virtues. From it there sprang other characteristics which I will merely mention: in the first place, the care, or rather the cult of friendship, which had a very wide scope in him; his constant interest in the young, whom he knew in large numbers and whom he assisted and helped in various ways. His solicitude for them was assiduous, just as his advice was frequent and appreciated.

3. But it is now time to pass from affectionate remembrance of our deceased brother to the more elevated atmosphere in which the Word of God, just proclaimed,

wishes us to be and to which it leads us. There has rung out in our ears, beloved brothers and sons, the important evangelical warning *"Estote parati"* (Lk. 12:40): The Lord has spoken to us of vigilance, readiness and preparation— "let your loins be girded and your lamps burning"—while waiting for His coming.

This is a lesson which retains its full force permanently, because it is linked up with the littleness of our life on this earth; it reminds us of the "relativity" of our temporary stay here below and at the same time its decisive importance in relation to the other and definitive abode in heaven. It is for this reason that the sad occasion that has gathered us here, as, moreover, any case of death, is revealed in the light of faith as being a salutary reality, as an opportunity for meditation and a source of grace. We, too, must always be prepared psychologically, spiritually, in possession of that interior liberty which, keeping us free from the ties of the world and maintaining us in the tension of desire, facilitates and hastens in hope our meeting with Christ the Lord up above, in our homeland.

It seems to me that Cardinal Pignedoli, also in the way in which he left us, offers us such a spectacle of serenity and detachment. Certainly I wish to, in fact I must, thank him for the manifold and always diligent service he carried out for the Holy See and the Church for long years; but I wish now to express a special reason for gratitude, also on your behalf, for the fruitful lesson he left us in his death.

So I will conclude with the book of Wisdom: "The righteous man, though he die early, will be at rest." Truly, through his life as a good and faithful servant, through his death as a prepared and vigilant servant, he has already found rest in God, that is, consolation, reward and peace. Amen!

Today the Church Wishes To Be "the Church in the Modern World"

On the occasion of the celebration of the feast of St. Peter and St. Paul, the Holy Father met the members of the Sacred College and all the collaborators of the Roman Curia, Vatican City, and the Vicariate of Rome, ecclesiastics and laity. After listening to an address of homage delivered to him on behalf of the assembly by the Dean of the Sacred College, Cardinal Carlo Confalonieri, John Paul II delivered the following address.

Lord Cardinals,

And all of you present here, my collaborators in the organizations of the Roman Curia!

I greet you all very cordially, on this eve of the feast of the holy Apostles Peter and Paul, and I express to you my joy at finding myself with you. I thank Cardinal Carlo Confalonieri, Dean of the Sacred College, who has expressed, with the great delicacy of spirit that always characterizes him, the sentiments of you all, presenting to me your good wishes on this eve of the feast of the Fisherman of Bethsaida, whose latest and humble Successor I am.

CURIA SANCTI PETRI

1. I so much wanted us to be together on this precise day because it is our feast. It is the feast of the *Curia Sancti Petri in Ecclesia Romana*. Here, not far from the place where Peter gave the supreme proof of his love for Christ, following Him on the cross—*tu me sequere* (Jn. 21:22)— we are gathered, all of us who form the Curia at every level and degree.

I was so anxious to celebrate this feast together with you because we must feel, all together, a living part of this holy Church of God which is in Rome, and experience the noble pride of belonging to it by virtue of our title: the Pope, who speaks to you as Successor of Peter, the Cardinals who form in a special way the presbyterium of the Roman Church as direct collaborators of the Pope, and all the others—superior prelates, officials, men and women religious, lay people—united in one bond of labor and affection, for a service of particular honor and special responsibility.

It is also my desire, in this period that precedes the holidays, to thank you for the careful, valuable and generous work which you carry out for my ministry as Pope of the universal Church and Bishop of Rome. I am well aware that my apostolic work, if it has such a wide range and scope to meet the growing requirements raised by the implementation of the Second Vatican Council, can reach these purposes with the help of God, precisely because it takes its place in a wider and more vast collaboration of other posts, other persons, other vital cells. Many, a great many, of these remain unknown, hidden in the shadows. But to carry on such a superhuman mission, so many hidden, discreet and silent activities are necessary. I thank you for this contribution, which I consider irreplaceable.

ACTIVITY OF THE CHURCH *AD INTRA*

2. I intend to take a look with you at facts and elements, very important ones, which this year have marked the action of the Church *ad intra*, in her own life, autonomous and sovereign, which is unfolded in time for the continuation of the evangelical proclamation. We wish together to seek the identification of the way that the Church must follow, fearlessly and very confidently, in the unique awareness she has of being led by the Holy Spirit, who, according to the Lord's solemn promise, acts in the Church. As the conclusion of the second millennium approaches, we see better and better how the Second Vatican Council was a particular and very special "moment" of the action of the Church in our age, and that our duty is to implement it fully. In this light, it is necessary to see how much, humbly but firmly, the Holy See has tried to proceed, with your collaboration, along this main line of the implementation of the Council in all fields of ecclesial life.

3. The feast of the holy Apostles Peter and Paul stimulates these reflections, beloved brothers and friends, for they are at the foundations of the Church of Rome.

After His resurrection, Christ said three times to Peter: "Feed"; but first He asked him: "Simon, son of John, do you love me?" (Jn. 21:16) In this way He reconfirmed the mission He had already entrusted to him earlier, in the brotherly community of the "Twelve": a mission that various important and significant moments contributed to prepare. The Gospel lists them to us in a continual "crescendo," up to the climax of the words spoken by Christ at Caesarea Philippi, which we will hear again at the Mass tomorrow (cf. Mt. 16:13-19), at the Last Supper (Lk. 22:31f.) and at the Sea of Tiberias, which I have just recalled. However, perhaps the most important moment, considering the circumstances, is the following: "Lord, to whom shall we go? You have the words of eternal life" (Jn. 6:68). In the "words of eternal life" the Church finds her ultimate *raison d'être*. They constitute the basis of the true life of the Church in the dimensions of the individual stages of history as well.

The modern Church has a particular "historical" sensitivity: she wants to be, in the full meaning of the term, "the Church in the modern world." It is precisely for this reason that the Church must deeply "feel" the power of the Gospel, contained in the full dimension of the mystery of Christ: "the mystery hidden for ages in God" (Eph. 3:9), revealed in time, and in a certain sense always more and more corresponding to the necessities of history, that is, "the signs of the times." The correct proportion between "verticality" and "horizontality" consists in this: There is no truly evangelical "horizontality" without "verticality," and vice versa.

In this sense Vatican II is the "gift" that the Holy Spirit bestowed on the Church at the great turning point of the millenniums: as I was happy to point out in the Encyclical *Redemptor hominis*, that is, "what the Spirit said to the Church through the Council of our time...cannot lead to anything else—momentary restlessness notwithstanding—but a still more mature solidarity of the whole People of God, aware of their salvific mission.... The Church's consciousness, enlightened and supported by the Holy Spirit and fathoming more and more deeply both her divine mystery and her human mission..." (no. 3).

EPISCOPAL COLLEGIALITY AND PETER'S "PRIMATIAL" MISSION

4. The Council showed that Peter's mission is a "primatial" one in a strong "framework" of collegiality. We must always go back, and in various ways, to this truth of the "existential principle" of the Church (cf. LG 20-23), and it is lived daily by the Church herself, in a form more and more adapted to the requirements of the present time, according to the indications of the Council.

In the first place, the Synod of Bishops opens great possibilities to this collegial collaboration of the episcopal body of the whole world round Peter's Successor.

But it must not be forgotten that there are also in the Church other collegial forms, more ancient than the Synod, for example, the very ancient, institutionalized form of the Sacred College of Cardinals. This College, made up of bishops of the whole Church, incardinated in Rome with their Suburbicarian Sees and Titles, surrounds and sustains with its wisdom, its experience and its advice, the work of the Pope "in pastoral solicitude for the Church in her universal dimensions," as I said at the opening of the plenary meeting which took place from November 6-9 of last year (*Insegnamenti*, II, 2, 1979, p. 1048). If I decided to call that meeting, which was defined a historic one because —apart from the meetings during the two conclaves in 1978—the possibility of convening it had not been offered for centuries (far less in the vast dimensions offered today by the composition and number of the Sacred College), it was precisely and principally in view of a special exercise of episcopal collegiality.

Since I have recalled that first solemn session of the Sacred College, I am happy to mention here, in the light of the same principle of episcopal collegiality *cum Petro et sub Petro*, the first Consistory of my pontificate, celebrated last year, on June 30, when fourteen new Cardinals, called from various dioceses of the world and for the service of the Roman Curia, were added to your ancient College: vital new sap transfused into the old trunk of the Roman Church!

Then there are the National Conferences of Bishops, which aim in various ways at expressing that *iunctim* which is the point of contact between the "collegial" character of the bishops and the "primatial" one of Peter in the exercise of their respective pastoral ministries in the Church.

5. At this point I am happy to recall with special gratitude, in this framework of collegiality lived in intense prayer and in lucid examination of the problems of the moment, the celebration, here in the Vatican, of two extraordinary sessions of particular synods: the particular Synod of Ukrainian Bishops, convened on March 24, 1980, for the nomination of the Coadjutor, with the right of succession, of the venerated and dear major archbishop and metropolitan of Lwow, Cardinal Joseph Slipyj; this had been preceded by the particular Synod of Dutch bishops, celebrated from January 14-31, which aroused a deep and universal interest in the Church. For over two weeks we worked together, allowing ourselves to be guided by the unity of the Father, the Son and the Holy Spirit, who gathers the People of God (cf. LG 4). The decision to convoke the Synod had matured in the many meetings that took place with the bishops of that nation, and the deep meaning of the decision can already be grasped from the title of the agenda: "The exercise of the pastoral work of the Church in the Netherlands in the present circumstances, in order that the Church may be manifested more and more as communion." This deep significance was also understood by the faithful, as is shown by the observations

put forward by them, but above all by the fervent prayer with which they accompanied the work of their bishops together with the Pope. I was able to be present in all those days, and take part in most of the working sessions. Together we prayed, together we celebrated the Eucharist, together we invoked the Blessed Virgin. I wish here to pay tribute to the availability, devotion and objectivity of the Dutch pastors, who let themselves be guided solely by the reality and the fundamental requirements of ecclesial communion—both local and universal communion.

This form of dialogue within the Church herself serves to strengthen the bonds of a communion, the organic and constructive principle of which is always charity.

The final conclusions of that Synod take on fundamental importance, rich in hopes, in the first place for the Church in the Netherlands, but also for the whole Church, since the problems examined there in the light of Vatican II concern also other local Churches. But in the first place it is the witness of communion and collegiality, given during all the phases of the Synod, which make it a historic event for the whole Church.

6. But how could I forget, as special and unique moments of episcopal collegiality—in the "primatial" framework—lived alongside the bishops themselves in their own countries, therefore in direct contact with their problems and their pastoral anxieties, the memorable meetings I had with pastors during the visits I have paid so far to the various countries, taking part on those occasions in the sessions of the various National Episcopal Conferences? I bear deeply engraved on my heart, with a memory that will never fade, the experience I had in Puebla, in Mexico, together with all the bishops of the Latin American continent; the one with my confreres of the episcopates of Poland, Ireland, the United States of America, Zaire, the Congo, the Central African Republic and Chad, Kenya, Ghana, the Upper Volta, Ivory Coast, France, as well as the meetings with the Italian Episcopal Conference here in Rome.

7. I am glad to recall here, furthermore, the very precious and rich experiences constituted by the visits *ad limina* of the various episcopates of the world that come, like Paul of Tarsus, *videre Petrum* (Gal. 1:18), and to give him a living picture of their individual Churches, whose pulsating life can be felt, as it were, in its riches of human energy and divine grace, in its hopes, in its tribulations: up to now I have had the consolation of meeting, even on several occasions, the bishops of Colombia, Argentina, Chile, Peru, Papua-New Guinea and the Solomon Islands, Mexico, Venezuela, Ecuador, Nicaragua, Japan, Malaysia, Singapore and Brunei, Indonesia and Vietnam.

It was a mutual giving and giving of oneself, the bishops to the Pope, the Pope to the bishops: These visits really offer the possibility of a personal talk with every single pastor of the various particular Churches, and of collegial meetings, I would say recapitulatory and more concise, with the various groups of the episcopate of the country or the region, taken together.

8. I consider it also very important to point out the intense and continuous exchange of correspondence between the Holy See and the single dioceses in the world, in all their elements, which call to mind the human face of the People of God, its requirements, its problems, its sufferings, its joys. What this Apostolic See "receives" and "hears" is so precious, in order to be able, in its turn, to "give" and "reply" adequately. I am happy on this occasion, which sees us gathered as the members of one family, to acknowledge the praiseworthy and constant common effort that all the congregations and departments carry out—and of which I have the consoling confirmations every day—to put into practice the collegiality *sui generis* that exists within the Roman Curia. This collegiality is carried on in everyday duty, which has the sole and specific characteristic of collaboration in the exclusive service of the Vicar of Christ and Successor of Peter for the proper functioning of the whole Church; and this

cooperation is accompanied by a close and responsible "co-responsibility" of all its members, from the Cardinal Prefect down to the ushers.

The Apostolic Constitution *Regimini ecclesiae* highlighted the necessity and the advantages of increasingly close collaboration, especially in matters of joint competence (cf. Chap. II, nos. 13-17), and that is yielding its fruit. I cannot, therefore, omit a word of praise and encouragement both for the consultation and study meetings which take place within the single departments or various departments together (between Prefects, Secretaries, Under-secretaries with their collaborators), and particularly for the meetings of all the heads of departments of the Roman Curia, advocated by *Regimini* itself *(ibid.* no. 18), and in which I felt it was my duty always to take part, right from the beginning of the pontificate.

I take this opportunity to thank Cardinals König, Philippe and Bafile, who have left their high office at this time. I am very much obliged to them for the precious assistance they gave to me and to the Roman Curia; and I greet, with my best wishes, those who are taking their places.

At the above-mentioned plenary meeting of the Sacred College, I pointed out that "the prospect of the further implementation of the Second Vatican Council depends to a great extent on the efficient operation of the structures of the Roman Curia—and on their planned cooperation with similar structures within the local Churches and episcopal conferences" *(Insegnamenti,* II, 2, 1979, p. 1056). Therefore it is necessary to ask ourselves continually: What must the Curia be? How must it operate to meet in an ever better way its vocation, the specific tasks it has towards the universal Church, on the basis of the "primatial" and at the same time "collegial" character which is typical of the bishop's ministry and of the hierarchical structure of the Church, as well as of her apostolic and pastoral mission?

To the extent to which we answer these questions, which are a challenge to our conscience, we can say that we have met the confidence that the Lord has placed in us by calling us to be members of such a complex and delicate organism.

APOSTOLIC JOURNEYS

9. The Magisterium of Vatican II contains a stupendous and rich vision of the Church, which calls for persevering "realization." Many things are still to be done, perhaps even more than what has already been accomplished. At the center of the self-realization of the Church is awareness of the mission. We participate in the "trinitarian mission" (cf. LG 2-4; AG 2-9); it is a participation that must be expressed in the missionary-mindedness of the Church herself (*Ecclesia in statu missionis*). The mission is the revelation of "the power of God for salvation to every one who has faith, to the Jew first and also to the Greek" (Rom. 1:16), in the significance and in the actual capacity of those to whom it is addressed.

Vatican II has taught us how to "manifest" this power of God with full understanding and respect for every man, and also for the individual nations and peoples, cultures, languages, traditions as well as for religious differences and even differences of faith and non-belief (both in the acknowledgment and in the denial of God).

10. In this context one and all of the Pope's pilgrimage-journeys take on their full significance as regards each one specifically and also globally. These journeys are visits paid to the individual local Churches, and serve to show the place these have in the universal dimension of the Church, and to emphasize the peculiar aptitude they have in constituting the universality of the Church. As I stated on another occasion, every journey of the Pope is "a real pilgrimage to the living sanctuary of the People of God" (October 17, 1979, *Insegnamenti*, II, 2, 1979, p. 765).

In this perspective the Pope travels, sustained like Peter by the prayer of the whole Church (cf. Acts 12:5), to proclaim the Gospel, to "strengthen brothers" in the Faith, to console the Church, to meet man. They are journeys of faith, of prayer, the heart of which is always meditation and proclamation of the Word of God, the Eucharistic Celebration, and invocation of Mary. They are likewise opportunities for itinerant catechesis, for evangelical proclamation in extending to all latitudes the Gospel and the apostolic Magisterium, expanded to the worldwide spheres of today. They are journeys of love, peace and universal brotherhood (cf. *Insegnamenti, ibid.*, pp. 710f.). Mexico, Poland, Ireland, the United States, Turkey, Africa, France, and soon Brazil: at these meetings of souls, even though in immense crowds, there can be recognized the charism of Peter's daily ministry in the streets of the world.

Such, and such only, is the purpose of the Pilgrim-Pope, although some people may attribute to him other motives. The aim of pastors is to "gather the People of God" in different rank and dimension. In this "gathering" the Church recognizes herself and at the same time realizes herself. Among various methods of putting Vatican II into practice, this seems to be fundamental and particularly important. It is the apostolic method: it is the one of Peter, and, even more, the one of Paul. How can we fail to be moved on reading of the journeyings of the Apostle of the Gentiles, as the Acts propose them to us so vividly? How can we fail to be moved by that daring, that defiance of all obstacles, all difficulties? The technical means offered by our time facilitate this method today and in a way "force" us to adopt it. John XXIII already felt this, but it was Paul VI who gave it full realization, and on a vast scale. John Paul I would certainly have continued it.

11. In those truly plenary assemblies of ecclesial communities in the various countries, the second chapter of *Lumen gentium*, a fundamental one, is put into practice. It deals with many "spheres" of membership of the Church as the People of God, and of the bond that exists with her, even on the part of those who do not yet belong to her.

In this manifold view of the reality of the Church in the world, the visits have led sometimes to a society that is mainly "Catholic" (such as Mexico, Ireland, Poland, France, and in a short time Brazil), but equally often also to countries where "Catholics" live side by side with brothers of other Churches and Christian denominations (such as in the United States of America), often forming a minority; and also to countries where Catholics live side by side with followers of other religions, and are one of the various groups operating in the individual nations (such as in the African countries visited so far), or even as a small minority (such as in Turkey). Finally, the journeys also take place in various situations that take shape between believers and non-believers.

12. It can be said that, after the Second Vatican Council (on the basis of the above-mentioned chapter II of *Lumen gentium*, and of other particular documents), the pilgrim Pope feels "at home," as it were, everywhere, even "among strangers." And he has the proofs of this also in the relationship they maintain towards him.

I cannot forget the meetings with the Chief Rabbi and his collaborators in Istanbul; with the Jewish community at Battery Park in New York; with the Muslim leaders in Nairobi, Accra and Ouagadougou; with the Hindu leaders also in Nairobi; with representatives of the Muslim community, and of the Jewish, in Paris. It is the continuation of a conversation which the Apostolic See continues to carry on with the representatives of non-Christian religions (I recall the audiences with various groups of Buddhists and Shintoists in the Vatican), thanks also to the intelligent and discreet work of the Secretariat of the same name, whose late president I recall once more: Cardinal Pignedoli!

13. Everywhere, regardless of tradition or religious membership, the Pope brings with him the deep awareness that God "desires all men to be saved and to come to the knowledge of the truth" (1 Tm. 2:4); awareness of Christ's redeeming work, which was accomplished in His blood

shed for all men, without distinguishing between believers and non-believers. The Pope also brings with him everywhere awareness of the universal brotherhood of all men, in the name of which they must feel united around the great and difficult problems of the whole human family: peace, freedom, justice, hunger, culture and other problems, which, with the help of God, I dealt with abundantly at UNO, in New York, for the General Assembly of the United Nations, on October 2 of last year; at the Organization of American States, on October 6; at FAO, in Rome, on November 12; and finally at UNESCO, in Paris, on last June 2. The Gospel is the fundamental *magna charta* of this awareness.

ECUMENICAL CONTACTS

14. The special task of the way that concerns the mission of the Church is ecumenism: the trend to the union of Christians. It is a question of a priority that is imposed on our action, in the first place because it corresponds to the very vocation of the Church. The ecumenical effort is not engaged in for reasons of opportuneness and it is not dictated by contingent situations or conditions, but is based on God's will.

On the strength of this conviction, I visited the Ecumenical Patriarch, His Holiness Dimitrios I, in Istanbul. It was necessary for me to visit the first see of the Orthodox Church, with which we are united by deep communion. We have become newly aware of this communion in the last few years, during which there developed the dialogue of charity, which led to the theological dialogue. The latter has just started in Patmos with a spiritual dynamism that arouses in me joy and hope. The dawn of the century that is approaching must find us united in full communion. The theological dialogue will have to overcome the disagreements that still exist, but, as I had occasion to say elsewhere, it will be necessary to learn again to breathe fully with two lungs, the Western and the Eastern.

I recently received, here in Rome, delegations from the Patriarchates of Moscow and Bulgaria. But also, and above all, I had the joy to have in this month of June the visit of the Catholicos-Patriarch of Georgia, Elia II. I am not forgetting the Ancient Eastern Churches. My meeting in Istanbul with Patriarch Snork Kaloustian marks the determination to carry on what has been undertaken by my venerated Predecessor and by the Catholicos of the Armenian Church. With the Copt Church, a document is being completed, whose preparation started with the visit I received last year from an important delegation of that Church. I have also recently received the visit of a metropolitan of the Syrian Church in India, and of a delegation of the Church of Ethiopia, whose Patriarch I hope to meet. But above all, last May, H. H. Mar Ignatius Yacoub III, the Patriarch of the Syrian Church, who died just a few days ago, led an important delegation to renew the visit he paid to the Church of Rome in 1971.

I also like to hope that those who are most directly charged with promoting unity—those who are responsible for ecumenism in the dioceses, ecumenical commissions in the episcopal conferences, the Secretariat for the Union of Christians within the Roman Curia, which I wish to thank publicly here—are closely associated in a fruitful collaboration.

15. The effort to re-establish full communion with the Churches that are heirs to the various Eastern traditions does not make us neglect, however, the concern to overcome the divisions that came into being in the 16th century in the West. In less than two years, and in a spirit of Christian friendship, I have had exchanges with two Archbishops of Canterbury: Dr. Coggan, who kindly attended the solemn inauguration of my pontificate, and Dr. Runcie, who met me in Africa. At these meetings I saw reflected the intentions of so many Anglicans for the restoration of unity.

This intention instills strength in so many dialogues and so much collaboration in progress in the English-speaking world. This is an experience that must lead us to follow in prayer the work carried out by the joint commission between the Catholic Church and the Anglican Commission, the results of which, very important ones, will be presented at the end of next year.

The Methodists followed the Second Vatican Council closely, and they found in the renewal that it has produced many inspirations close to their ideals of holiness of life.

In the official dialogue with the Lutheran World Federation, the numerous controversies of the 16th century, still not without effect today, have been studied in a joint theological effort.

In the framework of these contacts with the Lutheran Christians, the discussion on the *Confessio Augustana* has assumed particular significance in these times. The 450th anniversary of this fundamental document, which dates back to 1530, occurs at this time. A special statement on it was made, as you know, last Wednesday.

Also, in the dialogue with the World Alliance of Reformed Churches, reflection has been carried out on our common origins and we have reached agreement in reflecting on Christian responsibility in the face of the world of today.

A dialogue is being carried on with the Pentecostal Churches, and many misunderstandings are being removed.

Parallel to "bilateral" contacts and dialogues with the different Churches, collaboration has been developed at the same time with the World Council of Churches and its various departments. I have asked for this collaboration to be increased, since I am convinced—in spite of the difficulties—of the importance of this multilateral dialogue and of the benefits it may have. In this connection I had useful conversations with the Secretary General of that organization, Pastor Philip Potter, at the beginning of last year.

During each of my journeys I endeavored to meet my brothers of other Churches and ecclesial communities. This happened particularly in Ireland, in the United States of

America, in various African countries, and in Paris. These meetings made it possible, with the help of experience, to carry out brotherly exchanges progressively and they permitted mutual listening and mutual understanding. And I hope they will grow and develop in this direction during future journeys.

16. But since only God allows us to advance in fulfillment of Christ's supreme desire *ut unum sint* (Jn. 17:21ff.), the essential importance of prayer can be understood, as the Second Vatican Council stressed (cf. UR 8). Once more and insistently, I urge the Catholic faithful, and especially those called to the contemplative life, to raise incessantly their supplication for the real and complete unity of all disciples of Christ. The Week of Prayer for the Unity of Christians must be, every year, the very special time—the heart—of this supplication. In this way the Catholic principles of ecumenism, established by the Second Vatican Council, will be able to be fully realized; in this way we shall be able to follow the present and future impulses of the Holy Spirit with discernment, in complete docility and generosity (cf. UR 24).

17. However, as I stressed in my recent letter to the German episcopate, according to the above-mentioned Conciliar Decree *Unitatis redintegratio,* the union of Christians cannot be sought in a "compromise" between the various theological positions, but only in a common meeting in the most ample and mature fullness of Christian truth. This is our wish and theirs. It is a duty of mutual loyalty. The Second Vatican Council stated: "Nothing is so foreign to the spirit of ecumenism as a false irenicism which harms the purity of Catholic doctrine and obscures its genuine and certain meaning" *(ibid.,* no. 11).

True ecumenical dialogue demands, therefore, on the part of theologians particular maturity and certainty in the truth professed by the Church; it demands particular faithfulness on their part to the teaching of the Magisterium. Only by means of such a dialogue "can ecumenism, this great heir of the Council, become an ever more mature reality, that is, only along the way of a great commitment of the Church, inspired by the certainty of faith and by confidence in the power of Christ, in which, right from the beginning, the pioneers of this work distinguished themselves" (Letter to the German Episcopate, *L'Osservatore Romano*, May 23, 1980). In this effort we take as our basis solely the doctrine of the Council and we wish to see verified the programmatic words of its decree on ecumenism: *Unitatis redintegratio*, the "restoration of unity."

FAITHFULNESS TO THE HOLY SPIRIT

18. In the whole process of the Church's "self-realization," according to the view that, benignly assisted by the Holy Spirit, she traced for herself during the Council, it is necessary to maintain fully faithfulness to the Holy Spirit: which means the faithfulness of the Church to herself also, to her own identity.

This faithfulness is the condition, and at the same time the verification of reliance on Christ, trust in Christ, who promised: "I am with you" (Mt. 28:20); and the very root of the life and development of the Church is "innervated," so to speak, in this trust. As I said at the *Angelus* on the first Sunday of Lent: "The Church, in the present age, has no other need as great as this faith—inflexible and inviolable—in the power of Christ, who wishes to operate in human hearts as Redeemer and Bridegroom of the Church, and reveals the mystery of that love which is eternal and lasts throughout the centuries" (February 24, 1979).

The real way of the Church is faithfulness to Christ. Therefore the Church must continue in "His truth" and guard the "deposit" in the spirit of love and through the love in which God reveals Himself more fully, because "God is love!" (1 Jn. 4:8) It is not possible, in all honesty, for this faithfulness to coexist with other ways that gradually lead away from Christ and the Church, questioning fixed points of doctrine and discipline, which, as such, have been entrusted to the Church and her mandate, in the guarantee of faithfulness assured by the Holy Spirit. Faithfulness to Christ is faithfulness to the indefectible guidance of the Spirit: *Ubi enim Ecclesia, ibi et Spiritus Dei, et ubi Spiritus Dei illic Ecclesia et omnis gratia: Spiritus autem veritas:* these are the famous words of Saint Irenaeus *(Adv. Her.* II, 24, 1). And Cyprian: *Unus Deus est, et Christus unus, et una ecclesia eius, et fides una, et plebs una in solidam corporis unitatem concordiae glutino copulata: scindi unitas non potest (De Unitate Eccl.,* 23).

Therefore it is the mandate of the episcopal college, gathered closely round the humble Successor of Peter, to guarantee, protect and defend this truth, this unity. We know that, in the exercise of this mandate, the teaching Church is assisted by the Spirit with the specific charism of infallibility. This infallibility is a gift from above. Our duty is that of remaining faithful to this gift, which does not come to us from our poor powers or capacity, but only from the Lord. And it is that of respecting and not disappointing the *sensus fidelium,* that is, that special "sensitiveness," whereby the People of God perceives and respects the riches of the Revelation entrusted by God to the Church and demands their absolute guarantee.

From the principle of collegiality and from the pastoral and magisterial mission of the bishops, there can be deduced their common co-responsibility in safeguarding the purity of the doctrine of the Church. They are called to collaborate closely with the competent departments of the Roman See, the center of the ecclesial community, in order to enable it more and more to carry out its mission, that is, of gathering and unifying in the same common Faith the individual local Churches and all the faithful. The German Cardinals and bishops have recently given proof of this reality, which is sometimes difficult.

19. Actually the bishops, as pastors and teachers, are promoters of a real dialogue with all the faithful, particularly with the theologians who have the task of teaching on behalf of the Church, by virtue of a special mission. As I

wrote in my recent letter to the German episcopate, there must be "taken into due account also the special responsibility of theologians. Nor must it be forgotten that it is the right and the duty of the Magisterium to decide what is in conformity or not with the doctrine of the Church on faith and morality. It is part of the prophetic mission of the Church to check, approve, or reject a doctrine."

As my Predecessor, Paul VI, stressed in the first five years of activity of the International Theological Commission, it is necessary "to affirm that all theologians, as if according to a norm inherent in their office, participate, though in different degrees of authority, in the specific office of pastors in this field: that is, that of causing the Faith to bear fruit and vigilantly averting errors that threaten their flock" (October 11, 1973; *Insegnamenti di Paolo VI*, XI, 1973, p. 990). It is, therefore, a complementary duty, based on the principle of subsidiarity, which is entrusted with great hope to theologians by the Church. By means of the instruments of theological research carried out in living faith in the living God, they must indicate to the People of God the main route of the Church, faithfulness to the Word Incarnate, which continues its mission in the world. Unfortunately, after the Second Vatican Council, a new ecclesiology, strongly supported by some media of social communication, has come forward, claiming to indicate to the Church ways that are not those of the Second Vatican Ecumencial Council. Theologians have the duty of giving an authoritative and authorized confirmation to the teaching of the Church, a direction to follow in order to understand the true doctrine of the Church more and more thoroughly. Certainly, doing this, they have the right to carry out free analysis and research, but always in conformity with the very nature of the "science of God." Every "theology" is a speaking about God: in fact, according to the main tenor of the great Fathers of the Church, especially the Eastern ones, it is also, and cannot but be, a "theory," a "theopsy": a seeing God, an immersion in Him in contemplation and adoration. A theology that does not pray is destined to become barren; in fact, what is more harmful, it is destined to make barren the hearts of the faithful and of future priests, casting on them the shadow of doubt, uncertainty and superficiality. All this calls for reflection on the serious responsibility that theologians have in the Church, and on the duties to which they must adhere in order to do honor to their name.

20. At this point I cannot but recall the merits that the International Theological Commission has acquired in this field since 1968. Nor can I forget the role and the activity of the Pontifical Biblical Commission. They are all organizations that let themselves be guided by the light that comes from Christian wisdom and to be led to it, in order to unify "in one vital synthesis" human activities together with religious values, "under the direction of which all things are coordinated with one another for the glory of God and for man's complete development" (cf. SC; *AAS* 71, 1979, p. 469).

CHURCH AND CULTURE

21. In this light of research and contemplation of heavenly Wisdom, special significance goes to the role that universities and theological faculties are called to carry out in preparing the clergy of the future and cultured youth, who wish to deepen their knowledge of Holy Scripture in order to teach religion in schools and to carry out better their tasks as catechists. I recall with particular joy the visits I paid to these centers of diffusion of Catholic doctrine, both here in Rome, to the Pontifical Universities —St. Thomas Aquinas (November 17, 1979), Gregorian (December 15), and Lateran (February 16, 1980)—and, during the apostolic journeys, to the Theological Faculty of Krakow (June 8, 1979), to the Catholic University of Washington (October 7, 1979), to the Catholic Institute of West Africa at Abidjan (May 11, 1980), and to the Catholic Institute of Paris (June 1, 1980).

22. Always in the understanding that moves the Church along the way to the implementation of the Coun-

cil, it is necessary to mention the effort that is being made in the field of relations between the Church and culture and science. It is a field as old as Christianity itself, which has always sought contacts with the great stages of the human spirit, from the Didaskaleion of Alexandria, to the safeguarding and custody of the Greek and Latin classical masterpieces by the *Scriptoria*, attached to the convents and episcopal sees, and to the foundations of the *Universitates Studiorum* in the Middle Ages.

In the Pastoral Constitution *Gaudium et spes* (nos. 53-62), the Council gave new impetus to "promotion of the progress of culture," a task which is to be considered a fundamental one at this moment, when the spread of the mass media brings rapidly to public opinion, and then to current mentality, not only scientific theories but also ideologies which challenge, in a continual critical judgment, the intelligence of modern man and also the faith of the believer. It is a challenge that we must accept. A positive relationship between the world of science and of culture cannot but lead to an answer to the vital problems of man and faith. I explained at the plenary meeting of Cardinals the importance I attribute to this primary task; and I acknowledge publicly the commitment and the youthful enthusiasm with which Cardinal Garrone, resigning his previous office, has dedicated himself to relations with culture and science. I am happy to recall, in addition to the meetings I have had, and have, with various representatives of culture, the solemn session with which the Pontifical Academy of Sciences commemorated the first centenary of the birth of Albert Einstein, on November 10.

Let us continue along this way to seek, according to the spirit of *Gaudium et spes*, "an adequate expression of the relationship of the Church with the vast field of modern anthropology and of humanistic sciences" *(ibid.)*, always in the exalting vision of the Word, of Wisdom, "the true light that enlightens every man" (Jn. 1:9), that came down into the world and became flesh (Jn. 1:14) in order that man might find the fullness of truth, the synthesis of created elements, attained in the superior consistency between reason and faith, between the innate nobility of the intellect and the transcendent fulfillment given to it by divine truth. I heartily thank all those who carry out their work, silent and active, so that the relations between religion and science may be developed more and more.

SELF-REALIZATION OF THE CHURCH IN HER MAIN ELEMENTS

23. It is necessary, furthermore, that the Church —whose duty is to serve God and men in Christ—continually concentrate on the way of her own self-realization, on the various spheres and structures of her apostolic organization. It is a whole articulation pulsating with life, which gives and receives contributions from its individual components and which the Pope, whose duty it is to "strengthen brethren," must therefore follow and encourage with might and main. But, in doing so, he is well aware that he is in debt to so many persons, especially to the competent departments of the Curia, to which deep and due gratitude must therefore go.

24. In the first place: the seminaries, which have the very delicate responsibility of receiving, sifting and strengthening vocations, the key problem of the Church today. In this light I would like to recall the visits paid here in Rome to the Polish College, the English College, the Mexican College, the Irish College, the Capranica College, the Dutch College, the Roman Major and Minor Seminaries, the North American College, as well as the audience granted to the Apulian Regional Seminary of Molfetta. Outside Rome, in the pilgrimages made so far, I have visited the Seminary of Guadalajara in Mexico, the Seminary of St. Charles in Philadelphia, that of Quigley South in Chicago, that of Kumasi in Ghana, and of Issy-les-Moulineaux in Paris; and furthermore there was in every nation a warm and cordial meeting with young seminarians, the fundamental hope of the Church of tomorrow.

Of equal importance in ecclesial life today is the presence of men and women religious, the living witness to the kingdom of God, the paschal proclamation of the resurrection, and the spirit of the evangelical beatitudes. For this reason I met the central leaders of the Society of Jesus, the International Union of Superiors General, the Council of the Union of Superiors General, the General Chapter of the Society of St. Paul, the Plenary Assembly of the Sacred Congregation for Religious and for Lay Institutes.

25. Then there is youth, which is open to the Gospel, to spiritual values, with the whole thrust of its enthusiasm, with its thirst for authenticity and truth, with its confrontation with the essential problems of its own spiritual and moral life. It is always a joy for the Pope to meet the young. And it is a reciprocated joy. What enthusiasm I have always found in their midst!

I recall the evenings at Castel Gandolfo with the groups that succeeded one another. I recall the holy Masses and audiences in Rome, with secondary and university students of various nations. And during all my apostolic journeys, the direct conversation, face to face, eye to eye with the hosts of young people joyful and thoughtful who surrounded me, was a feast for everyone. I go back in thought to the university students of Mexico, at Guadalupe; to those of Poland, at Krakow; to the Mass at Galway, in Ireland; to the meeting at Madison Square Garden, New York. I think of the young people of Norcia, of Turin, of the students of Zaire, of the Ivory Coast, of the young workers of Catholic Action in Paris, then of the meeting at Parc des Princes.

26. A special place in the attention of the Church and of the Pope is held by the family, which Vatican II defined as the first and vital cell of society (AA 11), the meeting of generations (GS 52), the domestic Church (LG 11), the apprenticeship of apostolate (AA 11, 30), the first seminary and training-ground of vocations (OT 2; AG 19, 41). How could we fail today to concentrate all attention,

corresponding to the care that God the Father has, in Christ, for mankind, on this nerve center of modern life, threatened by so many dangers and become so vulnerable, due to the inoculation of deadly germs—sometimes legalized by the interventions of civil law—such as permissiveness, free love, the institution of divorce, the liberalization of contraceptives, the introduction of abortion? One trembles before really tragic statistics, which reveal dark abysses in moral behavior today. It is the family that is most directly threatened. That is the reason for the subject, of vital importance, proposed to the Synod of Bishops next autumn, which is dedicated precisely to the family, and the preparations for which are in full swing. To this end I have dedicated, since the summer of last year, the catechesis of the general audiences on Wednesdays, to offer the People of God a global reflection—from the biblical and theological point of view—on the reality of love, of giving and mutual fulfillment through the sexes, according to the original plan of God and according to the teaching of Christ, which brings us back to the "beginning."

27. Then I wish to make at least a reference to the parishes, the visible expression of the unity of the Church and her life of liturgical prayer and charity, in the ties that are woven in them through all the social classes in the bond of the one love of Christ. As Bishop of Rome, I have a direct pastoral responsibility with regard to the individual Roman parishes: for this reason I started to visit them one by one, right from the beginning of my pontifical service, and there would not be time to list all those that have welcomed me. The Cardinal Vicar keeps a note of them! I thank him and his collaborators for the stupendous reality established by these meetings of the Bishop of Rome with his parishes!

28. Christian life is daily unfolded in the exercise of the individual professions and of human labor. Hence, the pains to reach and meet, in Rome, in Latium, and in the journeys in Italy and in the various continents, the reality of men engaged in the building of the earthly city, in order

that they may be able to proceed, with the help of God, in the consistency of moral and ethical principles, in brotherhood and respect for man: entrepreneurs and executives, workers in industry in its various branches, artisans, farmworkers, fishermen, men of international and national politics, journalists, artists and actors, sportsmen, etc. None of them, when the opportunity was offered, has lacked the word of the Pope to tell them that the Church is waiting for them with open arms, and is relying on them so much for the building of a world "proportionate to man," and in order that God may be loved.

29. To love God! Liturgical life is the very special place where this exchange between God and man takes place; and the altar of the Eucharist, where Christ Jesus, the true and eternal Priest, offers Himself as a victim to the Father for mankind, is the meeting point between heaven and earth. The Second Vatican Council gave a magnificent impetus to liturgical renewal, which had been prepared by a whole movement that had flourished all over the world ever since the innovations introduced by St. Pius X. The Constitution *Sacrosanctum concilium* was the first document solemnly approved by the Council Fathers, from which there started that constant work of reform, carried on humbly and courageously by the great Pontiff Paul VI. It is well known, however, that—alongside that dangerous ecclesiology which I mentioned before—there have developed movements and mentalities, both of regression and of arbitrary experimentation, which have sometimes led to serious disturbance of the faithful, priests, and the whole Church. The most evident contradictions have come to light precisely concerning the Eucharist, precisely at the altar, where the *regula fidei* must inspire, on the contrary, the utmost respect for Him who, in the Mass, renews His sacrifice in a sacramental form, and leaves it to His Church as a perpetual memorial of His immolated love. This was the origin of the letters which I addressed to the bishops and, through them, to the priests, on Holy Thursday of last year and of the recent *Dominicae cenae*. There fol-

lowed the liturgical norms of the competent Sacred Congregation in regard to the cult of the Eucharistic Mystery. I ask the whole Church to live in that spirit of respect and love, which these documents wish to instill.

MARY LEADS US TO CHRIST
AND HOLINESS

30. Complete reliance on Christ, which is, as it were, the condition and consequence of His giving Himself to the Church, with all the powers of redemption that are His, is fundamental and vital for the Church herself, for her true self-realization, for her progress: I mean for her real progress, and not for a problematic "progressiveness" which destroys without leaving behind anything valid.

This gives rise, therefore, to the necessity of a continual renewal in a special union with Mary, Mother of Christ and Mother of the Church. "To her"—I said before Christmas—"I entrusted the beginning of my pontificate, and to her I have brought, in the course of the year, the expression of my filial piety, which I learned from my parents. Mary has been the star of my way, in her most famous or most silent sanctuaries" (Insegnamenti, II, 2, 1979, p. 1497). In these six months there have been added to the list of those places, so dear to my heart, other sweet names: the Consolata and the "Great Mother," in Turin; Our Lady of Zaire, in Kinshasa; Our Lady of the Rosary, in Kisangani; Notre Dame, in Paris; and in the Ivory Coast I laid the first stone of the Church of "Our Lady of Africa."

It is an appeal which, with a symbolic gesture, with my word, with the prayer of the Angelus or Regina Caeli, I address to the Church and to the world in numerous circumstances, taking advantage of the riches of tradition, of the Marian piety of the individual local Churches, and of the various nations, which have blossomed in numberless gracious and moving forms in honor of the Blessed Virgin. Here, too, the fundamental doctrinal inspiration comes from the Council, from the Dogmatic Constitution Lumen *gentium,* which, in chaper VIII, gave a global synthesis, sober in its extraordinary richness, of Marian theology, and called upon all believers to set out with greater commitment along the royal way of true Marian piety, which leads to Christ.

The post-conciliar age, albeit in the midst of some shadows, has led to a rich deepening of this doctrine, by means of the contribution of theologians, and, above all, thanks to this Apostolic See. The teachings of my Predecessor Paul VI will never be forgotten; in his stupendous Apostolic Exhortations *Signum magnum* and *Marialis cultus,* he left a monument of his devotion and his love for Mary, and a complete synthesis of the biblical, theological and liturgical motives that must guide the People of God in continual growth of the veneration owed to her who is the Mother of God, our Mother, and Mother of the Church.

Also in the ecumenical sphere, especially in relations with the sister Churches of the East, this inspiration to renewal comes to us from confidence in the intercession of Mary, who considers us all her children, and in which we can already find a strong impetus to a unity which, in devotion to Mary, we already find realized.

31. Furthermore, Mary is present in the Church to stimulate the holiness of her best sons, to direct them along heroic ways of evangelical and missionary surrender in favor of the poor, children, the simple, the suffering, those who are waiting for Christ's message. Mary is the inspirer of holiness in the Church, and we find a moving confirmation of this also in those new Blesseds, whom the Lord has given me the incomparable consolation of holding up to the devotion and admiration of the faithful of the whole world: Francis Coll, James Laval, Henry de Ossó y Cervelló, Joseph de Anchieta, Mary of the Incarnation (Guyart), Peter De Betancur, Francis de Montmorency-Laval, Kateri Tekakwitha.

CONCLUSION

32. Revered and dear brothers! I considered it my duty to express all this confidentially on the eve of the day

which is the feast of the Roman Church. What I have said, summarizing as far as possible the pontifical activity of a whole year, is set, I would say, in the same line of continuity with the profession of Peter at Caesarea Philippi (cf. Mt. 16:16), which I already renewed on October 22, 1978, at the beginning of my pontifical service.

On this feast, in a special way, it is necessary to go back to the very roots to see how there develops and grows from them that tree which sprang from "the smallest of all seeds" (Mt. 13:32) on the soil fertilized by the precious blood of the Redeemer—and here, in Rome, also by the blood of His holy Apostles Peter and Paul. We feel holy pride in belonging to this place: *Ista quam felix Ecclesia, cui totam doctrinam apostoli cum sanguine suo profuderunt, ubi Petrus passioni dominicae adaequatur, ubi Paulus Ioannis exitu coronatur* (Tertullian, *De Praescript. Haer.* 36): really, the two great Apostles bequeathed to us "the whole doctrine together with their blood." We wish to carry such a precious inheritance in our hearts and in our ministry, with humility and love, before the "mighty works of God," which they handed down to us in the heritage which perpetually gives life.

Enthusiasm and Courage in Evangelizing Mission

After the official welcome by the President of Brazil, on June 30, 1980, John Paul II drove to the capital in an open car. Before celebrating Mass on the esplanade adjacent to the Cathedral of St. John Bosco, he entered the Cathedral where he delivered the following address to the bishops and clergy of Brasilia, of the suffragan dioceses and of other dioceses, especially of the state of Minas Gerais.

1. Precisely with you, beloved brothers in the episcopate and dear priests, I have my first meeting with a particular group in the land of Brazil: I do not hide the fact that this gives me joy and satisfaction. I can apply to you,

in all sincerity and without rhetoric, the words of the Apostle: "You are my crown and joy" (cf. Phil. 4:1).

I know that many of you have come from far away and with a certain sacrifice; I come from Rome...but there are no distances in the Church of God and we are gathered here, united in the same ideal, in the name of the Lord Jesus of Nazareth. And impelled by the same mission: to proclaim Jesus Christ and His Gospel, "the power of God for salvation to everyone who has faith" (Rom. 1:16), to serve the cause of the kingdom of God, for which we are ready to give everything—even life, if it were necessary. In this spirit of unity you have come to Brasilia, to manifest esteem for the Pope, to bear witness through him to your adherence to Peter's mission. Thank you for the delicacy of your gesture and for the support you give thereby to this pastoral visit of mine. May God reward you!

2. I said at once on my arrival that I was coming to encourage and stimulate the Church. This is the mandate I have received from the Lord. Accept in this sense the brotherly and friendly word that I now wish to leave with you in memory of this rapid meeting. You are the pastors of a good and simple people, which manifests great hunger for God. Discharge, therefore, with enthusiasm, the evangelizing mission of the Church. To carry it out, assume courageously the task of satisfying this hunger by leading this people to the meeting with God. In this way you will also contribute to making it more human. In the spirit of a mother and always faithful to her Lord, in respect of the legitimate institutions which must serve man's cause, the Church must offer the specific collaboration of her mission, in view of the common good, in the construction of the civilization of love.

3. Of course, difficulties will always arise. But take heart: Christ, who died and rose again, always gives, with His Spirit, light and strength in order that we may correspond to our sublime vocation (cf. LG 10).

Be bearers also of a word of encouragement for those who form your communities; especially for the little ones and those who need it more because they are suffering in body or in spirit. Tell everyone, without exception, that, as universal Pastor of the Church, like the Apostle John, "no greater joy can I have than this, to hear that my children follow the truth" (3 Jn. 1:4). This truth is Jesus Christ who Himself proclaimed that He was "the way, and the truth and the life" (Jn. 14:6). Take to everyone the certainty of my affection and my prayer, with the apostolic blessing.

Thank you. May you be happy. God bless you!

Let Us Realize in the Church the Marvels of God's Love

On July 2, 1980, John Paul II met 150 Latin American bishops in the Cathedral of Rio de Janeiro, with whom he celebrated the twenty-fifth anniversary of the foundation of the Latin American Episcopal Council. The Holy Father delivered the following address.

Revered and beloved brothers in the episcopate,

In the framework of my pastoral visit to Brazil, I come with real joy to this meeting with you, bishops of Latin America, gathered in this beautiful and welcoming city of Rio de Janeiro, where CELAM was inaugurated.

I. BIRTH OF *CELAM*: ITS STAGES

1. Twenty-five years have passed since that Conference in 1955, during which there developed the idea of asking the Holy See to create a Latin American Episcopal Council, which would collect and channel the new needs felt at such a wide level.

With a great vision of the future and with joyful hope in the promise of abundant ecclesial fruits, my Predecessor Pius XII anticipated a favorable response: "We cherish the certain hope that the benefits now received will one day be returned immensely multiplied. The time will come when

Latin America will be able to give back to the whole Church of Christ what it has received" *(Ad Ecclesiam Christi, AAS,* XLVII, pp. 539-544).

Today, the Successor of Peter and the representatives of the Church in Latin America, which is nearly half of the whole Church of Christ, are meeting to commemorate a significant date and evaluate the results with a glance at the future.

Before the abundant fruits gathered in these years, in spite of the inevitable deficiencies and gaps; before this Latin American Church, truly a Church of hope, my heart opens in gratitude to the Lord with the words of St. Paul: "We give thanks to God always for you all, constantly mentioning you in our prayers, remembering before our God and Father your work of faith and labor of love and steadfastness of hope in our Lord Jesus Christ" (1 Thes. 1:2-3).

It is the gratitude that springs also from your pastors' hearts, because the Holy Spirit, the soul of the Church, inspired at the right moment that new form of episcopal collaboration forged by the birth of CELAM.

2. The first organization of its kind in the whole Church because of its continental dimension, a pioneer as the expression of collegiality when the episcopal conferences had not yet been consolidated, an instrument of contact, reflection, collaboration and service of the Conferences of Bishops of the Latin American continent, CELAM has recorded in its annals a rich and vast pastoral action. For all these reasons, the Pontiffs, my Predecessors, considered it a providential organization.

3. The life of CELAM is, as is known, set in the framework of three great moments, corresponding to the General Conferences celebrated by the Latin American episcopate.

The first General Conference is a historical milestone of particular importance, because it was during its course that the idea of founding CELAM arose. This first stage is bound up especially with the persons of Cardinal Jaime de

Barros Camara, the outstanding Archbishop of this Arch-diocese of San Sebastian of Rio de Janeiro, the first presi-dent of CELAM, and of Bishop Manuel Larrain of Talca, also president of the Council. May the Lord reward them, who are now in the Father's house, and may He reward all those who made possible the creation of the Latin American Episcopal Council or who served it with praise-worthy and generous commitment.

The second General Conference, convened by Pope Paul VI and celebrated at Medellin, reflects the phase of CELAM's expansion and growth. Its subject was: "The Church in the present transformation of Latin America in the light of the Second Vatican Council." CELAM, in close collaboration with the episcopates, contributed to the application of the renewing force of the Council.

The third General Conference, which I had the hap-piness of opening at Puebla, is the fruit of the intense collaboration of CELAM with the various episcopal con-ferences. I will speak of it further on.

4. In successive stages there took place a progressive adaptation of the structures of CELAM; and new forms of participation on the part of the bishops—for whom it exists and works—were established or expanded. The episcopal conferences as such were present, right from the begin-ning, through their delegates, and, from 1971, also with their presidents, members by right. Forms of coordination have gained a great deal, thanks to regional meetings and with the new services distributed in the various pastoral areas. Numerous pastors have taken part in its direction, convinced that their great mission, in solicitude for all the Churches, goes beyond the boundaries of their particular Churches (cf. CD 6).

I am happy to note that frequent and cordial collab-oration has been maintained with the Apostolic See and with its various departments, particularly with the Pon-tifical Commission for Latin America, which, from the heart of the Church—according to the happy image used by Paul VI *(Sollicitudo Omnium Ecclesiarum)*—follows the activities of the Council with diligent interest, encouraging and sustaining its initiatives in view of greater efficiency in all areas of the apostolate.

II. A SPIRIT IN THE SERVICE OF UNITY

If all this has been possible during these twenty-five years, the reason is that CELAM was animated by a fundamental orientation of service, which has very definite characteristics:

1. CELAM, one spirit.

CELAM, in its collegial spirit, is nourished by communion with God and with the members of the Church. For this reason it wished to remain faithful and available to the Word of God and to requirements of communion in the Church, and it endeavored to serve the various ecclesial communities in respect to their specific situation and the particular character of each of them. It tried to discern the signs of the times, and to give adequate answers to the changeable challenges of the moment. This spirit is the greatest wealth and the greatest asset of CELAM and at the same time the guarantee of its future.

2. CELAM, a service for unity.

The Church is a mystery of unity in the Spirit. This is the longing that emerges from Christ's prayer: "That they may all be one; even as you, Father, are in me, and I in you, that they also may be in us, so that the world may believe that you have sent me" (Jn. 17:21). Therefore, St. Paul also exhorts to "maintain the unity of the Spirit in the bond of peace. There is one body and one Spirit, just as you were called to the one hope that belongs to your call, one Lord, one faith, one baptism, one God and Father of us all..." (Eph. 4:3-6).

Well, this unity does not consist in something received passively or statically, but it must be built dynamically, to consolidate it in this rich and mysterious ecclesial reality, which is the indispensable premise of pastoral fruitfulness. This is the attitude that characterizes the early ecclesial community: "And day by day, attending the temple together and breaking bread in their homes, they partook of food with glad and generous hearts" (Acts 2:46-47). "The company of those who believed were of one heart and soul" (Acts 4:32). And so "the Lord added to their number day by day those who were being saved" (Acts 2:48).

Therefore, the more serious the problems are, the deeper must be unity with the visible Head of the Church and of the pastors with one another. Their unity is a precious sign for the community. Only in this way will they obtain the fruits of evangelization efficaciously. This is the reason why I observed with real joy, approving the Puebla conclusions: "The Church of Latin America has been strengthened in its unity, in its own identity..." (Letter of March 23, 1979).

3. Unity "in the Spirit," a unity of faith.

It is derived, in fact, from the mystery of the Church, built on the will of the Father, by means of the salvific work of the Son, in the Spirit. It is a union which then descends to members of the ecclesial community, associated with one another in a sublime way by the bonds of faith, sustained by hope and vivified by charity. To us is entrusted the serious responsibility of effectively safeguarding this unity in true faith.

The first service of Peter's Successor is to proclaim the faith of the Church: "You are the Christ, the Son of the living God" (Mt. 16:16). The Pope, as Peter's Successor, must strengthen his brothers in it (cf. Lk. 22:31). For your part, you, too, pastors of the Church, must strengthen your communities in the Faith. This must be your permanent concern, well aware that it is a question of a fundamental requirement of your mission, letting yourselves be guided by the principles of the Gospel and without any motivations extraneous to it. In this way you will be able to direct the faithful clearly and avoid dangerous confusion.

Let your unity continue to be nourished by the charity that emanates from the Eucharist, the root and foundation of the Christian community (cf. PO 6), the sign and cause of unity. It is clear, furthermore, that this unity that should exist among you, the bishops of the Church, should also be reflected in the various ecclesial divisions: the priests, the religious and lay people.

4. The unity of the priests with the bishops springs from the same sacramental brotherhood. You rightly declared at the Puebla Conference: "The hierarchical ministry, the sacramental sign of Christ, the Pastor and Head of the Church, is principally responsible for the building up of the Church in communion and for the dynamism of its evangelizing action" (Puebla, 59). And you added: "The bishop is the sign and builder of unity. He exercises his authority evangelically in the service of unity...; he instills confidence in his collaborators, especially the priests for whom he must be a father, brother and friend" (Puebla, 88).

Unity in pastoral work must continue to be stimulated and strengthened with this spirit in the various centers of communion and participation in the parish, in the educative community, in the smaller communities.

5. Union with the hierarchy by those who have embraced consecrated life is of great importance. So many positive aspects pointed out at Puebla, such as "the desire of internalizing and deepening the way of living the faith" (Puebla, 726) and the insistence that "prayer succeed in becoming an attitude of life" (Puebla, 727); the effort of solidarity, of sharing with the poor, must be seen in the perspective of full communion.

In this way consecrated life is "a privileged means of effective evangelization" (EN 69). Therefore, in my opening address at the Third General Conference I pointed out that the bishops cannot "lack the responsible and active, yet at the same time docile and trusting, collaboration of the religious" (II, 2).

Doctrinal orientation and the coordination of pastoral action falls to the bishops. Therefore, all those who carry out the apostolate must support, generously and responsibly, the guidelines indicated by the hierarchy, both in the doctrinal field and in ecclesial activities. This applies to the competence of bishops in their particular Church and, according to the principles of a sound ecclesiology, to the episcopal conferences or, in due measure, to the service carried out by CELAM. It is clear, on the other hand, that attentive care for the spiritual good of men and women religious must be a pre-eminent feature of the diocesan or supradiocesan apostolate.

6. Nor can ecclesial communion with the pastors be lacking in such an important field as the world of the laity. The Church needs the formidable contribution of the layman, whose range of action is a very wide one.

The Puebla Conference stressed the fact that the layman "is responsible for organizing temporal realities in order to put them in the service of the establishment of the kingdom of God" (Puebla, 789) and that "the laity cannot shirk a serious commitment to the promotion of justice and the common good" (793). With special emphasis on political activity (cf. 791), the layman must promote defer.se of man's dignity and his inalienable rights (cf. 792).

In this specific mission of lay people, it is necessary to give them the place that belongs to them, especially in participation in, and leadership of, political parties, or in the exercise of public offices (cf. Puebla, 791). The principle you indicated, which is inspired by the Medellin Conference (Priests, 19) and the 1971 Synod of Bishops, is a solid one: "Pastors..., having to devote themselves to unity, will strip themselves of all politico-party ideology.... In this way they will be free to evangelize the political scene following the example of Christ, starting from a Gospel without party bias or ideologization" (Puebla, 526). These are directives of profound pastoral consequences.

7. The pursuit of ecclesial unity takes us to the heart of ecumenism: "And I have other sheep, that are not of this fold; I must bring them also, and they will heed my voice. So there shall be one flock, one shepherd" (Jn. 10:16). The ecumenical dialogue, which takes on special characteristics in Latin America, must be set in this perspective. Prayer, trust, faithfulness must be the climate of real ecumenism. The dialogue between brothers of different confessions does not erase our own identity, but presupposes it. I know very well that you are endeavoring to create an atmosphere of greater rapprochement and respect, which is hindered by some people who have recourse to methods of proselytism that are not always correct.

8. The unity of the Church, in the service of the unity of peoples.

The Church takes her place within the reality of peoples: in their culture, their history, the rate of their development. She lives, in deep solidarity, the sorrows of her children, sharing their difficulties and assuming their legitimate aspirations. In these situations she proclaims the message of salvation that knows no boundaries or discrimination.

The Church is aware that she is the bearer of the efficacious Word of God, the Word that created the universe and that is capable of recreating, in the heart of man and in society at its various levels, attitudes and conditions in which the cultivation of love can be carried out. With this purpose, the Puebla document was officially presented to the UN and to the Organization of American States.

By virtue of the proclamation of the Gospel, when man's eminent dignity is trampled on, when his collapse is maintained or prolonged, the Church speaks out. This is part of her prophetic service. She denounces everything that is opposed to God's plan and prevents the fulfillment of man. She speaks out in defense of man wounded in his rights, in order that his wounds may be healed and that attitudes of real conversion may be brought about.

Serving the cause of justice, the Church does not intend to produce or deepen divisions, intensify conflicts or spread them. On the contrary, with the power of the Gospel the Church helps to see and respect a brother in every man; she invites persons, groups and peoples to dialogue, in order that justice may be safeguarded and unity preserved. Under certain circumstances she may even act as mediator. This, too, is a prophetic service.

Therefore, when in the exercise of her own mission she feels the obligation to speak out, the Church conforms to the requirements of the Gospel and of the human being, without serving the interests of economic or political systems or the ideologies of conflicts. Beyond groups or social classes, she denounces instigation to any form of violence, terrorism, repression, class struggles, wars, with all their horrors.

Before the tragic curse of war and the arms race, which cause increasing underdevelopment, let the Church in Latin America and in each of the peoples born again in the Gospel raise the cry of the venerated Pope Paul VI: "No more war!" I myself echoed this cry before the Assembly of the United Nations. Let there not be added to the painful situations new conflicts, which aggravate the condition of oppression, particularly of the poorest.

The Church, as history proves with eloquent examples, has been in Latin America the strongest factor of unity and of meeting between the peoples. Continue therefore, beloved pastors, to make your total contribution to the cause of justice, of a rightly understood Latin American integration, as a service of unity, full of hope. And in this task of making your critical voice heard at times, particularly in collegial service of the common good, always continue to let your actions be guided by strict objectivity and timeliness, in order that, in due respect for the legitimate authorities, the voice of the Church may challenge consciences, protect persons and their freedom, and demand due remedies.

III. *CELAM* AND PUEBLA
IN THE WAKE OF MEDELLIN

1. On this occasion on which we are looking at the past twenty-five years of CELAM to project them towards the future, two equally important and significant conferences must be mentioned: Medellin and Puebla.

Let us thank God for what they gave to the Church. The first one "wished to be an impetus of pastoral renewal, a new 'spirit' in the face of the future, in full ecclesial faithfulness in the interpretation of the signs of the times in Latin America" (Homily in the Basilica of Our Lady of Guadalupe). Therefore, I myself said to you that it would have to "take as its point of departure the conclusions of Medellin, with all the positive elements that they contained, but without ignoring the incorrect interpretations made at times, and which call for calm discernment, timely criticism, and clear choices of position" (Opening Address at Puebla, January 28, 1979).

The second one picked up and undertook the legacy of the preceding one, in the new ecclesial context. It is the present that concerns us as pastors. But wishing to guide the present moment, we are well aware that the past relives in it, giving it roots and inspiration. In this sense allow me to refer now in a special way to some aspects connected with the Puebla Conference.

I consider it all the more important in that I am well aware that in CELAM, at its regional meetings, and in a good many episcopal conferences, the main guidelines of the Third General Conference have been incorporated in their own pastoral plans. The same thing can be seen in the five-year reports of many dioceses.

I was greatly pleased by the rapid spread and permeation of the Puebla Document in the communities of Latin America, and outside it. I had hoped that that would happen. In fact, the Puebla Conference, as I have said on other occasions, is in a way an answer that goes beyond the borders of this beloved continent.

In the meetings that took place during your visits *ad limina*, I often had recourse to the Puebla Document, which I knew in detail and approved with joy after the clarification of some concepts. In this way I wished to emphasize its rich doctrinal and pastoral orientations.

2. At the beginning of the conference, I stressed your noble mission as teachers of truth.

In the pastoral approach to our communities, is there a form of presence that the people love more than this one of teachers? Could a true pastoral action, or a genuine ecclesial renewal, be based on any foundations other than those of the truth about Jesus Christ, the Church and man, such as we profess? Consistency with these truths puts the pastoral seal on the directives and options that the conference formulated. You dedicated great attention to these truths, as can be seen in the various chapters of the Document.

3. You tackled, in fact, serious problems of Christology and ecclesiology, which had been requested by the episcopates themselves and which cause concern also among you.

Fidelity to the faith of the Church with regard to the person and the mission of Jesus Christ is of vital importance, with enormous pastoral repercussions. Continue, therefore, to demand a commitment to consistency in the proclamation of *Redemptor hominis*. Let this faithfulness shine forth in preaching in its various forms, in catechesis, in the whole life of the People of God.

4. The Church is for the believer an object of faith and love. One of the signs of real commitment with regard to the Church is sincere respect for her Magisterium, the foundation of communion. The antithesis that is sometimes made between an "official," "institutional" Church and the Church-Communion is not acceptable. They are not, they cannot be, separated realities. The true believer knows that the Church is the People of God, by reason of

being called together in Christ, and that the whole life of the Church is determined by belonging to the Lord. It is an elect "people," chosen by God.

5. The work of theologians deserves particular attention. This ministry is a noble service, which the vast majority carry out faithfully. The theologian's work implies a firm attitude of faith. Together with freedom of investigation, the oral or written communication of his investigations and reflections must be carried out with a complete sense of responsibility, in agreement with the rights and duties that belong to the Magisterium, placed by God to guide the whole faithful people in faith.

6. The Puebla Conference also wished to be a great stand on man's behalf. It is not possible to consider the service of God as opposed to the service of men, the right of God as opposed to the right of men. Serving the Lord, dedicating our life to Him in saying that "we believe in one God," that "Jesus is the Lord" (1 Cor. 12:3; Rom. 10:9; Jn. 20:28), we break with everything that claims to set itself up as an absolute, and we destroy the idols of money, power, sex, and those that are hidden in ideologies, "lay religions" with totalitarian ambitions.

Recognition of the lordship of God leads to discovery of the reality of man. Recognizing the right of God, we will be capable of recognizing the right of men, of "man in all his truth, in his full magnitude..., each man, for each one is included in the mystery of the redemption and with each one Christ has united Himself forever through this mystery..." (RH 13).

7. In view of the reality of such vast poverty-stricken areas and in the presence of the gap between the rich and the poor—which I mentioned at the beginning of the historic days of Puebla—you rightly called for a preferential option for the poor, not an exclusive nor an excluding one (cf. Puebla, 1145, 1165). The poor are, in fact, God's dearest loved ones (cf. Puebla, 1143). Christ, the Servant of Yahweh, is reflected in the poor. "Their evangelization is par excellence the sign and proof of the mission of Jesus"

(cf. Puebla, 1142). You rightly indicated that "the best service of one's brother is evangelization which prepares him to fulfill himself as the son of God, frees him from injustices and enhances him integrally" (Puebla, 1145). It is, therefore, an option that expresses the dearest love of the Church, within her universal mission of evangelization and without any area remaining excluded from her attention.

Among the elements of an apostolate marked by special love for the poor there emerges: interest in preaching that is solid and accessible; in a catechesis that embraces the whole Christian message; in a liturgy that respects the sense of the sacred and avoids the risks of political instrumentalization; in a family apostolate that defends the poor man from unjust campaigns that offend his dignity; in education, causing it to reach the underprivileged areas; in the piety of the people, in which the very soul of peoples is expressed.

One aspect of the evangelization of the poor consists in strengthening an active social concern. The Church has always been sensitive to this and today this awareness is growing: "Our social conduct is an integral part of our following of Christ" (Puebla, 476). In this connection, in obedience to the directives I gave you at the beginning of the Puebla Conference, you stressed, beloved brothers, the validity and necessity of the social doctrine of the Church, whose "primary object...is the personal dignity of man the image of God, and the protection of all his inalienable rights" (Puebla, 475).

A concrete aspect of evangelization, which must be addressed particularly to those who enjoy economic means—in order that they may collaborate with those in greatest need—is the correct concept of private property, which "involves a social obligation" (Opening Address, III, 4). Both at the international level and within each country, those who possess goods must be more attentive to the needs of their brothers. It is a question of justice and humanity, and also of a view of the future, if we desire to preserve the peace of nations.

For this reason I express my satisfaction with the message sent from Puebla to the peoples of Latin America, and at the same time I am confident that CELAM's "Operational Service of Human Rights" will echo the voice of the Church where situations of injustice or violations of the legitimate rights of man demand it.

8. An important subject at the Puebla Conference was that of liberation. I had exhorted you to consider the specific and original presence of the Church in liberation (Opening Address, III, 1). I pointed out to you how the Church "does not need to have recourse to ideological systems in order to love, defend, and collaborate in the liberation of man" (III, 2). In the variety of statements and movements of liberation, it is indispensable to distinguish between what implies "a correct Christian idea of liberation" (III, 6), "in its integral and profound meaning, as Jesus proclaimed and realized it" (ibid.), loyally applying the principles that the Church offers, and other forms of liberation which are far from, and even inconsistent with, the Christian commitment.

You dedicated timely considerations to the signs for discerning what is real Christian liberation, with all its value, urgency and richness, and what follows the ways of ideologies. The contents and attitudes (cf. Puebla, 489), the means they use, help in this discernment. Christian liberation uses "evangelical means, with their particular efficacy, and does not resort to any form of violence or dialectics of the class struggle..." (Puebla, 486), or to Marxist practice or analysis, because of "the risk of ideologizing to which theological reflection is exposed, when it is carried out on the basis of a praxis which has recourse to Marxist analysis. Its consequences are the complete politicizing of Christian existence, the dissolution of the language of faith into that of social sciences and the elimination of the transcendent dimension of Christian salvation" (Puebla, 545).

9. One of the most original pastoral contributions of the Latin American Church, as it was presented at the 1974 Synod of Bishops and incorporated in the Apostolic Exhortation *Evangelii nuntiandi*, was that of the ecclesial grassroots communities.

May these communities continue to show their vitality and yield their fruit (cf. Puebla, 97, 156), avoiding at the same time the risks they may meet, to which the Puebla Conference referred: "It is deplorable that, in some places, clearly political interests should claim to manipulate them and detach them from true communion with their bishops" (Puebla, 98). In light of the fact of ideological radicalizing, which is met with in some cases (cf. Puebla, 630), and for the harmonious development of these communities, I call you to take up the commitment assumed: "As pastors we resolutely wish to promote, guide and accompany the ecclesial grassroots communities, according to the spirit of Medellin and the principles of *Evangelii nuntiandi*" (Puebla, 648).

10. The Puebla Conference wished to give an impetus to "a more decisive option for the overall apostolate" (cf. Puebla, 650), necessary for the effectiveness of evangelization and for the promotion of the unity of the particular churches (Puebla, 703). So let the various aspects of the apostolate be articulated in it, with dynamic unity of theological and pastoral principles. CELAM can do a great deal in this regard.

11. In this perspective of an adequate overall apostolate, allow me to stress the pastoral priorities I indicated at Puebla, which you accepted with such marked interest. They retain all their vitality and urgency. I am referring to the apostolate of the family, of youth, and of vocations.

To make the family in Latin America, united by the sacrament of marriage, a real domestic Church is an urgent task. The cultivation of love must be built on the irreplaceable foundation of the home. We are expecting a strong stimulus for this priority from the forthcoming Synod.

Youth, as I often see in my ministerial contacts and my apostolic journeys, is ready to respond. Its generous capacity for committing itself to noble ideals, although they call for sacrifice, is not exhausted. It is the hope of the world, of the Church, of Latin America. So let us succeed in transmitting to it, without reductions or false shame, the great values of the Gospel, of the example of Christ. They are causes that the young perceive as worthy of being lived, as ways of responding to God and to men, their brothers.

The vocational apostolate deserves very special attention, as I said repeatedly to Latin American bishops during their visit *ad limina*. Vocations to the priesthood must be the sign of the maturity of communities; and they must also be manifested as a consequence of the blossoming of the ministries entrusted to lay people and of a timely apostolate in schools and families, which will serve as a preparation to listen to the voice of God.

Be thoroughly diligent, therefore, in solid spiritual, academic, and pastoral formation in the seminaries. Only in this way shall we be able to have a well-founded guarantee for the future. We need priests fully dedicated to the ministry, enthusiastic about their total commitment to the Lord in celibacy, convinced of the greatness of the mystery of which they are bearers.

God grant that you will be able, one day, to send more missionaries to help in areas that lack them, in your own nations and in other continents.

IV. CONCLUSION

I wish to conclude these reflections now by making a pressing call for hope. Certainly, there is still a long way to go in the building of the kingdom of God on this continent. There are many obstacles in its way. But there is no reason to despair. As He promised, Christ will be with us to the end of time, with His grace, His help, His infinite power. The Church for which we are struggling and suffering is His Church, in which the Holy Spirit continues to live and to spread the marvels of His love. In faithfulness to His inspirations, let us go forward with renewed enthusiasm in the work of evangelizing all peoples.

In cordial gratitude for so many efforts dedicated to the Church, I extend this call for hope to all the bishops of Latin America, to all those who work in CELAM, to priests, members of the various institutes of consecrated life and of the laity, who in so many different forms manifest in a marvelous way, often hidden, the magnificent variety of love of the Lord and of man.

I include in this sentiment of well deserved gratitude all those organizations of Europe and North America which collaborate so effectively, with apostolic personnel and with economic means, in the lives of many particular Churches. May the Lord reward them abundantly for this pastoral solicitude of theirs.

May the Blessed Virgin, Our Lady of Guadalupe, at whose feet you laid the Puebla Document with immense trust, accompany you on your way, lighten your toil in a motherly way, sustain your hope and guide you to Christ, the Savior, the eternal reward.

With the blessing and affection of Peter's Successor, with expanded love for the Church, bring all the peoples to Christ. Amen.

Going About Doing Good

After the solemn celebration of the twenty-fifth anniversary of the foundation of CELAM, on July 2, 1980, the Holy Father met the representatives of the clergy, sisters, and Catholic laity in the Cathedral of Rio de Janeiro.

Dear brothers and sisters in Christ,

In this pilgrimage of mine through Brazil, I have already had the joy of being able to see much of your beautiful country and the kindness, the noble sentiments, and spirit of faith of its people. Here I am seeing the same thing. God be praised.

I thank my dear brother, Cardinal Eugenio de Araújo Sales, and, through him, everyone, for the excellent welcome given to me now and which I received here in the archdiocese of Rio de Janeiro: from the preparations committee to the groups and all the persons who were present.

With the Cardinal Archbishop, I wish to greet his auxiliary bishops and all the diocesan and religious priests who compose the local presbyterium and share with the diocesan pastor, in a special and deep way, responsibility as messengers and distributors of the goods of salvation. As "the salt of the earth" and "the light of the world," you are trying to build up the Church here, with well drawn-up pastoral plans. Always be a visible presence of the sacred in this large metropolis, living and acting as each of you is in reality: an *alter Christus*, who goes about doing good.

To all I leave this memento of the meeting with the Pope: "Whatever your task, work heartily, as serving the Lord and not men." And, in all things and always, "serve the Lord Christ" (Col. 3:23-24).

With my apostolic blessing!

Called by God
To Act in His Name

In the afternoon of July 2, 1980, John Paul II presided over a solemn concelebration with five hundred priests in the course of which he conferred priestly ordination on seventy-nine deacons. The ceremony took place in the Maracana Stadium in Rio de Janeiro and over one hundred and fifty thousand faithful were present. The Holy Father delivered the following homily after the presentation of the candidates.

Revered brothers and beloved sons,

1. This is a solemn hour. The Lord is present here in our midst. His promise would suffice to give us this cer-

tainty: "Where two or three are gathered in my name, there am I in the midst of them" (Mt. 18:20). It is in His name that we are gathered for the priestly ordination of these young men who are here in front of this altar. Upon them, chosen from the marvelous land of Brazil with special affection, Jesus will shortly cause the Spirit of the Father and of Himself to descend. The Holy Spirit, marking them with His seal by means of the imposition of the bishop's hands, enriching them with graces and special powers, will realize in them a mysterious and real configuration to Christ, the Head and Pastor of the Church, and will make them His ministers forever.

At this solemn point of the rite, it is well to stop and meditate. The Gospel which we have heard and the liturgical ceremony which preceded its reading are subjects capable of fixing our minds in endless contemplation. It is natural that, at this moment of intense joy, I should address you particularly, beloved ordinands, who are the reason for this celebration. I do so with the words of the Apostle Paul: *"Os nostrum patet ad vos...cor nostrum dilatatum est."* "Our mouth is open to you...; our heart is wide" (2 Cor. 6:11). My ardent desire is to help you to understand the greatness and the significance of the step you are about to take. This solemn hour will certainly have a reflection on all the other hours that will follow in the course of your life. You will have to return often to the memory of this hour in order to receive the incentive to continue, with renewed ardor and generosity, the service that you are called today to exercise in the Church.

ANSWER FOUND IN CHRIST, IN THE FAITH

2. "Who am I? What is asked of me? What is my identity?" These are the anxious questions that are raised most frequently for the priest today, who is certainly not immune from the repercussions of the crisis of transformation that is shaking the world. You, beloved sons, certainly

do not feel the necessity of asking yourselves these questions. The light that penetrates you today gives you almost a palpable certainty of what you are, of what you have been called to. But tomorrow you may meet brothers in the priesthood who, in the midst of uncertainty, are questioning themselves about their own identity. And once the first fervor has passed a little, it may happen that you, too, will ask yourselves these things. For this reason I would like to propose to you some reflections on the priest's true character, which will serve as a great help for your priestly faithfulness.

It is certainly not in the sciences of human behavior, nor in socio-religious statistics, that we shall seek our answer, but in Christ, in the Faith. We will humbly question the Divine Master and ask Him who we are, what He wishes us to be, what is, in His eyes, our true identity.

THE CALL OF JESUS

3. A first answer is given to us at once: we are *called*. The history of our priesthood begins with a divine call, as happened in the case of the Apostles. In choosing them, Jesus' intention is clear. It is He who takes the initiative. He Himself will point this out: "You did not choose me, but I chose you" (Jn. 15:16). The simple and moving scenes, which present to us the call of each disciple, reveal the precise realization of determined choices (cf. Lk. 6:13) on which it is useful to meditate.

Whom does Jesus choose? He does not seem to consider the social class of the ones He chooses (cf. 1 Cor. 1:27) nor to take into account superficial enthusiasm (cf. Mt. 8:19-22). One thing is certain: We are called by Christ, by God. This means: We are loved by Christ, loved by God. Have we reflected sufficiently about this? Actually, the vocation to the priesthood is a sign of predilection on the part of Him who, choosing you among so many brothers, called you to participate, in a very special way, in His friendship: "No longer do I call you servants, for the servant does not know what his master is doing; but I have called you friends, for all that I have heard from my Father I have made known to you" (Jn. 15:15). Our call to the priesthood, marking the highest moment in the use of our freedom, has brought about the great and irrevocable option of our life and, therefore, the finest page in the history of our personal experience. Our happiness consists in never underestimating it!

RITE OF ORDINATION
CONSECRATES YOU

4. With the rite of Holy Ordination you will be introduced, beloved sons, to a new kind of life, which separates you from everything and unites you to Christ with an original, ineffable, irreversible bond. In this way your identity is enriched with another characteristic: you are *consecrated.*

This mission of the priesthood is not a mere juridical title. It does not consist just in ecclesial service rendered to the community, which is delegated by the latter, and for this reason can be revoked by the community itself or renounced by the free choice of the "official." It is a question, on the contrary, of a real and deep change through which your supernatural organism has passed thanks to a divine "seal," the "character" that entitles you to act *"in persona Christi"* (in the place of Christ) and for this reason qualifies you with regard to Him as living instruments of His action.

You now understand how the priest becomes *"segregatus in Evangelium Dei"* ("set apart for the Gospel of God," Rom. 1:1), and no longer belongs to the world, but is henceforth in a state of belonging exclusively to the Lord. The sacred character affects him at such depth as to direct completely his whole being and actions for a priestly purpose. Thus there no longer remains in him anything that is at his disposal as if he were not a priest, far less as if he were in conflict with this dignity. Even when he carries out actions which, by their nature, are of the temporal order, the priest is always God's minister. In him everything, even what is secular, must become priestly as in Jesus, who was always a priest and always acted as a priest, in all the expressions of His life.

To such an extent does Jesus identify us with Himself in the exercise of the powers which He has conferred on us, that our personality disappears, in a way, before His, since it is He who acts through us. "With the sacrament of Ordination," someone said appropriately, "the priest becomes definitively suitable to lend Jesus our Lord his voice, his hands and his whole being. It is Jesus who, in Holy Mass, changes the substance of the bread and wine into that of His body and His blood" (cf. I. Escrivà de Balaguer: *Sacerdote per l'eternità*, Milan, 1975, p. 30). And we can continue. It is Jesus Himself who, in the Sacrament of Penance, speaks the authoritative and fatherly word: "Your sins are forgiven" (Mt. 9:2; Lk. 5:20, 7:48; cf. Jn. 20:23). It is He who speaks when the priest, exercising his ministry in the name and in the spirit of the Church, announces the Word of God. It is again Jesus Christ Himself who takes care of the sick, children and sinners, when the love and pastoral solicitude of the sacred ministers encompass them.

As you can see, we are here at the peak of Christ's priesthood, in which we participate and which made the author of the letter to the Hebrews exclaim: *"grandis sermo et ininterpretabilis ad dicendum,"* "about this we have much to say which is hard to explain" (Heb. 5:11).

The expression *"sacerdos alter Christus,"* "the priest is another Christ," created by the intuition of the Christian people, is not just a way of speaking, a metaphor, but a marvelous, surprising and consoling reality.

THE GIFT OF PRIESTHOOD
REALIZED IN YOU

5. This gift of the priesthood, always remember, is a miracle that was realized in you but not for you. It was

realized for the Church, which is equivalent to saying, for the world that must be saved. The sacred dimension of the priesthood is completely ordained to the apostolic dimension, namely, to the mission, to the pastoral ministry. "As the Father has sent me, even so I send you" (Jn. 20:21).

The priest is, therefore, someone who is "sent." This is another essential connotation of priestly identity.

The priest is the man of the community, bound entirely and irrevocably to his service, as the Council clearly illustrated (cf. PO 12). From this point of view you are destined to carry out a double task, which in itself would be sufficient for an inexhaustible meditation on the priesthood. Clothed in the Person of Christ, you will exercise in a way His function as mediator. You will be interpreters of God's Word, stewards of the divine mysteries (cf. 1 Cor. 4:1; 2 Cor. 6:4) for the people. And you will be, with God, the representatives of the people in all its components: children, the young, families, workers, the poor, the lowly, the sick, and even the distant and adversaries. You will be the bearers of His offerings. You will be His voice of prayer and supplication, of exultation and groaning. You will be His expiation (cf. 2 Cor. 5:21).

For this reason let us keep engraved in our memory and in our heart the words of the Apostle: *"pro Christo legatione fungimur, tamquam Deo exhortante per nos,"* "We are ambassadors for Christ, God making his appeal through us" (2 Cor. 5:20), to make our life a deep, progressive and firm imitation of Christ the Redeemer.

CARRYING OUT
YOUR PRIESTLY ACTIVITIES

6. Dear sons, with this rapid exposition I have tried to illustrate to you the fundamental features of the priest.

I now wish to draw some practical consequences which will help you in carrying out your priestly activity inside and outside the ecclesial community.

First of all in the ecclesial world. You know that the doctrine of the common priesthood of the faithful, so amply developed by the Council, has offered the laity a providential opportunity to discover more and more the vocation of every baptized person to the apostolate and his necessary active and responsible commitment in the task of the Church. From that there has blossomed a vast and consoling flowering of initiatives and activities which constitute an inestimable contribution for the proclamation of the Christian message both in mission lands and in countries such as yours, in which the necessity of supplementing the presence of the priest with the help of the laity is felt more acutely.

This is certainly consoling, and we should be the first to rejoice at this collaboration of the laity and encourage it.

Nothing of all this, however—and it is well to say so at once—reduces in any way the importance and the necessity of the priestly ministry, or can justify a lesser effort for ecclesiastical vocations. Far less can it justify the attempt to transfer to the congregation or to the community the power that Christ conferred exclusively on His sacred ministers. The priest's role remains irreplaceable. We should, indeed, request the collaboration of the laity in every way. But in the economy of redemption there exist functions and tasks—such as the offering of the Eucharistic Sacrifice, forgiveness of sins, the office of the Magisterium—which Christ willed to link essentially to the priesthood and in which no one, without having received Holy Orders, can replace us. Without the priestly ministry, religious vitality runs the risk of seeing itself cut off from its sources, the Christian community of disintegrating, and the Church of becoming secularized.

It is true that God's grace can act just the same, especially where it is impossible to have a minister of God and where the fact of not having one is not anyone's fault. It is necessary not to forget, however, that the normal and certain way for the benefits of Redemption passes through the means instituted by Christ and in the forms established by Him.

It can also be understood from this how each of us must be concerned with the problem of vocations. We exhort you to dedicate to this field the first and most intense cares of your ministry. It is a problem for the Church (cf. OT 2). It is an extremely important problem. On it depends the certainty of the religious future of your country. You may, perhaps, be discouraged by the real difficulties of bringing the invitation of the Church to the world of youth. But be confident! The young people of our time also feel strongly the attraction for the heights, for difficult things, for great ideals. Do not be under the illusion that the prospect of a priesthood that is less austere in its requirements of sacrifice and renunciation—such as, for example, in the discipline of ecclesiastical celibacy—can increase the number of those who intend to commit themselves to following Christ. Quite the contrary. What is lacking and must be created in our communities is rather a mentality of strong and conscious faith. Where the daily sacrifice keeps the evangelical ideal awake and raises love of God to a high level, vocations continue to be numerous. This is confirmed by the religious situation of the world. The countries in which the Church is persecuted are, paradoxically, those in which vocations flourish most, and are sometimes even abundant.

TO BE AS LIGHT AND SALT
OF THE EARTH

7. It is necessary, furthermore, that you should become aware, beloved priests, that your ministry takes place today in the atmosphere of a secularized society, the characteristic of which is the gradual decline of the sacred, and the systematic elimination of religious values. You are called to effect salvation in it as signs and instruments of the invisible world.

Prudent but confident, you will live among men to share their worries and hopes, to encourage their efforts for freedom and justice. But do not let yourselves be possessed by the world or by its prince, the evil one (cf. Jn. 17:14-15). Do not adapt yourselves to the opinions and tastes of this world, as St. Paul exhorts: *"Nolite conformari huic saeculo"* (Rom. 12:1-2). Rather, conform your personality with its aspirations to the line of God's will.

The power of the sign is not in conformism, but in distinction. Light is different from darkness to be able to illuminate the path of one who walks in darkness. Salt is different from food to be able to give it taste. Fire is different from ice to warm limbs stiff with the cold. Christ calls us the light and salt of the earth. In a dissipated and confused world such as ours, the power of the sign lies precisely in being different. The more apostolic action calls for greater insertion in the human mass, the more different it must be.

In this connection who does not realize that to have absorbed a certain worldly mentality, to have frequented dissipated environments, and also to abandon an external way of presenting oneself, distinctive of priests, can reduce the sensitivity of one's own value as a sign?

When these luminous horizons are lost sight of, the figure of the priest is dimmed, his identity enters a state of crisis, his special duties no longer find their justification and contradict one another, and his very *raison d'être* is weakened.

Nor is this fundamental *raison d'être* recovered if the priest becomes a "man for others." Should not one who follows the Divine Master already be so?

The priest is, certainly, a "man for others," but by virtue of his particular way of being a "man for God." Service of God is the foundation on which to construct the genuine service of men, the one that consists in liberating souls from the slavery of sin and in bringing men back to the necessary service of God. God, indeed, wishes to make mankind a people that worships Him "in spirit and truth" (Jn. 4:23).

Let it remain quite clear, therefore, that the priestly service, if it wishes to be really faithful to itself, is an excellent and essentially spiritual service. Let this be emphasized today in face of the manifold trends to secularize the priest's service, reducing it to a purely philanthropical function. His service is not that of the doctor, the social worker, the politician or the trade-unionist. In certain cases, perhaps, the priest will be able to carry out these services, though in a supplementary way, and, in the past, he carried them out excellently. But today they are adequately discharged by other members of society, while our service is specified more and more clearly as a spiritual service. It is in the sphere of souls, of their relations with God and of their interior relationship with their fellow men, that the priest has an essential function to carry out. It is here that his assistance for the men of our time must be realized. Certainly, if the circumstances demand it, he will not dispense himself from giving also material assistance, by means of works of charity and the defense of justice. But as I said, this is, in the last analysis, a secondary service, which must never make us lose sight of the principal service, which is that of helping souls to discover the Father, opening oneself to Him and loving Him above all things.

Only in this way will the priest never feel useless, a failure, even if he were obliged to renounce some external activity. The Holy Sacrifice of the Mass, prayer, penance, the best, or rather, the essential part of his ministry, would always remain integral as it was for Jesus in the thirty years of His hidden life. In this way immense glory would also be given to God. The Church and the world would not be deprived of a real spiritual service.

CLOSE TO MARY
AS THE APOSTLES WERE

8. Dear ordinands, dear priests, at this point my address becomes a prayer, a prayer which I wish to entrust

to the intercession of the Blessed Virgin, the Mother of the Church and Queen of the Apostles. In your anxious expectation of the priesthood, you certainly took your place near her, like the Apostles in the Upper Room. May she obtain for you the graces you most need for your sanctification and for the religious prosperity of your country. May she grant you especially love, her love—the love that gave her the grace of generating Christ—in order to be capable of carrying out your mission of generating Christ in souls, too. May she teach you to be pure, as she was; may she make you faithful to the divine call, and make you understand the whole beauty, joy and power of a ministry lived unreservedly in dedication and immolation for the service of God and of souls. Finally, let us ask Mary, for you and for all of us here present, to help us to say, following her example, the great word: "Yes," to the will of God, even when it is demanding, even when it is perhaps incomprehensible, even when it is painful for us. Amen.

Love and a Spirit of Sacrifice Make the Gospel Advance

The Mass in honor of Blessed José de Anchieta was the Pope's first meeting with the population of São Paulo, in the vast area of the civilian section of the military airport of "Champs de Mars," early on July 3, 1980. The Pope delivered the following homily to the congregation of more than a million.

1. I am really happy to be with you, in this dear city of São Paulo, whose city council, with a delicate gesture, has made me an honorary citizen, because of the fact that, as Sovereign Pontiff, I recently decreed the beatification of Father José de Anchieta, of the Society of Jesus, rightly considered one of the founders of your city.

This manifestation of cordiality moves me and leads me to express my deep and sincere thanks.

Now I wish to reflect with you on the fascinating figure of Blessed Anchieta, so bound up with the religious and civil history of this beloved Brazil.

Blessed Anchieta arrived here, in this part of your great nation, Brazil, in 1554. The city did not yet exist; there were only a few scattered groups of natives. He arrived on January 24, on the eve of the feast of the Conversion of St. Paul. Therefore the first Mass celebrated here was precisely the one in honor of the Apostle of the Gentiles, and to him was dedicated the village that was to spring up around the hut—the "little church"—which was to be its heart. Hence the name of this city of yours, Sao Paulo, the largest city in Brazil.

Born in the Canary Islands, educated in Portugal, José de Anchieta came from those nations which, in that age, contributed so much to the discovery of the world. From Spain and from Portugal there set out sailors and pioneers, who, plowing the waves, arrived at lands hitherto unknown. Conquistadors, settlers, traders, explorers followed in their wake.

Did Father Anchieta come as a soldier in search of glory, a conquistador in search of lands, or a trader in search of good business and money? No! He came as a missionary to proclaim Jesus Christ and spread the Gospel. He came with the sole purpose of leading men to Christ, transmitting to them the life of sons of God, destined for eternal life. He came without asking anything for himself; on the contrary, ready to give his life for them.

Well, I too come to you for the same reason, moved by the same love: I come to you as the humble messenger of Christ.

This has always been the only motivation of the journeys that have taken me to the various continents: apostolic journeys of the one who, as the Servant of Christ, wishes to strengthen his brothers in the Faith.

Today, too, this is the reason why I am in your midst.

It unites me deeply with your Blessed José de Anchieta.

Welcome me just as you welcomed Anchieta: May my passing in your midst have something of the passage and the permanence of the great apostle in the midst of your people, in your villages of that time, in your great country. May it be the passage of the Lord's grace.

ATTENTIVE TO GOD'S INSPIRATION

2. Young, full of life, intelligent, joyful by nature, great-hearted and loved by all, a brilliant student at Coimbra University, José de Anchieta succeeded in winning the affection of his companions, who liked to hear him recite poetry. Owing to the timbre of his voice, they called him the "canary," recalling in this way the singing of the birds of his native island, Tenerife, in the Canaries.

So many paths to success opened before him. But, young in faith, he was attentive to the inspirations and the movements of God, who drew him along other ways, called him and guided him to a path very different from the one that others had perhaps imagined for him. In moments of spiritual darkness, the youth sought silence, solitude, in order to pray. Often, laying his books aside, he would walk alone along the banks of the river Mondego.

It was during one of these walks that José entered the cathedral of Coimbra and, before the altar of the Virgin Mary, he suddenly found the peace and serenity that he had desired so much. So he decided to devote his life to the service of God and men. In order to live this ideal, he made a vow of chastity, then and there consecrating himself to the Virgin; he was then seventeen years old.

From that day he intensified his prayer and continued his studies with ardor. Though young, he showed a great sense of maturity toward the meaning of life. The gift of himself which he had made to the Mother of God began to take on concrete shape as a call to religious life.

At that time, the letters that Francis Xavier—the great missionary—wrote from the East were being read at

Coimbra University. They also contained urgent appeals to the young students of European universities. Deeply impressed by what Father Xavier said about what so many peoples and countries lacked, and wishing to follow such an eloquent example of dedication to the glory of God and the good of men, Anchieta decided to enter the Society of Jesus: He wanted to be a missionary.

So, some years later, he came to Brazil.

Now I want to address you, young people of São Paulo, the young people of the whole of Brazil, of the great nation that can be called "young" because its population has such a high percentage of young people: Look to your Anchieta!

He was young like you, but open to God and His invitations. He was full of life like you, but in prayer he sought the answer to life. In this contact with the living God he found the way that leads to true life, to a life of love for God and for men.

The Lord, who lived on earth, passing from village to village doing good (cf. Mt. 9:35), still passes today in search of hearts open to His invitation: "Come, follow me!" (Mt. 19:21; Lk. 10:2)

Remember: José de Anchieta answered generously, and the Lord made him the "Apostle of Brazil," who contributed in an outstanding way to the good of your people.

TO SAVE SOULS: GOAL OF HIS LIFE

3. Once a missionary, Anchieta lived the spirit of the Apostle of the Gentiles, who in his letters spoke of the vicissitudes, difficulties and dangers he faced, bearing in his heart the "daily pressure of his anxiety for all the Churches" (cf. 2 Cor. 11:26-28).

In a letter of June 1, 1560, revealing his great desire to lead the peoples of this country to the Lord, Father Anchieta wrote verbatim: "Therefore, without letting myself be intimidated by calms, storms, rain, and the foaming, impetuous currents of the rivers, we are trying unceasingly to visit all the villages and houses of both the Indians and the Portuguese; and even by night we rush to the sick, through dark forests, at the price of great fatigue, both because of the difficult roads and because of the bad weather" (Letter to Father Diego Laynez, Superior General of the Society of Jesus). Describing even more clearly the conditions of those who, with him and like him, dedicated themselves to the "Brasis" (Brazilians: *editor's note*)— as he used to call them—he reveals even more deeply the greatness of his love and spirit of sacrifice and, above all, the purpose of his existence: "Nothing is difficult for those who cherish in their hearts and have as their only aim the glory of God and the salvation of souls, for which they do not hesitate to give their own life" *(ibid.)*.

To save souls for the glory of God: that was the goal of his life. This explains the amazing activity of Anchieta in seeking new forms of apostolic activity, which led him to become everything to everyone for the Gospel; to become the servant of everyone to win as many men as possible to Christ (cf. 1 Cor. 9:19-22).

He spared no effort to understand his "Brasis" and share their life. If he learned their difficult language—and so well that he was the first to compose a grammar of it—it was out of the love that drove him to incorporate himself among them, in order to speak to them of Jesus and trans-mit the Good News. Thus—following the example of Christ the Lord, God-become-man to reveal the Father—he be-came an excellent catechist who spoke of God to the men among whom he lived, in a simple way, adapting himself to their mental levels and their customs.

For this same purpose, taking into account the natural gifts and qualities of the Indians, their thirst for knowledge, their generosity and hospitality and their com-munity spirit, he promoted and developed the "aldeias" (villages), centers in which the life of each one merged with that of others, in an adequate way, in work, in solidarity, in cooperation. The heart of each of these centers was always the house of God, where the Eucharistic Sacrifice was celebrated regularly and the Lord was present in the Blessed Sacrament. Yes, because a social group cannot last that is not animated by charity, which only God can instill into hearts (cf. Rom 5:5), nor can it offer what the heart of man and the whole of mankind seek with great desire.

In Puebla, speaking of the liberation of man, I insisted that it must be seen in the light of the Gospel, that is, in the light of Christ, who gave His life to redeem mankind, liberating him from sin. More recently, speaking in Africa, where the community spirit is so much alive, I urged the peoples of that continent to try to develop their social spirit in a truly Christian way, without letting themselves be influenced by extraneous movements, materialistic on the one hand, and of the consumer society on the other. I repeat this to you, too. Fr. Anchieta succeeded in understanding the mentality and customs of your people. With his prudent social action, inspired by the Gospel and rooted in it, he was able to stimulate a growth and development capable of integrating this same mentality and customs—in their truly human elements, therefore willed by God—in the lives of persons and of the civil and Christian community.

Appreciating the thirst for knowledge of the "Brasis," their outstanding talent for music, their ability and other gifts, he created for them centers of cultural and artisan formation which gradually contributed to raising the general level of subsequent generations: Sao Paulo, Olinda, Bahia, Porto Seguro, Rio de Janeiro, Reritiba—where he died and which today is called Anchieta—are places which, together with others not mentioned, speak to us of the tireless apostolic activity of the Blessed.

In all this immense effort of his, with the help of many confreres, unknown by many but nonetheless admirable, there was a vision and a spirit: the complete vision of man redeemed by the blood of Christ; the spirit of the missionary who does everything in order that the human beings whom he approaches to help, support and educate, may reach the fullness of Christian life.

Allow me now to address particularly you bishops, priests, men and women religious, who have given your lives to serve God in the Church. Let the purpose of your pastoral action, individually or collectively, never deviate from what—as I said in my Encyclical *Redemptor hominis*—is the real purpose for which the Son of Man became a man and worked in our midst. Let His mission of love, peace and redemption be really yours. Remember that Christ Himself indicated to us what His mission consisted of: *Veni ut vitam habeant et ut abundantius habeant:* "I came that they may have life, and have it abundantly" (Jn. 10:10).

If you wish to be extensions of the life and mission of Christ, be faithful to your vocation. Father Anchieta did everything, he even studied the fauna and flora, medicine, music, literature, but he directed everything to the real good of man, destined and called to be, and live as, a son of God.

SECRET OF BLESSED
JOSÉ DE ANCHIETA'S DRIVE

4. Whence did Fr. Anchieta derive the strength to carry out so many works in a life entirely spent for the benefit of others, to the extent of dying, exhausted, when he was still at the peak of his activity?

Certainly not from an iron constitution. On the contrary, his health was always uncertain. In his apostolic journeys, made on foot and without any comfort, he always suffered in his body the effects of an accident he had had as a young man.

Did he find strength, perhaps, in his talents and human gifts? Partly, yes; but this does not explain everything. With this assertion alone, we do not arrive at the real source.

This man's secret was his faith: José de Anchieta was a man of God. Like St. Paul, he could say: *Scio cui credidi*:

"I know whom I have believed, and I am sure that he is able to guard until that day what has been entrusted to me" (2 Tm. 1:12).

From the moment when, in Coimbra Cathedral, he had spoken to God and to the Virgin Mary, the Mother of Christ and ours, from that moment to his last breath, the life of José de Anchieta was straightforward and clear: to serve the Lord, to be at the disposal of the Church, to do everything in his power for those who were, or who were to become, sons of the Father who is in heaven.

Certainly, he did not lack sorrows and grief, disappointments and failures; he, too, had his share of the daily fare of every apostle of Christ, of every priest of the Lord. But in his tireless activity and in continual suffering, he never lacked the tranquil, serene and manly certainty founded on the Lord Jesus, whom he found and with whom he united himself in the Eucharistic Mystery, to whom he offered himself constantly to let himself be molded by His Spirit.

José de Anchieta had understood what was God's will for him on the day when he knelt humbly before an image of our Lady: The Mother of the Savior began to take care of him and he began to cherish a very tender love for her. He taught his "Brasis" to know her and love her. He dedicated to her a poem which is a real song of the soul, written in very difficult circumstances when, taken hostage, his life was continually in danger. Having neither paper nor ink at his disposal, he wrote his poem lovingly on the sand of the beach and learned it by heart: *De Beata Virgine Matre Dei Maria*.

Deep and ardent union with God; living and affectionate attachment to the crucified and risen Christ, present in the Eucharist; tender love for Mary: This is the source from which there sprang the richness of the life and activity of Anchieta, a true missionary, a real priest.

May God, through the intercession of Blessed José de Anchieta, give you the grace to live as he taught, as he invites us with the example of his life.

Convincing Witnesses of Jesus Christ

On his arrival at Porto Alegre on July 4, 1980, the Holy Father was welcomed by Cardinal Alfredo Vicente Scherer, by the State Governor and his wife, and by other civil and ecclesiastical authorities. Despite the almost freezing temperature of two degrees centigrade, His Holiness drove in an open car to the cathedral. From the balcony of the church he delivered the following address to the vast gathering of people that had assembled in Deodoro Square.

1. I warmly thank the beloved pastor of this Archdiocese, dear Cardinal Vicente Scherer, for the noble words he addressed to me and in which I again find the virtues that I already know to be his: simplicity, sincerity, absolute fidelity to the Successor of Peter.

I gather from his words that you were all waiting for this moment. I can tell you that I, too, have anxiously awaited the day when, in the course of this pilgrimage of mine through Brazil, I would come to meet you in Porto Alegre. Blessed be the Lord for this opportunity.

At the side of His Eminence Cardinal Scherer, I greet his auxiliary bishops. I greet my brother bishops of the ecclesiastical province of Rio Grande do Sul. I greet the priests, deacons, and religious present here. I greet the faithful of every race, age, and status.

A special greeting to those who have come from further away to see the Pope—from the neighboring state of Santa Catarina, which I have not been able to visit this time, from Argentina, and from Uruguay. I know that it is not my person that counts: What counts is the mission that the Lord has wished to entrust to me. I am happy to know that, beyond the Pope, it is to the Successor of Peter, and therefore to Peter himself, it is to the Vicar of Christ, and therefore to Christ Himself, that your homage is addressed. To Him alone praise and glory for centuries without end.

2. I come, therefore, as Pastor of the Universal Church, to meet face to face the sheep that the Good Shepherd, in His loving designs, has entrusted to me. I come as the Successor of Peter, to give continuity to his mission of strengthening brothers. I come as the Vicar of Jesus Christ, bringing His blessing and His peace.

I know that the faith is deeply rooted in your land, and is lived intensely in your hearts.

I know, too, that the secret of this great vitality in faith lies in the families that have been formed in a Christian way, and in the missionaries, excellent priests, who over a century ago intensely evangelized this region.

To be convincing witnesses of Jesus Christ, we must seek ever greater authenticity; we must remain firm in the Faith. Now, I think (and I tried to explain this in my Apostolic Exhortation *Catechesi tradendae*) that in our days it is not possible for Faith to survive and spread without a deepening of the faith itself. That is, without a catechesis adapted to the circumstances, but always in conformity with the mind of the Church. Therefore, I do not wish to let this opportunity pass without exhorting you pastors, bishops, and priests, you fathers and mothers of families, you teachers, to make a courageous and persevering catechetical effort for children, young people, and adults.

3. A word of friendship to the presbyterium, represented here in such large numbers. I do not need many words to tell you that you are in the Pope's heart. He always prays for you and asks the Lord to give you the grace of fidelity to the gift already received, to make each of you a *sacerdos in aeternum*. Live the mystery of the unity of the Church, remaining united with your bishops "like the strings of the lyre," to recall the vivid comparison of St. Ignatius of Antioch. This is the secret of the apostolic fruitfulness of the presbyterium.

And what shall I say to men and women religious? You occupy in the Body of Christ, the Church, a place that is solely yours. You are the expression of her vocation to holiness, to which you must give concrete form. May God bless your lives, making them fruitful in His love, which will certainly be to the benefit of your brothers.

Here in your city I am to meet a group of "the called," together with those engaged in their formation. While waiting for this gratifying meeting, it is enough for now to tell you that the Church must always preserve in her soul a deep compassion: There is a multitude of people who are "tired and exhausted, like sheep without a shepherd"; and a prayer: "Send, Lord, laborers into your harvest" (cf. Mt. 9:36-38).

I know that your state is rich in vocations and, with you, I thank the Lord. I hope that you will always be able to appreciate this gift, to take up these vocations and help them to mature in love of God and unconditional fidelity to the Church, for the good of the whole community.

God bless your families, rich in fine traditions, centers of the radiation of Christian values, and reservoirs of numerous vocations.

4. Finally, I greet the whole people of Porto Alegre and of the state of Rio Grande do Sul. You experience here the harmony of the meeting of so many races, merged into an authentic Brazilian character. You are a living lesson that it is possible for man to live in brotherhood with his fellow man.

From this archdiocese, born with the title and under the protection of the apostle Peter, the Successor of the same Peter greets everyone and invokes God's blessings for everyone, but particularly for the old, the sick, those who are suffering in body or in soul, and for the children.... The Pope embraces you all with sincere affection. The Pope prays for everyone, and blesses everyone.

May the Virgin Mary, "the Mother of God"—as you lovingly invoke her in your cathedral—help you and lead you to her beloved Son.

Listening to the Lord, the Great Friend

On July 5, 1980, the Pope met over ten thousand priests and "voca-cionados," that is, all those who feel "called" to the priesthood or religious life, most of whom came from the State of Rio Grande do Sul, but many also from the State of Santa Catarina, as well as from Uruguay, Paraguay, Argentina, and Chile. The following are excerpts from the Holy Father's address.

Beloved sons,

You will certainly not be surprised if I confide to you that this meeting was one of those most anticipated by me among the many that Providence grants me in this great nation. It is a joy to be able to meet you young people, ready to follow Jesus Christ, who calls for a complete gift of oneself in witness to love for Him and service for brothers; with you priests and religious who are responsible for the formation of those preparing for the priesthood, religious life or a direct commitment in apostolic activity. On you there depends to a great extent the future of the Church in Brazil.

"Grace to you and peace from God the Father and the Lord Jesus Christ" (2 Thes. 1:2). Many thanks for the cordiality and enthusiasm of your welcome, which I greatly appreciate. It is another expression of the traditional Brazilian hospitality that I have experienced in these days.

PRIESTLY AND RELIGIOUS FORMATION

Beside you [young people], as ministers of Christ and interpreters of his internal aspirations, are those to whom the Church has entrusted the delicate task of your formation. Turning my attention to them, I am happy to recall in the first place the long tradition of commitment for priestly formation in Brazil, with some characteristics recognized by everyone. It goes back to the first experiences in the colleges of Bahia, Sao Paulo and Rio de Janeiro; it passes through the period formerly designated as "the Age of

Convents," and through alternate times of trial and prosperity, until it reaches the first ecclesiastical organization. In the 18th century there appear seminaries properly so-called, among which those of Mariana, Olinda, and Caraça, to name a few, have left a mark in the history of Brazil.

At this point, how could I fail to recognize the merits and appreciate the important role of the orders and religious congregations?

Subsequently, with seminaries such as were recommended by the Council of Trent established in many parts of the immense territory, there continued the formation of successive generations of priests, some of whom, in this last century, came to Rome to complete their studies and formation, first at the Latin American College, then in the Brazilian College, or in the Roman houses of religious institutes, valuable means to maintain the traditional ties between Catholic Brazil and St. Peter's See, in the communion of the universal Church.

Before these glorious traditions of the past, a question imposes itself on the heart of the Pope, worried by the *sollicitudo omnium ecclesiarum* (2 Cor. 11:28): In a decisive moment for its destiny and for that of the world, such as the present, will Brazil have the seminaries, religious houses, or other ecclesiastical institutes; will it have, above all, the rectors and teachers capable of preparing priests and religious who will be equal to the problems raised by a continually growing population, with increasingly vast and complex pastoral needs?

The question involves a fundamental point of ecclesial life. I would like to pause for a few moments to speak about it to you who have, in various capacities, responsibility for the seminaries and houses of formation. The centuries-old experience and the considered reflection of the Church prove the absolute necessity of these structures for the preparation of priests and religious. The Second Vatican

Council has confirmed that the way followed by the Church through the centuries is the right one, and that it must not, therefore, be abandoned.

The formation of a priest and of a religious cannot be left to improvization. It is God's grace that inspires the vocation; it is God's grace that creates the priest and the religious. But this grace is given in the Church and for the Church: so it is up to the Church to test the authenticity of a call and guide its development up to the goal of Holy Orders and religious vows. Now for the Church, on the basis of her tradition and experience, all this cannot be fully carried out without an institution called by a highly significant name: the seminary, and other similar institutions for religious formation.

Certainly, the seminary and other educational institutions need to be updated. The Church knows this. It is one of her constant concerns. The Church knows that reality changes according to times and places; she reflects on reality and follows reality, which bears within it the signs of divine Providence. Therefore, she proposes precise norms, and in this way tries to help those responsible for priestly and religious formation in their difficult work which, to be efficacious, must always be carried out in the Church, with the Church, and for the Church.

For this reason my venerated predecessors have taken care, with admirable solicitude, to deal with the subjects of priestly and religious formation, such as modern pastoral needs required. For the same reason the Holy See has not failed to recall, comment on, and explain the requirements pointed out by the Council through a series of documents, in which those responsible for priestly and religious formation must see a renewed testimony of trust, understanding, and love.

As I speak to you, I have in mind the difficulties which disturb the modern world and which have repercussions in the life of the Church. Seminaries and other institutions of formation could hardly be spared. The very proposal of priestly and religious life has quite often found obstacles even in those who should have proclaimed it courageously or might have accepted it generously.

Even if the difficulties were greater than those we know, our sacred duty remains that of evangelizing the People of God with regard to the divine dignity of the ministerial priesthood and the lofty ideal of consecrated life. For this reason, beloved priests and religious, I call upon you to meditate again on the Constitution *Lumen gentium* and the Decrees *Presbyterorum ordinis* and *Perfectae caritatis* of the Second Vatican Council. In particular, I call upon you to reread the letter I addressed to all the priests in the Church on the occasion of Holy Thursday, 1979, to reaffirm the sacred doctrine of the Church on the ministerial priesthood, which is participation in the priesthood of Christ by means of Holy Orders, and the gift of Christ to His and our community (cf. nos. 3 and 4).

If we are deeply convinced of this truth, if we communicate it in its entirety to the People of God, if we bear witness to it with our lives, then the difficulties of our times will not frighten us.

BALANCE AND COURAGE ARE NECESSARY

Having reaffirmed these fundamental principles which spring from faith, allow me to mention some practical aspects which deserve prudent consideration for the good of the Church and of priestly and religious life.

The Church wishes the most adequate means and methods to be sought for the formation of the priest and religious of today. The directives of the Council and the subsequent ones of the Holy See are all aimed in this direction. The Council rightly suggested dividing seminary communities that are too large. It proposed that aspirants to the priesthood keep in touch with the community and offer assistance for pastoral activity in the places their formation took place. There can be no doubt about the pedagogical value of these guidelines.

However, after a sufficient period of experimentation, we all have the duty to re-examine some initiatives, undertaken certainly with good intentions, but which may distort the directives of the Council and lead to disappointing and harmful results. What things must be corrected or completed, for example, in the various undertakings, not always happy ones, aimed at replacing seminaries, especially by means of the so-called "little communities"? What are the pro's and con's of a formation of future priests exclusively within the communities in which they will subsequently have to carry out their ministry? How to avoid reducing to a minimum the program of studies and of the seminary curriculum to the evident detriment of the specific intellectual and spiritual formation which belongs to the new minister of God?

Balance and courage are necessary, especially on the part of the bishops, to direct clearly all the points concerning the formation of new ministers, especially priests. We rejoice to see that the farsighted norms of the Second Vatican Council are again taken into due consideration, accepted, and put into practice, while experiments which have not yielded fruit, or have turned out to be negative, are reshaped, made relevant, and, when necessary, abandoned.

But above all, I am anxious to stress that in this task, the work of priests and religious remains fundamental, be they superiors, teachers, or masters of novices. Your mission is a marvelous but difficult one. The pastors of dioceses and those responsible for religious life have reflected and prayed before choosing you and entrusting to you one of the most delicate ministries that exist in the Church: to form those who will form the People of God.

Having accepted this mission, you must feel responsible for your personal preparation. The Council stressed this point (cf. OT 5). The First Synod of Bishops gave precise guidelines. Your bishops and religious superiors will help you. But your continual improvement on the spiritual, intellectual, and pastoral levels depends on you, on awareness of your duty.

Your spirituality must draw from the pure spring that is Christ, the Teacher of teachers, Pastor of our souls, the supreme Model of all educators and of all education. Your intellectual preparation must always be updated, in total fidelity to the Magisterium and to the living Tradition of the Church, in humble and affectionate acceptance of the Word of God which surpasses all human wisdom. Your pastoral efficiency cannot but increase with integration in the diocesan presbyterium, which experience enriches you, and which you enrich with your experience.

With this complete preparation, your mission will be carried out laboriously, but also joyfully, under the blessing of God who does not leave without help anyone who offers Him his unconditional cooperation. Thus prepared, you will find light and strength to carry out a work of authentic evangelical pedagogy.

You will guide the aspirants entrusted to you to achieve the height of spirituality, that height which will then sustain them in the labors of apostolic ministry and in fidelity to the commitments assumed on behalf of the Church. You will guide them to discern their vocation clearly, to strengthen their character, to accept the sacrifice of a life dedicated wholly to God and to the Church. You will guide them to acquire a solid, healthy, and open education, which is required today of anyone who is to be, in his turn, a teacher of the People of God. You will guide them towards pastoral knowledge and wisdom, which is the proclamation of the Word of God, the celebration of the divine Mysteries, spiritual care for the community and for individual souls. In a word: Your disciples will draw upon your riches, as you draw on the inexhaustible riches of Christ's heart.

SHOULDER YOUR RESPONSIBILITIES

This is, beloved sons, the exhortation that wells up from my heart; this is the instruction I wish to entrust to each of you: Put your mind, your heart, your energies generously at the disposal of Christ. I say it to you, superiors and educators who, in daily dedication to your delicate task, are called to be a sign and instrument of the service of Christ who is building up His Body. I say it to you young people who have accepted the call and have agreed to set out in the footsteps of Christ, in order to be tomorrow the witnesses to His love among your brothers.

Christ needs the contribution of all to bring to other hearts the word that "not all men can receive" (cf. Mt. 19:11), that is, the word of the call to unreserved surrender to the cause of the kingdom.

Grow in Grace and in Knowledge of the Lord

In the afternoon of July 6, 1980, the Holy Father reached Salvador da Bahia, the eighth stage of his pilgrimage in Brazil. In the Cathedral, addressing thirty bishops and about eight hundred priests and religious of the state of Bahia, the Holy Father delivered an address. The following are excerpts.

Lord Cardinal Archbishop,
Most Reverend Coadjutor Archbishop João de Souza Lima,
Most Reverend Auxiliary Bishop Thomas Murphy,
My brothers in the episcopate and in the ministerial priesthood,
Men and women religious,
Dear brothers and sisters,

The traditional hospitality of Bahia, of which I am the recipient at this moment, could not find a better expression for my joy and happiness than the eloquent and sincere words of your Archbishop, beloved Cardinal Avelar Brandão Vilela. Grateful to him and to the whole of Bahia, I wish to express to you my "Thank you very much" for the welcome given to me.

I address my greeting to you. And with the words of St. Paul, I hope and pray that "the goodness and loving kindness of God our Savior will appear" (cf. Ti. 3:4). The goodness of the Savior for the pastors of this archdiocese and of all suffragan dioceses; for the faithful of these various particular Churches; for the rulers and those in charge of the common good of the state, in this capital and in all cities; for those who exercise responsibilities; for families, and especially for those that are suffering tribulations or are in mourning; for the young and children, as also for the old; for the sick and for those who are lonely. May the kindness and the "love of the Savior" be with you all and with all your dear ones.

Allow me a special greeting to the priests of each of the local dioceses, the image of which I wish to see in the priests present here. Ministers of Christ the Priest, called to act *in persona Christi*, live also as if Christ Himself lived in you. It is the only way of being real educators to faith, pastors and guides of the faithful who, sometimes aloud, but nearly always with a silent supplication, ask you for guidelines for their lives, a light for their path.

Accept, all of you, beloved sons, the greetings and good wishes of the Pope, with the affection he places in you. And may the apostolic blessing, which I willingly grant you, be a token of the divine grace which will make you "live sober, upright, and godly lives in this world, awaiting our blessed hope, the appearing of the glory of our great God and Savior" (Ti. 2:12-13).

Growth of Communion and Participation Makes Evangelization More Perfect

On July 10, 1980, the Pope met the bishops of Brazil at the Centro de Covenções in Fortaleza and delivered the following address.

Your Excellency, the President,
Lord Cardinals,
Beloved brothers in the episcopate,

1. In joyful anticipation of the visit I am now paying to your country, in the last few months I often thought of the various meetings I would have. Each of them seemed to me very important, but I can tell you with the sincerity of a brother: none is more important than this one with you, bishops of Brazil.

Today you are the most numerous episcopal body in the world; and the intense activity you carry out in the apostolate of a young and dynamic Church, such as yours is, corresponds to the number. Because of this and the promising prospects of your country, the episcopate to which you belong has a prestige and a responsibility that go far beyond the borders of your dioceses and of the nation itself: a responsibility before the whole Church.

Therefore, in the schedule of this apostolic pilgrimage, my greatest desire was to be personally among you, to greet you *"in osculo sancto"* (Rom. 16:16; 1 Cor. 16:20), and *"in vinculo pacis"* (Eph. 4:3), to express to you directly my sentiments as Pastor of the universal Church. The Lord Jesus will understand why, applying them to this occasion, I say to you words that He Himself uttered at a crucial moment of His life: "I have earnestly desired to eat this passover with you" (Lk. 22:15). As a matter of fact, this meeting is a Passover, a passing of the Lord in our midst. God be praised for offering me this opportunity, and may He assist us in this hour so that this meeting may be for you a source of renewed pastoral fruitfulness, as it is for me a source of joy and comfort.

THE NATIONAL CONFERENCE OF THE BISHOPS OF BRAZIL (CNBB)

2. I wish my first words to be a brotherly greeting to the National Conference of the Bishops of Brazil.

I cannot forget the almost pioneering character of this Conference. Created with this name of Conference of Bishops in far-off 1952, it was one of the first in the world to be formed. And this was long before the Second Vatican Council shed new light on the doctrine of episcopal collegiality, and rightly recommended the episcopal conferences, as a special expression and particularly appropriate organ of this collegiality.

In these twenty-eight years—everyone recognizes this —it has tried to carry out a mission and accomplish a work in keeping with its nature: to make possible the meeting and dialogue of the increasingly numerous bishops in the country; to facilitate the concentration of pastoral action, thanks above all to an overall plan and apostolate which have been, right from the beginning, the dominant concern of the CNBB; as authentically as possible to represent the Brazilian episcopate to other institutions, including the civil ones.

Certainly the conference, far from resting on its laurels, will have to endeavor constantly to be more and more faithful to its mission. This faithfulness to its original vocation, to the goals that the Church's wisdom indicates to it, and to the ways that she has laid down, is the condition for the effectiveness of its action. For the conference, therefore, as for every living organism, especially an organism in the service of Christ, to seek improvement is a sign of inner health; it is a necessity; it is a duty.

In what areas should improvement and growth be sought? The Puebla document suggests the answer: in communion, in participation, in evangelization.

COMMUNION WITHIN THE CNBB

3. In communion first of all. Because this is the *raison d'être* and the prime purpose of every episcopal conference: to create and always keep alive communion among the bishops that compose it. These are necessarily men who are very different from one another, just as the first Twelve chosen by the Lord Jesus Himself were different. The more numerous they are, the greater is this difference. However, the pastoral service which they carry out calls for strong communion among them, at the deepest level conceivable. The bond of this communion—far stronger than anything that could divide or separate them—is the one Lord who called the bishops and made them His ministers; the one truth of which they are both teachers and servants; the one salvation in Christ which they proclaim and make present; the brotherly charity which "gathers them in unity" (cf. Hymn *Ubi caritas*).

Pastors of a Church which, according to the theology of the Second Vatican Council, likes to define herself as a "sacrament of unity" (LG 1), the bishops are called to be the first to bear living witness to unity. Let us not be under any illusion: The best preaching the bishops of a nation can give, the most fruitful service they can render to their own people, the most efficacious action they can perform, will certainly be the true and visible demonstration of their communion. Otherwise, without this communion, everything else is seen to be dangerously precarious. In their own conference the bishops wish, and have the right, to find an incentive to unity and an instrument of unity.

If I may draw upon my personal experience as a bishop, and also as a member of a national conference, I would not hesitate to say that any manifestation of an episcopal conference produces an impact (I am speaking of a real, deep, lasting, and not necessarily sensational impact) that is only as great as the unity that is reflected in it as the soul of the episcopal collegiality concretely embodied in this group of bishops. Consider, brothers: the evidencing of effective collegiality will be facilitated only insofar as it is accompanied by affective collegiality. This presupposes authentic dialogue among all its members, which, as you know, goes from the continual cultivation of poverty of spirit to the constant opening to divine grace which is its perfection. Attention to others in the little acts of everyday life is necessary. Thus is created the climate which causes mutual trust to grow—this trust that is never limited to mere cordiality in mutual relations, but must arrive at that deep sentiment which enables us to accept with simplicity, in the area of matters of opinion, views or positions different from one's own, provided we safeguard the common good of the Church on the local level and in her universal dimension. It was, in fact, with a vivid awareness of episcopal collegiality and an attitude of brotherly confidence that I came here to you, and that I find myself here a brother among brothers, to speak to you and listen to you, as much as time permits.

I would like to add—but perhaps it is superfluous —that growth in communion calls for ever deeper mutual knowledge, understanding of the other, respect for his conscience, frankness and loyalty. All of this is the fruit of a charity, which on this level is called brotherly love and communion, which leads to overcoming biases, party spirit, or disputes among groups, and leads to the integration of conceivable differences within a certain healthy pluralism. A conference cannot but thank God when it is immune from these problems, and must beseech Him humbly and fervently that it may always be so. God grant that it may always be so. God grant that in the documents and pronouncements of this episcopal conference this harmony may always be manifested because "by this, men will know that you are my disciples," the Lord says, "if you love one another."

PARTICIPATION IN THE CNBB

4. To grow in participation is the second goal. An episcopal conference is a joint venture: spiritually rich if all the bishops feel fully members and are present with pleasure and without embarrassment; impoverished whenever for any reason someone feels, or says he is, or sets himself, on the perimeter.

Growth in participation takes place in some matters, perhaps humble, but nonetheless worthy of considerations. Participation grows to the extent that sincere efforts are made to perceive and consider stands in the name of the whole conference, to consider the deep sentiment and convictions of parts of the whole, of considerable number even though not in the majority.

In a large episcopal conference, the greater representation the bishop members have in policy-making organs, the greater is the participation. Participation grows when in practice the bishops see their own conference as the place where they can meet in the exercise of their role as persons called in a special way to share in the mission of Christ the Prophet. By virtue of this union with Christ Himself, the bishops serve divine truth in the Church. They help to mold the life of the Church herself with respect to her basic scope, and they are constituted teachers of faith of the People of God, in continuity with the one Divine Master (cf. Mt. 23:8). They have an individual and collegial responsibility, which cannot be renounced, before Christ Himself and before the whole Church. However, who could doubt the value of a competent collaboration which in various areas priests, lay people, men and women religious offer to the bishops within the episcopal conference? They deserve praise for this contribution of theirs. Of course, it is the bishops who remain responsible for the decisions, the pronouncements, and the documents of the conference as such, and therefore they must answer for them to their own conscience and to God. To surround themselves with collaborators may be a way of supporting the effort of fidelity to divine truth and of greater service to the People of God. However, no one should be surprised by the fact that at assemblies and in their conferences, the bishops should try to have at their disposal sufficiently long periods to meet and dialogue with one another without the presence of others, to strengthen their own unity as teachers of faith, to share the common responsibility of being, to an ever increasing extent, the strength and guarantee of the fundamental unity of the Church.

All of us who look with understanding and admiration to your conference hope and pray that it may always make progress in participation, that no one will withhold his presence, not just physical, but also active and efficient presence. This participation will be the greatest grace of the conference.

THE CNBB AND EVANGELIZATION

5. In any episcopal conference, improvement in communion and in participation necessarily results in an improvement in its principal task, which is evangelization.

In the Apostolic Exhortation *Evangelii nuntiandi*, which is certainly the magna charta of evangelization for this last quarter of a century and one of the most outstanding documents of the Magisterium of Paul VI, this great and unforgettable Pope recalled that evangelization is something rich, complex, and dynamic (no. 17), involving various elements. But he added: "To evangelize is first of all to bear witness, in a simple and direct way, to God revealed by Jesus Christ, in the Holy Spirit" (no. 26); the foundation, center, and summit of evangelization is salvation in Jesus Christ (no. 27). The Puebla document closely follows the inspiration of *Evangelii nuntiandi* when, speaking of the content of evangelization, it presents as "essential content" (no. 351) the "central truths" (no. 166) on Jesus Christ (no. 170ff.), on the Church (no. 220ff.), and on man (no. 304ff.), calling all the rest an "integral part" of evangelization.

Especially in our world threatened by atheistic secularism—and this can never be recalled too often—it is the duty of the Church to proclaim the absolute reality of God, the mystery of Jesus Christ, the transcendence of salvation, of the faith, and of the sacraments of faith. It is the duty of her pastors. You will certainly agree with me if I state that we, as ministers of Christ in His Church, will have credibility and efficacy in speaking of temporal realities only if first (or at least at the same time) we are careful to proclaim "a salvation which exceeds all these (temporal) limits in order to reach fulfillment in a communion with the...divine Absolute" (cf. EN 27), to proclaim "the prophetic message of a hereafter, man's profound and definitive calling" *(ibid.,* no. 28).

I mention this to say that I am happy when an episcopal conference gives room in its program of assemblies to subjects pertaining to urgent questions of a temporal nature which affect the men of our time. The very nature of this organization always requires that such questions be included in evangelization and in the paramount search for the kingdom of God and His justice (cf. Mt. 6:32), which the Lord indicated to us in a panorama of all our concerns. He Himself left us the example. To all without exception He proclaimed the Good News, although His immediate attention went to the humblest, the poor, and the suffering. In the exercise of our ministry, the things concerning God will always have to prevail, if we want our office as men appointed to act on behalf of men (cf. Heb. 5:1) to remain in all its vitality. Thus the assemblies, the episcopal conferences, must concern themselves with comparing the emergent problems in the life of men and of society with the thought of God, known, sought, studied, and shared in a brotherly way, without omitting to deal opportunely and surely with the specific problems of the life of the Church, such as those that pertain to the liturgy, prayer, priestly vocations, religious life and its correct renewal, catechesis, the religious formation of the young, popular piety and its requirements, the challenge of erroneous sects, the avalanche of immorality, etc.

The strength and identity of our Church lies mainly in this. In this way and with this attitude not only will the Church in Brazil benefit, in your case, but also Brazilian society itself, and especially the upcoming generations.

Recently, from the time my intention to make this pastoral visit to Brazil became known, the number of letters that daily reach me from this country greatly increased. They are moving letters, in the poverty and simplicity they reveal on the part of the writers, and they do not conceal the difficulty of some of them who have barely learned to handle a pen. They manifest a hunger for God, an openness to the sacred, and sometimes an explicit thirst for the truth of the Gospel and supernatural life. This cannot leave us indifferent. We, pastors of the Church, cannot fail to give them the spiritual goods which they request, like children asking for bread, looking for someone to break it for them, as Scripture says. Actually, with the spiritual goods and the specific means of the Church at our disposal, through adequate apostolic programs, animated by a conscious concern for concrete man in his total reality, the Church, without having to resort to means that are alien to her, can very well contribute to the transformation of society, helping it to become increasingly just, based on objective justice. This makes evident the necessity of catechesis and emphasizes its importance.

Reading your quinquennial reports, I am impressed by the way many of you deplore the lack of depth of faith in a people which is nevertheless religious, good, and to use Tertullian's expression, "naturally Christian" (Apologetics, 17: Ed. Rauschen, 58). This superficiality in knowledge of the doctrine of faith causes not a few disadvantages, among which you yourselves mention: a certain vulnerability with regard to erroneous doctrines; a certain tendency to a superficial piety, to sentiments more than convictions; the ever imminent risk of an external faith, detached from life.... In this situation catechesis is urgent.

I cannot but admire the zealous pastors who, in their Churches, try to meet this urgent need concretely by making catechesis a real priority.

Therefore, catechesis must always be the main task of evangelization, as the 1974 Synod of Bishops pointed out. I am of the opinion that catechesis must be a constant concern of the episcopal conference as such, and of its various organizations, which will not fail when necessary to have recourse to theologians and experts in the art of teaching, for clarification of doctrine and adaptation of catechisms to the various ages and levels of the persons for whom they are intended.

As for the content and methods of this catechesis, I will not repeat here what I tried to explain as much as possible in the Apostolic Exhortation *Catechesi tradendae.* I mention only that the faithful called to the communion of the Church have the right to receive "the word of faith" (Rom. 10:8) "in all its rigor and in all its vigor" (CT 30) by means of an effective, active, and adequate catechesis; a catechesis which, with the integrity of its content, brings the whole message of Jesus Christ to the man of our time. In this field we bishops of the Church, in our conscience as pastors, will always find ourselves faced with the question of texts for catechesis: How are they drawn up? What is their content? What message do they transmit? What image of God, of Christ, of the Church, of Christian life, of the vocation of man, do they communicate? Here is a field in which zeal and pastoral vigilance will have to be exercised as in few others.

This would be the right place for some words concerning the ecclesial "Base Communities" outlined by my venerated Predecessor Paul VI in the Apostolic Exhortation *Evangelii nuntiandi* (no. 58). I take the liberty of calling your attention to some points of his. These communities are a reality in Latin America today, especially in this country, and must be accompanied, assisted, and studied, to yield the fruits desired by everyone, without deviating towards ends that are extraneous to them. I do not wish to dwell on this point. I entrust to your episcopal conference the special text concerning these "Base Communities." I would have liked to have brought it personally and orally to those for whom it is intended, were it not for the lack of time due to the complexity of the program.

PERSONAL RESPONSIBILITY
OF EACH BISHOP

6. Rightly conceived and realized, the episcopal conference is an incomparable point of meeting and dialogue for the bishops of a country. In it each one will certainly find assistance, guidance and encouragement.

However, it neither can nor intends to limit, far less suppress and replace, the personal responsibility that every bishop assumes with episcopal ordination, on receiving the mission and the charisms necessary to carry it out. This mission, which binds him to his particular Church, but also opens him to concern for all the Churches, is carried out by every bishop as a personal commitment: it is his task as pastor.

Recalling this pastoral *munus*, I cannot pass over in silence a matter that accompanies me at this meeting as a cause for joy: it is the image, Brazilian bishops, that you project in the whole Church and in the world. It is an image of poverty and simplicity, of total dedication, of closeness to your people, of perfect integration in its life and in its problems. It is an image of bishops who are deeply evangelical and in conformity with the model proposed by the Second Vatican Council. Through much evidence, I already knew this aspect of your character as bishops. But reading your quinquennial reports, receiving you and talking to you at home, on the occasion of your visits *ad limina Apostolorum*, to my joy and edification, as well as to the edification of your faithful, I can tell you that I thank God for your witness of poverty and presence in the midst of your people. Is it necessary to encourage you on this point? I gladly do so, asking God to make you more and more capable of true sharing, that is, of rejoicing and suffering, living together and collaborating with those whom He has entrusted to your pastoral care.

Involved in this way in the life of your people, you must feel more determined to exercise your mission, all the aspects of which Christ the Pastor invites you to assume. Your people need you to assume them and, although silently, urge you to do so. I, too, called to strengthen you in your mission (cf. Lk. 22:32), hope that you will do so. What are these aspects?

6.1 In the midst of your people which says to you, as the disciples said to Jesus: "teach us to pray" (Lk. 11:1), be teachers of prayer. You are the chief liturgists of your Churches; with them and for them celebrate the sacramental mysteries, especially the Eucharist. You are also the primary ones responsible for getting your people to pray and for promoting dignified liturgical prayer. It is important that, in communion with your priests, you should make every effort toward a wholesome liturgical renewal. Avoid, on the one hand, an unjustified attachment to liturgical forms useful in the past, but meaningless today; on the other hand, avoid liturgical abuses, prolonged experimentation in liturgical matters, the rule of subjectivism and anarchy, all of which shatter true unity, confuse the faithful, and compromise the beauty and depth of celebrations. As bishops, one of your principal concerns is that of ensuring the purity and nobility of liturgical celebrations, certain that, far from being detrimental to the liturgy, the liturgy in Brazil, this makes it more efficacious.

6.2 Imitating those whose unworthy but mindful and responsible successors we are today, proclaim Jesus Christ and His message constantly. It was above all for this that we were called, consecrated by the "Holy Spirit...put to feed the Church of God" (Acts 20:28): to reveal to men the mystery of Christ, to make His Good News resound, to make many men His disciples. We can repeat with St. Paul that we have not come to teach any human science, but Jesus Christ and Jesus Christ crucified (cf. 1 Cor. 1:23;

2:1-2), because in the midst of our people we are not experts in politics or economics, we are not leaders with regard to any temporal enterprise, but ministers of the Gospel.

This is, so to speak, the most delicate point of communion among bishops. They can differ with regard to incidental temporal options, but they cannot but be inseparably united when it is a question of their fundamental task: the evangelical proclamation of Jesus Christ.

6.3 Be constructors of the ecclesial community. The Second Vatican Council says with great emphasis and in various documents that we pastors are sacraments—signs and artisans—of communion. Thereby it stresses an essential dimension of our ministry: that of calling together those who are scattered, of gathering those who are separated, of constructing the Church in this way and maintaining it in unity, despite all the forces of rupture and disunion.

6.4 Be teachers of truth, of the truth that the Lord wished to entrust to us—not to hide it or bury it, but to proclaim it humbly and courageously, to promote it, to defend it when it is threatened. I reminded those of you whom I met in Puebla last year of the threefold truth: about Jesus Christ, about the Church, about man. In the service of this truth there are the theologians, and happy is the Church which finds within it teachers capable of studying this truth, teachers illuminated by Revelation, the word of God and Tradition, by the Magisterium of the Church, and who in this light are helped by the human sciences. Let the bishops attentively follow the ministry of these theologians, integrating it into the totality of ecclesial service; nothing is more fruitful nor more enriching for the Church. The true theologian knows, also through a supernatural intuition, that it is up to the bishop to watch over his theological activity with pastoral care for the benefit of the faith of the People of God.

We would all be happy if errors and deviations in these three fields—Christ, the Church, man—were something remote. This is perhaps possible, but unreal for the moment, and you know this. Therefore, it is your duty—a painful and distressing one, but unavoidable—to point out these errors serenely and firmly and propose the truth in exact terms to the faithful. May the Lord give you the charism of discernment in order to have these truths always present, and the freedom and certainty of teaching them always, refuting everything that is in contradiction to them.

6.5 Be fathers and brothers of priests, your collaborators in the work of the Gospel (cf. Phil. 4:3). I am certain that your experience as bishops cannot but confirm my twenty years' experience as bishop of Krakow: if it is stimulating and encouraging for a priest to be able to count on the acceptance and collaboration of his people and on the friendship of colleagues, it is no less necessary—in fact, I would say it is more necessary—to be able to rely on understanding, closeness, and support in difficult moments, on the part of the bishop. The priests of a diocese understand, by and large, that the bishop may lack gifts as an administrator, as an organizer, as an intellectual, but they suffer if they do not find in him the confidence of a brother and a security imbued with the affection of a father. Give the best of yourselves to be always close to your priests. But above all remember that for a bishop nothing can be more urgent and precious than the holiness of his priests. *Forma gregis*, the model of the flock; it is not exaggerated nor utopian to ask that the bishop should also be *forma pastorum*, the model of his priests in everything that constitutes the spirituality—personal holiness and apostolic zeal—of his presbyterium.

6.6 Be careful and watchful fathers of future priests. I would be happy if, as a result of this meeting, there should remain in your hearts as pastors the firm conviction of doing even more in your dioceses to foster vocations for the priestly ministry and for religious life. A bishop can be sure that the time, talents, and energy that he expends for this purpose are never wasted. So watch over your seminaries, aware that any imperfection or deviation there may be in the formation of future priests; any compromise for fear of being too demanding, or insufficient attention on your part, or by those you have chosen as directors, does harm to the seminarians themselves today and a greater harm to the Church tomorrow.

6.7 Be fathers and brothers of the religious who, living their consecration fully, are at the heart of the Church in the service of the kingdom. Let communion between the bishop and men and women religious of the local Church always be as perfect as possible. This communion will consist, above all, in respecting and promoting the general charism of religious life with its essential dimensions, and the particular charism of each religious family. In the bishop, religious must always be able to find the one who calls them to live their own vocation better and better. Then, too, communion will consist in summoning and helping men and women religious for an increasingly vital and natural integration in the pastoral dynamics of the diocese. One of the requirements of this integration will be, on the part of religious, the sound decision to accept and respect the charism of bishops in the Church as teachers in faith and as spiritual guides, "placed by the Holy Spirit...to feed the Church of God" (Acts 20:28). If inspired by the Christian virtues of confidence, respect, loyalty, charity, and the spirit of service, more than by mere juridical norms, "mutual relations" between bishops and religious are seen to be immensely useful for the Church. All the more so in a country such as Brazil, where the presence and activity of religious has been outstanding throughout its history.

6.8 Be generous and receptive fathers of the laity of your Churches. The Second Vatican Council set forth a theology of the laity as one of the most important elements of its ecclesiology. It reminds us that the layman is, by definition, a disciple and follower of Christ, a man of the Church present and active at the heart of the world, to manage temporal realities and ordain them to the kingdom of God. Above all, these lay people expect from their pastors nourishment for their faith, certainty with regard to the teachings of Christ and of the Church, spiritual support for their lives, and firm guidance for their function as Christians in the world. They also expect the legitimate amount of freedom for their commitment in temporal matters. They expect help and encouragement to be laity without the risk of clericalization (and they likewise expect their pastors to be fully such without risks of laicization...). May the vast numbers of laity here in Brazil, who dedicate themselves unreservedly with ever greater commitment in the service of the Church, find in you everything they need for an even better service.

6.9 Be, in the name of the Gospel, promoters of the great human values: above all, that of the real dignity of man, a son and image of God, a brother and heir of Jesus Christ. Your vocation as bishops forbids you, quite clearly and without half measures, anything that resembles political party-spirit or subjection to this or that ideology or system. Rather than prevent you, it instead invites you to be close to, and at the service of, all men, especially the weakest and neediest. You know that the preferential option for the poor, forcefully proclaimed at Puebla, is not an invitation to exclusivism, and would not justify a bishop's refusal to proclaim the Word of conversion and salvation to this or that group of persons on the pretext that they are not poor—besides, what substance is given to this term?—because it is his duty to proclaim the *whole* Gospel to *all* men, that *everyone* should be "poor in spirit." But it is a call to a special solidarity with the humble and the weak, with those who are suffering and weeping, who are humiliated and left on the fringes of life and society, in order to help them to realize ever more fully their own dignity as human persons and sons of God.

As I have already said several times in this pastoral journey, particularly in my meeting with brothers of the Vidigal Favela in Rio de Janeiro—and the Cardinal is my witness—the Church of Brazil does well to reveal herself as the Church of the poor, the Church of the first beatitude: "Blessed are the poor in spirit, for theirs is the kingdom of heaven" (Mt. 5:3). By doing so, the Church also serves the good of society in the exercise of her mission. She does not claim to assume political activities as her own function. She respects the constituted authority (cf. 1 Pt. 2:13-17). She does not fail to proclaim that authority is necessary for the good of society, for the maintenance and exercise of society's sovereignty. On the other hand, however, the Church claims as her own right and duty the practice of a social apostolate, not along the line of a purely temporal project, but as the formation and guidance of consciences, with her specific means, so that society may become more just. And the Church must do the same, bishops must do the same, in the various countries of the world and in the various systems that exist in the modern world.

It is the task of the episcopate to prepare and propose the program of this social apostolate and to carry it out in collegial unity. In Brazil it is possible to organize this action with the promise of great fruitfulness, because in this country the Church and the episcopate constitute a real social power. But to achieve this goal some fundamental conditions must be met.

In the first place, this social program must be authentic, that is, consistent with the nature and identity of the Church. It must correspond to her principles (which are those of the Gospel), and be inspired by her magisterium, especially her social magisterium. In other words, this social apostolate cannot be based on premises which, whatever merits and qualities they may claim, are contrary to Catholic truth in its very foundations.

In the second place, the social apostolate will have to be genuinely Brazilian, without ceasing to be also universal. It must correspond to the complete truth with regard to the modern world. It must keep its eyes open to all injustices and all violations of human rights, wherever they may be, in the field of both material and spiritual goods. If it should lack this fundamental perspective, it runs the risk of becoming an object of one-sided manipulations.

Furthermore, the program of social action of the Church must be organic: it must consider the bond that exists between the various economic and technical factors on the one hand, and cultural needs on the other. In this context special attention must be paid to instruction and education, indispensable prerequisites for access to social advancement equal for everyone. Bold reforms, which are necessary, do not have as their only aim the communizing of the means of production, especially if by that is meant the concentration of everything in the hands of the state, converted into the only real capitalist power. The purpose of these reforms must be that of permitting everyone the access to property, since property is, in a way, the indispensable condition of man's freedom and creativity. It is what enables him to emerge from anonymity and "alienation," when it is a question of working in conjunction for the common good.

Lastly, the social action of the Church must be the commitment of all those on whose shoulders weigh the significant parts of the mission of the Church, each one according to his specific function and responsibility.

In this way, theologians will not be exposed to all kinds of objections, if they give their teaching a direction that is completely evangelical and Christian, faithful to the teachings of the Church. Ministers of the Church—bishops and priests—will be aware that their best and most effective participation in this social apostolate does not consist in becoming involved in party struggles or in options of groups and systems, but in being true "educators in faith," reliable guides, spiritual stimulators. Religious will not change what constitutes their charism in the Church—complete dedication to God, prayer, witness of the future life, pursuit of holiness—for political commitments that are of no use either to themselves—who lose their own identity—or to the Church, which remains impoverished with the loss of one of her essential dimensions, or to the world and society, equally deprived of that original element which only religious life can bring to legitimate pluralism. The activity of laymen also will assume its genuine dimension, because it acquires the view of the whole man and every part of man "including his openness to the absolute, even the divine Absolute" (EN 33).

6.10 At this happy meeting with you I could not neglect a final plea: Be brothers of Peter's Successor, united with him affectively and effectively *"in opus ministerii"* (cf. Eph. 4:12). Only *"cum Petro et sub Petro"* (AG 38), independently of the person of the one who happens to be invested with the office of Peter, do the episcopal college and each bishop find the fullness of their ecclesial mission.

I consider it superfluous to recall that this communion with the Pope is expressed in the acceptance of his word, not only when spoken by him personally, but also when it comes through the organs that collaborate with him in the pastoral government of the Church and speak in his name, with his approval, or by his mandate.

Nothing is more comforting for me, as the fruit of your visit *ad limina* and of my visit to you, than to know that I can rely on this sincere and generous communion with Peter's See, the principle of unity and the seed of universality. United with you *"in cruce et spe episcopatus,"* the Bishop of Rome, the Pastor of the universal Church, finds renewed courage in the extraordinary ministry that God's mysterious plan has willed to entrust to him.

REMEMBRANCE OF BROTHER BISHOPS

7. I do not want to conclude these words and end this meeting without recalling the names of bishops who, for four and a half centuries, were the legitimate successors of the Apostles in these countries and dedicated their whole life and all their energies to the construction of the kingdom of God. The historical and cultural circumstances

in which they were called to exercise their mission are different, their human characteristics are different, and their personal histories are different; but they were all men who left signs of their passage, beginning with Dom Pedro Fernandes Sardinha, who was the first bishop of Brazil. Any mention of names is necessarily a limited one, but how could we fail to recall figures such as Dom Vital Maria de Oliveira, Dom Antônio Macedo Costa, Dom Antônio Ferreira Viçoso; the first two Brazilian Cardinals Dom Joaquim Arcoverde and Dom Sebastião Leme da Silveira Cintra; Dom Silvério Gomes Pimenta, Dom José Gaspar de Alfonseca e Silva? How could I fail to mention here in Fortaleza the admirable figure of Dom Antônio de Almeida Lustosa, who is buried in this cathedral and who left in this diocese the shining image of a wise and holy man? May the memory of these brothers and of so many others who preceded us with the sign of faith stimulate us more and more in the service of the Lord.

The Church of Amazonia Is Particularly Missionary

On July 10, 1980, the Holy Father met the clergy, religious, and faithful of the diocese of Manaus, in the Cathedral dedicated to Our Lady of the Conception. The following are excerpts of an address delivered by the Holy Father.

Most Reverend Archbishop Apostolic Administrator
    of Manaus,
Most Reverend Archbishops and Bishops,
Beloved brothers and sisters in Christ,

Divine Providence has again been generous with the Pope, reserving for him, after such great joys, that of coming here to Manaus, in the heart of fabulous Amazonia, to conclude the vigorous schedule of this pastoral visit. I am deeply grateful to Providence for this meeting with you in a setting that speaks of the Creator and proclaims that "he alone does great wonders" (Ps. 135:4), and I offer praise and homage to the one and triune God in whose name I am here.

I am happy to be able to meet the Church of this region—so markedly missionary—and to meet the civil society, particularly its rulers and representatives. I am very grateful for the warm welcome of everyone, well expressed in the kind words of the Archbishop Apostolic Administrator.

WORD OF LIFE AND TRUTH

Present everywhere, the Lord has wished to be present here among us in other particular ways: really present in body, blood, soul, and divinity in the most holy Eucharist which we shall celebrate; present in His Word, committed to the Church as a trust and a heritage, the Word of life and truth which the Pope wishes to proclaim here, too; present in the Vicar of Christ to whom was given the power "to feed his lambs and his sheep" (cf. Jn. 21:15ff.); present in each of His "saints," that is, those who live the divine life; present in the community of all of us gathered here in His name; and present, finally, in the "little ones," in those "poor in spirit" whom the Lord proclaims blessed (cf. Mt. 5:3), because they are empty of themselves in order to receive the kingdom and because the Lord identifies Himself with them in some way: "As you did it to one of the least of these my brethren, you did it to me" (Mt. 25:40).

Present before Him and united in Him by the bond of charity, may it be the Lord who speaks to you through "Peter": to Him I lend my voice and my visible affection so that a sign of His love may reach everyone.

INTIMACY NOURISHED WITH PRAYER

A greeting first of all to my beloved brothers in the episcopate, who, collegially united with me, share concern for all the Churches. With them I greet the group of priests, diocesan and religious. You are a gift that God makes to His Church. Through the sacrament of Holy Orders, the Lord, who chose you and called you, consecrates you with a new title to be servants of His Gospel of salvation (cf. Gal. 1:7): It illuminates for us all the view of the Church as Christ willed it, universal though clothed in every part of the world in different aspects and exterior expressions, always one and unique. For this reason, while you strive to be very close to the people and its problems, you do well to cultivate ecclesial unity, "rooted and grounded in love" (cf. Eph. 3:17).

4. I also greet—and you know with what affectionate esteem—you, dear men and women religious. Through your consecration you have put your life in the hands of the Lord. Let yourselves be fashioned by Him in the intimacy that is nourished with prayer and worship "in spirit and truth," as the Father wants His worshipers to be. Let the Spirit of love always lead you along the ways of spiritual ascent with simple poverty, manifest chastity and generous obedience.

To all of you, equally beloved sons who fill posts of responsibility or who are engaged in more simple work as Christians, to all, the same affectionate greeting is extended. In direct union with your pastors and in the communion of the whole Church, you are those who in the reality of everyday life bear witness to the Good News in your life and action.

Look to Christ, our model and teacher: He passed, "doing and teaching" (cf. Acts 1:1). He reminds us all of the duty of fidelity to the vocation received from God and to the commitments personally assumed in Baptism. To accomplish them may we be continually enriched with grace upon grace.

I remind you on this occasion that only one thing is necessary: consistency with our being as Christians, faithfulness to the love with which God loved us first and awaits our love. The truth is that we are all called —let us not be afraid of the word!—to holiness (and the

world today needs holiness so much!), a holiness cultivated by everyone, in the various kinds of lives and in the
different professions, and lived according to the gifts and
tasks that each one has received, advancing unhesitatingly
along the way of living faith, which brings forth hope and
operates by means of charity (cf. LG 41).

Liturgical Renewal
in the Oriental Churches
According to the Spirit
of Vatican Council II

*On August 29, 1980, the Holy Father received in audience a group of
Indian bishops of the Malabar and the Malankar Rites on the occasion
of their* ad limina *visit. The group was led by Cardinal Joseph Parecattil,
Archbishop of Ernakulam for the Syro-Malabars. The Holy Father
delivered the following address.*

Venerable and dear brothers in our Lord Jesus Christ,

1. I am very grateful to you for your visit today; it is
indeed with great joy that I address my affectionate
greeting to all of you who, together with Cardinal Joseph
Parecattil, Archbishop of Ernakulam and President of the
Pontifical Commission for the Revision of the Eastern
Code of Canon Law, have come from different parts of
India for this *ad limina* visit and for your collegial meeting.

2. In you I sense the presence here of the whole Syro-
Malabar Church, this Eastern and authentically Indian
Church which for centuries has been a marvel of Christian
witness in fidelity to its primitive faith and to its legitimate
traditions. And hence my greeting goes today to your
entire Church: to the priests, to the men and women religious, to the members of secular institutes, to the young,
to the old, to the fathers and mothers of families, to the
workers, to the children and to all the faithful, especially
those who are in sickness and in pain.

My greeting and good wishes go also to the faithful and pastors of the other Churches who live alongside of you in the different parts of Kerala and in the rest of India, as well as to the brethren of the Christian communities which are not yet in full communion with us. They go likewise to all the members of the non-Christian religions.

3. In this collegial visit, I wish officially to express my gratitude for the diligent reports which you have placed at my disposal and at the disposal of my collaborators in the Apostolic See, for a greater knowledge of your eparchies with their many clergy and religious. These eparchies are teeming with pastoral and missionary activity; their activities are also manifested in the field of culture through colleges and schools, in the field of charitable and social assistance through hospitals and dispensaries, and wherever there is need to work for the human, social and spiritual advancement of your communities or of anyone without distinction of belief, race or rite. I have noted your commitment, full of dedication and of love for all. This is an honor and a duty for the whole Catholic Church, and this is also the task of your Church. It has always been so, and today especially this commitment shines with new luster. I am happy to render testimony to your zeal.

4. This perspective of openness to all people without any distinction is a challenge to my own apostolic service, which is described by *Lumen gentium* in these words: *"Universo caritatis coetui praesidet, legitimas varietates tuetur et simul invigilet ut particularia, nedum unitati noceant, ei potius inserviant"* (no. 13).

I have desired this encounter with you and I wish to thank you for the praiseworthy responsibility with which you have accepted the invitation of the Sacred Congregation to participate in a study meeting on the reform of the sacred liturgy of your own Church. This is a meeting from which it seems right to expect the happiest of results with respect to a clear liturgical discipline and a liturgical renewal according to the directives and spirit of the Second Vatican Council. You may be sure that the Successor of

Peter, on every occasion, as in this fraternal encounter, has only one desire and proposal, that of being what the Council has called: *"unitatis tum episcoporum tum fidelium multitudinis, perpetuum ac visibile principium et fundamentum"* (LG 23).

5. What fundamentally does this encounter of ours and your collegial meeting with the competent congregation of the Holy See look to if not to the realization of perfect communion *in vinculo pacis?* The liturgy manifests and effects unity in an altogether special way. "Liturgical actions are not private functions, but are celebrations of the Church, which is the 'sacrament of unity,' namely, a holy people united and organized under their bishops. Therefore, liturgical actions pertain to the whole body of the Church; they manifest it and have effects upon it" (SC 26).

Besides setting forth with such vigor this general fundamental theological concept, the Council draws attention to other principles of the greatest importance: The Church desires to respect and foster in a special way "the spiritual adornments and gifts of the various races and peoples. Anything in their way of life that is not indissolubly bound up with superstition and error she studies with sympathy and, if possible, preserves intact. Sometimes, in fact, she admits such things into the liturgy itself, as long as they harmonize with the true and authentic liturgical spirit" *(ibid.,* no. 37). Moreover, *Lumen gentium* states: "By divine providence it has come about that various Churches established in diverse places by the Apostles and their successors have in the course of time coalesced into several groups, organically united, which, preserving the unity of faith and the unique divine constitution of the universal Church, enjoy their own discipline, their own theological and spiritual heritage.... This variety of local Churches with one common aspiration is particularly splendid evidence of the catholicity of the undivided Church" (no. 23).

But, at the same time, the Council wishes these Churches to be faithful to their traditions: "For it is the mind of the Catholic Church that each individual Church or rite should retain its traditions whole and entire, while adjusting its way of life to the various needs of time and place" (OE 2). This same decree also proclaims: "All Eastern rite members should know and be convinced that they can and should always preserve their lawful liturgical rites and their established way of life, and that these should not be altered except by way of an appropriate and organic development" *(ibid.,* no. 6).

To attain their aim it is necessary to have a rigorous and severe application of the conciliar directives on fidelity to the traditions of one's own rite: "Easterners themselves should honor all these things with the greatest fidelity. Besides, they should acquire an ever greater knowledge and a more exact use of them. If they have improperly fallen away from them because of circumstances of time or persons, let them take pains to return to their ancestral ways" *(ibid.,* no. 6). Difficulties will not be lacking in the field of returning to the genuine sources of one's own rite. It is a question, nevertheless, of difficulties which must be faced *viribus unitis* and *Deo adiuvante.*

The liturgical renewal is hence the fundamental element for the ever fruitful life of your Church: a renewal founded on fidelity to your own genuine ecclesial traditions and open to the needs of your people, to your culture and to possible changes owing to your own organic progress. You will be usefully guided by the fundamental principles which are set out in the letter *Dominicae cenae,* and which will assist you not to err in a matter that is so important and so delicate.

6. After these reflections on the liturgy, I am pleased to speak about the memorandum that you wished to make known to me through the Sacred Congregation for the Eastern Churches. The content of this document, despite the brevity imposed on it by reason of circumstances, invites me to reflect on the history of your glorious

Church, which in the free world is the Eastern Church that is most numerous and flourishing, the one with the greatest number of priests, men and women religious, seminarians and laity.

How can we fail to emphasize with joy and with true satisfaction the contribution of your Church to the cause of the missions, not only in India but also elsewhere, to the promotion of priestly and religious vocations, to the activities of teaching and of charitable assistance, etc.? There is no question of underestimating the many human factors that have their own influence in these phenomena, but rather of noting how these factors are also indebted to the Christian faith of your Syro-Malabar families, who are always open to giving their children to the cause of the universal Church even beyond the boundaries of your particular Church. I wish to express my heartfelt thanks to you the bishops, to your priests, to the religious, the members of secular institutes, the seminarians and the generous families, for what you have done and continue to do for the universal Church. What at one time the missionaries of Europe and America did and are still doing *in auxilium Orientalium*, you have done and are doing *in auxilium Ecclesiae Latinae*. I sincerely thank you. All of this is in perfect harmony with the spirit of the Council which wants the particular Churches to feel in their heart responsibility for the other Churches and for the universal Church.

7. After a glance at your Church, my thought turns to the *desiderata* that you have presented. The importance of what you set forth, as well as the canonical, ecclesiological, pastoral, doctrinal and practical implications thereof, explain why it is not possible on this occasion to give an immediate and complete response to your proposals.

When there is a question of matters that concern the whole Church, and the creation of supra-episcopal structures in which the interests of different bishops and particular Churches are involved, the Holy See adopts serious and wise procedures that are sanctioned by the practice of many centuries. I wish to assure you how happy I am to see that you are endeavoring to affirm and deepen your identity as a particular Eastern Church. I am pleased to quote here the thought of my great Predecessor, Paul VI, in his concluding discourse at the 1974 Synod of Bishops: *"Eodem tamen tempore exoptamus, ut sedulo caveatur ne altior pervestigatio essentialis huius aspectus rerum, quae Ecclesiae sunt, ullo modo noceant firmitati 'communionis' cum ceteris particularibus Ecclesiis et Petri successore, cui Christus Dominus grave, perenne atque amoris plenum hoc officium commisit, ut agnos et oves pasceret* (Jn. 21:13-17), *ut fratres confirmaret* (Lk. 22:32) *ut fundamentum esset et signum unitatis Ecclesiae"* (October 26, 1974: *AAS* 66, p. 636).

With reference to some phrases of your memorandum, I would like to recall an aspect of the collegial teaching of the Second Vatican Council: *"Romanus enim Pontifex habet in Ecclesiam, vi muneris sui, Vicarii scilicet Christi et totius Ecclesiae Pastoris, plenam, supremam et universalem potestatem, quam semper libere exercere valet"* (LG 22). On the occasion of the above-mentioned synod, Paul VI added: *"unum potius adest propositum, quo videlicet omnes—pro suo quisque munere suscepto fideliterque impleto—Dei voluntati respondeant, maxima impulsi dilectione" (ibid.).* I wish, however, to assure you that everything will be done compatibly with the good of the universal Church and with the necessary gradualness.

8. In the same order of ideas there is also the problem of the assistance of your faithful outside your eparchies. On the one hand, my unforgettable Predecessor John Paul I, in his brief pontificate, had the opportunity and joy of being able to appoint Archbishop Antony Padiyara as Apostolic Visitor for the Malabar faithful living in different regions of India outside the territories of Eastern jurisdiction. The Archbishop has striven with exemplary solicitude to fulfill the task entrusted to him, and I wish to express my gratitude to him *coram vobis.*

Also involved, on the other hand, in this question are the Papal Representative in India and the Latin Ordinaries of those places where these Malabar faithful are living. I can assure you that there will be rendered accessible to these faithful all the helps which the laws of the Church foresee, particularly by the prescriptions, which you yourselves have cited, of the Decree *Christus Dominus.* It is well known how, after the Council, the Church wished to revise the Apostolic Constitution *Exul familia,* and my Predecessor Paul VI in *Pastoralis migratorum cura* did not omit any effort to place every spiritual help at the disposal of emigrants. The common concern of the bishops of the emigrants' places of origin and the bishops of their new homes requires a harmony of relationships and a spirit of fraternal collaboration. It is my most earnest desire, and my conviction, that the episcopal conferences, whether of India or the regional ones, will find a way to develop a just manner of providing for this need.

In this effort to help the most needy faithful, either spiritually or materially, the Malabar bishops will find in the Holy See a sincere support and an animating force, which, in an ecclesial perspective that embraces the needs of the individual particular Churches and the common good of the whole Church, seeks to create a climate of mutual knowledge and esteem among all people, especially among the faithful of different races, nations and rites.

I would like to add yet a word about your eparchies. I am not only thinking of your Church in terms of numbers, statistics and the outstanding activities of each of your eparchies, but I am contemplating the rich spiritual life that exists therein.

I am thinking of your priests, so numerous and generous. I am thinking of the men religious who are members of Eastern institutes, as well as orders and congregations of Latin origin, and who are docile to the call of Christ and in the vanguard of the Church's life. I am thinking of the great numbers of women religious of contemplative and active life, whose consecrated oblation reflects that of

Mary, and becomes the basis for a selfless service that mirrors the maternal care of the whole Church, especially for the little ones, for the weak, the poor and the suffering.

I am thinking of the young people, and particularly of the seminarians: each of you has a minor seminary for candidates for the priesthood, and there are two major seminaries—the Pontifical Seminary of Alwaye and the Apostolic Seminary of Kottayam—besides the Scholasticate of the Carmelites of Mary Immaculate, with two theological faculties and a third one already envisioned. In this regard it is worthwhile to call attention to the following exhortation: "The formation of future priests should be considered as one of the most important ministries in a diocese and, in some ways, the most demanding. In fact, the work of teaching unites the professor very closely to the work of our Lord and Master, who prepared His Apostles to be witnesses of the Gospel and dispensers of the mysteries of God" (Sacred Congregation for Catholic Education, *The Theological Formation of Future Priests*, IV, 1, 3).

In conclusion, I present to your reflection a profound desire of my heart: you are here united with Peter *"communione fraternae caritatis atque studio permoti universalis missionis Apostolis traditae"* (CD 36). This is a propitious occasion for recalling the supreme theme of unity: fraternal unity among bishops; unity between the different rites; unity between the bishop and the priests; between the bishop and religious; between the bishop, priest and laity; between the poor and the well-to-do. The unity which in these days of grace you have sought in the liturgical and pastoral fields must be the first fruit of this particular experience of harmony and collaboration.

My thoughts go to the bishops of the other rites who work in the same territory and who must be not only brothers who coexist with you but who live alongside of you, in profound ecclesial communion with you and with the whole Church. My thoughts go also to the various groups and communities of separated brethren who look with sincere admiration to your bond with the Successor of Peter.

My last word is one of hope and prayer to Mary, Mother of the Church. May she protect you always and through her intercession may your eparchies continue to have a great flowering of vocations and great holiness of life. May she enable all of us to fix our gaze constantly on her Son, Jesus Christ, the great High Priest and chief Shepherd of the Church of God.

And now a word to the Malankar bishops, who are associated in a fraternal way with the group of Malabar prelates.

I wish to extend a very special greeting to you, since this year is the anniversary of an extraordinary event in your Church. You are celebrating the golden jubilee of that spiritual movement of which the late and esteemed Mar Ivanios was a pioneer, and which brought into full communion with Rome himself, other prelates, and the communities which he founded: the Brothers of the Imitation of Christ and the Sisters of Bethany.

As a sign of my own sharing in this golden jubilee, I am happy to announce my decision to send as my representative and as the bearer of my message Cardinal Wladislaw Rubin. Prefect of the Sacred Congregation for the Eastern Churches, who will be present for the solemn celebrations that are scheduled for next December 26-28.

I assure you of my prayers, my blessing and my fraternal affection in Christ Jesus our Lord.

Adherence to Truth and Witness of Life

On August 30, 1980, in the Basilica of St. Bernardine, after a welcoming address by the President of the Episcopal Conference of Abruzzi and Molise, Most Rev. Vincenzo Fagiolo, Archbishop of Chieti and Vasto, the Holy Father delivered the following message to the priests, religious, and leaders of Catholic associations.

Beloved brothers and sisters, sons and daughters,

Having arrived at the highlight of my pilgrimage, after offering fervent prayer for the most urgent intentions of Christianity at this time, I am glad to spend some moments together with you, dear priests, men and women religious, and leaders of the Catholic associations of the Churches of Abruzzi and Molise, here in front of Saint Bernardine's urn, which preserves his incorrupt and venerated remains, in this splendid basilica which the piety and love of the people of Aquila erected in his honor only thirty years after his happy death.

Even before addressing my greeting to you, I am happy to confide to you the spiritual emotion that wells up in my heart at the thought that the construction of this temple, the sign of uninterrupted devotion to the holy religious, was willed and encouraged by another saint, John of Capestrano, a great apostle and defender of Europe and so venerated in Poland for his incisive and reforming pastoral activity. In fact, he addressed from Krakow—as you well know—a warm appeal to the citizens of Aquila to erect a worthy monument to his own confrere and teacher, raised to the honors of the altar by Pope Nicholas V, in 1450, six years after his death. St. Bernardine and St. John of Capestrano are intimately connected in the veneration and faith of the Poles.

And now I address my sentiments of gratitude to the Most Reverend Father John Vaughan, Minister General of the Order of Friars Minor, who, on behalf of the four great Franciscan Families, greeted me at the threshold of this basilica with words of fervent welcome. With equal affection and sincere satisfaction, I express my gratitude to Archbishop Vincenzo Fagiolo of Chieti, President of the Episcopal Conference of Abruzzi and Molise, who wished to manifest with such cordial expressions, animated by deep faith, the affection and the spiritual communion of your hearts, your concerns, and your resolutions with those of the humble Vicar of Christ.

I thank you, priests and religious, for your work, your commitment, your service, which ensure that pastoral action of evangelization and witness, indispensable for the growth of the Church of Christ. You carry out your mission with intense and exemplary dedication, aware of being servants of a sublime cause, for which Christ the Lord continuously chooses His worthy followers. You keep alive awareness of the grandeur of the task received and the necessity of continually striving to be worthy of it. It is a high and exalting service, which demands deep conviction about your own priestly identity, that is, as men who are stewards and administrators of God's mysteries, irreplaceable instruments of forgiveness and grace, ministers of an eternal kingdom, who lend their words, their hands, their hearts to Jesus the Redeemer of man.

I now call on you all to turn your attention and admiration to the priestly and apostolic figure of the great "speaker" of the Renaissance, fascinating—even according to experts—in his inimitable and colorful Italian dialect, who led such crowds of faithful to conversion and to evangelical happiness, while he reconciled families and towns in the name of Jesus the Savior; from him we draw motives of comfort and encouragement in our particular mission as consecrated persons, evangelizers and qualified witnesses; to him we address the vibrations of our hearts as convinced and joyful children of the Church.

By the inscrutable design of Providence, St. Bernardine concluded his busy earthly days within the walls of this beloved city in the comforting evening of the Ascension, in 1444, while his friars, as if sealing with a significant motto a life spent entirely in the proclamation of salvation, were singing in chorus the antiphon *"Pater manifestavi nomen tuum hominibus quos dedisti mihi"* (Jn. 17:6). The Gospel phrase, which the saint used to repeat every day and which has rightly been adopted by iconography, inserting it in the halo round his head, assumes a symbolic value and contains the whole meaning of the great preacher's apostolic activity.

He who wanted to be able to speak with extreme clarity and boldness in every circumstance (cf. San Bernardino da Siena, *Prediche*, Lib. Ed. Fior., 1964, p. 219) offers us an example of adherence to truth and of adherence to the revealed Word, an attitude which must prevail in anyone who wishes, even in the silence of the cloister and through the daily exercise of a hidden consecration, to carry out the ecclesial commitment of transmitting God's loving plan with regard to man.

The sentence of the psalm, *"Declaratio sermonum tuorum illuminat et intellectum dat parvulis"* (Ps. 119 [118]:130), was dear to the saint, and he considered it a necessary commitment to have to speak openly "so that the listener may go away happy and enlightened and not all mixed up" *(op. cit.,* p. 45). This love for truth and for the clarity of its exposition must sustain our catechetical and evangelizing service, so that we will not go astray along paths of human interpretations and compromises with the spirit of the world, thus moving away from faith, which alone ensures us victory (cf. 1 Jn. 5:4).

Certainly, truth must be guaranteed and accredited by the witness of our life. "You must"—the saint said— "follow Christ, you who want to be a preacher" *(op. cit.,* p. 46). This pattern of behavior which is required in the "speaker" of the revealed Word cannot be separated from humble and sincere adherence to the ecclesiastical Magisterium, which makes it binding on him "to leave heresy and hold what the Holy Church and her holy doctors hold, and never contradict what has been ordered" *(op. cit.,* p. 47). There can be no authentic exercise of the ministry of the Word within the Church, without the heart's obedience to Him who, though covered with weakness and frailty, has received the mandate to ensure purity of doctrine. Today such trusting obedience, which is not justified as adherence to the will of men, but only as reliance on the Lord and on His action in the Church, is urgently necessary.

Our work as evangelizers, finally, must be dictated and sustained by love for Christ the Lord and for souls. It is not possible to commit oneself thoroughly in this sublime task without the strength that comes from a generous, spiritual, and complete love, manifested to the world as a bright light. In this sense St. Bernardine is of great relevance today, both for his examples and for his lucid teachings.

Let our service, dear brothers and sisters, which has the supreme aim of making men convinced of the heavenly Father's love, be entrusted entirely to the Mother of God and our Mother, so greatly loved and celebrated by our saint, who has expressions of extraordinary tenderness for her, admirably exalting her in her mission as bestower of grace.

In this perspective of hope and confidence, I call down upon all of you the fullness of heavenly gifts and I gladly impart my affectionate blessing to you and to all your dear ones.

"Like Ministers of Truth and Grace"

On September 3, 1980, the Holy Father concelebrated Mass with two hundred priests at his summer residence. The priests represented two groups, the Ecclesiastic Consultants for the Farmers, and the Apostolic Movement for the Blind. The Pope delivered the following homily on this feast of St. Gregory the Great.

1. On the day the liturgy of the Holy Mass recalls to us the splendid figure of Pope St. Gregory the Great, I am happy this morning to be able to concelebrate the Eucharistic Sacrifice with you, Ecclesiastic Consultants for the Farmers, and with you, Consultants of the "Apostolic Movement for the Blind," who are in Rome for your respective national meetings.

Before the altar, let us first of all give our thanks to the Lord for this particular liturgical encounter and for all the ineffable gifts that He continuously grants to the Church, His elect Spouse, to all the priests in the spiritual care of souls, and to you priests who perform a ministry, not always easy, of guidance and Christian inspiration among the generous workers in the fields and the dear sightless brothers and sisters. We invoke light and comfort on the labors that await you in these days and from which many expect your assistance for the solution of so many spiritual and social problems which harass them daily.

In your gentle apostolate, you are aware of the necessity of always having the heart of true pastors, thoughtful not only of material assistance—certainly necessary and right—but also, and above all, spiritual assistance, following the example of St. Gregory the Great, who in his tireless pastoral care could harmonize so well the promotion of legitimate temporal needs with spiritual ones, to which he naturally attached supremacy, so as to merit the eulogy of Good Shepherd, dedicated to him by the Church with the readings we have just heard from the book of the prophet Ezekiel (34:11-16) and the Gospel according to John (10:11-16).

2. The task of the ecclesiastical diocesan consultants for the farmers assumes an importance and a delicacy easy to imagine if one considers that you are sent by the Church to work "like priests," and hence like ministers of truth and grace. It is your mission to see to it that the economic promotion of the rural world is always inspired with the great spiritual and moral values of the Gospel, as they emerge and are presented by the social teaching of the Church.

Such teaching, continually reproposed in its integrity and actuality, calls for choices, at times demanding, that cannot be wholly accepted if the individual persons and families do not have orientations of faith truly in mind.

To this end it behooves me to renew the exhortation, previously directed to you by my venerated Predecessor Paul VI, to carry out "a more intense formative and religious activity, especially among the young," to whom must be offered an integral vision of man in all his dimensions and values, without which it is impossible to give an adequate, coherent, and stable response to the questions connected with marriage and the family in the present hour.

To you, consultants of the Movement for the Blind, I express a special appreciation and encouragement for everything you are doing in favor of a category of persons so tried, but also so generous in their invaluable services to society. How lovely and meaningful is your presence as friends and priests, and how much consolation and light you can bring to them! May you awaken in their souls energy and good will for the good of the Church and society, and be for them instruments of Christian joy and ministers of eternal salvation.

3. Finally, I congratulate all of you present for the ecclesial sensitivity with which you link and coordinate the specific educative activity you carry on, for the pastoral programs of the particular Churches which you bring forward in order to make the various experiences of evangelization increasingly integrated and relevant.

Upon these tasks I now invoke with great trust the Lord's grace for the intercession of the most Holy Virgin and St. Gregory, as I warmly impart the conciliatory apostolic blessing, extended to your assistants and to all your dear ones.

Method and Doctrine of St. Thomas in Dialogue with Modern Culture

On September 13, 1980, the Holy Father received in audience the participants in the Eighth International Thomistic Congress, dedicated to the study of the origin and contents of the encyclical Aeterni Patris, *of its implementation by the successors of Leo XIII, and of the Thomistic renewal that brought the pontifical document to maturity at the turn of the century.*

The Pope delivered the following message after an address by Cardinal Luigi Ciappi, President of the Pontifical Roman Academy of St. Thomas Aquinas.

Venerated and very dear brothers!

I am truly glad to be able to welcome in a cordial meeting today the participants in the Eighth International Thomistic Congress held on the occasion of the centenary of the encyclical *Aeterni Patris* of Leo XIII, and likewise of the foundation at the bidding of the same Supreme Pontiff of the "Pontifical Roman Academy of St. Thomas Aquinas."

I greet those present with all my affection, and in particular the venerated brother Cardinal Luigi Ciappi, President of the Academy, and Msgr. Antonio Piolanti, Vice-President.

CONCLUDING THE CENTENARY

1. The holding of the Eighth International Thomistic Congress, organized by the Pontifical Roman Academy of

St. Thomas Aquinas and of Catholic Religion, concludes the commemorative celebration of the centenary of the encyclical *Aeterni Patris*, issued August 4, 1879, and the foundation of the academy itself by the great pontiff Leo XIII, which occurred on October 13, 1879.

From the first meeting held in the University of St. Thomas Aquinas in November of last year up to today, the celebrations multiplied in Europe and other continents. These closing academic sessions, which saw illustrious qualified teachers meeting in Rome from every part of the world in the name of Pope Leo XIII and St. Thomas Aquinas, were able simultaneously to strike a balance between the celebrations held this year and those of the centenary of the encyclical.

Since the beginning of my pontificate I have not let pass a propitious occasion without recalling the sublime figure of St. Thomas, as, for example, on my visits to the Pontifical Angelicum University and the Catholic Institute in Paris, in the address to UNESCO, in an explicit and implicit manner, in my meetings with the Superiors, lecturers and students of the Pontifical Gregorian and Lateran Universities.

THE ENCYCLICAL'S PRINCIPLES

2. The hundred years of the encyclical *Aeterni patris* have not passed in vain, nor has that celebrated Document of pontifical teaching gone out of date. The encyclical is based on a fundamental principle which lends it a profound inner organic unity: It is the principle of harmony between the truths of reason and those of faith. It is this that was uppermost in the heart of Leo XIII. This principle, always consequential and relevant, has made considerable progress in the last hundred years. Suffice it to consider the consistent Magisterium of the Church from Pope Leo XIII to Paul VI and what was completed in Vatican Council II, especially in the documents *Optatam totius, Gravissimum educationis, Gaudium et spes.*

In light of Vatican Council II, we see, perhaps better than a century ago, the unity and continuity between authentic humanism and authentic Christianity, between reason and faith, thanks to the directives of *Aeterni Patris* of Leo XIII, who with this document subtitled *De philosophia christiana...ad mentem Sancti Thomae...in scholis catholicis instauranda,* showed awareness that a crisis, a rupture, a conflict, or at least an obscuration in the relationship between reason and faith had occurred.

Within the culture of the 19th century two extreme attitudes in fact can be singled out: rationalism (reason without faith) and fideism (faith without reason). Christian culture moves between these two extremes, swinging from one part to the other. Vatican Council I had already had its say on the matter. It was then time to mark out a new course in the internal studies of the Church. Leo XIII farsightedly prepared for this task, presenting again—in the sense of establishing—the perennial thought of the Church in the clear, deep methodology of the Angelic Doctor.

The dualism setting reason and faith in opposition, not at all modern, constituted a renewal of the medieval doctrine of the "double truth," which threatened from within "the intimate unity of the man-Christian" (cf. Paul VI, *Lumen ecclesiae,* no. 12). It was the great scholastic doctors of the 13th century who put Christian culture on the right road again. As Paul VI stated, "In accomplishing the work signaling the culmination of medieval Christian thought, St. Thomas was not alone. Before and after him many other illustrious doctors worked toward the same goal: among whom St. Bonaventure and St. Albert the Great, Alexander of Hales and Duns Scotus are to be recalled. But without a doubt St. Thomas, as willed by divine Providence, reached the height of all "scholastic" theology and philosophy, as it is usually called, and set the central pivot in the Church around which, at that time and since, Christian thought could be developed with sure progress" *(ibid.,* no. 13).

It is for this reason that the Church has given preference to the method and doctrine of the Angelic Doctor. Quite other than exclusive preference, this deals with an exemplary preference that permitted Leo XIII to declare it to be *"inter Scholasticos Doctores, omnium princeps et magister" (Aeterni Patris,* no. 13). And truly such is St. Thomas Aquinas, not only for the completeness, balance, depth, and clarity of his style, but still more for his keen sense of fidelity to the truth, which can also be called realism. *Fidelity to the voice of created things so as to construct the edifice of philosophy: fidelity to the voice of the Church so as to construct the edifice of theology.*

LISTEN TO AND QUESTION THINGS

3. In philosophic scholarship, before listening to what humanity's sages say, St. Thomas' opinion is that it is necessary to listen to and question things. *"Tunc homo creaturas interrogat, quando eas diligenter considerat; sed tunc interrogata respondent" (Super Job. II, Lect. I). True philosophy should faithfully mirror the order of things themselves, otherwise it ends by being reduced to an arbitrary subjective opinion. "Ordo principalius invenitur in ipsis rebus et ex eis derivatur ad cognitionem nostram"* (S. Theol., II-IIae, q. 26, a. 1, ad 2). Philosophy does not consist in a subjective system put together at the pleasure of the philosopher, but must be the faithful reflection of the order of things in the human mind.

In this sense St. Thomas can be considered a true pioneer of modern scientific realism, which has things speak by means of empirical test, even if its interest is limited to having them speak from the philosophical point of view. It is rather to be questioned if it is not precisely philosophical realism that historically has stimulated the realism of the empirical sciences in all their branches.

This realism, far from excluding the historic meaning, creates bases for the historicity of knowledge without letting it decline into the fragile circumstance of historicism, widespread today. Therefore, after having given precedence to the voice of things, St. Thomas takes an attitude of paying respectful attention to what the philosophers have said and say in order to evaluate it, comparing them with the concrete reality. *"Ut videatur quid veritatis sit in singulis opinionibus et in quo deficiant. Omnes enim opiniones secundum quid aliquid verum dicunt"* (I Dist. 23, q. 1, a. 3). It is impossible to think that human knowledge and the opinion of men are completely without every truth. It is a principle that St. Thomas borrows from St. Augustine and makes his own: *"Nulla est falsa doctrina quae non vera falsis intermisceat"* (S. Theol. I-IIae, q. 102, a. 5, ad 4). *"Impossibile est aliquam cognitionem esse totaliter falsam, sine alique veritate"* (S. Theol. II-IIae, q. 172, a. 6; cf. also S. Theol. I, q. II, a. 2, ad 1).

TRUTH IS LIKE A BRIDGE

This presence of truth, even if it be incomplete and imperfect and at times distorted, is a bridge uniting every man to other men and makes understanding possible when there is good will.

In this view, St. Thomas has always given respectful attention to all authors, even when he could not entirely share their opinions; even when pre-Christian and non-Christian authors are concerned, as for example the Arab commentators on Greek philosophy. This leads to his invitation to approach with human optimism even the early Greek philosophers—whose language is not always clear and precise—trying to go beyond linguistic expression, still rudimentary, in order to scrutinize their deep intentions and spirit, not heeding *"ad ea quae exterius ex eorum verbis apparet"* but the *"inentio"* (De Coelo et mundo, III, Lect. 2, no. 552), that guides and encourages him. When it comes to the great Fathers and Doctors of the Church, he then always tries to find a point of agreement, more in the completeness of truth that they possess as Christians than in the way, apparently different from his, with which they express themselves. It is well known, for example, that he tries to attenuate and almost make every divergence with St. Augustine disappear as long as the right method is used: *"profundius intentionem Augustini scrutari"* *(De spirit. creaturis,* a. 10 ad 8).

Furthermore, the basis of his attitude, sympathetic towards everyone, but without failing to be openly critical every time he felt he had to—and he did it courageously in many cases—is in the very concept of truth. *"Licet sint multae veritates participatae, est una sapientia absoluta supra omnia elevata, scilicet sapientia divina, per cuius participationem omnes sapientes sunt sapientes"* *(Super Job,* I, *Lect.* 1, no. 33). This supreme wisdom, which glows in creation, does not always find the human mind disposed to receive it, for very many reasons. *"Licet enim aliquae mentes sint tenebrosae, id est sapida et lucida sapientia privatae, nulla tament adeo tenebrosa est quin aliquid divinae lucis participet...quia omne verum, a quocumque dicatur, a Spiritu Sancto est"* *(ibid., Lect. 3,* no. 103). Hence the hope of conversion for every man, however intellectually and morally misled.

This realistic and historic method, fundamentally optimistic and open, makes St. Thomas not only the *Doctor Communis Ecclesiae,* as Paul VI calls him in his beautiful letter *Lumen ecclesiae,* but the *Doctor Humanitatis,* because he is always ready and available to receive the human values of all cultures. The Angelic One can rightly state: *"Veritas in seipsa fortis est et nulla impugnatione convellitur"* *(Contra Gentiles,* III, c. 10, no. 3460-b). Truth, like Jesus Christ, can be denied, persecuted, fought, wounded, martyred, crucified; but it always comes back to life and rises again and can never be uprooted from the human heart. St. Thomas put all the strength of his genius at the exclusive service of the truth, behind which he seems to want to disappear almost for fear of disturbing its brightness so that truth and not he may shine in all its brilliance.

EXEMPLARY MODEL
OF THEOLOGICAL RESEARCH

4. Faithfulness to the voice of things, in philosophy, corresponds, according to St. Thomas, to faithfulness to the voice of the Word of God transmitted by the Church in theology. And its rule, which never fails, is the principle: *"Magis standum est auctoritati Ecclesiae...quam cuiuscumque Doctoris" (S. Theol.* II-IIae, q. 10, a. 12). Truth suggested by the authority of the Church assisted by the Holy Spirit, is therefore the measure of truth as expressed by all the theologians and doctors—past, present and future. The authority of St. Thomas' doctrine is here resolved and replenished in the authority of the Church's doctrine. That is why the Church has proposed it as an exemplary model of theological research.

In theology, too, St. Thomas therefore prefers not the voice of the Doctors or his own voice, but that of the Universal Church, almost anticipating what Vatican II says: "The totality of the faithful who have received the unction of the Holy Spirit cannot be mistaken in believing" (LG 12); "when both the Roman Pontiff and the body of the bishops with him define a doctrinal point, they do it in accordance with revelation itself, which everyone must stay with and conform to" (LG 25).

It is not possible to review all the reasons that induced the Magisterium of the Church to choose St. Thomas as a sure guide in theological and philosophical disciplines; but one is doubtless this: his having set the principles of universal value which bear out the relationship between reason and faith. Faith contains the values of human wisdom in a superior, different, and eminent way: therefore, it is impossible for reason to be in disagreement with faith, and if in disagreement, it is necessary to look at and reconsider the conclusions of philosophy: In this sense faith itself becomes a priceless aid for philosophy.

The recommendation of Leo XIII is still valid: *"Quapropter qui philosophiae studium cum obsequio fidei christianae coniungunt, ii optime philosophantur: quando quidem divinarum veritatum splendor, animo exceptus, ipsam juvat intelligentiam; cui non modo nihil de dignitate detrahit, sed nobilitatis, acuminis, firmitatis plurimum addit"* (AP 13).

Philosophical and theological truth converge into a single truth. Truth of reason goes back from creatures to God; truth of faith descends directly from God to man. But this diversity of method and origin does not take away their fundamental oneness, because there is a single identical Author of truth manifested through creation, and truth communicated personally to man by means of His Word. Philosophical research and theological research are two different directions of movement of a single truth, destined to meet, but not collide, on the same road, in order to help each other. Thus reason, illuminated, strengthened, and guaranteed by faith, becomes a faithful companion of faith itself, and faith immensely widens the limited horizon of human reason. On this point Saint Thomas is truly an enlightening teacher: *"Quia vero naturalis ratio per creaturas in Deo cognitionem ascendit; fidei vero in nos, e converso, divina revelatione descendit, est autem eadem via ascensus et descensus, oportet eadem via procedere in his quae supra rationem credentur, qua in superioribus processum est circa ea quae ratione investigantur de Deo"* (Contra Gentiles, IV, 1, no. 3349).

The difference in the method and instruments of research greatly differentiates philosophical knowledge from theological. Even the best philosophy, which is of the Thomist style, which Paul VI has so well defined as "natural philosophy of the human mind," flexible in listening and faithful in expressing the truth of things, is always conditioned by the limits of intelligence and human language. However, the Angelic One does not hesitate to declare: *"Locus ab auctoritate quae fundatur super ratione humana est infirmissimus"* (S. Theol. I, q. 1, a. 8, ad 2). Any philosophy, in that it is a product of man, has man's limits. On the contrary, *"locus ab auctoritate quae fun-*

datur super revelatione divina est efficacissimus" (ibid.). Divine authority is absolute; therefore, faith enjoys the solidity and security of God Himself; human science always has man's weakness, to the extent that it is founded upon man. Yet, even in philosophy there is something absolutely true, unfailing and necessary: its first principles, the foundation of every knowledge.

LOVE OF TRUTH AND OF GOOD GO TOGETHER

A correct or honest philosophy raises man to God, as Revelation brings God closer to man. For St. Augustine: *"verus philosophus est amator Dei" (S. Augustinus, De Civ. Dei,* VIII, 1: Pl. 41, 225). St. Thomas, in echoing him, says the same thing in other words: *"Fere totius philosophiae consideratio ad Dei cognitionem ordinatur"* (Contra Gentiles, I, c. 4, no. 23). *"Sapientia est veritatem praecipue de primo principio meditari"* (Contra Gentiles, I, c. 1, no. 6). When they are authentic, love of truth and love of good go together always. The idea of St. Thomas as a cold intellectual, advanced by some, is disproved by the fact that the Angelic One reduces knowledge itself to love of truth when he puts as a principle of every knowledge: *verum est bonum intellectus" (Ethic.* I, Lect. 12, no. 139; cf. also *Ethic.* VI, no. 1143; *S. Theol.* q. 5, a. 1; ad 4; I-IIae, q. 8, a. 1). Hence the intellect is made for truth and loves it as its innate good. And when the intellect is not satisfied by any partial truth acquired but always reaches beyond it, the intellect reaches beyond every particular truth and is naturally extended to total and absolute Truth which can really be none other than God. Desire for truth is transfigured into a natural desire for God and finds its clarification only in the light of Christ, Truth made Man.

Thus all of St. Thomas' philosophy and theology are not posited without, but within, St. Augustine's famous aphorism: *"fecisti nos ad te; et inquietum est cor nostrum, donec requiescat in te" (S. Augustinus, Conf.* I, 1). And when St. Thomas passed from the inherent tendency of man towards the truth and the good to the order of grace and redemption, he is transformed, not less than Saint Augustine, St. Bonaventure and St. Bernard, into a supreme poet of charity: *"Caritas est mater et radix omnium virtutum in quantum est omnium virtutum forma"* (S. Theol. I-IIae, q. 62, a. 4, cf. also I-IIae, q. 65, a. 2; I-IIae, q. 65, a. 3; I-IIae, q. 68, a. 5).

MAN—THE NOBLE CREATURE

5. There are still other reasons that make St. Thomas timely: his very deep sense of man, *"tam nobilis creatura"* (Contra Gentiles, IV, 1, no. 3337). The idea he has of this *"nobilis creatura,"* the image of God, is easy to observe every time he begins to talk of the Incarnation and redemption. From his first great youthful work, the Comment on the Judgments of Pier Lombardo in the prologue to the Third Book, in which he starts to deal with the Incarnation of the Word, he does not hesitate to compare man to the "sea," in that he collects, unifies, and elevates in himself the less than human world, as the sea collects all the waters of the rivers which flow into it.

In the same prologue he defines man as the horizon of creation in which sky and land join, like a link between time and eternity, like a synthesis of creation. In the last years of his life, when beginning the treatise on Incarnation in the third part of the *Summa Theologica*, still inspired by St. Augustine, he affirms that by merely taking on human nature, the Word could show *"quanta sit dignitas humanae naturae ne eam inquinemus peccando"* (S. Theol. III, q. 1, a. 2). And right after that he adds: by being incarnated and taking on human nature, God was able to show *"quam excelsum locum inter creaturas habeat humana natura"* (ibid.).

UPDATING ST. THOMAS

6. Among other things, in the meetings of your Congress it has been observed that the principles of the

philosophy and theology of St. Thomas were not perhaps utilized in the moral area, such as is demanded by the times and which it is possible to obtain from the great principles set forth by St. Thomas to be firmly connected to metaphysical bases for a greater organic unity and vigor. More has been done in the social area, but there is still a great gap to be bridged so as to meet the deepest and most urgent problems of man today.

It is possible that this is something to be taken up by the Pontifical Roman Academy of St. Thomas Aquinas for the immediate future, staying alert to the signs of the times, to the demands of greater organic unity and penetration, in accordance with the directives of Vatican II (cf. OT 16; GE 10), and the currents of thought of the contemporary world, for not a few aspects differing from those of St. Thomas' times and also from the period in which the Encyclical *Aeterni Patris* was issued by Leo XIII.

St. Thomas has pointed out a path that can and should be followed and updated without betraying its spirit and fundamental principles, but also keeping in mind modern scientific conquests. Science's true progress can never contradict philosophy, just as philosophy can never contradict faith. The new scientific contributions can have a cleansing and liberating function in the face of the limits imposed on philosophical research by medieval backwardness, not to speak of the non-existence of a science such as we possess today. Light can never be dimmed but only strengthened by light. Science and philosophy can and should work together so that both remain faithful to their own method. Philosophy can illuminate science and free it from its limits, as in its turn science can throw new light on philosophy itself and open new roads to it. This is the teaching of the Master from Aquino, but still before that is the Word of Truth itself, Jesus Christ, who assures us: *"Veritas liberabit vos"* (Jn. 8:32).

AN OUTSTANDING
PONTIFICAL ACADEMY

7. As is well known, Leo XIII, rich in wisdom and pastoral experience, did not content himself with issuing theoretical directives. He exhorted the bishops to create academies and Thomistic study centers, and he himself gave them the first example by establishing here in Rome the Pontifical Academy of St. Thomas Aquinas to which was then joined in 1934 the older Academy of Catholic Religion. The Congress meeting in these days also had the purpose of celebrating the centenary of your own Academy—and with good reason, because famous personages, illustrious Cardinals, many of the best talents and teachers of the sacred sciences of Rome and the world are its members as presidents and associates. It is an Academy that was always especially dear to all my Predecessors up to Paul VI, who received it twice in audience on the occasion of the previous congresses, addressing them and giving memorable directives.

It is impossible to pass over in silence the principal characteristics that have permitted your Academy to be faithful to the commitments assigned to it from time to time by the Supreme Pontiffs: its Catholic universality because of which it has always had among its associates personalities residing in Rome and outside of Rome (how can Jacques Maritain and Etienne Gilson not be remembered?), members of the diocesan clergy and religious of every order and congregation; its timeliness in making the study of contemporary problems the subjects of analysis in the light of Church doctrine: *"Ecclesiae Doctorum, praesertim Sancti Thomae vestigia premendo"* (GE 10), almost as a prelude to Vatican Council II.

The most convincing evidence is the works of the Academy: the numerous cycles of conferences, the publications, the periodic congresses requested by Pope Pius XI and carried out with exemplary precision and great profit to Catholic studies.

Nor can I fail to recall among the students who obtained their degrees from the Pontifical Roman Academy of St. Thomas Aquinas two of my illustrious Predecessors: Pius XI and Paul VI.

WITH GREAT COMMITMENT AND SERIOUSNESS

Dear venerated brothers!

Vatican Council II, which gave new impetus to Catholic studies with its decree on priestly training and Catholic education along the lines of the teaching of Saint Thomas (S. Thoma magistro: cf. OT 16), serves as a stimulus and omen for a renewed life and more abundant fruits in the near future for the good of the Church!

In expressing to you my deep pleasure in the International Thomistic Congress, that in these days has truly made a notable scientific contribution both because of the qualifications of its participants and rapporteurs, and the careful preparation of the various historical and philosophical problems, I urge you to continue, with great commitment and seriousness, to accomplish the goals of your Academy so that it can be a living, pulsing, modern center in which the method and doctrine of St. Thomas can be put into continuous contact and serene dialogue with the complex leavens of contemporary culture in which we live and are immersed.

With these wishes, I renew my sincere, kind feelings and heartily bestow my apostolic blessing.

Reconciliation of the World with God

During his pastoral visit to Siena on September 14, 1980, the Holy Father met with the bishops of the episcopal conference of Tuscany. The following is the text of his talk.

Your Eminence; venerated, dearest brothers of the Tuscan episcopate!

I am extremely happy to be here with you today on the occasion of this visit to Siena that I am making to venerate St. Catherine in a special way. If the meetings on this day all have a great importance for me, the one with you obviously is especially meaningful. It is the meeting of the Pope, whom Catherine so loved as "the sweet Christ on earth," with the bishops, so venerated by her: she says, in fact, that to them also, as to the "glorious apostle Peter," God left "the key of the blood of (His) only-begotten Son, which key imparted eternal life" (cf. *Dialogue*, CXV, ed. Cavallini, Rome, 1968, p. 277). In the most intense recollection of that gigantic figure, of that woman whose name is renowned in Italy and in all the world, we bishops—rather, I will say, you bishops of the Tuscany that gave so great a saint to the Church—must draw the inspiration for a commitment, an offering, an even greater sacrifice for the Church itself, for the souls which have been entrusted to us as the priceless treasure, because they cost the blood of Christ.

COMPLETELY DEDICATED TO THE CHURCH

1. Catherine speaks to us of just this love for the Church. We are in the service of the Church; our lives are completely dedicated to the Church. Writing to Pope Urban VI, whom she told about a supernatural vision, the saint repeated the words she heard regarding the Church, the Bride of Christ: "You see her quite empty of those who

seek her sum and substance, that is, the fruit of the blood...because the fruit of the blood belongs to those who bear the price of love; since she is based on love, and is love itself. And for love (said God Eternal) I want each one to give to her, in accordance with what I give to minister to my servants in different ways, as they have received. But I am sorrowful that I do not find one to minister to us" (*Letter* no. 371). And Catherine's whole life, passing like a fiery meteor that illuminates and warms the Church and civilized society with its fire, was spent for this "Bride," so that it could truly be what Christ wanted and loved her to be, "in splendor, without spot or wrinkle or any such thing, that she might be holy and without blemish" (Eph. 5:27). To her confessor, Blessed Raymond of Capua, she wrote after the rebellion of the Romans against the Pope: "Be assured that if I die, I die of passion for the Church" (cf. I. Taurisano, *S. Caterina da Siena*, p. 410).

This passion for the Church must also be ours: by word, example, prayer, sacrifice. We are sent by Christ as His representatives before men. "For the love of Christ controls us, because we are convinced that one has died for all. God, who through Christ reconciled us to himself and gave us the ministry of reconciliation; that is, God was in Christ reconciling the world to himself, not counting their trespasses against them, and entrusting to us the message of reconciliation. So we are ambassadors for Christ, God making his appeal through us" (2 Cor. 5:14, 18ff.).

NEED TO BE IMMERSED IN GOD AND CHRIST

2. It is necessary to be deeply, totally immersed in God in order to penetrate and understand the full power of these words, as Catherine was immersed in Him and in the model Jesus. It is necessary to be immersed in God and in Christ, my venerated and dear brothers, so that our mis-

sion may become life and life-giving truth for others, just as it was in her and for her.

And we must be, like she was, in love with Christ, with a love of the greatest trust and sacrifice, so that the reconciliation of man and the world with God holds, for our contemporaries and for those who will come after us, the meaning of the expressive sign and convincing reality.

When, six centuries after the death of that unusual figure in the history of the Church and Italy, we meet in medieval Siena, we feel how much the contemporary world has need of that reconciliation with God, which was accomplished once and for all in Christ. We also feel how necessary it is for us, the Church; for us, bishops— together with our priests, the sisters and the brothers of consecrated life, and even with all the Christian laity—to have the same faith and strength deriving from that reconciliation, that "word of reconciliation" that was entrusted to us for the good of humanity and the world.

LEST WE DISAPPOINT GOD'S TRUST

3. St. Catherine of Siena knew this "word of reconciliation." She knew how to say it forcefully and effectively before men, great and small: before the society of Italy of that time; before the pastors of the Church; before the Pope and princes.

She knew this "word of reconciliation." She carried it as deeply within herself as she was immersed in God through the love of Christ and absolute submissiveness to the Holy Spirit promised to the Apostles, that He does not leave anyone wanting in the Church—it is enough to know how to open our hearts, open all our reserve and shout: Come! Come! Come! Fill me up!

Immersion in God, the culminating example of which we find in St. Catherine, means leaving full freedom for the action of God in our souls, for His action in man, and through man, in the world.

Then the divine mysteries—drawn from the same source by St. Catherine—are no longer for us the shadow of distant problems but become a Reality: the higher, fundamental Reality which embraces within itself all reality, created and human, and gives it its proper significance. God, who has reconciled the world to Himself in Christ, and continually accomplishes in Him the work of reconciliation, acts by means of simple beings, poor in spirit, mild and humble of heart. Such was St. Catherine of Siena —in keeping with the spirit of the beatitudes of the Sermon on the Mount. Casting a glance at her brief life—thirty-three years!—we must notice that to those who offer themselves to God in Christ and with that self-oblation give the entire world—humanity and the Church—to such as these God responds with a special trust, and entrusts to them the Church, humanity and the world, and gives the grace necessary not to disappoint this trust of God's.

St. Catherine certainly did not disappoint God's trust. She did not disappoint the trust of her Bridegroom towards the Church, humanity and the world. And so we, bishops of the Church of God, must not disappoint God's trust. We must respond. We must be the agents of His grace, just as was Catherine, modest virgin, daughter of simple people, without special education, who, entrusting herself wholly to God, became the incomparable instrument of His grace, His forgiveness, His reconciliation. Like her, "ambassadors for Christ"! In this way our souls remain attuned to this beloved saint, the sixth centenary of whose death has brought us together here.

ST. CATHERINE PROVIDES A REMINDER

4. Reconciliation with God in Jesus Christ embraces and penetrates different times, days, months and years, eras and generations. What was that time of the Church and the world before which St. Catherine of Siena was given the mission of pronouncing this "word of reconciliation" entrusted to her in a special way by God?

It certainly is not necessary here for me to remind you of the events, at times tempestuous, the tragedies, the dangers of the historic period in which St. Catherine lived: the mission she performed to the benefit of Church unity before the return to Rome of Pope Gregory XI; then in calling for all the forces of the Church to come together around his Successor, Urban VI, against the anti-Pope Clement VII; the work of pacification she carried out in the Italian cities—suffice it to mention Florence and Rome for all of them; the apostolate she performed in reawakening dulled, uneasy consciences and recalling them to the meaning of God, of the supremacy of inner life, to purity of morals. All this in the name of love, all this in the blood of Christ that bedews the garden of the Church and is the font of personal sanctity of the clergy, of its ministerial function, and likewise of the incorruptibility and integrity of families and lay life.

5. St. Catherine today reminds us bishops, in the difficulties of today's ministry, that if we want our efforts to be fertile in Christ we must begin with the same root by which she lived and gave herself: love of Christ. How real are the words written to the Cardinal of Ostia, Pietro d'Estaing: "You, then, as a true son and servant ransomed by the blood of Christ crucified, I want you to follow in His footsteps, with a manly heart and ready dispatch; never wearying yourself with either suffering or pleasure, but persevere up to the end in this and every other work that you take on to do for Christ crucified. Apply yourself to eradicating the injustices and miseries of the world, the many wrongs committed: those which revile the name of God" (*Letter* no. 7).

With this strength, this conviction, we bishops must fight to have God's mercy triumph, to announce that God "so loved the world that he gave his only Son, that whoever believes in him should not perish but have eternal life" (Jn. 3:16). This is the starting point for that love for the blood of Christ that impelled Catherine to give of herself for the Church until she was immolated like a flame, up to the last spark. This is the starting point also for us to commit ourselves to leave no stone unturned so that the love of Christ may have the highest supremacy in the Church and society.

I am pleased here to acknowledge to all of you everything you are doing for your dioceses so that Christian life in the families, youth, the flourishing of vocations, the forms of civil society may be completely, firmly manifested. And in particular I direct my praise to Cardinal Giovanni Benelli, Archbishop of Florence, for his clear commitment, for his pastoral zeal in supporting efforts for the protection of human life.

I well know, dear brothers, the difficulties involved in your mission of reconciling men with God in the environment of today, ensnared by worldliness, dominated by ideologies, corroded by consumerism and hedonism.

I am, therefore, glad for your generous dedication to the apostolic ministry in remembrance of St. Paul's counsel: "Preach the word, be urgent in season and out of season..." (2 Tm. 4:2). Do not let yourselves become discouraged, but continue with the indomitable fortitude of St. Catherine in your tireless efforts to proclaim the need for a sincere return to the Faith and the practice of Christian virtues, so that the true soul of your people emerges in all its human qualities and all its supernatural gifts.

Let the Spirit of the Lord sustain you; let the prayers and encouragement of the Vicar of Christ be of comfort to you.

The Church of our times believes, with the certitude of faith itself, that God reconciled the world to Himself in Christ once and forever; and at the same time she is trying to pronounce the "word of reconciliation" that God entrusts to her for the world of today and orders her to pronounce, in keeping with the signs of our times and in complete unity with the message of eternal salvation. This message greatly broadens the heart of the Church, just as it broadened Catherine's heart to hope even against every hope, to work beyond the limit of human endurance, to sacrifice herself to the last for the Church, for Christ's triumph of love, for the children's return to the Father of all consolation. In fact, in the heart of the Church there is a persistent image of the Father who awaits the prodigal son and welcomes him with open arms when he returns to the paternal home.

The Church of our era, which in Vatican Council II defined herself as the Sacrament of Salvation and the Sign of Union of all mankind with God, also sought to pronounce in the Council itself, in a particularly ample and abundant manner, that "word of reconciliation" entrusted to her by God. Let Catherine of Siena, patron saint of Italy, with her love for Christ and the Church, make it resound with unchanged power, today and in the future, and lend protection, courage, hope, and strength to our ministry as "Ambassadors for Christ."

My apostolic blessing is a pledge of these ardent wishes.

Closer and More Organic Coordination

The meeting with the clergy and religious of the diocese of Siena and of all Tuscany took place on September 14, 1980, in the Cathedral. After a welcoming address by Cardinal Benelli, President of the episcopal conference of Tuscany, the Holy Father delivered the following message.

Venerated brother bishops and you very dear priests, male and female religious of Tuscany:

1. I wish to respond to the splendid address of His Eminence, Cardinal Giovanni Benelli, with cordial thanks and, since he has officially spoken on behalf of all of you, I very gladly extend my feelings of gratitude to all of you gathered here.

I well know that you expect from me—your spokesman has just now said it—a special word of encouragement, which, inspired by the occasion which brought me today to this illustrious city, has a more direct relation to your vocations and to your lives as consecrated souls, and can, therefore, help you both in the permanent work of personal sanctification and in the fulfillment of the special duties of the ministry entrusted to each of you.

LIVING EXAMPLES OF HOLINESS

2. You see, I came to Siena to honor the saint who for the past six centuries has not ceased to irradiate in the Church and in the world, quite beyond the geographical and national confines of Tuscany and Italy, the prestigious example of her love for Christ and His Vicar on this earth, and her zeal for the salvation of souls. In St. Catherine's name it has been, and is, my intention to take up again the inexhaustible discussion surrounding holiness, which constitutes the fullness and culmination of a life truly Christian, and to which—as the Council has reminded us—all the faithful "of whatever status or rank" (LG 40) are called. But such a discussion—I ask myself and I ask you—what good is it in the first place if not for those who through a free and conscious decision have chosen to follow Christ, personally assuming very special commitments, both professed and lived? Yes, it is especially worthwhile for us who, because of our direct participation in the unique priesthood of Christ or the formal profession of evangelical counsels, must travel the way of perfection and holiness. We are the ones who must offer the example of a Christianity lived under daily tensions to the Christians who live in the world and are so often tempted by its thousands of seductions, and who can also find themselves defenseless. It is we who must present them with convincing proof that it is possible and actually easy, even in the midst of the difficulties of our days, to live in consistent fidelity to the Gospel and to be totally Christian. What would become of us, dearest brothers and sisters, if such an example of proof were lacking on our part? Remember what I would call the two perceptive images offered us in

the Sermon on the Mount: Every Christian should be the light of the world and the salt of the earth (cf. Mt. 5:13-16); but this duty of good example assumes a special significance for us who have given ourselves to Christ irrevocably in a selfless, total giving. I would say this entails a precise *obligation of our state*, and I am sure that the vivid images of the two saints whom we are solemnly honoring today could help us fulfill it.

ECCLESIAL LIFE DEPENDS ON THE EUCHARISTIC LIFE

3. A second thought is connected with the act of Eucharistic worship that we have now completed: the adoration of the "most holy Particles" that have been preserved in the Basilica of St. Francis for two and a half centuries. The Eucharist is the vital center; it is the heart of the Church which unceasingly draws from it the faith, the grace, the energy that are necessary for her journey through history. Where Eucharistic life flourishes, there the ecclesial life flourishes: This, brothers, is an axiom whose validity not only touches theological doctrine, but also reaches and must reach the existential dimension on the community and personal levels.

Therefore, it is necessary to see to it that the Eucharistic Mystery, perpetual memorial of Easter and Redemption, always has in each of our communities—parishes, families, religious houses, seminaries, associations—that central position which fully and rightfully belongs to it. But it is likewise necessary that in the life of each of us as well, this exalted Mystery is and always remains the essential point of reference for our growing and increasingly perfect "link" with Christ the Lord. Therefore, let the Eucharist be the sure road for communion, that is, the union and unity we must establish with Him: "In the breaking of Eucharistic Bread"—the Council yet again reminds us (LG 7)—"as we actually partake of the body of the Lord, we are elevated to communion with Him (personal relationship) and among ourselves (communitarian relationship)." I wish to add that also from this point of view—I mean that of a special Eucharistic spirituality—it behooves us to have that selfsame duty of good example of which I have just spoken.

HISTORIC ANNIVERSARY
OF THIS CHURCH

4. Finding myself in this magnificent Cathedral, I cannot remain silent about an event which recently occasioned special celebrations. I refer to the "Year of the Cathedral," proclaimed to commemorate the eighth centenary of the dedication of this temple in honor of Mary's assumption into heaven. Like Santa Maria del Fiore and so many other churches of your Tuscany, the Cathedral of Siena, too, has a history going back many centuries which concerns not only art in its highest aesthetic expression, but also and above all the spiritual life of a people. It is a fact that such life has found right here, within these walls, its point of convergence and radiance throughout all the communities of the archdiocese.

Taking this historic anniversary as a starting point, I invite you, my very dear brothers and sisters, to reflect on the function that concerns every Cathedral as a dynamic center of each particular church, and concerns, above all, the bishop who has his See there. Together with the other colleagues in the episcopate as well as the Successor of Peter, he bears the primary responsibilities of "building" his ecclésial community, since he takes part in a unique manner, on a level of high, great prestige, in that triple function of Christ, which belongs to the faithful as well: He is by right, and must be, in fact, the *teacher* who teaches the faith and moral doctrine, the *priest* who offers the sacrifice of the New Covenant, the *shepherd* who leads his flock. If every cathedral is a meaningful symbol of these duties, it does not, however, speak only to the conscience of the bishop: it is a call for all the members of the particular Church, beginning with those who, like you, are called to collaborate with the bishop in the diocesan pastorate.

From this thought springs another one which I want to mention to you. Without ignoring or denying the "canonical" distinction between the secular and regular clergy, in our days—and it is a great lesson of the Council which so rightly has been called pastoral—a closer and more organic coordination is necessary between the priests and the bishops. It demands, on the one hand, the most mature ecclesiological conscience for the unity existing between them in relation to the unique priesthood of Christ; and on the other hand, it demands the increasing questioning that comes from whoever has no knowledge of the Faith or doubts it to the point of rejecting it. I am not speaking in terms of efficiency and human success, almost as if the cause of the Gospel depended on a certain type of organization and is, therefore, reduced to the choice of determined structures or new technical organs. I am speaking of the "inner necessity" springing from what the Church is by reason of her very make-up, and which today she must be in the socio-cultural travail of which we are at one and the same time witnesses and participants.

It is not right today to linger on positions of ordinary administration or bureaucratic sluggishness, nor can one insist too much on subtle distinctions about the competence and right of doing this thing or that: Today it is more than ever necessary to act for the Gospel and act with vigilant and courageous zeal, ready for sacrifice and open to the vehemence of an inexhaustible charity for which bishop and priests, regular or secular as they may be, work in unity of intent, combining—like the disciples of the early Church—one heart and one soul (cf. Acts 4:32). And the same duty is imposed in due proportion upon the religious and upon those who, because of a special call from the Lord, have received, or prepare themselves to receive, the various ecclesial ministries. This is a subject that certainly deserves to be developed: If for lack of time this is not possible for me now, I ask you to take it and probe it in your personal reflections and in the brotherly discussions you hold under the guidance of your superiors and pastors.

The meeting in this cathedral, therefore, in order to be a more dear and lasting memory, should conclude with a strong appeal to apostolic action: In the name of Christ, whose humble Vicar and Servant I am, I invite you always to keep in mind the "building of the Church" I mentioned as a work of permanent actuality to which you, as consecrated persons, are called to collaborate in a completely special manner. Only from a profound conviction, matured in prayer, will you be able to evolve renewed proposals and concrete initiatives. This, too, it seems to me, refers to good example which the Lord Himself summarized with His great and reassuring words: "Let your light so shine before men, that they may see your good works and give glory to your Father who is in heaven" (Mt. 5:16). Amen!

Look at the Present with Realism, at the Future with Hope

In the afternoon of September 20, 1980, the Holy Father met the priests, men and women religious, and leaders of the Catholic laity of Montecassino in St. Germanus Church. The following are excerpts from the Pope's address.

Beloved priests, men and women religious, and beloved leaders of the Catholic laity!

I would have felt a pang of remorse if, on this happy opportunity offered to us by St. Benedict's jubilee year, I had not set aside a moment of my visit entirely for you, who bring about, inspire, and are responsible for the Christian spirit of the People of God in this land of Cassino, so deeply marked by the memory and the protection of the Western Patriarch.

CONCERN FOR SOULS

First of all, I wish to thank you for the joy you give me on knowing and seeing you so animated by a deep spirit of faith in Christ our Lord and of affectionate allegiance to His Vicar. I thank you above all for the pastoral work which you, in various capacities, carry out with concern for the salvation of souls. Your Vicar General has asked me, as you have just heard, for words of encouragement for your "daily pastoral commitment." I willingly fulfill his wish, expressing my esteem and good will, in the first place, to you pastors of souls, who, in generous collaboration with your bishop, carry out such a delicate service for the Church of Cassino. Your presence stirs up in my mind unforgettable memories connected with my pastoral experiences as priest and bishop in my native diocese in Poland, where I spent most of my youthful energies among souls whom I have always found so eager for that *Word* which comes from above and for that special *power* which comes from the sacraments of salvation.

So let the expression of my brotherly solidarity and my sincere appreciation go to you for the generous dedication with which you carry out the priestly ministry, and for the good will with which you cope with the many difficulties which you confront due to the scarcity of pastoral aids or the lack of collaboration. To you, beloved brothers, who as worthy workers of the Gospel put the Lord's commandments into practice every day, according to the Benedictine spirit: *Praecepta Dei factis quotidie adimplere* (Rule no. 4), I say: continue to work confidently for the salvation of all men and women, but pay particular attention to the poor, the segregated, abandoned children, weary workers, and all those who suffer in body and spirit. Rest assured that in your work of edification and salvation, the Pope follows you, understands you, loves you, and blesses you.

Be Teachers and Witnesses of the Truth Which Comes from God

On September 24, 1980, the Holy Father received in audience a group of bishops from Argentina on their visit ad limina Apostolorum. *The group was led by Cardinal Raul Francisco Primatesta, Archbishop of Cordoba. John Paul II delivered the following address.*

Revered brothers in the episcopate,

I thank God for allowing me to meet you and other bishops of Argentina, who have come to Rome for the visit *ad limina*, and to get to know better, in this way, the reality of evangelical work in those lands, distant geographically, but very close to my heart.

At this collective meeting I wish to reflect with you on some points which more particularly require your dedication as teachers and pastors of faith, and which call at the same time for the effort of the whole Christian community.

Opening the recent Puebla Conference, I pointed out concretely what constitutes the fundamental core of evangelization and how it is the main duty of bishops to be teachers and witnesses of the truth that comes from God: the truth about Jesus Christ, the Word and Son of God, who becomes man to draw close to man and offer him, through His mystery, salvation, God's great gift (Opening Address, I, 5). But truth that reaches man through the sacred Magisterium of the Church, which was established and instituted by the same Lord as a communion of life, charity and truth *(ibid.*, I, 6). Finally, it shows man in this way the principle and foundation of his dignity and his rights. In this connection I wish to tell you that I am pleased with the efforts you are making to be faithful to this program and to the duty you have to the souls entrusted to your pastoral responsibility.

Today I wish, however, to refer more specifically to two points that you, Lord Cardinal, mentioned in the words you have just uttered. The first is that of priestly and religious vocations. This year, on the occasion of Holy Thursday, I sent two letters to bishops and priests to stress the necessity of laying the foundations of your own priestly identity and giving the world the testimony of clear consecration to God. Learning now of the encouraging reality of the revival of vocations in your dioceses, I point out once more the prior importance of the pastoral care required, on the one hand, for the promotion of the vocations of young men and adolescents and the formation of seminarians and aspirants to religious life; and, on the other hand, for the continual spiritual renewal of priests.

Christian priesthood has no meaning outside of Christ. Traditional teaching repeats to us constantly: *sacerdos alter Christus,* and it does so not by marking a parallel meaning, but by indicating how Christ becomes present in every priest and how the priest operates *in persona Christi.* How will this reality be possible if there does not exist a correspondence between that mysterious identity with Christ and the personal identity that is obtained through the actual acceptance of each priest? And how can we reach Christ if the Father does not draw us? For this reason, prayer must fill the priest's life: personal prayer, which, although it has to be expressed eminently through the Sacred Liturgy, will have to be nourished with continual recourse to Holy Scripture, in the light of the Magisterium of the Church. Daily participation in the Eucharist will seal this deep and irreplaceable contact with the Lord.

Obviously, there is also required of the priest an effort of study and research in the sources and expressions of this same Magisterium of the Church, with the prudent complement of secular sciences, in order to be more adequately prepared for the service of the Lord in favor of men.

On the other hand, the true identity of the priesthood involves humble submission and use of the intelligence and natural gifts to get to know and accept God's ways, abandoning oneself confidently to His plan of salvation. Only under the action of grace does one arrive at the wisdom—a gift of the Holy Spirit—through which the priest has a transcendent view of human life, acquires the real meaning of things, and draws from the principles of faith the conclusions that will direct every man, in every situation, along the ways of Truth and Life.

There has been no lack in Argentina of exemplary priests and religious, who bore and bear a testimony of faithfulness and dedication in their own consecration to Christ and to the Church. Therefore, I renew my confident exhortation to your priests, seminarians, and religious men and women, to continue generously in their vocation.

The second point to which I wish to refer is that of lay associations and particularly Catholic Action. Apostolic activity organized at the level of the faithful is necessary; with structures adequate for the conditions of our time, and which at the same time reflect and coordinate the activity of parishes and ecclesial communities, integrating them in the apostolate of the bishop and of the hierarchy of the Church.

The Second Vatican Council presented the greatness of the vocation of the laity who, by their presence and activity in the order of temporal things, must be living witnesses to the Faith. It also showed that this witness can be an individual and personal apostolate, but it clearly pointed out the conditions of organized apostolate, which correspond to the social nature of man, and specified its close relationship with the specific apostolate of the hierarchy (CD 33).

As regards Catholic Action more concretely, beyond activities of exclusively temporal character or of mere social assistance, it brings its members deep awareness of their apostolic vocation in their own situation as lay people. As the Second Vatican Council rightly teaches: "The Church is not truly established and does not fully live, nor is it a perfect sign of Christ, unless there is a genuine laity existing and working alongside the hierarchy" (AG 21).

For this reason, making my own what Paul VI wrote to the bishops of Argentina: "We wish our brothers in the episcopate and priests, too, to see in Catholic Action an indispensable collaborator of the ministry, as a sign and token of the living presence of the laity in communication of the Lord's redeeming grace" (Letter to the Argentine Episcopate, June 12, 1977), I wish to repeat what I said to the young people of Italian Catholic Action on last May 26, about the necessity and commitment of "receiving the message of Jesus and passing it on to others," so that it may grant members of Catholic Action and apostolic associations serenity of spirit, nobility of soul and unfailing consistency in evangelical witness within the environment in which they are called to live and act. It will be necessary to be able to listen, study, discover and live what one has "received." And what one has received must not remain inert in each one, but must be handed on, communicated to others, as was done by the Apostles who spread over the world to communicate and announce to all peoples the message of salvation received from their Master (cf. *L'Osservatore Romano*, English edition, June 18, 1979). To all those who work in this field, I wish to express my esteem, praise and encouragement.

Dear brothers in the episcopate: these are the reflections I wished to communicate to you. I thank you for your generous ecclesial commitment and I encourage you not to weaken in your apostolic work. On your return to your dioceses, think that Peter's Successor, whom you visited in Rome, accompanies you with his prayer and his affection in your pastoral care of every day.

You are now beginning the National Marian Year. May the Blessed Virgin, "mediatrix before the Mediator," obtain for you the grace of growing with your faithful and the whole Argentine people in knowledge of the truth, in order that you may have life, love and peace. With these desires, take with you my blessing, which I extend to all your diocesans and to the Argentine people in general.

The Family Gives Life to Society

On September 26, 1980, John Paul II presided at the solemn concelebration of the opening of the Fifth General Assembly of the Synod of Bishops. The 216 synodal fathers concelebrated with the Pope in the Sistine Chapel. The following is the translation of the Holy Father's homily, delivered in Latin.

1. Venerable brothers in the episcopate and dearly beloved brothers and sisters participating in this session of the Synod of Bishops, which is about to begin:

It would be fitting to start our work by going straight to the heart of the priestly prayer of Christ. We know how important and how profound the moment was when He uttered the words of this prayer. Let us listen to the deep meaning which fills these words: "Holy Father, preserve in your name those you have given to me, so that they may be one, as we are one" (Jn. 7:11).

When the Church prays for her unity, she simply goes back to these words. With these words we pray for the unity of Christians. And using the same words, we seek from the Father, in the name of Christ, that unity which we should bring about during the assembly of the Synod of Bishops, which begins today and, after a period of long and thorough preparation, undertakes its work on the theme: the role of the Christian family.

THE CHURCH LIVES THROUGH CHRISTIAN FAMILIES

2. This theme has been chosen, prepared after thorough examination, as a result of suggestions which had been sent to the secretary general of the Synod of Bishops by many bishops and episcopal conferences. This theme, during the next weeks, will make up the basis for our considerations, also because we are deeply convinced that through the Christian family the Church lives and fulfills

the mission given to her by Christ. Therefore, we can say in all honesty that the theme of the present session of the Synod sees itself as a continuation of the preceding two sessions. Both evangelization, theme of the 1974 Synod, and catechesis, theme of the 1977 Synod, not only look to the family but also receive their authentic vitality from the family. The family is the fundamental object of the Church's evangelization and catechesis, but it is also the necessary subject for which nothing else can be substituted: the creative subject.

"DOMESTIC CHURCH"

3. The family must, being the subject, be conscious of the mission of the Church and of its participation in this mission; not only to persevere in the Church and to draw from its spiritual resources, but also to constitute the Church in its fundamental dimension, like a "miniature Church" (domestic Church).

The present Synod's job is to show all the families their particular role in the mission of the Church. This participation includes, at the same time, the realization of the actual ends of the Christian family, as much as possible in its full dimension.

In the work of the synodal assembly, we would like to perceive again the rich teachings of the Second Vatican Council which pertains to the truths about the family and how the families have translated these teachings into daily life. The Christian families must fully find their place in this work of great importance. Above all, the Synod intends to render service to this end.

SHARING GIFTS

4. St. Paul teaches us in the second reading of today's liturgy: "We are one body in Christ and each one is a part of one another" (Rom. 12:5). Therefore, although the synodal assembly is by its nature a particular form of activity of the episcopal college, within this assembly we

feel the need for the presence and the testimonies of our dear brothers and sisters who represent the Christian families of the world. "We therefore have different gifts given to us in accordance with the grace given to each of us" (Rom. 12:6). It is really necessary at the time of this assembly, whose theme is the Christian family and its role, to have the presence and the testimony of those whose gifts, according to the grace given them, are the gifts of life and of vocation to marriage and family life.

Beloved brothers and sisters, we will be grateful to you if during the work of this Synod in which we are involved, in our episcopal and pastoral duty, you would share with us these gifts of your condition and your vocation, at least through the testimony of your presence and your experience, rooted in the sanctity of this great sacrament, this sacrament which is proper to you: the sacrament we call Matrimony.

THE CHURCH LOOKS TO SPOUSES

5. When Christ the Lord, before His death, at the threshold of the Paschal Mystery, prays: "Holy Father, preserve in your name those you have given to me, so that they may be one, as we are one" (Jn. 17:11), He is seeking in a special way the unity of married couples and of families. He prays for the unity of His disciples, for the unity of the Church; and the mystery of the Church is compared by St. Paul with marriage (cf. Eph. 21:33). Within its duties, the Church not only has special responsibilities to the family but it also finds its reflection in the family. Inflamed with love of Christ her Spouse, who loved us till the end, the Church looks toward spouses who promise love to one another through the course of their whole life, even unto death. The Church considers it her particular duty to foster this love, this faithfulness, this honesty and all good things which come from the human person and society. It is actually the family which gives life to society because in the

family, through the work of education, the actual structure of humanity is formed, proper to every person in this world.

In today's Gospel, the Son speaks thus to the Father: "The words which you have given me I have given to them; they have received...and believed that you have sent me.... All things mine are yours and all your things are mine..." (Jn. 17:8-10).

Doesn't the echo of this dialogue resound in the hearts of all generations? Don't these words vividly portray the history of each family and, through the family, of each person?

Don't we feel, through these words, specially connected to the mission of Christ Himself: of Christ the Priest, the Prophet, the King? Isn't the family born by reason of this mission?

CONSCIOUS OF ITS MISSION

6. "Therefore I exhort you, brothers, for the love of God, to offer yourselves as a living sacrifice, holy and pleasing to God; this is your spiritual worship" (Rom. 12:1).

This sacrifice and this rite give testimomy to your participation in the royal priesthood of Christ. You have no choice but to obey the words of exhortation which God, Creator and Father, has spoken. In the first reading from the book of Deuteronomy, these words are said: "This word is very close to you, it is in your mouth and in your heart because you put it into practice" (Dt. 30:14).

And in this manner Christ prays for His disciples: "I don't pray that you take them from the world but that you keep them from evil. Sanctify them in truth.... I sanctify myself for them that they may be sanctified in truth" (Jn. 17:15-19).

The Word of God, announced in today's liturgy, describes the duties which it is fitting that we propose to Christian families in the Church and in the modern world:

—consciousness of one's own mission, which comes from the saving mission of Christ and is fulfilled as a special service;

—this consciousness is fed by the Word of the living God and by the power of Christ's sacrifice. In this way the testimony of life is developed, capable of forming the life of others and of sanctifying others in truth;

—from this consciousness flows the good which alone "preserves from the evil one." The duty of the family is altogether like the duty of Him who in the Gospel said of Himself: "When I was with them, I preserved in your name and guarded those you gave me; none of them was lost..." (Jn. 17:12).

Yes, the duty of each Christian family is to guard and preserve the fundamental values. To do this is to guard and preserve humanity itself.

SERVICE TO HUMANITY

7. May the Holy Spirit guide and sustain all our work during this assembly which begins today.

It is fitting that we begin in the words taken from the heart of the priestly prayer of Christ. It is fitting that we begin with the Eucharistic Celebration.

All our work during the following days will be nothing but a service rendered to humanity: to our brothers and sisters, to spouses and parents, to youth, to children, to generations, to families,

to all to whom Christ revealed the Father,

to all whom the Father gave "from the world" to Christ.

"I pray for them whom you have given me, because they are yours" (Jn. 17:9).

Importance of the Work of Pope Paul VI and of the Brief Pontificate of Pope John Paul I

On September 28, 1980, John Paul II went to St. Peter's Basilica to preside at the solemn concelebration of suffrage for the Supreme Pontiffs Paul VI and John Paul I.

Approximately 300 concelebrants participated in the rite: Cardinals, Synodal Fathers and bishops of the European episcopal conferences. About 25,000 faithful and pilgrims were present.

After the Gospel, John Paul II delivered the following homily.

1. "But you, man of God, fly from these things; incline to justice, to piety, to faith, to charity, to patience, to meekness. Fight the good fight of faith, seek to gain eternal life, to which you have been called and for which you have made a beautiful profession of faith before many witnesses" (1 Tim. 6:11-13).

These words of the Apostle, taken from this Sunday's liturgy, allow us, two years after his death, to renew the memory of Pope John Paul I, who was called to the See of Peter on August 26, 1978, and was called back to the house of the Father to gain eternal life on September 28, after having ended in this See his service which lasted barely thirty-three days:

"Seek to gain eternal life, to which you have been called and for which you have made a beautiful profession of faith before many witnesses."

A SMILE FOR EVERYONE

2. How much these words tell us! How much they tell all those who joyfully greeted the elevation of Cardinal Albino Luciani, Patriarch of Venice, to the See of Saint Peter; to all those who still remember and almost visualize

his good and calm face, so readily illuminated by a serene smile for every person. How much these words say to priests, for whom he was both brother and father, especially for those priests to whom he willingly preached spiritual exercises.

A short time ago, I had occasion to read the text of these marvelous exercises, full of his spirit, from the figurative language, adapted in every step to the reality of priestly life and centered around the figure of the Good Samaritan. We can see how dear this figure was to him, how much he identified with it. We can also guess that such a figure would have been the inspiration for that pontificate, which barely had the time to begin. Truly he was, for the Church and for the world, *magis ostensus, quam datus!* (More shown than given!)

PRESENT AT 1977 SYNOD

3. We bishops, reunited for the present session of the Synod, still remember him as a member of the 1977 session. In the Synod Hall, I was seated near him, right in front of him. Eleven months after that session, he was called to the See of St. Peter, and a year later he was no longer alive! He didn't even have the time to publish the document on the theme of catechesis, in which he wanted to express, as requested by the Synodal Assembly, the fruit of his work on a theme which was very dear to him. However, during barely four weeks of his pontificate, he found the time to give us a particularly special expression of his religious teachings during the Wednesday general audiences dedicated to faith, hope and charity.

On the other hand, we cannot forget the words on the Synod of Bishops' theme pronounced in his first radio message the day after his election. After having declared, as his first intention, that of developing without intermission the heritage of the Second Vatican Council, by striving to apply its wise norms, he directed his attention to the Cardinals of the Sacred College and to all the bishops of the Church of God, "whose collegiality"—he added —"we wish strongly to reinforce, taking advantage of their work in the government of the universal Church, through the instrumentality of the Synod and through the structure of the Roman Curia" (cf. *Teachings of John Paul I*, pp. 15-17). These fairly clear words are a demonstration of his formal promise to give value to the Synod.

That is why today, in the moment in which we are again united in the Synod, we consider it a particularly heartfelt need to remember our brother and father before God, Pope John Paul I, bowing our heads before the inscrutable mystery of Providence, which was manifested in his coming and in his going, and giving thanks because he kept "the commandment without stain or wrinkle until the manifestation of our Lord Jesus Christ" (1 Tm. 6:14).

HIS TWO PREDECESSORS

4. The personality of John Paul I will always direct our thoughts toward his two Predecessors in the See of St. Peter, whose combined names he chose as an inheritance, as if he wished to confirm the fact that it wouldn't be right to separate them and that, being in the service of the See of St. Peter, it is necessary to continue their work.

Today if, through the names of John and Paul, we direct our thoughts to his two Predecessors, who in a certain way inaugurated a new era for the Church, we must in particular direct this thought along with prayer and sacrifice to Pope Paul VI, first of all because the second anniversary of his death was only some weeks ago and shortly precedes today's commemoration of the anniversary of the death of his immediate Successor.

Among his many works, Paul VI will be remembered in history as the person who, putting into practice the teachings of the Second Vatican Council about collegiality, gave life to this actual Synod of Bishops, for which we have met in ordinary session for the fifth time.

Fundamental to this point is the text of the constitutive document *Apostolica sollicitudo*, because, three months before the conclusion of the Council itself, it fixed the still valid lines of this new ecclesiastical organism, conceived as *peculiare sacrorum Antistitum consilium* (a special consultative body of the holy bishops), and it clearly indicated to us its spirit and its purpose: to promote closer union and fruitful cooperation between the Sovereign Pontiff and the bishops of the whole world (cf. Motu proprio, *Apostolica sollicitudo* in *AAS* 57 [1965], pp. 775ff.).

WORDS OF POPE PAUL VI

5. While inaugurating the preceding ordinary session of the Synod of Bishops with a concelebration in the Sistine Chapel, Paul VI greeted the assembly as a "splendid example of ecclesial communion" and, addressing himself to the personal conscience of each bishop present, he said, among other things:

"We are chosen, we are called, we are invested by our Lord with a transforming mission. As bishops, we are the successors of the Apostles, the pastors of the Church of God. We are qualified by one obligation: to be witnesses, to be bearers of the Gospel message, to be teachers for humanity. We want to remember all of this, venerable brothers, to revive the consciousness of our election, of our vocation, of our responsibility in this great, dangerous, and uncomfortable role which has been given to us; but, above all, to strengthen our confidence in the help of Christ in our sufferings, in our work, in our hopes."

And again:

"To be true apostles of Christ today is a great act of courage and also a great act of faith in the power and assistance of God: assistance that God will certainly not fail to provide, if the heart of the apostle remains open to the delicate and powerful influx of His grace."

And also:

"The panorama of the world, upon which our responsibility as evangelizers looks, gives us the idea of the immensity of our mission and makes us able to feel the weight of our mission. There is still an inadequacy on our part which makes us seem totally insufficient. But it is because of this that we must affirm and confirm our task: The glance at the world and at the future ought not to generate carelessness. Just the opposite: far from overdoing it in reacting to the temptation to inertia, we should be certain that the *virtú* (power), that is to say, the force, the aid, the help of the Lord is with us" (cf. *Teaching of Paul VI*, XV [1977], pp. 888-890).

These, then, were the strengthening words we heard on September 30, 1977. Today, it was necessary that they resound anew among us, to give witness to the continuity of this great cause, to serve which we are reunited here.

PILGRIMAGE TO SUBIACO

6. However, at this point, because I will be going on pilgrimage to Subiaco this afternoon with the representatives of the episcopal conferences of the European countries, I cannot but refer, if even briefly, to another of the outstanding merits of Paul VI. I am alluding to what he said, decided, and did to keep alive always in the consciousness of modern Europe, as an active yeast, the memory of the great contribution of thought and of works given to this continent by St. Benedict and, more generally, by the Benedictine tradition. After having proclaimed the saint the patron of Europe, he went to Monte Cassino to visit his tomb, consecrated the church of the restored archabbey, and, in a memorable discourse, spoke of a society "so in need of gaining new energy at its roots...," the Christian roots that in great part St. Benedict gave it. And he opportunely named the higher motives, that is to say, the "two heads that make us desire the austere yet suave presence of Benedict among us: for the faith, which he and his order preached in the family of peoples, especially in the one called Europe: the Christian faith, the religion of our civilization, that of the Holy Church, mother and teacher of the peoples; and for unity, to which the great solitary and social monk educated us as brothers

and for which, therefore, Europe was Christianity. Faith and unity: what better things could we want and invoke for the whole world and, in particular, for the large and elect portion called Europe?" (cf. *Teachings of Paul VI*, II [1964], p. 606)

On the basis of this historic inheritance, the same Pontiff, having on different occasions received groups of prelates belonging to the European nations, stressed many times the task or, rather, the mission to stimulate other nations and to cooperate with more responsibility in the diffusion of faith. He reminded the representatives of some of the European episcopal conferences of the "value of the examples of Churches on this continent for other areas of the Catholic world, above all for the recently formed Churches, which await needed help from the older Churches" (cf. *Teachings of Paul VI*, V [1967], p. 495).

He repeated the same concepts in March 1971 to the presidents and delegates of the Conferences of Europe meeting in Rome to establish the special "Council" of the European episcopates. On such an occasion, he wanted to recall again the unitary character of tradition, of civilization and of customs of the inhabitants of the continent, and he urged "giving a Gospel witness of faith, of hope, of charity, of justice and of peace, having considered the important causes which in Europe call forth the help of the Church and of human society," without forgetting, however, the needs of the universal Church, especially in the Third World (cf. *Teachings of Paul VI*, I [1971], pp. 221-222).

7. May "the King of kings and Lord of lords, who alone has immortality and dwells in inapproachable light, whom no man has ever seen or can see" (1 Tm. 6:15-16), reveal in a blessed eternity the splendor of His sanctity "face to face" and admit to communion with Him in eternal charity our two venerable brothers and fathers: Paul VI and John Paul I.

"May His be the honor and the power forever."

St. Benedict—a Man of God

On September 28, 1980, the Sacro Speco *at Subiaco—the humble cave in which St. Benedict spent three years in penitential prayer—was the goal of a solemn pilgrimage made by the Holy Father with the bishops of Europe and other continents who were at the Vatican for the Synod of Bishops. John Paul II delivered the following address.*

Venerated and beloved brothers,

1. Today the great jubilee of St. Benedict has brought us all to Subiaco. It has already given you the opportunity to preside, in your countries and in your dioceses, over important celebrations, not only for monks or cloistered nuns, but for the whole People of God entrusted to your care, as I myself have done at Nursia and Monte Cassino. But today, the choice of the place sanctified by St. Benedict—the *Sacro Speco*—and the makeup of your assembly highlight this celebration in an exceptional way.

A millennium and a half has passed since the birth of this great man, who merited in the past the title of Patriarch of the West, and who was called in our days, by Pope Paul VI, the Patron Saint of Europe. These titles already testify that the influence of his person and his work went beyond the frontiers of his country, nor was it limited to his Benedictine family. The latter, moreover, experienced a magnificent expansion, and a week ago its sons and daughters, coming from numerous countries and continents, met at Monte Cassino to venerate the memory of their common father and the founder of western monasticism.

Today, at Subiaco, it is the representatives of the European episcopates that are gathered to bear witness, in the presence of the bishops of the whole world meeting in synod, how deeply and organically St. Benedict of Nursia is integrated in the history of Europe, and in particular how much the societies and Churches of our continent owe to him, and how they turn their eyes at this critical time to him who has been designated by the Church as their common patron.

Consecrating Monte Cassino abbey, resurrected from the ruins of war, on October 24, 1964, Paul VI noted the two reasons which make the austere and sweet presence of St. Benedict always desired among us: "The Christian faith that he and his order preached in the family of peoples, especially in the family of Europe..., and the unity through which the great solitary and social monk taught us to be brothers and through which Europe was Christendom.... It was so that this ideal of the spiritual unity of Europe might be sacred and inviolable" that my venerated Predecessor that day proclaimed St. Benedict "Patron and Protector of Europe." And the solemn brief *Pacis nuntius* which consecrated this decision, recalling the merits of the holy abbot, "messenger of peace, maker of unity, master of civilization, herald of the religion of Christ and founder of monastic life in the West," reaffirmed that he and his sons "with the cross, the book, and the plough," brought "Christian progress to the populations stretching from the Mediterranean to Scandinavia, from Ireland to the plains of Poland."

THE SOLITUDE OF SUBIACO

2. St. Benedict was above all a man of God. He became so by following, constantly, the way of the virtues indicated in the Gospel. He was a real pilgrim of the kingdom of God. A real *homo viator*. And this pilgrimage was accompanied by a struggle that lasted all his life: a battle in the first place against himself, to combat the "old man" and make room more and more in himself for the "new man." The Lord permitted that, thanks to the Holy Spirit, this transformation should not be restricted to himself, but should become a source of influence, penetrating the history of men, penetrating above all the history of Europe.

Subiaco was and remains an important stage of this process. On the one hand, it was a place of retreat for St. Benedict of Nursia: he withdrew there at the age of fifteen in order to be closer to God. And at the same time a place that shows clearly what he is. His whole history will remain marked by this experience of Subiaco: solitude with God, austerity of life, and the sharing of this very simple life with some disciples, since it was there that he began a first organization of monastic life.

That is why I, too, have come with you to this high place of the *Sacro Speco* and of the first monastery.

THE MAN OF GOD

3. Benedict became a man of God by continually rereading the Gospel, not just for the purpose of getting to know it, but also of entirely expressing it in his whole life. It might be said that he reread it in depth—with the whole depth of his soul—and that he reread it in its fullness, in the dimension of the horizon he had before his eyes. This horizon was that of the ancient world which was on the point of dying, and that of the new world which was being born. In the depth of his soul as well as in the horizon of this world, he established the whole Gospel: the whole of what constitutes the Gospel, and at the same time each of its parts, each of the passages that the Church rereads in her liturgy, and even each sentence.

Yes, the man of God—*Benedictus*, the Blessed, Benedict—is penetrated with the whole simplicity of the truth contained in it. And he lives this Gospel. And living it, he evangelizes.

As a heritage, Paul VI has left us St. Benedict of Nursia as patron saint of Europe. What did he want to tell us by this? Above all, perhaps, that we must incessantly give ourselves up to expression of the Gospel, that we must express it completely and in our whole life. That we must reread it with the whole depth of our soul and in its full dimension, in the dimension of the world horizon we have before our eyes. The Second Vatican Council has firmly set the reality of the Church and her mission against the background of the world's horizon, which day by day becomes contemporary.

Europe is an essential part of this horizon. As the continent in which our countries are situated, it is for us a gift of Providence, which entrusted it to us at the same time as a work to be realized. We, as the Church, as pastors of the Church, must reread the Gospel and proclaim it in accordance with the tasks inherent in our age. We must reread it and preach it in accordance with the expectations which are continually manifested in the life of men and societies, and at the same time in accordance with the conflicts we meet with in their life. Christ never stops being "the expectation of peoples," nor does He ever stop being at the same time a "sign that is contradicted."

Yes, in the steps of St. Benedict, the task of the bishops of Europe is to undertake the work of evangelization in this modern world. Doing so, they refer to what was worked out and constructed fifteen centuries ago, to the spirit that inspired it, to the spiritual dynamism and hope that marked this initiative; but it is a work to be undertaken in a renewed way, at the cost of new efforts, related to the present-day context.

CHRISTIAN RESPONSIBILITY

4. It is in this framework of evangelization that the declaration of European bishops, which has just been read: "Responsibilities of Christians with regard to the Europe of today and tomorrow," takes on its whole meaning. This document, worked out in common, is an appreciable fruit of the collegial responsibility of the bishops of the European continent as a whole. It is, undoubtedly, the first time that the initiative has assumed such proportions. It is a question, as it were, of a document of the Catholic Church in Europe, which is represented, in a particular way, by the bishops, as pastors and teachers of faith. I joyfully hail this encouraging sign of a collegial responsibility which is progressing in Europe, of a better asserted unity among the episcopates. These episcopates are, in fact, in countries whose situations are very different, whether it is a question

of their social or economic systems, of the ideology of their states, or of the place of the Catholic Church—which now forms an unquestionable majority, now a small minority as compared with other Churches, or in a very secularized society. Trusting in the beneficial and stimulating character of exchanges and cooperation, as I have often said, I willingly encourage the pursuit of this collaboration, which is in keeping with the line of the Second Vatican Council. Moreover, it is not unconnected with the Benedictine and Cistercian practice of interdependence and cooperation between the various monasteries scattered throughout Europe.

In the declaration made public today and in this high place, you rightly express concern with a widened ecclesial unity. Europe is, in fact, the continent in which ecclesial divisions had their origin and were manifested in a sensational way. This means that the Churches in Europe—those descended from the Reformation, Orthodoxy, and the Catholic Church—hold a special responsibility on the way to unity, on the plane of mutual understanding, theological work, and prayer.

Likewise, with regard to the Catholic communities of other continents represented here, the Church of Europe must be characterized by mutual welcome, service, and exchange, in order to help these sister-Churches to find their own physiognomy, in the unity of faith, the sacraments, and the hierarchy.

In a word, it is a common testimony of your pastoral concern that you give today, dear brothers, that we give today, related to needs and expectations. I do not have to take up again here what is set forth abundantly in this common document. It is a question of marking out a way of evangelization for Europe, and of following it, with our faithful. It is a task to be continued and taken up again incessantly. Does not the next symposium of the bishops of Europe have as its theme "the self-evangelization of Europe"? And that brings us back to the great project, the peerless initiative of St. Benedict, certain specific characteristics of which have enormous human, social and spiritual consequences.

NEW PLEA FOR PEACE IN EUROPE

5. St. Benedict of Nursia became the spiritual patron of Europe because, like the prophet, he made the Gospel his food, and immediately tasted its sweetness and its bitterness. The Gospel constitutes, in fact, the whole truth about man: It is at once the Good News and at the same time the word of the cross. Through it we see the problem of the rich man and poor Lazarus—with which today's liturgy has familiarized us—come to life again, in different ways, as a historical drama and as a human and social problem. Europe has inscribed this problem in its history; it has taken it far beyond the frontiers of its continent. With it, it has sown restlessness in the whole world. Since the middle of our century, this problem has returned, in a way, to Europe; it is raised also in the life of its societies. It does not cease to be a source of tensions. It does not cease to be a source of threats.

I already spoke of these threats on the first day of the year, referring to this great anniversary of St. Benedict; I recalled, before the dangers of nuclear war that threaten the very existence of the world, that "the Benedictine spirit is a spirit of salvation and promotion, born from the awareness of the divine plan of salvation and reared in the daily union of prayer and work." It is "at opposite poles to any program of destruction whatsoever."

The pilgrimage we are carrying out today is, therefore, another great cry and a new plea for peace in Europe and in the whole world. We pray that the threats of self-destruction that the last generations have caused to rise on the horizon of their own lives may move away from all the peoples of our continent and all other continents. We pray that the threats of oppression of some by others may also move away: the threat of the destruction of men and peoples who, in the course of their historical struggles and at the cost of so many victims, have won the moral right to be themselves and to self-determination.

THE GOOD NEWS OF EQUALITY AND BROTHERHOOD

6. Whether it is a question of the world which, at the time of St. Benedict, was limited to ancient Europe, or of the world which, at the same time, was ready to be born, their horizon passed through the parable of the rich man and poor Lazarus. At the moment when the Gospel, the Good News of Christ, penetrated into antiquity, the latter bore the weight of the institution of slavery. Benedict of Nursia found on the horizon of his time the traditions of slavery, and at the same time he was rereading in the Gospel a disconcerting truth about the definitive readjustment of the fate of the rich man and Lazarus, in accordance with the order of the God of justice. And he was reading also the joyful truth about the brotherhood of all men. Right from the beginning, therefore, the Gospel was an appeal to go beyond slavery in the name of the equality of men in the eyes of the Creator and Father. In the name of the cross and redemption.

Was it not St. Benedict who put into practice, as a rule of life, this Good News of equality and brotherhood? He put it into practice not only as a rule of life for his monastic communities, but, even more, as a system of life for men and for peoples. *Ora et labora.* Work, in antiquity, was the lot of slaves, the sign of degradation. To be free meant not to work, and therefore to live on the work of others. The Benedictine revolution puts work at the very heart of man's dignity. The equalizing of men around work becomes, through work itself, a foundation, as it were, of the freedom of the sons of God, of freedom thanks to the climate of prayer in which work is lived. Here we indeed have a rule and a program. A program that consists of two elements. The dignity of work cannot be drawn, in fact, solely from material, economic criteria. It must mature in man's heart. And it can mature in depth only through prayer. For it is prayer—and not just the criteria of production and consumption—which tells humanity, finally, what working man is, he who works by the sweat of his brow and also with the toil of his mind and his hands. It tells us that he cannot be a slave, but that he is free. As St. Paul affirms: "He who was called in the Lord as a slave is a freedman of the Lord" (1 Cor. 7:22). And Paul, who did not think it unworthy of an Apostle to "labor, working with (his) own hands" (1 Cor. 4:12), is not afraid to show the Ephesians his own hands which provided for his needs and those of his companions (cf. Acts 20:34). It is in faith in Christ and in prayer that the worker discovers his dignity. It is again St. Paul who states: "God has sent the Spirit of his Son into our hearts, crying, 'Abba! Father!' So through God, you are no longer a slave but a son" (Gal. 4:6-7).

Have we not recently seen men who, before all Europe and the whole world, united the proclamation of the dignity of their work with prayer?

WORK AND PRAYER: THE MESSAGE OF FREEDOM

7. Benedict of Nursia, who through his prophetic action sought to bring Europe out of the sad traditions of slavery, seems therefore to speak, after fifteen centuries, to the many men and multiple societies that must be freed from the various contemporary forms of the oppression of man. Slavery weighs on the one who is oppressed, but also on the oppressor. Have we not, in the course of history, known powers, empires, which oppressed nations and peoples in the name of the even stronger slavery of the society of the oppressors? The watchword *ora et labora* is a message of freedom.

Moreover, is not this Benedictine message today, on the horizon of our world, an appeal to shake off the slavery of the consumer society, of a way of thinking and judging, of drawing up our programs and determining our whole lifestyle solely in terms of the economy?

The fundamental human values disappear in these programs. The dignity of life is systematically threatened. The family is threatened, that is, this essential mutual tie based on the trust of generations, which has its origin in the mystery of life and its fullness in the whole work of upbringing. It is also the whole spiritual heritage of nations and countries that is threatened.

Are we able to check all that? To reconstruct? Are we able to take the weight of coercion from the oppressed? Are we capable of convincing our world that the abuse of freedom is another form of coercion?

PATRON SAINT OF EUROPE

8. St. Benedict has been given to us—a patron saint of the Europe of our time, of our century—to testify that we are capable of doing all that.

We must just assimilate the Gospel again in the depths of our souls, in the framework of our present age. We must accept it as the truth and consume it as food. The way to salvation and restoration will then gradually be discovered, as in those distant times when the Lord of lords placed Benedict of Nursia, like a lamp on a stand, like a beacon on the road of history.

It is He, in fact, who is Lord of the whole history of the world; Jesus Christ who, though He was rich, became poor for our sake, so that by His poverty we might become rich (cf. 2 Cor. 8:9).

Honor and glory to Him forever!

St. Gerard—Monk, Apostle and Martyr

On the occasion of the celebrations of the millennium of the birth of St. Gerard, bishop and martyr, the Holy Father sent the Church in Hungary the following letter which was read on Sunday, September 28, 1980, during the solemn Eucharistic concelebration held in the metropolitan basilica of Esztergom.

To His Eminence, Cardinal Laszlo Lekai,
Archbishop of Esztergom,
to the archbishops, bishops and clergy,
to men and women religious,
and to all the faithful,

So soon after my last letter, I have the joy to be able to address you again, because of a happy occasion.

This year the universal Church celebrates the 1,500th anniversary of the birth of St. Benedict, the patriarch of Western monasticism, and the local Hungarian Church also commemorates in this same year the millennium of the birth of St. Gerard, bishop and martyr, one of the great sons of St. Benedict. A surprising coincidence of two anniversaries!

St. Gerard was a monk of the Venetian cloister of St. George, who was elected abbot when still young *(Legenda minor* and *Legenda major S. Gerhardi,* ed. E. Madzsar, *"Scriptores rerum Hungaricarum"* 2 [1938]).

From his biographies, the figure of St. Gerard appears to us in three successive forms typical of Christian life: as a monk, as an apostle, and as a martyr. The *monk* is the man of God who, in prayer and work, dedicates his life completely to God; the *apostle,* the proclaimer of the good news of salvation of the Gospel, who educates the Christian to holiness of life and leads the pagan to Christianity; the *martyr*, one who, as extreme testimony of his love, gives himself, his prayer life, and his apostolic activity completely to God.

St. Gerard was a man of God: a monk who followed the Rule of St. Benedict, dedicating his life to God in prayer and in work. In St. Benedict's Rule *(Szent Benedek Regulaja*, bilingual edition of D. Soveges, Pannonhalma, 1948) the criterion of the monastic vocation is whether the monk really seeks God, *si revera Deum quaerit* (chap. 58). The practical means of this search is to follow Christ without surrender or compromise along the way of monastic obedience. That is fitting—the Rule writes—for those *qui nihil sibi a Christi carius aliquid existimant* (who consider nothing more precious to themselves than Christ), who, precisely for this reason, follow Him in what is the most characteristic feature of His earthly life and which Christ Himself defined in this way: *"Non veni facere voluntatem meam, sed Eius qui misit me"* ("I have not come to do my own will but that of Him who sent me") (Rule 5; cf. Jn. 6:38).

Well, St. Gerard was a man of God because he dedicated his whole life to God with this intention of obedience, adopting what Christ had enunciated. How? The answer is clear and univocal: according to the dictates of the Rule, in the dual harmony of prayer and work.

St. Gerard, as a man of God, was a man of prayer, if we consider prayer in the monastic tradition as an organically connected triple union of *lectio, meditatio* and *contemplatio* (reading, meditation and contemplation). He willingly renounced the office of abbot to be able to move to the Holy Land in order to immerse himself there, following the example and the teaching of St. Jerome, in study of the Bible. Let it not be forgotten that this *lectio divina* (divine reading), that is, study of the Bible and of the biblical comments of the holy fathers, is not, according to monastic tradition, scientific research primarily, but—in the form both of community liturgy and of meditation—a source of prayer which leads to love and contemplation of God, to the perfection of interior prayer.

But interior prayer expands and grows in the soul only if it is continually nourished by the spiritual activity of *lectio divina*, and brings its fruits only if it leads to the daily accomplishment, to the living actions, of fraternal service. The double concept of prayer and work: this is Saint Gerard's form of life. His work was permeated by the spirit of prayer, and in his prayers he incessantly offered his laborious life to God.

The unity of prayer and work is an ideal that keeps its relevance even for the believer of our days. Modern society, founded on work and on the constant increase of economic production, must be able to find an adequate moral and spiritual motive in order not to become slaves of those forces which it succeeds in dominating with technique and with the commitment of work.

How is it possible to make work, even the humblest and most tiring work, worthy of man? Where is the spirit derived from, which confers moral strength on the worker and human value on work? St. Gerard teaches us what a source prayer is for all these things, because the praying man understands better than others what God's will is, and in prayer he also finds the strength to carry out what God wants.

The gradual formation of his apostolic personality deserves particular attention in St. Gerard's life. Divine Providence directed him in such a way that, ever more forgetful of himself, he became a man for others. In the first place, he had to renounce his journey to the Holy Land and his study plans, to do what he had never thought of: to work as the collaborator of King Stephen and tutor of Prince Emericus, to strengthen the young Hungarian Christian community. Later he had to sacrifice his solitude in Bacony Wood, to dedicate his strength, as a missionary bishop, to organizing the new diocese of Csanad.

St. Gerard, as monk and abbot, knew very well the two classical chapters of the Rule regarding the duties of the abbot (Rules 2 and 64). Both are permeated with the evangelical parable of the Good Shepherd, since St. Benedict considered the abbot the vicar of Christ, the Good Shepherd, in the monastery. The Rule points out above all in this connection that the abbot, before God, is responsible for those entrusted to him: *"Semper cogitet quia animas suscipit regendas, de quibus et rationem redditurus est."* ("Let him always be aware of the souls he must guide, of whom he will have also to give an account....") But he also stresses that the abbot must carry out his task as guide in a spirit of fraternal service: *"Sciat sibi oportere prodesse magis quam praeesse."* ("He must know that it is necessary to be of service rather than to be first.") This service must be guided by love stripped of personal preferences and adorned with a wise sense of moderation, which makes the abbot capable of adapting himself to the particular nature and degree of intelligence of those who are entrusted to him: *"Sciat quam difficilem et arduam rem suscipit, regere animas et multorum servire moribus."* ("He must know how difficult and hard it is to care for souls and to cope with the different characters.")

This spirit of the Good Shepherd, to which Saint Gerard, as monk and as abbot, had been educated by the Rule, also made him fit to become the counselor of King Stephen and the tutor of Prince Emericus.

In modern society, as in any other time, is it not a blessing to have such counselors and such tutors who, whether they are ecclesiastics or laymen, are aware of their responsibility not only before men, but also before God, and concern themselves with the destiny of the people and particularly with the education and guidance of youth, with that spirit which, following the principles of brotherly love and wise moderation, dedicates them generously to service of the community? Is not Christ, who did not come to reign, but to serve and to sacrifice His own life for the good of mankind, an admirable example for all times? (cf. Mt. 20:28)

For this spirit to be formed not only in the conscience of those who have responsibility, but also in the conscience of every member of the Church and society, and for it to become increasingly operative, knowledge of Christian doctrine is necessary. In my letter, sent to you all on Easter day of this year, I recalled the essential importance of catechesis for the formation of Christians in our time, and that not only for children and for the young, but also, and above all, for adults. It is Christian doctrine that forms the spirit of the Good Shepherd necessary for those who feel called to renew the Church and society.

This spirit conferred on St. Gerard also the strength to assume—renouncing his solitude in Bacony Wood—the missionary work of organizing the diocese of Csanad. His sacrifice reminds us of the words of St. Martin, born in Pannonia over half a millennium before, a monk and bishop in Gallia. On his deathbed, when his disciples implored him not to abandon them, the holy bishop addressed Christ with the following words: *"Domine, si adhuc populo tuo sum necessarius, non recuso laborem: fiat voluntas tua."* ("Lord, if I am still necessary to Your people, I do not refuse to work: may Your will be done.") St. Gerard shows a similar readiness for sacrifice, deriving from the sentiment of brotherly responsibility and the spirit of service.

The missionary bishop set to work with twelve monks, chosen from Hungarian convents, which were blossoming—four of whom were called from St. Martin's monastery on Mount Pannonia, the present Pannonhalma. In Csanad they not only erected the cathedral and the convent church in honor of the Blessed Virgin, but they also organized a school, intended particularly for the education of the future generation of priests and monks.

What is particularly interesting for modern man is the method of missionary activity: that is, that it should not remain superficial and exterior, but lead to real conversion, that is, to the interior spiritual change which is called *metanoia* in the Gospel. One chapter of *Deliberatio* bears witness to what the spirit of St. Gerard's missionary activity was. Explaining the verse *"Aperiatur terra et germinet salvatorem"* ("Let the earth open and salvation bud forth") of Isaiah (45:8), he writes: *"Vis audire quomodo aperta exstitit haec terra ad germen rorantibus coelis et pluentibus nubibus?... Ait (Scriptura): Poenitentiam agite et baptizetur unusquisque vestrum in nomine Domini Iesu Christi, in remissione pecnum Spiritus Sancti.... Sic aperta est catorum vestrorum et accipietis donum Spiritus Sancti.... Sic aperta est terra, atque tali aperitione germinavit salvatorem, id est praedicavit Christum suum redemptorem ad omnes gentes. Quando doceo gentiles et Christum nescientes, et ipsi veniunt ad divinam perceptionem, audito verbo ex ratione, verbo et fide germino illis Christum...suo itaque verbo et fide germinatur Christus ad illum confluentibus...."* ("Do you wish to hear how this earth lies open to the bud dropped down by the heavens and raised by the clouds? [Scripture] says: do penance and be baptized, every one of you, in the name of Jesus Christ, for the remission of sins, and you will receive the gift of the Holy Spirit.... Thus the earth has opened and from this opening has budded forth the Savior, that is, it preached its Redeemer, Christ, to all nations. When I teach the Gentiles and those who do not know Christ, and they themselves come to the perception of the divine, having heard the word in their mind, I generate Christ in them by word and faith.... Thus, by word and faith Christ is begotten in those who come to Him.") *(Gerardi Morosense Ecclesiae seu Csanadensis Episcopi Deliberatio supra hymnum trium puerorum, VII, 583 sqq., ed. G. Silagi, Corp. Christ., Cont. Mediaevalis 49, Turnholti 1978)*

Is this not the missionary method that we must adopt today too, if we wish to bring the peoples to Christ? Christ must first be born in souls, in order that the Church as the community of faithful may be born again from within. It is unquestionable, in fact, that—as the Second Vatican

Ecumenical Council teaches (LG 8)—the Church is a "community of faith, hope and charity"; but her mission is not only to live Christ's salvation in faith, hope and charity, but also to be the mediator of this salvation and, through Christ, "to spread truth and grace to all."

With his life, St. Gerard bore a witness of assiduous service to evangelization. He did not seek to proclaim his own ideas, but the Good News of Christ. He also realized that an orderly ecclesial community can come into being only in this way: by seeking communion with Christ and offering one's own life in the service of brothers. The communion lived with Christ and with brothers reveals the true meaning of the institution of the Church: to lead to communion by means of faith in a God who is Love and who is close to us. St. Gerard dedicated his energies to organizing the Church—the newborn local community—by inserting its roots in the universal community, that is, the Church of Christ. This unity, the source of life and faith, is the indispensable condition for fruitful evangelization; and we, too, must love and serve our earthly country, its culture and its values, always loving and serving God. Has the Hungarian Church a more important task than that of following the apostolic spirit in the footsteps of the example and teaching of its great apostle?

Martyrdom crowned this life dedicated to God in prayer and apostolic activity. The events are well known: Bishop Gerard, when he was going from Székesfehérvar to Buda to welcome King Endre and lay in trusted hands the heritage of St. Stephen—that is, the destiny of the young Hungarian Christian community—was killed by a group of pagan rebels. This martyrdom was the extreme testimony of St. Gerard's love for his new country, for his new people. *"Maiorem hac dilectionem nemo habet, ut animam suam ponat quis pro amicis suis."* ("There is no greater love than this: to lay down one's life for one's friends.") (Jn. 15:13) Martyrdom, in the Greek language from which the word came to us, means precisely "witness."

If it is true that the task of the Christian today is to bring about the interior harmony of prayer and work, and cause the apostolic spirit dedicated to others to develop, it is also true that all will have credit and power in the eyes of men only if we bear witness to our conviction with our whole life, lived and, if necessary, offered for brothers. The example and supreme teaching of St. Gerard the Martyr is that we, with the complete dedication of our talent, our strength, our commitment, should bear witness to the truth in which we believe and which we profess. *"Accipietis virtutem supervenientis Spiritus Sancti in vos, et eritis mihi testes"* ("You will receive power when the Holy Spirit comes down on you; then you are to be my witnesses") (Acts 1:8): this is the testament of Christ who is returning to the Father.

The monument to St. Gerard—the monk, the apostle and the martyr—rises in the center of your capital, over the Danube, and, with the crucifix raised aloft, he still exhorts you today: Be witnesses to faith in Christ and to the brotherly love which is distinctive of Christianity, in the midst of your people!

May the Spirit of Christ give you strength, through the powerful intercession of the Blessed Virgin, *Magna Domina Hungarorum.*

With my special apostolic blessing.

From the Vatican, September 24, 1980, Feast of Saint Gerard, Bishop and Martyr.

Living in the Church
an Experience of Real Brotherhood

On October 5, 1980, the Holy Father met with the bishops, priests, religious, seminarians and novices of Apulia, in the Cathedral-Basilica of Santa Maria dell'Annunziata. The Pope gave the following talk to these "collaborators" of the bishops.

Venerated brothers in the episcopate,

Beloved priests, men and women religious and you, seminarians of this beloved archdiocese and of the whole Apulian Region.

1. There is a word of the Apostle Paul which very well expresses the sentiments that welled up in me when I thought of this meeting, and that now fill my heart as I look at your faces and hear your voices: "I thank my God in all my remembrance of you, always in every prayer of mine for you all, making my prayer with joy, thankful for your partnership in the gospel from the first day until now. And I am sure that he who began a good work in you will bring it to completion at the day of Jesus Christ" (Phil. 1:3-6).

Yes, beloved brothers and sisters, I am grateful first and foremost to God for what He is carrying out in your lives, by means of the enlightened and wise action of His Spirit; and I am also grateful to all of you for the generous readiness with which, responding to the urgings of divine love, you put your intellectual, moral and physical energies in the service of the cause of the Gospel.

HISTORICAL BASILICA

2. Our meeting takes place in the inspiring setting of this ancient basilica, which has seen so much history pass by under its airy and solemn vaults. If there is a work capable of expressing in a harmonious synthesis the deep spirituality, the kindheartedness, and the creative vigor of

the people of Otranto, it is certainly the cathedral, over whose architectural structures our admiring glance passes at this moment.

The succession of the slim, slender columns; the majestic perspectives of the arches; the solemn grandeur of the vaults; the wave of light which pours from the windows and central rose-window upon the impressive floor mosaic—everything merges into a harmonious poem of faith and beauty. It is a poem that believers, at the beginning of this millennium, entrusted to future generations, immortalizing in stone their certainties and their hopes.

We Christians of the last part of the millennium are called to interpret this poem, to gather the message of those ancestors of ours in faith, and to express its perennial richness in the ways of life characteristic of our time. It is a message which challenges everyone, but which expects to be listened to and understood especially by those who, because of direct participation in Christ's priesthood or the formal profession of the evangelical counsels, have had a more intimate and deeper experience of the new life which redemption brought into the history of the world.

MOSAIC MASTERPIECE

3. The inhabitants of this land wanted this basilica to be majestic and solemn, because it was to be the cathedral church, that is, the sacred place in which the Archbishop would have his chair as teacher and pastor. They would come here to listen to the proclamation of the eternal Word of the Gospel; they would receive here the necessary instruction on the mysteries of the kingdom; and the truths capable of guiding life and illuminating death would be illustrated to them here in an authoritative way.

Is it not this very function of the cathedral that we see emphasized and exalted in that extraordinary masterpiece of the floor mosaic? In it, the whole of human life, in its joys and its sorrows, its outbursts of generosity and its falling back into selfishness, in its quiet passing amid agricultural and domestic activities, as well as in its sudden clash with the dark shadow of evil and death, the whole of human life—I say—comes into the Church to ask divine Revelation for a word that will interpret it, clarify it, direct it, and comfort it.

And the mosaic work develops the answer in the images of the original temptation and the fall, of the fatal consequences of sin and of the prophetic announcements of redemption: here is Noah's ark, the symbol of the Church; here is the lion of Judah, the symbol of Christ. Man is recalled to the responsibility of a choice: before him are good and evil, virtue and vice. He can abandon himself to the drive of passions, ending up a slave to them in brutishness, of which the vast sample of beasts in the mosaic offers an impressive illustration. Or he can, on the contrary, commit himself in the struggle for good, imitating the just of the Old and New Testaments and straining, like a running stag, towards the Promised Land, which is represented as a marvelous garden.

This is, substantially, the catechetical discourse carried out by that kind of "encyclopedia in images" that your magnificent mosaic is. It is interesting to point out that it was desired by the Archbishop of Otranto of that time, Gionata, and it was realized, with the generous contribution of all the faithful, by a priest-monk, Pantaleone. Is there not in all this a reminder of the importance of catechesis and of the commitment that bishops, priests and religious must dedicate to it? This is what the Christian people expect, in the first place, from their priests and from those who have a more intimate experience of God and His transcendent mystery: that they should be teachers of truth; not of their own truth or that of some other sage of this world, but of the truth that God revealed to us in Christ.

I am happy to recall here what I wrote in this connection in the Apostolic Exhortation *Catechesi tradendae:* "As the twentieth century draws to a close, the Church is bidden by God and by events—each of them a call from

Him—to renew her trust in catechetical activity as a prime aspect of her mission. She is bidden to offer catechesis her best resources in people and energy, without sparing effort, toil, or material means, in order to organize it better and to train qualified personnel. This is no mere human calculation; it is an attitude of faith. And an attitude of faith always has reference to the faithfulness of God, who never fails to respond" (no. 15).

GLORIOUS MONASTIC TRADITIONS

4. Another thought certainly guided your ancestors in the construction of this temple, which they wanted to be luminous and beautiful: the thought that there was to take place here liturgical worship, in which the community, under the guidance of the priests, would meet God and would dialogue with Him. The land of Otranto had centuries of glorious monastic traditions behind it when it set to work on this task: Alongside forms of eremitical life, there had flourished in it little communities of monks *(esichie)* and larger convents *(laure)*, among which the Monastery of St. Nicholas in Casole had a position of pre-eminence for centuries.

How could I fail to recall the testimony left to us in this connection by St. Paulinus of Nola, who, addressing his friend Niceta, Bishop of Remesina in Dacia in a poem of his, describes to him the welcome he would be given on passing through these lands? "When you pass through Otranto and Lecce, virginal hosts of brothers and sisters will surround you, singing to the Lord with one voice" (Poem VII, vv. 85-92: PL 61, 485).

Innubae fratrum simul et sororum catervae (virginal hosts of brothers and sisters) already populated this region, therefore, in those distant centuries, and with the example of their devotion they taught the people of the surrounding area to sing praises to the Lord. They are glorious traditions to which you, consecrated souls of today, must continue to look, in order to draw inspiration and incentive in your commitment of complete surrender to Christ and to the Church.

You must refer to those traditions, in particular, to learn to love the divine liturgy more and more intensely, to assimilate its inexhaustible riches with growing understanding, and to celebrate its various moments with shining faith and joyful fervor. The people expects this of you. For this reason, in fact, it built the marvelous cathedral in which we are gathered. From your words, your songs, and your whole attitude during the celebration of the Divine Mysteries, Christians expect to be able to have, to some extent, experience of the fascinating and tremendous reality of God, three times holy.

Let it be your care to surround with particularly eager attentions the great "Mystery of Faith": the Eucharist, in fact, if it has been given to all believers in Christ, "has been entrusted to us also for others, who expect from us a particular witness of veneration and love towards this sacrament, so that they too may be able to be built up and vivified 'to offer spiritual sacrifice' " (Letter of the Supreme Pontiff, Pope John Paul II, on the Mystery and Worship of the Holy Eucharist, no. 2).

TO COMFORT ONE ANOTHER

5. Among the reasons that drove your ancestors to build this vast and gracious temple, we could not omit one, to which I finally wish to call your attention: those ancient Christians wished to construct, in this basilica, an environment in which they, and then their children and their children's children, could gather on the Lord's Day to feel they were a "Church" and comfort one another, along the tormented ways of time, by means of confession of the same faith and the foretaste, in hope, of the same goods promised.

The Church is the house in which the family of the children of God gathers, to strengthen the bonds of brotherly communion, overcoming possible tensions, granting the necessary forgiveness, offering each one the spiritual or material aid that he needs. The Church is the place in which the individual, whatever his social extraction may be, must be able to live an experience of real brotherhood.

From this point of view, too, your land has significant traditions. The geographical position of Otranto, which makes it a bridgehead, as it were, towards the East, has stimulated in the course of the centuries an intense exchange with those regions, determining the meeting and the fusion of different races and cultures. The Church was able to take her place in this cosmopolitan world, gathering and strengthening its universal aspiration, so congenial with the catholicity of her mission. The monasteries of this area, the churches scattered in the territory, the cathedral itself, were as many very special meeting points between Orthodox and Latin thought, between the Greek and the Roman Liturgy, as also between the men on one shore of the strait and those on the other. Here, under God's eyes, persons who spoke different languages and belonged to cultures distant from one another, were able to feel united in brotherhood in invocation of the one Father, revealed in history through the Incarnation of the Son, the "mediator between God and men, the man Christ Jesus" (1 Tm. 2:5).

These are exalting historical testimonies, which must continue to inspire the activity of the present Church of Otranto. You priests, you religious, must be guides and models of this commitment of communion in charity—you who have grown up in the bed of these noble traditions and have been nourished on the teachings and examples of those pioneers. It is your task to repropose, in words and with your lives, in the context of the present generation, the eternal message of a love which, in Christ, can open to accept every human being, to make room for him at the table on which the one Bread is broken (cf. 1 Cor. 10:16-17).

THROUGH THE INTERCESSION OF MARY

6. Beloved children, in order that the joy of this meeting may last and be expressed in fruitful results of apostolic commitment, I entrust your good resolutions to the intercession of the Blessed Virgin, whose sweet image —respected even in the 1480 invasion—has remained on the walls of the cathedral. May our Lady watch over you and over what you do in the service of the kingdom of her divine Son. And may she also grant that numerous vocations may spring from this land, bathed by the blood of so many martyrs, so that the new generations will not lack courageous and inspired pastors who are able to point out, in the changed situations of the present, the way that leads to Christ, to Him who "is the same yesterday and today and for ever" (Heb. 13:8).

With these wishes, while I renew to you the testimony of my sincere affection, I impart to you all a special apostolic blessing.

Work with Enthusiasm for the Spread of God's Kingdom

On October 7, 1980, the Holy Father received in audience the bishops of the Chaldean Rite on their visit ad limina Apostolorum, *led by the Patriarch of the Chaldeans of Babylon. His Beatitude, Paul II Cheikho. John Paul II delivered the following address.*

Your Beatitude and venerable brothers,

To receive you on the occasion of your visit to the tombs of the Apostles is a deep joy for me. It was, in fact, in this illustrious city of Rome that the Prince of Apostles shed his blood. And his martyrdom made this same city the See of the Church which presides over charity and the chair of truth destined to strengthen our brothers.

We want this meeting to be a moment blessed by the Lord to express to Your Beatitude and to the bishops of the Chaldean Church my sentiments of satisfaction for your ardor in spreading God's Word, and for your pastoral zeal in the service of the Christian communities that are entrusted to you.

I am certain that, returning to your dioceses, which are more than ever awaiting your presence and your affectionate devotion, in view of the circumstances, you will work with new enthusiasm for the spread of God's kingdom, which is a kingdom of love and of peace.

Your fundamental concern will certainly be to encourage your Church to bear a resolute and faithful Christian witness. For this purpose, the desired reform of the liturgy, to be carried out according to the indications of the Holy See in view of stimulating a greater participation of the faithful in the celebration of the Divine Mysteries, will certainly be useful.

This work, venerable brothers, concerns you in the first place, as well as your diligent collaborators, the priests engaged in the pastoral service of Christian communities, so that God may be worshiped in an agreeable way, and that esteem and love of heavenly things may be communicated to souls.

I hope that the Lord will bless you, by granting you more and more numerous vocations which, consequently, will demand of you a permanent obligation to watch over their adequate spiritual and intellectual formation.

It is a pleasure for me to stress also the presence of and the work carried out by the religious congregations. It is thanks to them that the ideal of evangelical perfection shines forth for the honor and service of the Chaldean Church. To men and women religious, I express my joy and my encouragement to go further and further in their life of piety and charity, in conformity with the norms given by the Second Vatican Council and with the new pastoral requirements. Let them endeavor to bring about their "updating" judiciously and qualitatively, in order to reach a real renewal of spiritual life and better integration in pastoral activities, in harmony with the particular character of each institute, and under the enlightened guidance of the hierarchy.

May today's meeting with you all—a visibly collegial meeting round the Vicar of Christ—be an incentive to live your pastoral work together, whatever may be the country in which you have the mission to carry it out. The Holy See appreciates these meetings on the national plane, in the form of assemblies or of episcopal conferences, even among different rites. They correspond, in fact, to the directives of the Second Vatican Council and are an effective and practically indispensable instrument, if we want to guarantee unity of action among several countries and maintain harmony and brotherly understanding among the different rites "in bonds of peace." And all that can be done without interfering in any way with the assignments of the Patriarch and his synod.

Finally I wish to take the opportunity to assure you that the Holy See will make every possible effort to procure a more appropriate assistance for the faithful of Oriental rites who are at present scattered all over the world.

To you, Your Beatitude, and dear brothers in the episcopate, to you priests, men and women religious, and all of you, faithful of the Chaldean Church, I renew the assurance of my deep affection and impart a fatherly apostolic blessing.

Bear Witness to the Church as Expert Pastors

On October 9, 1980, the Holy Father received in audience participants in the First World Meeting of Chaplains General, which took place in Rome under the presidency of the Prefect of the Sacred Congregation for Bishops, Cardinal Sebastiano Baggio. John Paul II delivered the following address.

Dear brothers,

The International Congresses of the Military, in particular those which take place in Lourdes every year, have already stood the test of experience. But it is, I think, the first time that chaplains general have gathered from the various countries and continents. I was anxious to take the time to greet you, congratulate you on your initiative, and encourage you.

You have to pool experiences—different ones, it is true, but parallel—to compare the precise problems which arise for you, and what all of you undertake to cope with them. In this way the major questions will emerge, and you will try to study them more deeply in order to illuminate the ways of your ministry.

Certain fundamental questions of an ethical character will certainly emerge around, for example, the legitimacy of certain methods of defense, the notion of a "just" war in today's context, and the threat of the use of nuclear arms— of which I myself have spoken earnestly on several occasions—or other armaments of great power, the more and more frequent question of conscientious objection, etc. You are evidently placed in a position in which these problems assume greater acuteness. Theoretical questions, apparently, for the solution is not in the hands of military chaplains; but important questions which concern you, for you have a special part in the formation of the conscience of soldiers and of public opinion; you have witness to bear to the Church, as pastors specialized in these difficult problems.

I think, however, that the essential part of your brotherly discussions must deal with spiritual assistance for the soldiers: that is your *raison d'être*. What an immense field! What a complex task!

You are responsible, on the one hand, for regular soldiers and their families. In spite of their rather frequent changes, it is a relatively stable environment. You are not their only reference point in the Church: they have their parishes and various Christian associations. But you are, in a special way, their pastors, the confidants of their life, and the priests who can often help them best in their sacramental and apostolic life.

You are entrusted, on the other hand, with all the young soldiers of the contingent who are fulfilling their military service. The period they serve with the colors is of great importance in their evolution, even if they themselves often think that it must be an interruption without relevance to their family and professional life. When it is realized that nearly all young men pass through this experience, your ministry takes on considerable urgency. You are placed at the crossroads of the life of the new generations. For youths who were supported up to then by a traditionally Christian environment, this time is generally a test: the test of their freedom, on the spiritual and moral plane, the balance of which may be an abandonment of religious practice and faith, but also an appreciable maturing of their convictions. For others, it is a new opportunity to meet the Church, Christians, a chaplain. Their stay in barracks is more limited than formerly, and often it no longer includes Sunday. But social workers and all those who collaborate with them may contrive to bring them other opportunities to reflect, to pray, and to open to the needs of others. May the time of military service become more and more, thanks to your contribution, an additional and original time of human and spiritual preparation for life! Here the priestly, apostolic zeal of each of your chaplains plays an essential part. You would like, of course, to see them more numerous. Support their difficult ministry well, help them like brothers, encourage them to surround themselves with Christian laymen whose witness is indispensable, and to set their efforts well within the framework of the Church, in harmony with the complementary ministry of other pastors.

But I will stop here, for these are questions that you have already discussed, or will discuss precisely. May the Lord strengthen your hope! I pray to Him to make your apostolate fruitful, and I willingly bless you, dear brothers—you and those who collaborate with you in your different countries.

Heirs of Authentic Missionaries

On October 10, 1980, the bishops from Burma paid their ad limina *visit to the Holy Father. The following is the text of the Pope's message to them.*

Dear brothers in the episcopate,

It is a great joy for me, as Successor of Peter in the See of Rome, to welcome you, my brother bishops from Burma, and to embrace you in the charity of Jesus Christ, the eternal and incarnate Word of God.

1. On this *ad limina* visit of yours, you come as the ordinaries of four local Churches: Mandalay, Myitkyina, Bassein and Kengtung. You come likewise as representatives of all the bishops of Burma serving the entire Catholic people throughout your land. I greet you, therefore, with great respect and friendship, with deep esteem and love. I greet you as collaborators in the Gospel, as bishops of the Church of God, who are united with me and all the members of the episcopal college in the bonds of faith and charity, and who are called to exercise together —according to each one's role—responsibility for the universal Church.

2. I greet you as the spiritual heirs of authentic and generous missionaries, who worked patiently and perseveringly so that the Gospel would become incarnate in the

culture of your people and transform their lives by its own ennobling originality. In you the Church authenticates the labors of the missionaries, renders homage to their sacrifices, and perpetuates their memory. I greet you as spiritual leaders of the faithful, many of whom have demonstrated and exercised heroism in the Catholic Faith, thus giving a splendid witness to Jesus Christ and His Gospel.

3. This is truly an hour of thanksgiving. Together we express our gratitude to the the most Holy Trinity for the blessings bestowed upon your people, for the graces that have touched their lives. Through Jesus Christ we give thanks that the Word of God took root in the hearts of your ancestors and brought forth fruits of justice and holiness of life in generation after generation. We give thanks for the great gift of perseverance that has characterized the lives of so many individuals and communities.

We praise the power of the Paschal Mystery which could alone guarantee fidelity to Christ and His Church, which has been and remains an unquestioned reality in your Christian experience. Despite difficulties of various kinds, despite obstacles from various sources, despite the unchanging exigencies of the Gospel—before which human nature instinctively recoils in every age—the grace of Jesus Christ has repeatedly conquered human hearts and sustained the efforts of so many of the faithful who zealously endeavor to put on Christ and to follow in His footsteps.

Through the action of the Holy Spirit, Christ's death and resurrection have effected growth among your people: young people have responded to vocations to the priesthood and religious life; many of the laity have understood their Christian dignity and enthusiastically embraced their mission; catechists have helped to make the Church ever more an evangelized and evangelizing community. All of this, venerable brothers, is owing to the grace of Christ, who in each age must be recognized and proclaimed as the Redeemer of man and the Savior of the world.

4. Our meeting is likewise an hour of renewal. At the tombs of the Apostles Peter and Paul we are challenged to rededicate ourselves to the Gospel and to its integral and faithful proclamation. We are called in our own lives to embrace anew the Word of God with all its demands and propose it confidently and consistently to our people in the name of Him who was known as a "sign of contradiction" (Lk. 2:34) and who once said: "The gate is narrow and the way is hard that lead to life" (Mt. 7:14).

Ours is also a rededication to the pastoral office which we exercise in the name of the Good Shepherd. As bishops we are called to make visible and attractive in ourselves the selfless, sacrificing and compassionate love of Jesus for His people. Only in intimacy with Jesus will we find the inner force to persevere in genuine concern for all our brothers and sisters. Only through holiness of life will we be relevant ministers and representatives of a loving Christ.

5. This is an hour of thanksgiving and renewal; it is also an hour of hope!

Because the Spirit of God has been poured out in our hearts and because the final destiny of the Church is in the hands of Jesus, we are sustained by a great hope. Our hope is that each community of the faithful in Burma, gathered together in the power of God's Word and made strong by Christ's sacraments, may ever more effectively fulfill its evangelizing mission and serve in the cause of human advancement. In brief, that all the faithful will relate to their neighbors as Jesus did to His, as Jesus wants us to do to ours. Dear brothers, the words of St. Paul confirm us in our hope today: "For to this end we toil and strive, because we have set our hope on the living God" (1 Tm. 4:10).

And from this gift of hope implanted in your hearts may there spring up, in each one of you and in your brother bishops at home, a new trust in Christ, a new assuredness in your pastoral ministry—a trust and assuredness that are alien to every form of human complacency, but which derive from confidence in Christ and His word, and are strong in the promise of Jesus, who says *"Ecce ego vobiscum sum"* (Mt. 28:20).

6. In this spirit of thanksgiving and renewal, with this fresh hope and trust, I ask you to take my greetings to all the beloved faithful of Burma. To the clergy, to the men and women religious, to the seminarians and catechists, and to all who make up the ranks of the Catholic laity, I send my apostolic blessing, with the assurance of my prayers, especially for the sick and suffering, for those afflicted by loneliness and sorrow. And to all your non-Christian brethren, particularly to the members of the Buddhist communities, with whom you are called to live and work together, as well as to the authorities of the state, I offer my cordial and respectful greetings.

And to you, my dear brothers in the episcopate: "Grace, mercy and peace from God the Father and Christ Jesus our Lord" (1 Tm. 1:2).

The Spiritual Tragedy of Our Times

On October 10, 1980, the Holy Father received in audience participants in the International Congress on the subject: "Evangelization and Atheism," sponsored by the Superior Institute for the study of atheism of the Pontifical Urban University. The group was led by Cardinal Agnelo Rossi, Prefect of the Sacred Congregation for the Evangelization of Peoples and Chancellor of the Urban University. John Paul II delivered the following address.

Your Eminence,
Your Excellencies,
Dear brothers and sisters,

1. Thank you for your words. As can easily be seen, atheism is unquestionably one of the major phenomena, and it must even be said, the spiritual tragedy of our times.[1]

Intoxicated by the whirl of his discoveries, assured of apparently unlimited scientific and technical progress, modern man finds himself inexorably confronted by his destiny: "What is the good of going to the moon—according to the expression of one of the most outstanding men of culture of our age—if it is in order to commit suicide?"[2]

What is life? What is love? What is death? Ever since there have been thinking men, these fundamental questions have continually inhabited their spirit. For millennia, the great religions have tried to bring their answers. Did not man himself appear, to the penetrating gaze of philosophers, as being, inseparately, *homo faber, homo ludens, homo sapiens, homo religiosus?* And is it not to that man that the Church of Jesus Christ intends to propose the Good News of salvation, bringing hope for all, through the ebb and flow of generations and civilizations?

A MASS PHENOMENON

2. But lo, in a gigantic challenge, modern man, since the Renaissance, has risen against this message of salvation, and has begun to reject God in the very name of his dignity as a man. At first reserved for a small group of souls, the intelligentsia which considered itself an elite, atheism has become today a mass phenomenon which besieges the Churches. What is more, it penetrates them from the inside, as if believers themselves, including those who claim to follow Jesus Christ, found in themselves a secret intrigue that destroyed their faith in God, in the name of man's autonomy and dignity. It is a question of a "true secularism," according to Paul VI's expression in his Apostolic Exhortation *Evangelii nuntiandi:* "a concept of the world according to which the latter is self-explanatory, without any need for recourse to God, who thus becomes superfluous and an encumbrance. This sort of secularism, in order to recognize the power of man, therefore ends up by doing without God and even by denying Him."[3]

FACE UP COURAGEOUSLY

3. Such is the spiritual tragedy of our time. The Church cannot resign herself to it. She intends, on the con-

trary, to face up to it courageously. For the Council wished to be in the service of man, not abstract man, considered as a theoretical entity, but concrete, existential man, at grips with his questions and his hopes, his doubts and his very denials. It is to that man that the Church proposes the Gospel. So he must know it, with that knowledge rooted in love, which opens to dialogue in clarity and trust between men separated by their convictions, but convergent in the same love of man.

"Lay and profane humanism," Paul VI said at the closing of the Council, "has appeared in its terrible stature and, in a way, has challenged the Council. The religion of God who became man has met the religion—for it is one—of man who becomes God. What has happened? A clash, a struggle, an anathema? That could have happened, but it did not take place. The old story of the Samaritan has been the model of the spirituality of the Council."[4]

I myself, at the tribune of the United Nations in New York, on October 2, 1979, expressed this wish: "The confrontation between the religious view of the world and the agnostic or even atheistic view, which is one of the 'signs of the times' of the present age, could preserve honest and respectful human dimensions without violating the essential rights of conscience of any man or woman living on earth."[5]

Such is the conviction of our full humanism, which brings us to meet even those who do not share our faith in God, in the name of their faith in man—and that is the tragic misunderstanding to dispel. We want to say to all of them fervently: we too, as much and more so than you, if it is possible, have respect for man. So we want to help you to discover and share with us the joyful news of God's love, this God who is the source and the foundation of the greatness of man, himself a son of God, and who became our brother in Jesus Christ.

EMINENT PARTICIPANTS

4. This tells you, dear friends, how much I rejoice in these study days which bring you together in Rome, at the Pontifical Urban University, under the auspices of the Superior Institute for the study of atheism, the sponsor of your International Congress on *Evangelization and Atheism.*

With great interest, I examined the program you sent me. And I noted with pleasure the presence of eminent professors and scholars, whom I am happy to welcome here. Actually, it almost makes one feel dizzy to discover the vastness of the field considered, and the lines of research you have laid out on it: the phenomenological, historical, philosophical and theological aspects of contemporary atheism.

The phenomenon, in fact, is invading us on all sides: from the East to the West, from socialist to capitalist countries, from the world of culture to that of work. None of the ages of life escape it—from young adolescence, a prey to doubt, to skeptical old age, passing through the suspicions and rejections of adulthood. And there is no continent that has been spared.

That was what led my Predecessor Paul VI, of venerated memory, to erect within the Roman Curia, alongside the Secretariats for the Unity of Christians and for non-Christians, another organism dedicated by vocation to the study of atheism and to dialogue with non-believers.[6] It must, in fact, be clear to the eyes of all that the Church wishes to be in dialogue with all, including those who have become alienated from her and reject her, both in their affirmed and resolute convictions, and in their decided and sometimes militant behavior. Both, moreover, are closely intermingled. Motivations bring forth action. And action, in its turn, molds thought.

FOR DIFFERENT REASONS

5. So it is with gratitude that I welcome your reflections, to integrate them in the pastoral action of the

Church in the direction of those who, for different reasons and in many ways, it is true, more or less follow the diversiform atheism of our time. What is there apparently in common, in fact, between countries in which theoretical atheism, it could be said, is in power, and others, on the contrary, whose professed ideological neutrality covers up a real practical atheism? Without any doubt, the conviction that man is, alone, the totality of man.[7]

Certainly, the psalmist has already repeated: "The fool says in his heart, 'There is no God.' "[8] And atheism does not date from today. But it was reserved, as it were, for our time to carry out a systematic theorization of it, wrongly claimed to be scientific, and to put it into practice on the scale of human groups and even of important countries.

CHURCH'S CHALLENGE

6. And yet (how could we fail to recognize it with admiration), man resists before these repeated attacks and this crossfire of atheism in its pragmatic, neopositivistic, psychoanalytical, existentialist, Marxist, structuralist, and Nietzschean forms. The penetration of customs and the breaking down of doctrines do not prevent, but rather sometimes even bring forth, at the very heart of regimes that are officially atheistic, as within the so-called consumer societies, an undeniable religious awakening. In this situation of conflict, it is a real challenge that the Church must face, and a gigantic task that she must carry out, for which she needs the collaboration of all her children: to bring about the re-acculturation of faith in the various cultural spheres of our time, and re-incarnate the values of Christian humanism.

Is this not a pressing request of the men of our time who, sometimes desperately and groping their way, seek the meaning of meaning—the ultimate meaning? In spite of their differences of origin and orientation, modern ideologies meet at the crossroads of man's self-sufficiency, without any of them succeeding in quenching the thirst for the absolute which tortures him. For "man infinitely transcends man," as Pascal noted in his *Pensées*. That is why, from his overflowing certainties, as from the trough of his questions, there always springs up again the search for this Infinite, whose image he cannot erase within him, even when he flees it: "You were within me. And I, I was outside myself," St. Augustine already confessed.[9]

DIALOGUE OF SALVATION

7. In his Encyclical *Ecclesiam suam*, Paul VI questioned himself about this phenomenon, and saw in it the way of a dialogue of salvation: "The reasons of atheism, imbued with anxiety, colored with passion and utopia, but often generous too, inspired by a dream of justice and progress, straining towards divinized finalities of social order: as many substitutes of the Absolute and the Necessary.... We also see atheists sometimes motivated by noble sentiments, disgusted with the mediocrity and selfishness of so many modern social environments, and skillful in borrowing from our Gospel the forms and language of solidarity and human compassion: Shall we not be able one day to lead back to their true sources, which are Christian, these expressions of moral values?"[10]

Atheism proclaims the necessary disappearance of all religion, but it is itself a religious phenomenon. Let us not, however, make of it a believer who does not know it. And let us not reduce what is a profound tragedy to a superficial misunderstanding. Before all the continually renascent gods of progress, becoming, and history, let us succeed in again finding the radicalism of the first Christians with regard to the idolaters of ancient paganism, and say again with St. Justin: "Certainly, we confess, we are the atheists of these would-be gods."[11]

AN INHUMAN HUMANISM

8. So let us be, in spirit and in truth, witnesses to the living God, bearers of His Father's tenderness in the hol-

lowness of a universe closed in upon itself and fluctuating between Luciferian pride and disillusioned despair. How could we fail in particular to be sensitive to the tragedy of atheistic humanism, whose antitheism, and more precisely whose anti-Christianity, eventually crushes the human person that it had wished to liberate from the heavy burden of a God who is considered an oppressor? "It is not true that man cannot organize the earth without God. What is true is that, without God, he can organize it, when all is said and done, only against man. Exclusive humanism is an inhuman humanism."[12] Four decades later, everyone can fill these ominous lines of Father de Lubac with the tragic weight of the history of our time.

What an invitation to return to the heart of our faith: "The Redeemer of man, Jesus Christ, is the center of the universe and of history."[13] The collapse of deism, the profane concept of nature, the secularization of society, the growth of ideologies, the emergence of human sciences, the structural ruptures, the return of agnosticism, and the rise of technical neopositivism—are these not as many challenges for the Christian to find again in an aging world all the power of the newness of the Gospel, always new, the inexhaustible source of renewal: *Omnem novitatem attulit, semetipsum afferens?* And St. Thomas Aquinas, eleven centuries afterwards, prolonged St. Irenaeus' words: *Christus initiavit nobis viam novam.*[14]

It is up to the Christian to bear witness to it. Certainly, he bears this treasure in a clay vessel. But he is nevertheless called to put the light on the stand, so that it may illuminate all those in the house. This is the very role of the Church, about which the Council reminded us that she is the bearer of Him who alone is *Lumen gentium.* This witness must be at once a witness of thought and a witness of life. Since you are men of study, I will stress, in conclusion, the first necessity, since the second one, in fact, concerns us all.

To learn to think well was a resolution that was willingly professed yesterday. It is always a prime necessity in order to act. The apostle is not dispensed from it. How many baptized persons have become strangers to a Faith which, perhaps, had never really lived in them because no one had taught it to them well! In order to develop, the germ of faith needs to be nourished by the Word of God, the sacraments, the whole teaching of the Church, and that in an atmosphere of prayer. And, to reach minds while winning hearts, faith must present itself for what it is, and not under false pretenses. The dialogue of salvation is a dialogue of truth in charity.

Today, for example, mentalities are deeply imbued with scientific methods. Now a catechesis insufficiently informed about the problems of the exact sciences, as of human sciences in their diversity, may accumulate obstacles in an understanding, instead of opening up a way to the affirmation of God. And it is you, philosophers and theologians, that I am addressing: look for ways to present your thought in a way that will help the scientifically-minded to recognize the validity of your philosophical and religious reflection. For what is at stake is the credibility, even the validity of this reflection, for many minds influenced, even without their knowledge, by the scientific mentality conveyed by the media. And I already rejoice that the next plenary assembly of the Secretariat for non-believers next March-April will study this subject: *Science and Unbelief.*

I must conclude. Confronted more than ever with the tragedy of atheism, the Church intends today to renew her effort of thought and testimony, in proclamation of the Gospel. Whereas a swarm of questions creeps into the mind of man, a prey to modernity, the mystery remains beyond the problems. And, as the Second Vatican Council taught us, "it is only in the mystery of the Word made flesh that the mystery of man truly becomes clear."[15] May His Spirit of light inspire your intellectual work, and may His Spirit of power animate your witness of life! I accompany this wish and this prayer with my apostolic blessing.

FOOTNOTES

1. Cf. Apostolic Constitution *Gaudium et spes*, On the Church in the Modern World, no. 19.

2. André Malraux, Preface to *L'enfant du rire*, by Fr. Bockel, Grasset.

3. No. 55.

4. Paul VI, Allocution to the Second Vatican Council, December 7, 1965: *AAS* 68 (1966), p. 55.

5. Address to the United Nations, October 2, 1979, no. 20.

6. Apostolic Constitution *Regimini Ecclesiae Universae*, of August 15, 1967, in reference to the teaching of Vatican II, *Gaudium et spes*, nos. 19-21 and 92.

7. Cf. my homily of June 1, 1980, at Issy-les-Moulineaux..

8. Psalm XIV.

9. St. Augustine, *Confessions*, X, 27.

10. Paul VI, Encyclical *Ecclesiam suam*, Polyglot Printing Press, Vat., August 6, 1964, pp. 66-67.

11. St. Justin, *Premiere Apologie*, VI, no. 1.

12. Fr. Henri de Lubac, *Le drame de l'humanisme athée*, Spes, 1944, p. 12. Quoted by Paul VI, Encyclical *Populorum progressio*, Easter 1967, no. 42.

13. First sentence of the Encyclical *Redemptor hominis*.

14. *Prima Secundae*, q. 106, art. 4, *ad primum*.

15. *Gaudium et spes*, no. 22, 1.

Mary's Unique Role in the History of Evangelization

At the conclusion of the Third Argentinian National Marian Congress, which took place at Mendoza from October 8 to 12, 1980, the Holy Father sent the following message to Cardinal Paolo Bertoli, his special envoy to the congress, and to the bishops and faithful of that nation.

Your Eminence, my special envoy,
Venerable brothers in the episcopate,
Beloved sons and daughters:

The close of the Third National Marian Congress, the culmination of a constant and intense work of evangelization in the company of the Mother of the Savior, offers me the opportunity to greet you and to be with you, sons and daughters of the beloved Argentinian land. "My love be with you all in Christ Jesus" (1 Cor. 16:24).

Evangelization "is the great ministry or service that the Church carries out for the world and for men, the Good News that the kingdom of justice and peace reaches men in Jesus Christ" (Puebla Document, 679). Hence the Church, if she wishes to be really the bearer of the message of the Son of God, must proclaim, live and bear witness to the Gospel faithfully and consistently. In the evangelizing history of the Church, the Virgin Mary has occupied and continues to occupy a singularly unique place. It has rightly been said: "to Christ through Mary."

In the Latin American continent and in the Argentinian nation, devotion and manifestations of love for the Blessed Virgin go back to the age of the preaching of the first missionaries. The proclamation of the Gospel has always been accompanied by the kind presence of Mary, who "constituted the great sign, with her motherly and merciful face, of the nearness of the Father and of Christ, with whom she calls upon us to enter into communion" (Puebla Document, 282).

Beloved, the presence of Mary in your religious history and that of your country has been constant, so that there is hardly a part of your national territory that does not feel united with her. Let it be enough to recall, as examples, the Marian sanctuaries of Lujan, Itati, del Valle, del Milagro, de Sumampa, del Rosario, de la Merced and del Carmen. These sanctuaries are a perennial testimony of the love with which Mary has blessed the Argentinian land, so that it is possible to affirm that devotion to the Mother of the Savior belongs to the purest tradition of the Argentinian Catholic people. Your presence here today is a tangible proof of this.

The central theme of the congress, "Mary and Evangelization in Argentina," was the starting point for reflection during these days on some pastoral questions which coincide with the ones that I myself pointed out as having priority at the Third General Conference of the Latin American Episcopate gathered in Puebla: the family, priestly and religious vocations, and youth (cf. John Paul II, Opening Address of the work of the Third General Conference of the Latin American Episcopate, Puebla, January 28, 1980). These same subjects have also been gathered in the "Puebla Document" itself, as priority pastoral options, and they must be studied more deeply and applied through a renewed and intense evangelization. Thus this National Marian Congress wishes to make present in your society, through the mediation of the Virgin Mary, the kingdom of God and, consequently, it also wishes Christ to be present within your hearts and your families, in factories, universities, schools, farms, in a word, in all the living environments of the country.

Beloved brothers and all my sons and daughters of the Argentinian nation, I exhort and encourage you always to keep alive the spiritual heritage you have received as a precious gift from your ancestors and from the first evangelizers. Intensely cultivate devotion to our Mother, the Blessed Virgin Mary; remain faithful to Christ; believe in Him, trust in Him, love Him, and, like Him, love your brothers and sisters, particularly those who are suffering and weeping at present, so that Argentinian society, consolidated on the pillars of brotherly love and reconciliation, will be able to exclaim the truth: "Behold, how good and pleasant it is when brothers dwell in unity" (Ps. 133:1).

The Marian Congress closes today, but its fruits must not end here. There now begins for you all, sons and daughters, a new stage. Christ, who died and rose again, has left us a mission: "Go therefore...teaching them (all nations) to observe all that I have commanded you" (Mt. 28:19-20).

With these wishes, invoking upon each and every one of you the constant motherly protection of the Virgin

Mary, so that she may help you always to be tireless apostles of Christ in the Argentinian society, and that you may always be united by the bond of charity, I affectionately impart my blessing to you: in the name of the Father, the Son and the Holy Spirit. Amen.

Principles of Hierarchical Communion— the Basis of Church Law

On October 13, 1980, the Holy Father received in audience in the Consistorial Hall a large group of participants in the Fourth International Congress of Canon Law from October 5-11, at Freiburg in Switzerland. The Congress, in which 400 students from all over the world took part, was organized by the "International Association for promoting the study of Canon Law" and took for its theme, "The fundamental rights of the Christian in the Church and in society."

Present at the audience were Cardinal Joseph Ratzinger, Archbishop of Munich and Freising; Archbishop Oskar Saier, of Freiburg im Breisgau; and Bishop Antonio Ronco Varela, Auxiliary to the Archbishop of Santiago de Compostela.

After an address by the President of the Association, Professor Pietro Agostino D'Avack, the Holy Father gave the following discourse.

1. Dear sons, revered teachers, and all of you who are studying canon law!

We greet you from the bottom of our heart, and while we willingly grant you this audience, we thank you at the same time for your sense of duty and for your good will. You have just finished the Fourth International Congress of Canon Law and out of love and loyalty towards the Successor of Peter you have made this rather long journey here to Rome to hear personally what we have to say and to receive guidance from us.

2. Since the Second Vatican Council the International Congresses of Canon Law have been so many examples and proofs of your persevering work. Moreover, these congresses render a useful service to the Church. On this we congratulate you very much. You met in Rome in 1968

and again in 1970.[1] Then in 1973 you met in Milan,[2] in Pamplona in 1976, and again here in Rome in 1977.[3] Our distinguished Predecessor Paul VI wanted to reflect with you on the mystery of the Church and the place and function of law in it. Again and again he emphasized the importance of canon law, and he showed in what spirit this renewal should be carried out. Moreover, he favored greater cooperation between the sacred disciplines,[4] and in accordance with the teaching of the Second Vatican Council, he asserted the need for a true theology of Church law.[5] We also want to favor this idea. We wish to assert again the great importance of the Magisterium. Likewise, we want to go before you and with you on the same road.

THE CONCEPT OF PAUL VI

3. When he explained to you the ecclesial system within which the law of the Church is placed, Paul VI envisaged a law of communion as the work of the Holy Spirit, and the law of charity.[6] You have followed his teaching in order to decide upon a theme for your Congress in Freiburg. So often did he extol the importance of the fundamental rights of man,[7] and in this category he placed the principal rights of the Christian, from which some time in the future a new code of Church law might be drawn up after the Council.[8]

4. It is almost superfluous for us to say that your Congress has greatly aroused our interest and has attracted our attention. For what can be more important than to define more accurately the fundamental rights of Christians so that they can be respected? What is even more necessary today than the respect and the protection due to the principal rights of man?

In this area of human affairs the Church has a most important function which she must fulfill. For in her own mystery of communion, the Church is able to understand man and define more accurately the principal rights which express his nature and certainly protect his dignity. Your

Congress at Freiburg also provides an answer to the more pressing anxieties of the Church, and at the same time to the deep longings of the men of our time.[9]

TRUE HUMAN FREEDOM

5. Indeed the need arises to do this because it is necessary for the Church of her very nature to concern herself with something even better, namely *communion.* The Church brings about this communion when she recognizes the dignity of the human person in the freedom which his divine origin and his eternal destiny demand.

If the world is seeking freedom, this freedom is found in Christ. Christ lives in the Church. Therefore, the true freedom of man is realized through the experience of ecclesial communion.[10]

This ecclesial communion is "an intimate communion which is always renewed with the very Source of life which is the most Holy Trinity. It is a communion of life, of love, of the imitation of Christ by following Him. Indeed, as the Redeemer of man He brings us into a close union with God."[11]

Also "the measure of man is God! Therefore man must return to this Source and to this one measure which is God Incarnate, Jesus Christ. If he wants to be man, and if he wants the world to become human, man must constantly return to Him."[12]

For this reason the dignity of man must be seen in Christ, just as in this *whole Christ,* which is the Church, one must recognize the nature of Church law, its necessary structures, and the primary rights of its members.[13]

6. The ecclesial order, if properly understood, is the juridical order in the external forum. That same order strives to establish *peace in communion.* In order for this to happen, this peace will be charity.[14] No one can err about this. Law is not opposed to charity. On the contrary, charity requires law to express and safeguard its necessary requirements on this earth. On the other hand,

those requirements are much better understood if they are according to the will of God, the fundamental demands of His love, and the living structures of His Church. This is, so to say, a sort of extension of the Word Incarnate[15] who became man in order to save men, to bring them back to the Father as adopted sons, liberated indeed to share the freedom and glory of the children of God.[16] In Jesus Christ and through Him they make up the Mystical Body and sacred communion that is the Church.[17]

7. In this communion, which is hierarchical, we must see the baptized person. Each Christian there has his own position, rank, and duty. This communion is the work of the Spirit and it remains firm on account of the priesthood of the bishops who, through the apostolic succession, teach, govern and sanctify the People of God and preserve them in the unity and charity of faith. Moreover, the very communion of the bishops is ministerial. It is at the service of ecclesial communion and safeguards its coherence around Peter, who in a central position watches over the charity of that unity.

THE TRUE THEOLOGY OF LAW

8. These principles are the basis of ecclesiastical law and they also make up the true theology of law. Besides, they throw light upon and confirm the dignity of man and his principal rights. There has never been a time when the Church has not protected these rights. She has even laid down canonical penalties against those who attack life itself, those who act against the dignity of man or injure his good name or deprive him of his freedom.[18] Likewise, there has never been a time when the Church has not proclaimed the duty both of private individuals and of public authorities to respect and promote the rights of the human person. The Church has favored order among nations. She has asserted the right of all nations to freedom. She has appealed to them to be faithful to the agreements they

have made. She has advocated that some worldwide authority be set up to preserve society and world peace by promoting respect for these rights.

9. The mission of the Church is the salvation of mankind. Therefore, she must see to it that she has an even better understanding of the fundamental rights of man and that she fosters respect for them and their observance. We are speaking of the rights of the family, of social groups, of religious communities.[20] But it is necessary for these rights to be recognized by civil society and protected by the states themselves. Moreover, all Christians must observe these rights by living according to the teaching of Christ. In this age all Christians have a grave and urgent duty to work to see that these rights are recognized and respected in public morals and laws. From this springs the duty proper to each of you, who are both Christian laity and students of law, to make your special contribution of wisdom, technical learning, and love for mankind to the effect that the juridical regulations of the earthly state fully make known and express the law of the Divine Wisdom which is inscribed on the heart of man; and that laws which violate the fundamental rights should for moral reasons be repudiated and changed into norms which fully respect these rights—the right to life from the moment of its conception until its natural term, the right to dignity, integrity, and freedom.[21] It is also rather fitting that you have investigated these arguments and rights with an ecumenical approach.

RIGHTS MUST BE RESPECTED

10. But insofar as the primary rights of Christians are concerned, defining them involves really hard work. That work which has already been started by the Second Vatican Council, not without great difficulty, must continue. The law of the Church, when it is renewed, will for its part certainly see to it that these rights are retained and observed in practical life. This is all the more necessary

because these rights of Christians are founded on the primary rights of man. Moreover, these principal rights of man are solemnly stated in the Declaration of the United Nations and they have been further defined in subsequent conventions.[22] Among them must be mentioned the Declaration of the Rights of the Child even before it is born. It is necessary for all these rights to be better understood, more carefully examined and reflected upon. Alas! they are far from being respected everywhere.[23] Nor can Church law disregard these rights. Indeed, Church law will play its part in applying them, and in this way it will both promote and enhance them.

11. If in the past certain people advocated the absolute separation of Church and state—each of which institutions has its own authority and its proper powers—this cannot imply a separation of ecclesial communion and society.

Rightly has it been said that all the questions which are put to men at this time can in no way be solved by reason alone or by only the activity of purely human institutions. More and more it is being felt that the future destiny of man surpasses the political order. It is also felt that there is a danger that the natural and technical sciences will crush man, and that in the long run all these things necessarily have an effect on the world of the spirit. This judgment repeats what we recently said in Paris: "The measure of the things and events of the created world is man, but the measure of man is God."[24]

12. This is why—as we stated in Washington last year—it is incumbent on us by virtue of our office to bear witness to the greatness of man in the totality of his life and his existence. This excellence of man springs from the love of God who created us in His own likeness and gave us everlasting life.[25]

Dear sons: your labors and your efforts, and now your Congress in Freiburg, make you close associates with this mission of ours. Therefore we ask you to carry on with this helpful and social work of yours joyfully and steadily.

Church law can and must penetrate and stimulate human law. While you are examining the fundamental rights of Christians, you are certainly making the primary rights of man better known and more fully respected. According to the will of God you deepen the understanding and strengthen the defense of the true dignity of the human person more and more.

These are our best hopes and wishes for you, and at the same time they are signs of our great esteem and gratitude.

May the Lord Himself support your work and may the apostolic blessing, which you have confidently sought from us, help and strengthen you always.

FOOTNOTES

1. Cf. *AAS*, 60 (1968), 337-342; 62 (1970), 106-111.

2. Cf. *Communicationes* 5 (1973), 123-131.

3. Cf. *AAS*, 69 (1977), 208-212.

4. Cf. *Communicationes* 5 (1973), 123-124.

5. Cf. *Ibid.*, pp. 130-131.

6. Cf. *AAS*, 65 (1973), 98; *Communicationes* 5 (1973), 126-127; *AAS*, 69 (1977), 209.

7. Cf. *AAS*, 69 (1977), 147-148; *AAS*, 60 (1968), 338-339.

8. Cf. *AAS*, 69 (1977), 149.

9. Cf. *Allocutio* of October 6, 1979, *Doc. cath.*, 76 (1979), 931.

10. *Allocutio* of March 31, 1979, in *Doc. cath.*, 76 (1979), 414; cf. *Homilia* in Bourget, June 1, 1980, *Doc. cath.*, 76 (1979), 585.

11. Cf. *Ibid.*, March 31, 1979, *Doc. cath.*, 76 (1979), 414.

12. *Allocutio* of May 31, 1980, *Doc. cath.*, 77 (1980), 570.

13. Cf. *AAS*, 65 (1973), 102-103.

14. Cf. *AAS*, 69 (1977), 148.

15. Cf. *Lumen gentium*, no. 8a.

16. Cf. Rom. 8:19-21.

17. Cf. Col. 1:15-20.

18. Cf. *C.I.C.*, Can. 2350 par. 1; 2352-2355.

19. Cf. *Nuntius radiophonicus Natalicius* 1944, *AAS*, 37 (1945), 17-21; cf. *Litt. Enc. Summi Pontificatus*, *AAS*, 31 (1939), 437; *Allocutio ad Congressum Iuristarum Catholicorum AAS*, 45 (1953), 800, *Allocutio ad Congressum constituendae unioni Europaeae*, *AAS*, 49 (1957), 629.

20. Cf. *Allocutio* of October 6, 1979, *Doc. cath.*, 76 (1979), 931.

21. Cf. *Allocutio habita Aquilae*, August 31, 1980.

22. Cf. *Nuntius ad Unitarum Nationem Coetum*, December 2, 1978, *Doc. cath.*, 76 (1979), 1.

23. Cf. *Nuntius ad ONU*, December 2, 1978, *Doc. cath.*, 76 (1979), 1-3; *Allocutio habita initio III Conferentiae Episcopatus Americae Latinae*, *AAS*, 71 (1979), 201-202 III no. 5; *Doc. cath.*, 76 (1979), 171; Enc. *Redemptor hominis*, no. 17, *AAS*, 71 (1979), 295-300; *Doc. cath.*, 76 (1979), 312-314, *Allocutio* of December 14, 1979 in *L'Osservatore Romano*. December 14, 1979.

24. Cf. *Allocutio* of May 31, 1980, *Doc. cath.*, 77 (1980), 570.

25. Cf. *Allocutio* of October 6, 1979, *Doc. cath.*, 76 (1979), 1.

Satisfaction with Patriarchal Activity and Synod

On October 14, 1980, the Holy Father received in audience a group of bishops of the Greek Melkite Catholic Rite on their visit ad limina Apostolorum. *The bishops were led by His Beatitude Maximos V Hakim, Patriarch of Antioch of the Greek Melkite Catholics. John Paul II delivered the following address.*

Your Beatitude and venerable brothers,

You have come together from the various dioceses of the Greek Melkite Catholic Patriarchate to visit the Pope, in keeping with an ecclesial custom that is worthy of respect and beneficial. Now that you are close to the tomb of the Prince of Apostles, who received the inalienable power of leading and strengthening all his brothers in faith and charity, I am particularly happy to bid you welcome.

This fraternal welcome is that of the Bishop of Rome, the Successor of Peter, "the perpetual and visible source and foundation of the unity of the bishops and of the multitude of the faithful" (LG 23). Welcoming you, I am happy to take up again the words of the Apostle Paul, Peter's companion in the sufferings endured for Christ: "To this he called you through our gospel, so that you may obtain the glory of our Lord Jesus Christ. So then, brethren, stand firm and hold to the traditions which you were taught" (2 Thes. 2:14-15).

My greeting goes in the first place—and in a very special way—to His Beatitude Patriarch Maximos V, who will soon celebrate the fiftieth anniversary of his priestly ordination at the Patriarchal See of Damascus. Now, all together, we raise our prayers and our fervent wishes to Christ, the sovereign Priest and Redeemer of men.

The Greek Melkite Catholic Church which you represent has gathered, in the course of the centuries, faithful of Greek language and origin, but also Syrian and Egyptian, and finally, faithful of Arab origin who came to the Catholic Faith as early as the fifth century and belonged to the Patriarchate of Antioch, Alexandria and Jerusalem. In spite of certain historical and political vicissitudes that are now very far away, and the recent consequences of fratricidal wars which still disturb peace in the Middle East, the Melkite Patriarchate is a flourishing one. It is indeed a happy opportunity for me to express to Your Beatitude, and to all the bishops of the Patriarchate, my feelings of satisfaction and my encouragement to continue this good pastoral work in accordance with the example of the Lord Jesus Himself and with the frequent teachings of Fathers of the Eastern Church, such as St. Basil the Great (cf. *Moralia*, LXXX, 12-21, P.G. 31, 864, b-868, b).

Many Greek Melkite Catholics, like those of other Eastern rites, have been obliged—and again recently—to leave their homes and the land of their ancestors. Some of them crossed the oceans, while others mangaged to find hospitality closer in Europe. For the faithful of the diaspora, the Holy See has erected an eparchy in the United States and Brazil, and it has just erected an apostolic exarchate in Canada. It has also established apostolic visits in Western Europe, Argentina, Venezuela, Colombia, Mexico and Australia, in conformity with the norms fixed by the Second Vatican Council, for the purpose of strengthening the preaching of the Word of God, and spiritual assistance for all communities of emigrant faithful.

Furthermore, it is a consolation for the See of Rome to know the work which, in the light of the teachings of the Council, is gradually being carried out in the synods, presided over by the Patriarch, and in which also the major superiors of male orders take part, as regards, for example, the updating of liturgical texts, pastoral work, and catechesis, with particular solicitude for the increase of priestly and religious vocations.

The commitment of the hierarchy for a spiritual and intellectual formation corresponds to the needs of our time. We know, too, the activity you pursue within the framework of ecumenical dialogue with separated brethren, aware that real and stable communion is built in truth and charity, in collaboration with the Apostolic See.

Your meeting today expresses the bond of collegiality with the Successor of Peter: May it remind everyone of the unity of pastoral action which is necessary in all the countries in which you are called to lead the People of God, as the Council says with regard to bishops scattered all over the world, "teaching in communion with the Roman Pontiff" (LG 25).

As I did recently for the visit of the bishops of the Chaldean Rite, I encourage meetings in the form of episcopal assemblies on the national level, to guarantee unity of action among the various Churches, to ensure harmony and brotherly understanding among the different rites, without, however, prejudicing the right of the Patriarch or those of his synod, according to the law in force.

I do not want to conclude without first of all renewing the expression of my deep affection to Your Beatitude, to all of you venerable brothers in the episcopate, to all your priests, to men and women religious, who are concerned with bringing about a renewal in their spiritual life and in their consecration to God and the Church, and who are doing so worthily in the field of the apostolate, welfare and charity; my affectionate thought goes finally to the faithful of the whole Greek Melkite Catholic Church. Entrusting you all to the watchful and motherly protection of Mary, the most holy Virgin Mother of God, I give you the apostolic blessing from the bottom of my heart.

All Are Called
to Evangelization

On October 19, 1980, Mission Sunday, the Holy Father presided over a concelebration with forty missionaries about to leave for the destinations assigned to them. In the course of the Mass, the Pope bestowed crucifixes, the sign of the missionary task to which all Christians are called, to some hundred new missionaries: priests, sisters, and laymen.

The following are excerpts of the homily delivered by John Paul II.

Venerated brothers and sisters!

Nos autem praedicamus Christum crucifixum (1 Cor. 1:23).

I wanted this special celebration on the occasion of World Mission Sunday to be a call to stimulate the whole ecclesial community once more to reflect, in the meditation of prayer, on a cause which is in itself of prime importance and always relevant, such as is that of the proclamation of Christ to the peoples. And I wanted around me as concelebrants some missionaries, who wish to be direct agents and promoters of this same cause and who, precisely because they will shortly receive from my hands the crucifix—the symbol that expresses more than all others their work and their sacrifice—have a preferential right and a place of special importance in the context of this sacred rite. To them, as well as to their distant confréres and collaborators, men and women religious and lay people—also on behalf of all of you present—goes my grateful and affectionate greeting for the exemplary and qualified witness that they have offered and continue to offer to the Church and to the world.

The Church, just as she repeated more forcibly to herself that, by the will of her divine Founder, she must be a sign and instrument of salvation for men, so she likewise added that, in order to be equal to this function, to correspond to it concretely in her way through history, she must always have the spirit and the style, the watchful tension and the holy ambition to be and remain truly missionary.

It will never be permissible for the Church to use the conclusive formula "mission accomplished" in order to fall back and dispense herself in this way from insisting on the commitment assumed: the self-definition to which I referred above is, in a word, the demonstration and confirmation of the self-consciousness that the Council—this great event of light and grace—has developed and strengthened in her. It is as if the Spirit has repeated again: "Know yourself and be yourself! You are, in Christ, the organ of salvation for all peoples; therefore, be missionary!"

If Jesus, in fact, having imparted the order to go and preach, had warned that salvation depends on faith and on the reception of baptism (Mk. 16:16), Paul, by means of a lucid examination, logical and theological, picks out the various phases and the distinct moments that connect salvation and the mission closely with each other. How is one saved? He answers: One is saved if one calls upon the Lord; but to call upon Him it is necessary to believe; and to believe it is necessary to hear; and to hear it is necessary to preach; and to preach it is necessary to be sent (cf. Rom. 10:13-15). Here, therefore, are the necessary steps between the starting point and the point of arrival. This is how there depends on the sending or mission the desired final destination, which is salvation, through the crucial point of faith, received after careful listening to the one who preaches it and, when it has become a personal choice and deep conviction of the heart, also expressed in the confession of the lips (ibid., 9-10).

IT IS GOD WHO ACTS

In this way the Apostle taught us the fundamental and determining importance or, rather, the irreplaceable character of the mission and evangelical preaching in the life and for the life of the Church: it is a question, in fact, of tasks that configure her specific vocation and her deeper identity (cf. EN 14). So it happened in the time of St. Paul, when he and his fellow apostles, very faithful and obedient interpreters of the Master's will, facing hardships and difficulties of every kind, went to all the regions of the then-known world to proclaim the Gospel. Strengthened inwardly by the Spirit, but always deprived of resources and means on the human level, they worked with great zeal; but let us carefully note the evangelist's expression—it was God who acted in a sovereign and powerful way with them: "while the Lord worked with them and confirmed the message by the signs that attended it" (Mk. 16:20).

Today is as then! Today must be as then! On the one hand, we must obey the mandate of our Lord, not to be disregarded, and then we must work, all of us committing ourselves, albeit in the variety of forms and in the difference of services, but in organic and substantial unity of intentions, for the proclamation and the spread of the Gospel. Yes, brothers and sisters, even if we do not go to mission territories, we have *all*, we have *always*, we have *everywhere* the possibility and the obligation to collaborate in this evangelizing activity, which is presented as *officium Populi Dei fundamentale* in the aforesaid Decree (no. 35). Precisely for this supreme reason, the respective duties of the universal Church, of the individual Christian communities, of bishops, priests, institutes of perfection and of lay people, are therein reviewed separately for the purposes of missionary cooperation (cf. *ibid.*, nos. 36-41).

On the other hand, aware of our insufficiency and littleness, we will always have to remember that our industry —made up of diligence, faithfulness, and sacrifice—is not enough and can never be enough in itself: He who acts, who converts, who calls to faith by illuminating minds and touching hearts, He who actually leads to salvation, is the almighty and merciful God. From this second point of view we can certainly affirm that the mission is humility and, therefore, is necessarily accompanied by that interior attitude which makes us repeat: "We are unworthy servants" (Lk. 17:10), and calls for a generous spirit of service. This is what Jesus Christ Himself taught us with words, and even more with His example; He "came not to be served but to serve, and to give his life as a ransom for many" (Mt. 20:28).

This life that the Lord gave us—and we know very well in what way and at what cost—is still, as always, at our disposal and at the same time at the disposal of all men, our brothers. In a few moments, in the ineffable mystery of the Eucharistic Sacrifice, this life will be immolated again and offered on our altar "for us and for all." In close union with Christ, the priest and victim, we must draw upon it abundantly to save ourselves and to save.

Faithfulness to the Deposit of Faith

On October 23, 1980, John Paul II received in audience a group of bishops of Papua New Guinea and the Solomon Islands who had come to Rome on their ad limina *visit. The Holy Father addressed them as follows.*

Dear brothers in Christ,

1. With deep fraternal affection I welcome you to the See of Peter, and I greet you with the words of Paul: "Grace and peace to you from God our Father and from the Lord Jesus Christ" (Eph. 1:2).

It is a great joy for me to embrace in you all the faithful of the two nations that you represent: Papua New Guinea and the Solomon Islands. Through you I send greetings to every community that is found throughout the geographical expanses that you are called to traverse in the name of Christ and for the cause of His uplifting Gospel of salvation.

It is particularly satisfying to note the presence of autochthonous bishops in your midst, knowing well that the Church's life by its nature is directed to the full flowering of the local ecclesial communities. It is indeed a special moment in evangelization when Christ, through His Church, calls to the episcopacy a son of the people to whom He has communicated His saving Word.

And so it is right for me to render homage to all of you, and to all the missionaries who throughout generations have expended themselves to bring the Good News of Jesus Christ to the people of your vast areas. The history of that evangelization of which you are the present-day heralds is a record of God's grace infused into hearts; it is a record of the *mirabilia Dei* taking place in human history, despite multiple obstacles and setbacks. The universal Church today expresses deep thanks for what has been accomplished for the building up of the kingdom of God in your regions; through me the universal Church gives expression to a debt of gratitude owed to you and your predecessors—to all who have planted the Church—for your generosity of faith and love.

MYSTERY OF ECCLESIAL SOLIDARITY

2. Our meeting today has a deep meaning because it manifests the nature of Christ's Church and of the college of bishops. Assembled with the Bishop of Rome, and through him united with all your brother bishops throughout the world, you find a dimension of your own unity that has important consequences for your apostolate. Above all you have come to celebrate the mystery of the Church and to be confirmed by Peter in the faith of Jesus Christ, the Son of God. I am sure that this profound ecclesial dimension of our unity will continue to be a source of strength and joy for your ministry in the years ahead.

Your contacts, moreover, with the Roman Curia are useful in assisting it to render ever more effective service, in my name, to your local Churches. I am confident that by divine grace the exchanges of experiences will bear fruit in furthering worthy pastoral initiatives for the good of

God's people. But apart from every practical consideration, your meeting in Rome gives expression to the deep
mystery of ecclesial solidarity, and, in particular, to the
pastoral responsibility for the local Churches that belongs
to the entire college of bishops, and to its head, the Bishop
of Rome. As we acknowledge and celebrate together our
unity in the apostolate, we know that this unity has a
supernatural effectiveness in regard to your ministry at
home.

AN EVIDENT WITNESS OF LOVE

3. I would not let this opportunity pass by without
extolling, amid the many achievements of the Church in
your lands, the great witness of Christian love that has
been given by the missionaries. This witness has been
manifested for generations through personal and concerted
activity in the Church, through loving attention to the
material needs of the people, through educational
endeavors, through medical and health care initiatives,
and through a multiplicity of services freely rendered to
the cause of human dignity. Above all, this witness of love
has been evidenced in a burning desire to bring the Gospel
of Christ into the heart of every individual and community, to fulfill the Church's fundamental function, which is:
"to direct man's gaze, to point the awareness and experience of the whole of humanity towards the mystery of
God, to help all men to be familiar with the profundity of
the redemption taking place in Christ Jesus" (RH 10). And
may this witness of love go on forever in Papua New
Guinea and in the Solomon Islands.

COMPLETE ONENESS

4. It is evident that missionary service will be useful and necessary for the future of the apostolate in your
countries. The great initial phase has been accomplished,
and it remains a triumph of God's grace. But the consolidation and development of each local Church must con-

tinue. This progress has two dimensions: Each local Church has its own identity as an individual ecclesial community, with its distinctive gifts of nature and grace, situated within the variety and unity of all God's people. Each local Church is, therefore, a special offering of Christ to His Father; it gives unique expression to one aspect of Christ's fullness. At the same time, each local Church is authentic precisely to the extent that it exemplifies in miniature the one, holy, catholic and apostolic Church of Christ. For the universal Church there is but one holiness and justice, and it is that which is born of truth (cf. Eph. 4:24). And this truth is the everlasting truth of God's Word. For this reason, dear brothers, we find abundant energy to continue our apostolic preaching, despite all obstacles, with great patience and love, but with great fidelity to the deposit of God's Word as proclaimed by the universal Church. The perfect identity of the local Churches is found in complete openness to the universal Church; it is nurtured by an awareness of Catholic unity.

CHRIST GIVES GRACE

5. In every effort which we must make to bring the Gospel to our people and into every aspect of their lives—and this is indeed our calling—we must ensure that the message which we preach remains the unchanged Word of God. Let us never fear that the challenge is too great for our people: They were redeemed by the precious blood of Christ; they are His people. Through the Holy Spirit, Jesus Christ vindicates to Himself the final responsibility for the acceptance of His Word and for the growth of His Church. It is He, Jesus Christ, who will continue to give the grace to His people to meet the requirements of His Word, despite all difficulties, despite all weaknesses. And it is up to us to continue to proclaim the message of salvation in its entirety and purity, with patience, compassion and the conviction that what is impossible with man is possible with God. We ourselves

are only part of one generation in salvation history, but "Jesus Christ is the same yesterday, today, and for ever" (Heb. 13:8). He is indeed able to sustain us as we recognize the strength of His grace, the power of His Word and the efficacy of His merits.

UNITY THROUGH PRAYER

6. Our great strength is found in our ecclesial unity, which in turn is fostered by prayer. And it is prayer that constitutes our master program of the apostolate: *Actiones nostras, quaesumus, Domine, aspirando praeveni et adiuvando prosequere!* Through the prayer that unites us ever more closely with Christ's design for His Church, we can plan more effectively and confidently for the future. In this way, brethren, devote your best efforts to those great issues that confront all of you: the question of vocations, the importance of social communications, the role of catechists, and the general promotion of the laity—not only as a practical means of sharing responsibility for the Gospel, but as a fulfillment of the divine will to associate the laity in the Church's mission of salvation. In prayer you will find the strength and insights to continue on the path of evangelization, being confident of the power of the Word of God to uplift and transform all human cultures, bringing to them the original and incomparable contribution that comes directly from Jesus Christ, who embodies the fullness of humanity.

7. I would ask you to devote special attention to fostering the holiness of Christian marriage and to proclaiming the fullness of God's design for the family. This task is indeed great: human knowledge and sensitivity will assist you, but only divine wisdom will enlighten you sufficiently for this ministry. And remember always that, by the power of Christ's Word and in the unity of God's Church, you will be enabled to lead your people "in paths of righteousness for his name's sake" (Ps. 23:3).

8. My thoughts today go out to all your collaborators in the Gospel—to the men and women religious who assist in building up the Church by word and deed. Their reward will be immense in heaven.

In a special way I am thinking of your priests, to whom God's Providence reserves such an important role in the proclamation of the Gospel. In this regard permit me to address to you the words I recently spoke to the bishops of Ireland: "Our relationship with Jesus will be the fruitful basis of our relationship with our priests, as we strive to be their brother, father, friend and guide. In the charity of Christ we are called to listen to and to understand them, to exchange views regarding evangelization and the pastoral mission they share with us as co-workers with the order of bishops. For the entire Church—but especially for the priests—we must be a human sign of the love of Christ and the fidelity of the Church. Thus we sustain our priests with the Gospel message, supporting them by the certainty of the Magisterium, and fortifying them against the pressures that they must resist. By word and example we must constantly invite our priests to prayer" (Address of September 30, 1979).

9. And for all your local Churches I pray that they will enjoy peace and progress, and that they will be filled with the consolation of the Holy Spirit (cf. Acts 9:31).

Dear brothers in Christ: Let us go forward together, under the protection of our Blessed Mother Mary, in our common responsibility, for the glory of Christ's name, proclaiming the Good News of salvation—the "Good News of a great joy which will come to all the people" (Lk. 2:10). And to all your clergy, religious and laity I send my apostolic blessing, in the love of Jesus Christ, the Son of God and Savior of the world.

Upcoming Bicentennial of Korean Evangelization— Occasion for Thanksgiving

On October 23, 1980, the Holy Father received in audience a group of Korean bishops who were making their ad limina *visit. The following is the Pope's message to them.*

Dear brothers in our Lord Jesus Christ,

1. In the special unity that we are experiencing today, our heart is glad and our spirit rejoices. Together, we have a heightened sense of what it means to be "in Christ." For me personally it is a particular joy to welcome you, Cardinal Kim and my other brother bishops, since in the profound mystery of collegiality, divine Providence has reserved for both you and me a vital link with the history of salvation as it unfolds in the lives of all the Korean people.

Your presence here also gives expression to your awareness of the inestimable value of ecclesial communion. At the tombs of the Apostles your presence becomes a public act of thanksgiving—a solemn hymn of praise— for the *saving action of God* which takes place each day in the Church throughout Korea, and which has touched the lives of generations of your ancestors. In the words of the Psalm we can proclaim together: "Blessed be the Lord day after day, the God who saves us and bears our burdens. This God of ours is a God who saves…" (Ps. 68:19-20).

2. Indeed, the whole *history of evangelization in Korea* is recapitulated in this dynamic moment—which you are living today—of fidelity to the preaching of Peter and Paul. Your visit consolidates this history, from the first mention of the name of Jesus Christ in your land, and especially from that charismatic implantation of the Faith almost two centuries ago, which took place through the instrumentality of the layman Yi Sung-hun. Called to "the obedience of faith" (Rom. 1:5) through the action of the

Holy Spirit, your ancestors gave an heroic witness of faith, which reached its culmination in the fortitude of the Korean martyrs.

3. That same Holy Spirit is active today, and the grace of Christ is still bringing forth fruits of justice and holiness of life. How can we not praise our saving God for the signs of *Catholic vitality* found in your local Churches, for the gift of faith and Baptism constantly renewed to the edification of the universal Church! I still recall with joy how, during the Easter vigil of this year, I personally was able to baptize and confirm a number of those who had been zealously prepared at home in Korea for Christian initiation. The Church of God which is in your midst has indeed been able to accomplish great works of faith and charity—and all in the name of Jesus Himself.

4. With fidelity and perseverance you have pursued your Christian *mission of service,* giving an authentic response to Jesus' commandment of love. In schools and hospitals, through manifold works of mercy and a commitment to human advancement, your local communities have been able to give a true Christian response to human needs.

5. Although numerically small in proportion to your brothers and sisters, you have zealously rendered important service in contributing to the common good. In the religious, social, cultural, political and economic fields, Catholic citizens, individually and collectively, have made worthy and highly esteemed contributions. The Church must continue to exercise her *full solicitude for the human person,* for the rights of every man, woman and child. And thus the Church will always be attentive to the pastoral challenge extended to her in the field of human rights, in which she must not cease to place her response in the context of her own proper mission, which will ever be diligently concerned for the ethical and humanitarian dimension of every question that touches human existence,

recognizing indeed that, according to the teaching of Jesus, justice and mercy are among "the weightier matters of the law" (Mt. 23:23).

6. At the same time the Church will offer her original and distinctive contribution—which is her greatest: the proclamation of *the saving and uplifting Gospel of Jesus Christ in its fullness.* An aspect of her activity—but one which is the special inalienable right and duty of the laity—that deserves particular consideration is the activity of the laity on behalf of the renewal of the whole temporal order (cf. AA 7). There are many facets to this great task—clear goals to be envisioned and specific means to be employed—and it is not possible to treat them now. But may our Catholic laity always remember this: that they have a principal role in directing all creation to the praise of God, and of permeating the world with the spirit of Christ (cf. LG 36).

7. In 1984, you will be celebrating in Korea the bicentennial of your evangelization. It will undoubtedly be an occasion of grace, strength and renewal. In conjunction with that great anniversary, you are zealously preparing a national pastoral plan for the 1980's. In this coordinated effort you have indeed a providential opportunity to promote vigorously the unity of your local Churches. In every aspect of our ecclesial activity, Christ calls us to be one in Him. Hence everything that is done to promote *the unity of the episcopate and the unity of the clergy* will redound to the unity of the Body of Christ and to the effectiveness of the Church's mission. May every vital segment of the Church, every parish group, every community of religious and laity feel the need to be united in the acceptance of the Word of God and to be "faithful to the teaching of the apostles, to the brotherhood, to the breaking of bread and to the prayers" (Acts 2:42).

The preparation of a pastoral plan offers an excellent opportunity to embrace anew and ever more effectively— and with total priority—*the Church's mission of evangelization.* The foundation, center and dynamic summit of this evangelization is "a clear proclamation that, in Jesus Christ, the Son of God made man, who died and rose from the dead, salvation is offered to all men, as a gift of God's grace and mercy" (EN 27). And what greater offering can be presented through Christ Jesus to His Father on the occasion of your bicentennial than the oblation of unity—everyone, according to the injunction of Saint Paul, "united in the same mind and the same judgment"? (1 Cor. 1:10)

8. Dearly beloved brothers: The obstacles and difficulties that face the Gospel and imperil human life and dignity are many. But let us have faith in the action of Jesus Christ. Let us trust in His sustaining grace.

Worthy of your special affection and pastoral attention are your seminaries and your seminarians. Through the assistance of the Holy Spirit, many young men have heeded the divine invitation. Let us, on our part, make sure that their doctrinal and spiritual formation is solid, worthy of the Christ who called them to lifelong fidelity. If their training should be faulty, everything else would be defective. The only basis for priestly life and ministry is *the pure Word of God's revealed truth.* Let us guard this treasure and transmit it in all its vitality through our seminaries. It is hard to imagine any responsibility more awesome than this charge which Christ the chief Shepherd has given to us as bishops.

I ask you to assure all your priests, both diocesan and missionary, of my love in Christ. As they face the pastoral problems of each day, including those of an urbanized and migrant society, urge them to have confidence in Christ and in His abiding presence. Their greatest strength will always be in the *union with the Lord,* especially through prayer and the Eucharist.

For all men and women religious let us constantly hold up the ideal of *holiness and the wisdom of the cross.* The measure of their effectiveness is not judged by human standards; it is found in their capacity to love Jesus and His brethren.

I commend all of you to the saving grace of Christ our Lord, and I exhort you to be filled with trust, to go forward in hope. Jesus is truly telling us: *"Noli timere, pusillus grex, quia complacuit Patri vestro dare vobis Regnum"* (Lk. 12:32). My cordial and respectful greetings go to all your non-Christian brethren with whom you live and work, with fraternal esteem and love. My prayerful good wishes go likewise to all the authorities of your country, to all the citizens of good will.

9. At this time, my thoughts turn particularly to your brothers and sisters living in North Korea, especially to those who have suffered tribulation because of the name of Jesus and because of their fidelity to Him. May they know that they are indeed not forgotten. The Church universal offers to them the assurance of her prayers and her unfailing solidarity and love. As we speak of them before the world, we entrust them in hope to God, who "is able to do far more abundantly than all that we ask or think" (Eph. 3:20).

10. And even as we endeavor to fulfill our weighty pastoral responsibilities, we are profoundly convinced that the destiny of God's people is in the power of His grace, which in turn is abundantly dispensed through the hands of His blessed Mother Mary. She has long presided over the evangelization of your people and will continue to lead you all to Christ Jesus her Son, and through Him to the Father, to whom, in the unity of the Holy Spirit, be praise and thanksgiving for ever and ever.

Role of the Family in Charity and Truth

On October 25, 1980, in the Sistine Chapel, the solemn rite for the closing of the Fifth General Assembly of the Synod of Bishops began.

After an address of homage to the Pope by one of the delegate presidents, Cardinal Primatesta, the "Message to the Christian Family in the Modern World" was read; then, ending with the singing of Terce, John Paul II delivered the following homily in Latin.

Venerable brothers,

1. We have heard how St. Paul the Apostle thanked God for the Church of Corinth, "because it had become rich in Christ Jesus, in every word and in all knowledge" (cf. 1 Cor. 1:5). We now also feel compelled to express thanks above all to the Father, Son and Holy Spirit, before we bring an end to this Synod of Bishops; to celebrate this occasion, we who were members of this assembly or who participated in their work have been brought together in the mystery of that highest unity which is proper to the most Holy Trinity. To this ceremony, therefore, we bring a sense of gratitude that we have completed the Synod, which is an outstanding indication of the vigor of the Church and which has great importance for the life of the Church. For the Synod of Bishops—let us use the words of the Council, according to whose direction the Sovereign Pontiff Paul VI established the Synod—"as an instrument of the entire Catholic episcopate, signifies that all bishops are participants in a hierarchical communion of solicitude for the universal Church" (CD 5).

We are also grateful for these four weeks in which we have worked together. Indeed, this space of time, even before the last resolutions were offered—that is, the Message and the Propositions—was fruitful for us, insofar as truth and love seemed to grow more and more as the days and weeks went by.

This progress must surely be brought to light, and the characteristics which made it outstanding should be briefly described. In this way it will be evident how rightly and clearly there were manifested in it both freedom and responsible concern regarding the subject which was treated.

Today, above all, we want to offer thanks to Him "who sees in secret" (Mt. 6:4) and is active as a "hidden God," in that He directed our thoughts, our hearts and our consciences, and indeed endowed us with them so that we would focus on a spiritual work in fraternal peace and joy. Such was His gift that we scarcely felt the work or the fatigue. Nevertheless, how much fatigue there really was! You have truly spared no effort.

A SINGULARLY FRUITFUL SYNOD

2. It is likewise fitting that we give thanks among ourselves. Before all else, this must be said: that progress by which, in a gradually maturing manner, "we bore the truth in charity" we should all attribute to the constant prayers which the entire Church—standing around us, as it were—poured out at this time. This prayer was offered for the Synod and for families: for the Synod, insofar as it had reference to families; and for families, in regard to the roles which they must exercise in the Church and in the modern world. By reason of these prayers, perhaps, the Synod was singularly fruitful.

God was besieged with constant and copious prayers: This was most evident on October 12, when husbands and wives, who represented families throughout the world, came before St. Peter's Basilica to celebrate the sacred rites and pray together with us.

But if we ought to thank one another, this duty must at the same time be extended to so many benefactors who are unknown, but who helped us by their prayers throughout the whole world, offering also their sufferings to God for the intention of this Synod.

AN EXPRESSION OF GRATITUDE

3. Now we come to that expression of gratitude in which we embrace all those who contributed to the celebration of this Synod: there are the Presidents, the General Secretary, the General Relator, the members themselves in a special way, the Special Secretary and his helpers, the men and women Auditors, the communications media assistants, and all the others, from the ushers to the technicians and typists.

We are all grateful because we could complete this Synod, which was a singular manifestation of the collegial solicitude of the bishops of the whole world for the Church. We are grateful because we could see the family as it really is in the Church and in the modern world, as we considered the many different conditions which face the family: the traditions which, flowing from various forms of culture, touch it; the elements of a more sophisticated life which affect it and to which it is subjected; and other things of this type. We are grateful because, with the outlook of faith, we could re-examine the eternal plan of God concerning the family, manifested in the mystery of creation and confirmed by the blood of the Redeemer, the Spouse of the Church; finally, we are grateful that we could define, according to the eternal plan concerning life and love, the roles of the family in the Church and in the modern world.

FRUIT OF THE SYNOD

4. The fruit which this Synod of 1980 has already brought forth is contained in the Propositions accepted by the Assembly, the first of which says: "How to know the plan of God on the pilgrimage of the People of God. The sense of faith."

We have now received this rich treasure of Propositions, which number forty-three, as a singularly precious fruit of the labors of the Synod.

At the same time, we confirm the joy which the Assembly itself, in offering its Message, has addressed to the universal Church, which Message the General Secretariat, with the help of the offices of the Holy See, will take care to send to all to whom it is of interest, likewise using the help of the episcopal conferences.

NECESSITY OF SYNODS

5. Those things which the Synod of 1980 has pointedly considered and enunciated in its Propositions make us see the Christian and apostolic roles of the family in the modern world and make us in some way bring those responses from the whole abundance of things which the Second Vatican Council has taught. Thus we go forward along the way which will enable the doctrinal and pastoral proposals of the Synod to be effectively carried out.

In its achievements, this year's Synod is connected with past Synods and is their continuation—we speak of the 1971 Synod and especially of the 1977 Synod which served, and ought to serve, to draw the conclusion from the Second Vatican Council regarding life. These Synods help the work pertaining to this, so that the Church might in an appropriate way address itself to the conditions of our age.

ACCURATE EXAMINATION

6. Among the labors of this Synod, of the greatest usefulness must be considered the accurate examination of doctrinal and pastoral questions which certainly needed such scrutiny and, consequently, the sure and insightful judgment concerning each of these questions.

In the abundance of interventions, reports and conclusions of this Synod, which has aroused our admiration, there are two hinges on which the discussion has turned: namely, fidelity toward the plan of God for the family, and a pastoral way of acting, proper to which is merciful love and reverence shown to all men and women, and embracing them totally, touching their "being" and their "living"—in such abundance, we say, there are certain parts which were singularly taken to heart by the Fathers of the Synod, because they were conscious that they were interpreters of the expectations and hopes of many spouses and families.

Therefore, among the labors of the Synod, it is appropriate to remember these questions and to acknowledge this useful examination, which has been pointedly done: namely, the doctrinal and pastoral examination of questions, which, although they were not the only things treated in the Synod discussions, nevertheless had a special place there, insofar as their consideration was undertaken in a very sincere and free manner.

7. From this results the importance which is attributed to the opinions, which the Synod clearly brought forth concerning these questions, retaining at the same time that truly Christian perspective, according to which marriage and the family are considered gifts of divine love.

Therefore, the Synod, commenting on the pastoral ministry of those who have entered a new union after divorce, deservedly praised those spouses, who, although faced with great difficulties, nevertheless witness in their own life to the indissolubility of marriage; in their life there is carried the beautiful message of faithfulness to the love which has in Christ its strength and foundation. Besides, the fathers of the Synod, affirming once again the indissolubility of marriage and the practice of the Church of not admitting to Eucharistic Communion those who have divorced and have—against the rule—attempted another marriage, exhort pastors and the whole Christian community to help these brothers and sisters, who are not to be considered separate from the Church, but by virtue of their Baptism can and ought to participate in the life of the Church by praying, by hearing the Word, by assisting at the Eucharistic Celebration of the community, and by fostering charity and justice. Although it must not be denied that such persons can be received to the sacrament

of Penance, eventually and finally to Eucharistic Communion, when they open themselves with a sincere heart to
live in a manner which is not opposed to the indissolubility
of marriage: namely, when a man and woman in this
situation, who cannot fulfill the obligation to separate,
take on themselves the duty to live in complete continence,
that is, by abstinence from acts in which only married
couples can engage, and when they avoid giving scandal;
nevertheless, the deprivation of sacramental reconciliation
with God should not prevent them from persevering in
prayer, penance, and works of charity that they might find
the grace of conversion and salvation. It is fitting that the
Church present herself as a merciful mother by pouring
forth prayers for these persons and by strengthening them
in faith and in hope.

A PROMISE AND A GRACE

8. The fathers of the Synod are not removed in mind
and heart from the grave difficulties which many spouses
feel in their consciences about moral laws which pertain to
transmitting and fostering human life. Knowing that the
divine precept carries with it both a promise and a grace,
they have openly confirmed the validity and clear truth of
the prophetic message, profound in meaning and pertaining to today's conditions, contained in the Encyclical Letter
Humanae vitae. The same Synod urged theologians to join
their talents with the work of the hierarchical Magisterium
so that the biblical foundation and so-called "personalistic"
reasons for this doctrine might be continually illustrated,
explaining it so that the whole doctrine of the Church
might be clearer to all persons of good will, and so that
understanding might grow deeper by the day.

Directing their attention to those things which concern pastoral ministry for the good of spouses and of
families, the fathers of the Synod rejected any type of division or "dichotomy" between a pedagogy which takes
into account a certain progression in accepting the plan of

God, and doctrine, proposed by the Church, with all its consequences, in which the precept of living according to the same doctrine is contained; in which case there is not a question of a desire of keeping the law as merely an ideal to be achieved in the future, but rather of the mandate of Christ the Lord that difficulties constantly be overcome. Really, the "process of gradualness," as it is called, can't be applied unless someone accepts divine law with a sincere heart and seeks those goods which are protected and promoted by the same law. Thus, the so-called *ex gradualitatis* (law of gradation) or gradual progress can't be the same as *gradualitas legis* (the gradation of the law), as if there were in divine law various levels or forms of precept for various persons and conditions.

All spouses are called to sanctity in marriage according to God's plan; but this vocation takes an effect insofar as the human person responds to the precept of God, and with a serene mind has confidence in divine grace and one's own will. Therefore, for spouses, if both are not bound by the same religious insights, it will not be enough to accommodate oneself in a passive and easy manner to existing conditions, but they must try, so that, with patience and good will, they might find a common willingness to be faithful to the duties of Christian marriage.

CONSIDERING CULTURES

9. The fathers of the Synod have sought a deeper awareness and consciousness either of the riches which are found in various forms in people's cultures, or of the benefits which every culture brings with it—through which the unfathomable mystery of Christ is more fully understood. Besides, they have acknowledged, even within the purposes of marriage and the family, a vast field of theological and pastoral research, so that the accommodation of the message of the Gospel to the character of each people might be fostered, and so that it might be perceived in what ways, customs, outstanding characteristics,

the sense of life and the genius peculiar to each human culture are compatible with those things from which divine revelation is known (cf. *Ad gentes divinitus*, no. 22).

This inquiry, if it is instituted according to the principle of communion with the universal Church and under the impetus of local bishops, who are joined among themselves and with St. Peter's Chair, "which presides over the universal assembly of charity" (LG 13), will bear fruit for families.

DIGNITY OF WOMAN

10. In words both opportune and persuasive, the Synod has spoken of woman with reverence and a grateful spirit, especially of her dignity and vocation as a daughter of God, as a wife, and as a mother. Therefore, it commendably asked that human society be so constituted that women not be forced to engage in external work proper to a certain role or, as they say, profession, but rather, so that the family might be able to live rightly, that the mother might devote herself fully to the family.

TRUTH IN CHARITY

11. If we have remembered these outstanding questions and the responses which the Synod gave to them, we would not wish to think less of other matters which the Synod treated; for it has been shown how, in many interventions through these weeks, useful and fruitful, worthy questions were treated, which are explained either in the teaching or in the pastoral ministry of the Church, with great reverence and love, full of mercy toward men and women, our brothers and sisters, who come to the Church to receive words of faith and hope. Therefore, taking the example of the Synod, pastors should address these problems as they exist in married and family life with the same care and firm will so that we all might "bear the truth in charity."

We now wish to add something as the fruit of labors which we have undertaken for more than four weeks: namely, that no one can exercise charity other than in truth. This principle can be applied to the life of families no less than to the life and work of pastors who really intend to serve families.

Therefore, the fruit of this Synod session has been found in precisely this: that the roles of the Christian family, of which charity itself is the heart, are not fulfilled except in full charity. Moreover, all on whom it has been proposed to confer responsibility for a role of this type in the Church—whether lay people or clerics or religious of either sex—can do it in no other way than in truth. For truth is that which frees; truth is that which provides order; truth shows the way to holiness and justice.

It has been shown to us how great is the love of Christ and how great is the charity conferred on all those who establish any family in the Church and in the world: not only to the men and women joined in marriage, but also to children and young people, to widows and orphans, and to each and every person who participates in family life in any way.

To all of these, the Church wants to be and to remain a witness and, as it were, a portal to the fullness of that life of which St. Paul speaks at the beginning of the words just read: that we have become rich in all things in Christ Jesus, in every word and in all knowledge (cf. 1 Cor. 1:5).

And now we announce to you that we have appointed to help the General Secretary of the Synod of Bishops three prelates, whose nomination originates with the Roman Pontiff, to add to the twelve members of the same Secretariat elected by you. They are: Cardinal Ladislaus Rubin, Prefect of the Sacred Congregation for Oriental Churches; Archbishop Paulos Tzadua, Metropolitan Archbishop of Addis Ababa of the Ethiopians; Archbishop Carlo Maria Martini, Archbishop of Milan.

Finally, we wish you all well in the Lord.

All Are Called to Holiness

On October 26, 1980, in St. Peter's Square, the Holy Father presided over the solemn rite of beatification of Don Luigi Orione, Sr. Mary Anne Sala and Bartolo Longo. There were present thirty-five Cardinals, some hundred bishops, and over a hundred thousand faithful and pilgrims from various regions of Italy and numerous nations of the five continents. John Paul II delivered the following homily.

Esteemed brothers and beloved sons and daughters!

"Gaudeamus omnes in Domino, hodie, diem festum celebrantes sub honore Beatorum nostrorum!"

We can rightly sing this today, on this magnificent solemnity, while our spirits rise in contemplation of the heavenly glory reached by three new Blessed: Don Luigi Orione, Sr. Mary Anne Sala, and Bartolo Longo.

GIFT FROM THE ALMIGHTY

1. It is a day of rejoicing because the Church tells us that they officially enter the cult of the Christian faithful and can be invoked and prayed to, as already participating in eternal happiness. It is a day of rejoicing, because the Church, through them, indicates to us in an authoritative and certain way the goal of our life and the way to reach it, reminding us with St. Paul that "the sufferings of this present time are not worth comparing with the glory that is to be revealed to us" (Rom. 8:18); and it is a day of great rejoicing because the universal Church, and in particular Italy, delights together with the Sons of Divine Providence, the Sisters of St. Marcellina, and the citizens of Pompeii and Naples, in the honor publicly bestowed on these three champions of faith and charity.

Yes, the Lord is near us and makes us understand, through them, His will with regard to our earthly and eternal destiny: the salvation and sanctification of man, created "after the likeness of God in true righteousness and holiness" (Eph. 4:24). The three new Blessed, whom we in-

395 ALL ARE CALLED TO HOLINESS

voke today, along different ways and through painful trials, "fought the good fight, kept the faith, persevered in charity, thus reaching the reward" (cf. 2 Tm. 4:7). And now, together with the multitude of saints, they are for us light and comfort, support and consolation; they walk with us and for us, as teachers and friends; they are a gift from the Almighty, with their example, their word, their intercession.

Let our stirred-up gratitude, therefore, rise to God, the Author of grace, at this moment.

THE PRIEST: DON LUIGI ORIONE

2. Let us now concentrate in reflection, in particular, on the extraordinary message that each of the Blessed proposes to our meditation.

Don Luigi Orione appears to us as a marvelous and brilliant manifestation of Christian charity.

It is impossible to summarize in a few sentences the adventurous and sometimes tragic life of the one who defined himself, humbly but wisely, as "God's porter." But we can say that he was certainly one of the most eminent personalities of this century, due to his Christian faith, professed openly, and his charity, lived heroically. He was, entirely and joyfully, the priest of Christ, traveling all over Italy and Latin America, dedicating his life to those in greatest suffering from misfortune, want, and human wickedness. Let it be enough to recall his active presence among the victims of the earthquakes in Messina and Marsica. Poor among the poor, driven by love of Christ and brothers in greatest need, he founded the Little Work of Divine Providence, the Little Missionary Sisters of Charity, and later the Blind Sacramentine Sisters and the Hermits of St. Albert.

He also opened other houses in Poland (1923), in the United States (1934), and in England (1936), in a real ecumenical spirit. He then wished to give his love for Mary concrete shape by erecting at Tortona the wonderful Sanctuary of Our Lady of Custody. It moves me to think that Don Orione always had a special predilection for Poland, and suffered immensely when my dear country was invaded and torn apart in September, 1939. I know that the Polish red and white flag, which he carried triumphantly in a procession to the sanctuary of our Lady in those tragic days, still hangs on the wall of his modest room in Tortona: he himself wanted it there! And in the last greeting he uttered in the evening of March 8, 1940, before going to San Remo, where he was to die, he said again: "I love the Poles so much. I have loved them since my boyhood; I have always loved them.... Always cherish these brothers of yours."

From his life, so intense and dynamic, there emerges the secret and originality of Don Orione: He let himself be led only and always by the rigorous logic of love! Immense and complete love of God, Christ, Mary, the Church, the Pope, and equally absolute love for man—the whole of man, body and soul—and all men, little and great, rich and poor, humble and wise, holy and sinful, with special kindness and tenderness for the suffering, the underprivileged, the desperate. He enunciated his program of action as follows: "Our policy is the great and divine charity which does good to all. Let our policy be that of the 'Our Father.' We look at nothing else but souls to save. Souls and souls! That is our whole life; that is the cry and our program; our whole soul, our whole heart!" And he exclaimed with lyrical tones: "Christ comes bearing on His heart the Church, and in His hand the tears and blood of the poor, the cause of the afflicted, the oppressed, widows, orphans, the lowly, outcasts; new heavens open up behind Christ: It is, as it were, the dawn of God's triumph!"

He had the character and the heart of the Apostle Paul, tender and sensitive to the point of tears, tireless and courageous to the point of daring, tenacious and dynamic to the point of heroism, facing dangers of every kind, approaching high personalities of politics and culture, illuminating men without faith, converting sinners, always immersed in continual and confident prayer, sometimes accompanied by terrible penances. A year before his death he had summed up as follows the essential program of his life: "To suffer, be silent, pray, love, crucify oneself and worship." God is wonderful in His saints, and Don Orione remains a luminous example and comfort in faith for everyone.

ALL CHRISTIANS CALLED TO PERFECTION OF LOVE

Beloved in Christ!

Today the Church proposes for our meditation and our imitation a priest, a sister, and a layman: This coincidence of the three "states" of life is really significant! It can be said that it is an admonition and encouragement to all classes that form the People of God, that constitute the Church on her pilgrim way to heaven: We are all called to holiness; there are the necessary and sufficient graces for all; no one is excluded! As the Second Vatican Council stressed: "All Christians in any state or walk of life are called to the fullness of Christian life and to the perfection of love.... The forms and tasks of life are many, but holiness is one—that sanctity which is cultivated by all who act under God's Spirit and, obeying the Father's voice and adoring God the Father in spirit and in truth, follow Christ, poor, humble and cross-bearing, that they may deserve to be partakers of His glory" (LG chap. V, no. 40, b; no. 41, a). And again: "Therefore, all the faithful are invited and obliged to holiness and the perfection of their own state of life" (42, e).

Don Orione, Sister Mary Anne, and Bartolo Longo, reminding us of this fundamental doctrine, give us a lesson of supreme importance: the necessity of our own sanctification, pursued with earnestness, sincerity, humility, and steadfastness: "Seek first the kingdom of God and his righteousness!" Jesus admonished (cf. Mt. 6:33).

The most insidious and ever-recurrent temptation is to want to change society by transforming only the external structures; to want to make man happy on earth, satisfying only his needs and his desires. The new Blessed to whom we pray today tell everyone, priests, religious and laity, that the first and most important commitment is to change oneself, to sanctify oneself, in imitation of Christ, in methodical and persevering daily asceticism: The rest will follow.

We raise our prayer confidently to the new Blessed, who have already reached the eternal joy of heaven: Don Luigi Orione, Sister Mary Anne Sala, Bartolo Longo, intercede for the Church, which you loved so much!

Help us, enlighten us, accompany us on our way, always forward, with Mary!

Extend your glance and your love to the whole of mankind, in need of certainty and salvation!

And await us in the glory of heaven, which you already possess!

Amen! Amen! Alleluia!

Renew Ecclesiastical Commitment

On November 4, 1980, the feast of St. Charles Borromeo, the Holy Father received in audience the Sacred College of Cardinals who presented to him their best wishes for his feast day. John Paul II delivered the following address.

Venerated brothers of the Sacred College!

1. With an act of exquisite courtesy you have wished to gather round me today, to present to me your best wishes on my feast day. The beloved Cardinal deacon has expressed your common sentiments with noble and kind words, which have brought forth a deep and living echo in my heart.

I am cordially grateful to you for such delicate thoughtfulness, and while I in my turn present my sincere good wishes to Cardinal Confalonieri, who also celebrates his feast day today, I wish to testify to you the intense joy which this meeting gives me. The atmosphere of familiar intimacy, which reigns on an occasion such as this, effectively helps to strengthen the bonds of brotherly communion which, by the action of the Holy Spirit, link us together. There spontaneously rise to our lips the joyful words of the Psalm: *"Ecce quam bonum et quam iucundum habitare fratres in unum!"* (Ps. 132[133]:1)

2. I am happy on this occasion to renew to you the expression of my gratitude for the assiduous and intelligent collaboration that you offer me in carrying out the heavy tasks to which Providence has willed to call me. In particular I wish to thank you for the spiritual comfort that comes to me from your prayer, on whose indispensable support I particularly rely: It is necessary that, as for the Apostle Peter, "earnest prayer should be made to God by the church" (cf. Acts 12:5) also for his Successor, since today's difficulties are no less complex and serious than yesterday's.

Continue to be close to me with the generous dedication of your minds and your hearts. St. Charles is before you with the stimulating testimony of a service so similar to yours. For years, in fact, he was at the side of Pope Pius IV, to whom he offered the contribution of his wise diligence in the accomplishment of the weighty tasks of government, and particularly in the historic work of the reconvocation and happy conclusion of the Council of Trent. This is recalled by an authoritative biographer of his, who noted that the Pontiff *"negotium Borromeo dedit ut rem consiliis suis inceptam sollicitudine sua perficeret. Ita quidquid difficile ac periculosum incideret, Legati ad ipsum per litteras deferebant. Idque tam saepe fiebat, ut ne nocturnae quidem quietis certa tempora haberet"* (Giussano, *De rebus gestis S. Caroli*, Mediolani 1751, p. 35).

3. We look with admiration to the impressive example of this incomparable servant of the Church whose tireless dynamism amazed contemporaries, who were obliged to recognize that *"impares tot laboribus plures*

fore, quibus unus Borromaeus eo tempore sufficeret"
(testimony of the bishops of Lanciano and Modena, in *Lettere di S. Carlo IV*, p. 35). How could we fail to perceive the stimulus that comes to us from him to shoulder with renewed enthusiasm the *pondus diei et aestum*, connected with the fulfillment of the duties entrusted to us by the heavenly "Father of the family" in the mystical vineyard of His Church?

May St. Charles, who was not only the champion of the conclusive phase of the Council of Trent, but also the main artisan of its practical implementation, bestow his protection on us generously, so that the post-conciliar period, so rich in ferments and perspectives, which Providence has given us, too, to live, may find us farsighted and courageous ministers in daily ecclesial service, to the benefit of the People of God, for whom Christ died and rose again.

With these wishes to everyone I willingly impart the apostolic blessing, imploring every desired heavenly good.

Vocation to the Ministry —a Choice of Love

On November 4, 1980, over four hundred priests concelebrated the Eucharistic Liturgy with the Holy Father in the Vatican Basilica. With this celebration, the priests intended to open solemnly their meeting in Rome on the subject, "The spirituality of the diocesan priest today," organized by the Italian Episcopal Conference's Commission for the Clergy, and at the same time to take the opportunity to express in prayer their good wishes for the Holy Father on his feast day. The Holy Father delivered the following homily.

Beloved brothers!

I consider it a very special moment in my life to be able to concelebrate with you priests today at the Altar of the Chair of this Vatican Basilica, which is a symbol, center, and irradiation of faith and proclamation of the name of our Lord Jesus Christ.

1. The opportune circumstance which has gathered you from all over Italy, together with our venerated brother, Bishop Luigi Boccadoro, namely, the national meeting on the "Spirituality of the diocesan priest today," falls on the day on which the Church recalls to us the splendid figure of St. Charles Borromeo, the tireless pastor of the diocese of Milan, and also my heavenly patron saint.

The memory of St. Charles, which we are celebrating, can cast so much light on the vast and delicate problems which you are discussing in these days in Rome. It is summed up fundamentally in the pastoral reason of your being and your acting within the Christian community. A reason that demands not only the generous use of all the talents and resources with which the Lord has endowed you, but even the loss and complete surrender of your very lives, like the Good Shepherd, of whom the readings of today's liturgy speak, who does not hesitate to "lay down his life for the brethren" (1 Jn. 3:16) and to "lay down his life for the sheep" (Jn. 1:15), so that they "will heed his voice and become one flock and one shepherd" (cf. Jn. 10:16).

BEGINNING OF THE CHRISTIAN LIFE

2. It was precisely this pastoral consciousness that sustained and guided the spirituality and the work of St. Charles, who, rich and noble as he was, forgot himself to become everything to everyone in a priestly activity that has really something miraculous about it. Pastoral visits, meetings of priests, foundations of seminaries, liturgical directives for the two Roman and Ambrosian rites, catechesis at all levels, diocesan synods, the foundation of schools free of charge, of boarding schools for the young, and homes for the poor and the old: so many signs that manifest the intense and vibrant pastoral charity that strongly impelled his great heart, anxious about the salvation of souls.

But where did he draw such strength in this zealous ecclesial service, which subsequently became exemplary and symbolic for all bishops and priests after the reform of the Council of Trent? The secret of his success was the spirit of prayer. It is well known, in fact, how he dedicated a great deal of time, day and night, to contemplation and union with God both in his private chapel and in the parish churches where he went on pastoral visits. "Souls"—he used to repeat—"are won on one's knees." And in the address which he delivered at his last Synod, and which we meditate upon in the breviary today, he spoke to his priests as follows: "Nothing is so necessary for all ecclesiastics as the mental prayer which precedes all our actions, accompanies them, and follows them.... If you administer the sacraments, O brother, meditate on what you are doing; if you celebrate Mass, think of what you are offering; if you sing in the choir, think of whom you are speaking to, and about what; if you guide souls, meditate on what blood they have been redeemed by.... In this way we will have the strength to generate Christ in ourselves and in others" (*Acta Ecclesia Mediolanensis*, Milan, 1599, 1177-1178).

TO LAY DOWN ONE'S LIFE

3. Only on these conditions is one able to "lay down one's life" for souls, as we heard in the proclamation of the Word, that is, to be true pastors of the Church of God. Only in this way can that *pastoralis caritas*, of which the Second Vatican Council speaks (cf. PO 14), reach its maximum growth, and the priestly ministry really change into that *amoris officium* of which St. Augustine speaks (cf. *Tract. in Ioannem*, 123, 5: PL 35, 1967). Only in this way is the priest, who accepts the vocation to the ministry, able to make it a choice of love, as a result of which the Church and souls become his main interest, and, with this concrete spirituality, he becomes capable of loving the universal Church and that portion of it which is entrusted to him,

with all the eager love of a bridegroom for his bride. A priest who was not integrated in some way in an ecclesial community certainly could not present himself as a valid model of ministerial life, since it is essentially integrated in the concrete setting of the interpersonal relations of the community itself.

Celibacy itself finds its full meaning in this context. This choice of life represents a public sign, of very high value, of the primary and complete love that the priest offers to the Church. The celibacy of the pastor has not only an eschatological meaning, as witness to the future kingdom, but also expresses the deep bond that unites him with the faithful, since they are the community born of his charism and destined to comprise the whole capacity of loving that a priest bears within him. Furthermore, it sets him free interiorly and exteriorly, enabling him to organize his life in such a way that his time, his house, his habits, his hospitality, and his financial resources are conditioned only by what is the purpose of his life: the creation of an ecclesial community around him.

EXAMPLE OF ST. CHARLES

4. These are, beloved priests, some brief ideas—in view of the shortness of the time—for reflection for a priestly spirituality which comes to us from the figure and ministry of St. Charles, the admired and venerated pastor of the Church of Milan. Let us pray to him in the celebration of this Eucharist, that he will obtain from the Father, through the offering of the body and blood of Christ, that we may be prayerful and active priests for His greater glory and for the salvation of souls. Amen.

Fidelity and Perseverance in Communion with the Apostolic See

On November 11, 1980, the Holy Father received in audience a group of bishops from Taiwan making their canonical visit ad limina Apostolorum. *The Pope delivered the following message.*

Venerable and dear brothers in Christ,

1. I am very happy to have this meeting with you, the Bishops of Taiwan, in order to speak with you about the progress being made in your dioceses, about the problems which as pastors you have to face daily in the evangelization of the flock that you have been called to shepherd, and about your present anxieties and your hopes for the future. As you know, this forms part of the specific mission entrusted by Jesus to Peter and his Successors: the care for all the Churches: "Feed my lambs.... Tend my sheep" (Jn. 21:15-17), and the task of strengthening his brethren (cf. Lk. 22:32).

UNITED WITH THE POPE

2. The visit *ad limina Apostolorum* is an expression of that bond which links the bishops, individually and as a body, to the Bishop of Rome, who, by the will of Christ, is also the Pastor of the universal Church.

In fact, the Second Vatican Council clearly reaffirms the constant and unchanging doctrine of the Catholic Church: "The Roman Pontiff, as the Successor of Peter, is the perpetual and visible source and foundation of the unity of the bishops and of the multitude of the faithful. The individual bishop, however, is the visible principle and foundation of unity in his particular Church, fashioned after the model of the universal Church. In and from such individual Churches there comes into being the one and only Catholic Church. For this reason each individual bishop represents his own Church, but all of them together in union with the Pope represent the entire Church joined in the bond of peace, love and unity" (LG 23).

A GREAT PEOPLE

3. The Chinese people, scattered throughout the continent, in Taiwan, Hong Kong and Macau, and in the diaspora, is a great people, formed by a culture that is thousands of years old, formed by the thoughts of great and wise philosophers of ancient times, and by family traditions, such as that relating to the cult of ancestors. And well-known to all is the profound sense of kindness and urbanity that distinguishes it.

The Church, according to the different ways of thinking of the times, has sought to respect these traditions and cultural values, in the spirit of the Gospel, in the line of thought expressed by St. Paul when he exhorts the Philippians to prize "whatever is true, whatever is honorable, whatever is just, whatever is pure, whatever is lovely, whatever is gracious, if there is any excellence, if there is anything worthy of praise" (Phil. 4:8).

The Christian message, therefore, highlights and enriches the positive spiritual and human values existing in every culture and tradition; the Church seeks to attain a harmonious accord between the culture and traditions of a people on the one hand and faith in Christ on the other (cf. GS 57-62). This is a constant challenge for the Church, which must find in the culture and traditions of the people to be evangelized an important and indeed essential point for framing the method of proclaiming the Gospel message, according to the needs of every moment. The example of the great missionaries and apostles of China—as for example the Jesuit Matteo Ricci—should serve as a guide and inspiration for everyone.

A Christian is not just a person of faith, but one who is also called to be the leaven and salt in the civil and political society that he or she lives in. The Church, therefore, inculcates in her faithful a deep sense of love and duty towards their fellow-countrymen and towards their native land. She encourages them to live as upright and exemplary citizens and to work loyally for the all-round progress of the nation of which they are proud to be members.

DEDICATED TO EVANGELIZATION AND OTHER WORKS

4. I know that you, the Bishops of Taiwan, are deeply involved not only in the task of evangelization but also in works of education and social welfare. This, on the one hand, shows the pastoral zeal that animates you and your collaborators: the diocesan clergy, the men and women religious, and the laity. On the other hand, it honors the religious freedom that the Church in your territory enjoys.

The Holy See appreciates this attitude and encourages all the members of the Church in Taiwan to make good use of the situation of freedom and respect that it enjoys, in order to devote itself with ever greater fervor to the evangelization of the Chinese people and to those other good works that depend upon the local Churches.

On my part I hope for an ever greater increase of Chinese ecclesiastical and lay workers in the Lord's vineyard, an increase that will be the fruit mainly of a healthy Christian upbringing received in the family and in Catholic educational institutions. At the same time I express the earnest desire that these workers be given a solid and well-rooted formation both in the branches of knowledge necessary or useful for their future pastoral work, and also in the discipline of the Christian virtues, so that they will be effective collaborators of the Holy Spirit in building up that chosen portion of the kingdom of God that is in China.

RELIGIOUS SITUATION

5. Among the preoccupations that you have manifested to me, the present religious situation of the Catholic Church on the continent occupies a special place. I assure you that these preoccupations are also very much my own. From various parts of that immense territory I receive information that attests to the perseverance of very many Catholics in the Faith, in prayer and in religious practice, and that shows their firm attachment to the See of Peter. This news has moved me deeply, and it impels me to offer up a prayer, together with you my brother bishops, for that heroic Church, that the Lord may pour out upon those brave brethren and upon the faithful people the gifts of fortitude and perseverance, maintaining in them the ardent flame of hope that does not disappoint (cf. Rom. 5:5).

QUEEN OF CHINA

And finally, beloved brothers, I entrust the evangelization of China to the maternal protection of Mary, Queen of China. I pray for the prosperity and progress of the whole Chinese people, whom I affectionately remember every day in my prayers and in my pastoral concerns. With immense confidence in the power of the death and resurrection of the Lord Jesus, I repeat with the Apostle Peter: "Peace to all of you who are in Christ" (1 Pt. 5:14).

It is also a great joy for me to welcome, together with the bishops, the Chinese priests and religious resident in Rome. In you I render homage to the fidelity of all the Chinese priests and religious who follow the Lord Jesus with generosity and joy, sharing daily in His Paschal Mystery of death and resurrection.

Our unity in Christ and in His Catholic Church is indeed a wonderful gift of the Father—a gift which finds its supreme temporal expression in the Eucharist, and which prompts us to "wait in joyful hope for the coming of our Savior, Jesus Christ."

May your thoughts and resolutions, dear brothers and sisters, be centered today on the great fidelity to which you are called: fidelity to unity, fidelity to the Eucharist, fidelity to hope. This fidelity is essential to our baptismal calling, to our vocation, to our consecration. This fidelity embraces a whole attitude, a whole program of life; it is, moreover, an indispensable basis for any apostolate at the service of the Gospel. And may Mary, *Virgo fidelis*, sustain you in this fidelity, keeping you faithful to Jesus forever.

To Serve Truth in Its Multiple Aspects

On November 13, 1980, the Holy Father received in audience a group of bishops from Bolivia who had arrived in the Vatican to carry out the canonical visit ad limina Apostolorum. *John Paul II delivered the following address.*

Beloved brothers in the episcopate,

I welcome you with deep joy today, pastors of the People of God in Bolivia, who, after a postponement prompted by special events in your country, have come to Rome to carry out your visit *ad limina Apostolorum.* I feel close to you and to all the members of your respective ecclesial communities, and my affectionate thought goes to them too, assuring you with words of the Apostle St. Paul that "I do not cease to give thanks for you, remembering you in my prayers, that the God of our Lord Jesus Christ...may give you a spirit of wisdom and of revelation in the knowledge of him" (Eph. 1:17).

This brotherly meeting of Peter's Successor with you is the climax of your coming to Rome and the widened expression of that ecclesial communion which has already been manifested in the separate talks with each one of you. A beautiful way to make deeper and deeper the bonds of union in ecclesial love that mutually bind us.

I then thank God for all that and for the opportunity offered to me to share with you the hopes and problems of your dioceses, as well as to encourage you in your generous commitment to the Lord's cause. For this reason I longed to see you "that I may impart to you some spiritual gift to strengthen you, that is, that we may be mutually encouraged by each other's faith, both yours and mine" (Rom. 1:11f.).

SOLID UNION OF AIMS AND SENTIMENTS

I wish to express to you in the first place the deep satisfaction it gives me to see the solid union of aims and sentiments that exists among the various members of the Bolivian episcopate, morally present here in full force and led by the president and vice-president of the episcopal conference. I exhort you to maintain and strengthen this communion, the indispensable premise for effective pastoral work without the weakening effect of community tensions.

Another reason that gives me joy is the effort made by the episcopate of Bolivia to promote a catechesis adapted to the concrete circumstances of your own environment, following the directives indicated by *Catechesi tradendae.* It is unnecessary for me to stress this point, of such importance for arriving at this deep and generalized evangelization to which the Church in Latin America and in Bolivia in particular has dedicated and dedicates such generous energies.

I know that, precisely to give a valid response to this evangelizing need, you are engaged with renewed interest in the apostolate of native vocations to priestly life and to consecrated life in general. This is a chapter of decisive importance for the animation of ecclesial communities and for keeping them in faith. For this reason, all the initiatives you undertake to strengthen this fundamental area of the apostolate can depend on my satisfied approval and most cordial encouragement.

To prepare adequately the ground in which these vocations germinate, you are well aware how indispensable it is to give the most careful attention to the apostolate of the family, to which the recent Synod of Bishops rightly dedicated its diligent study. In its reflections and indications you will be able to find inspiration to give a new impetus to the family apostolate.

TO EDUCATE IN FAITH

This work will have to find its natural complement in the effort to educate the new generations, so that they may be strengthened in knowledge and experience of Christian principles and be capable of taking them in turn to the various environments of society. The achievements reached and the positive contribution offered by the Church in Bolivia and by Catholic schools—particularly by the Catholic University in La Paz—are an eloquent testimony of the spirit that animates the hierarchy and others invested with responsibility, to educate in faith and at the same time contribute to the welfare of the whole of society.

Although the mission to be carried out is a very vast one and many goals remain to be reached, I also see with pleasure that the Church in Bolivia has not forgotten at any moment the initiatives aimed at promoting also the human advancement of the neediest sectors of the population. I encourage you to intensify efforts in this direction, giving priority, which is not, however, exclusive or excluding, to attention to the poor, of which I myself and the Latin American Bishops have repeatedly treated (cf. my Address on the occasion of the twenty-fifth anniversary of CELAM, Rio de Janeiro, July 2, 1980, no. 7).

LOFTY PRONOUNCEMENT

I am also aware that, in the accomplishment of your duty and mission as leaders and guides of the ecclesial community in Bolivia, your voice has been raised at delicate moments for peaceful social life at the national level. Faithful to your office as pastors and guided by a Christian view of the human being, conscious also of the obligation to serve the truth in its multiple implications, you have made a pronouncement in favor of "the dignity of man and the freedom of the Gospel" (cf. Collective Letter of the Episcopal Conference of Bolivia on "Dignity and Freedom," Cochabamba, Sept. 8, 1980).

This is a dimension of her Magisterium which the Church cannot renounce, as an indivisible part of her service to God and to man.

Beloved brothers: I would be happy to talk to you about other concrete subjects, but we cannot prolong this meeting further.

Continue to work with renewed enthusiasm in the part of the Church that has been entrusted to you. God grant that your effort and the efficacious collaboration of your priests, men and women religious, seminarians, committed laity and that of so many other persons of good will, with the help of the Lord of the harvest who transcends all human capacity, will make available the forces necessary for faithful and continuous service of the Church and of man, our brother. With my prayer for all the sons and daughters of your beloved country, I assure you of my cordial favor and I give you my affectionate blessing.

Let Us Carry Christ's Love to a World Thirsting for It

On November 17, 1980, in Fulda's Cathedral, where St. Boniface, the Apostle of Germany, is buried, the Holy Father celebrated Mass and delivered the following homily to priests, deacons, and seminarians.

Dear brothers in Christ, Cardinals, archbishops and bishops, who form the episcopate of your homeland; my priests, beloved in Christ from the college of priests of every diocesan Church in Germany;

Dear deacons;

Dear seminarians, dear students of theology:

1. The words of the Apostle Peter which we have heard today in the second lesson of this liturgical celebration appear to me to have a very special sound here at the tomb of St. Boniface in Fulda: "So I exhort the elders among you, as a fellow elder and a witness of the sufferings of Christ, as well as a partaker in the glory that is to be revealed: Tend the flock of God that is your charge, taking care of it" (1 Pt. 5:1-2).

Nineteen hundred years have already passed since these words were written, and yet they still have the same freshness and force. They seem to me even to proclaim a very special message at this moment during your presence at the tomb of the bishop and martyr who is Germany's principal patron saint, precisely you to whom Peter's appeal is directed, certainly in different degrees: "Take care of the flock of God." Peter, who was the first to be called upon by the Good Shepherd to perform this task: "Feed my sheep" (Jn. 21:16), addresses himself as one of the "elders" to all those who together with him were shepherds of his time. With what deep emotion do we who are today shepherds of the Church hear these words, in the second millennium of Christianity which is drawing to its close! You who, according to the different ranks of your ministry—bishops, priests, or deacons—are shepherds of the Church in your homeland! And also you who have answered Christ's vocation and are preparing yourselves for your ministry as shepherds in time to come!

"Take care of the flock of God." Be shepherds of your brothers and sisters in your Faith, your baptismal grace, and your hope of sacred participation in the eternal grace and love!

ROOTED IN THE MYSTERY OF CHRIST

2. Peter reminds us in his Epistle of the suffering of Christ and likewise of the mystery of Easter to which he became a witness. With that testimony of the cross and the resurrection he then also links the hope of being "a partaker of that glory which is to be revealed" (1 Pt. 5:1).

The vocation to become shepherds of the Church and their various pastoral services always and everywhere have their roots in the comprehensive mystery of Christ: They lead from Him and to Him; in Him they find the strength for growth and full support; they serve Him with the fruit of their labor.

This mystery is then believed in true faith if those who serve Him are like to men "who wait for their Lord when he shall return from the wedding, that when he comes and knocks they may open immediately" (Lk. 12:36).

It is, therefore, the service of being alert for the Lord.

When Jesus began His time of suffering, He took the Apostles with Him into the Garden of Gethsemane. Three of them He led even deeper into the garden and asked them to watch with Him. But when, overcome with tiredness, they had fallen asleep, he returned to them and said: "Watch, and pray that you enter not into temptation" (Mt. 27:41).

Thus the service we are performing, dear brothers, is that of watching for the Lord. Watching means waiting beside that with which we have been entrusted. And that possession with which we have been entrusted is infinitely precious. We must constantly keep watch over it. We must submerge the roots of our faith, of our hope and love ever more in the "wonderful works of God" (Acts 2:11); we must identify ourselves ever more with the Revelation of the Father in Christ; and finally, we must be ever more sensitive to the influence of the Holy Spirit whom the Lord has bestowed upon us, and whom we want the Lord to keep on bestowing upon us through our ministry, through our holiness, through our priestly identity.

In the same way we must develop an ever deeper feeling for the greatness of man as revealed to us in the mystery of the Incarnation and the redemption: How precious is every human soul and how rich the treasures of grace and love.

Then we shall be able to act in accordance with Peter's exhortation, who has urged us to perform our duties "not by constraint but willingly, according to God...eagerly ...being examples to the flock" (1 Pt. 5:2-3).

GREAT MEN OF GOD

3. Let us consider the many outstanding bishops and priests whom this country has produced. I will name only a few of more recent times: Bishop von Ketteler and Adolf Kolping; Cardinals von Galen, Frings, Döpfner and Bengsch; Father Alfred Delp and the young priest, Karl Leisner; Karl Sonnenschein and Father Rupert Mayer; Romani Guardini and Father Kentenich.

Let us study them more closely! They all show us the meaning of this "watching"; what it means to have "one's loins girt" and to carry "lamps burning in your hands" (Lk. 12:35); how one can be a "faithful and wise servant, whom his master has set over his household to give them their food at the proper time" (Mt. 24:45).

These and many other model priests of the Church in your country can show us how our calling and all our ministry as bishops, priests or deacons are based on that glorious mystery of the human heart: the mystery of friendship with Christ, and how through the strength of that friendship the shepherd's true love of man grows, a mature, selfless love, which the world today thirsts for so greatly, especially the young generation.

I know that countless priests of the Church in your country experience the joy and the happiness of this deep spiritual affinity with Jesus Christ. But I know that there are also hours of anguish, of exhaustion, helplessness, and disappointment in the life of the priest today. I am convinced that this is also part of the life of those priests who devote their entire energy to the faithful accomplishment of their mission and perform their duties with great conscientiousness. Should it come as a surprise to us that the one who in his mission is so closely linked with Jesus Christ also shares the hours Jesus spent on the Mount of Olives?

FRIENDSHIP WITH CHRIST

4. What medicine can I offer you in this situation? Not that you should increase your activities, not that you should make desperate efforts, but that you should hold deeper communion with yourselves with regard to your calling, that very friendship with Christ, friendship with one another. Through you, Christ Himself wants to be visible as the friend of all in your midst and in the midst of your parishes. "No longer do I call you servants...but I have called you friends" (Jn. 15:15).

These words, which still resound in your hearts from the time of your ordination, should be the keynote of your life. To my friend I can say anything; I can confide my private thoughts with him: all my troubles and sorrows, all the unresolved problems and painful experiences.

I can base my life on His words, on the sacraments of the Eucharist and, not least, of Penance. That is the ground on which we stand. Have trust in Jesus Christ that He may not leave you, that He will assist you in the performance of your duties, even at times when success does not immediately appear to be at hand. Believe that although He expects everything of you, He does so as a friend expects it of his friends.

Friendship with Jesus Christ: that is also the deepest reason why a life of celibacy, indeed taken as a whole in the spirit of the evangelical counsels, is so important for the priest. To have one's heart and one's hands free for our friend, Jesus Christ, to be totally at His disposal and to carry His love to all men—that is a testimony which is not immediately understood by all. But if we inwardly fulfill that testimony, if we live it as our friendship with Jesus, then the understanding of this lifestyle which has its foundations in the Gospel will grow again in the community.

Friendship with Jesus has as both its fruit and consequence friendship with one another. The priests form a college around their bishop. The bishop is the one who represents Christ in a special way for you and with you. He who is a friend of Christ cannot bypass the mission of the bishop. Indeed, he will sense it; he will not pit his own views and standards against the mission which Christ has given the bishop. Unity with the bishop and the unity with the Successor of Peter are the firm foundation of a fidelity which cannot be lived without the friendship of Christ. That union is also essential if our ministry, the ministry of the bishops and the Pope, is to be performed in open, fraternal and understanding affection for you.

But that friendship demands still more. It demands that fraternal openness for one another, that we help to carry one another's burdens. It demands a common testimony so that we do not judge one another, mistrust one another, or think of our own prestige. I am convinced that if you conduct your ministry in the spirit of friendship and fraternity, you will achieve more than if everyone goes his own way. In the strength of such a friendship with the Lord you will be able to "watch" as was the Lord's hope of the "good servants" in the Gospel.

WATCHFUL MINISTRY

5. This "being watchful" on the part of the servant—the friend—waiting for the Lord relates also to the ultimate future in God and to the course of that history, to every moment. The Lord can come "in the second watch or in the third watch" (Lk. 12:38).

Through the instructions handed down by the Second Vatican Council, the whole Church has made it clear that it directs its mission in each case to the present, that is, to a world which is constantly developing, and above all to the hopes of the people in that world, to its joy and hope, but also its waywardness and errors (GS 1).

The ministry of the watchful and attentive shepherd also means, therefore, opening one's eyes wide to everything good and genuine, to everything true and beautiful, but also to everything grave and sorrowful in the life of man, and to do so full of love, full of readiness to be close at hand in a spirit of solidarity, even to sacrifice one's life (Jn. 10:11).

The shepherd's watchful ministry also means being ready to defend others against the ravaging wolf—as in the parable of the Good Shepherd—or against the thief, that he may not break into the house (Lk. 12:39). With that I do not mean a priest who keeps a strict, distrustful and merciless eye on the flock entrusted to him, but a shepherd who aims to free his flock from sin and guilt by the offer of reconciliation, who above all grants the people the sacrament of Penance.

"For Christ," the priest may and should call out to an irreconciled and irreconcilable world: "Be reconciled with God" (2 Cor. 5:20). In this way we reveal to the people the heart of God the Father and are thus an image of Christ the Good Shepherd. Our whole life can then become a sign and tool of reconciliation, the "sacrament" of the union between God and man.

But, together with me, you will note that the personal reception of the sacrament of Penance in your parishes has

fallen off very considerably in recent years. I earnestly
beseech you—indeed, I admonish you—to do everything
possible to make the sacrament of Penance in personal
confession something which all who have been baptized
will again regard as the natural thing to do. That is the aim
of penitential Church services, which play a very important part in the practice of the Church, but under normal
circumstances cannot be a substitute for the personal
reception of the sacrament of Penance. But also endeavor
yourselves to receive the sacrament of Penance regularly.

LIKE THE GOOD SHEPHERD

6. The watchfulness of the Good Shepherd is
expected of you in regard to the essence of all priestly activity, the celebration of the Holy Liturgy. Precisely after the
comprehensive reform of divine services, there are important pastoral tasks for you to perform. You will yourselves
first have to study and attentively practice the approved
rites. You should be in a position, as liturgists, to minister
to the deeper faith, the stronger hope and the greater love
among the People of God. I wish to thank you for all the
work you have put into the achievement of those important
aims, whose good fruit I have already been privileged to
see among you. It is all the more regrettable that the
celebration of the Mystery of Christ, here and there,
instead of spreading unity with Christ and among one
another, causes dissension and division. Nothing could be
more inimical to the will and the spirit of Christ.

I therefore beseech you, my priestly brothers and
friends, to proceed with responsibility along the path of
the Church which, true to its old tradition, it has today
resolved to follow, and to keep it from any spurious subjectivism. But I should like to emphasize that the special
liturgical arrangements which the German bishops have
requested on pastoral grounds have been granted by the
Apostolic See and are therefore legitimate.

Endeavor above all to proclaim the teaching of Jesus Christ in union with the entire community of the Church in a reverent and faithful celebration of the Mass—Jesus Christ, with whom you yourselves are united in friendship.

UNDERSTANDING YOUR CALL
AND MISSION

7. Dear brothers, dear sons in the Lord!

How deeply must we love our ministry and our calling! This I say to you all, to the older ones among you who are perhaps already tired and exhausted under the burden of your work; to those of you who are in the prime of your energy; and to those of you who are about to enter the priesthood. And I am also addressing the younger ones who hear God's secret calling. I want to encourage you to bring that vocation more firmly and more deeply into your lives and to follow it irrevocably and forever.

Today's first lesson from the prophet Jeremiah speaks very clearly of the miracle of that calling. An unprecedented but real dialogue between God and man. God-Yahweh says: "Before I formed you in the womb, I knew you: and before you were born, I consecrated you; I appointed you a prophet to the nations."

Man-Jeremiah replies: "Ah, Lord God, behold, I do not know how to speak, for I am only a youth."

God-Yahweh replies: "Do not say: 'I am only a youth'; for to all to whom I send you, you shall go, and whatever I command you, you shall speak. Be not afraid of them: for I am with you to deliver you" (Jer. 1:5-8).

How deep is the truth that lies in this dialogue! We should definitely make it the truth of our own life! We must grasp it with both hands and with our whole heart; we must live it, make it the subject of our prayers and become as one with it!

And this is at the same time the theological and psychological truth about our life! Man, who perceives his calling and his mission, speaks to God out of his weakness.

BE NOT AFRAID

8. The various advocates of a priesthood which differs from the image as developed by the Church and principally maintained in the Western tradition often appear today to make this weakness the fundamental principal of all else by almost declaring it to be a human right.

But Christ has taught us that man has above all a right to his greatness, a right to that which really towers above him. For it is precisely here that his special dignity emerges; here is revealed the wonderful power of grace: our true greatness is a gift deriving from the strength of the Holy Spirit.

In Christ, man has a right to such greatness. And the Church, through that same Christ, has a right to the gift of man: to a gift by which man offers himself totally to God, in which he also opts for celibacy "for the kingdom of heaven" (Mt. 19:12) in order to be the servant of all.

Man and the Church have a right to this. We should not weaken this certainty and conviction within ourselves! We must not abandon this illustrious legacy of the Church, nor should we hamper its growth in the hearts of the young.

Do not abandon your trust in God and in Christ! The Lord says: "Be not afraid of them: for I am with you to deliver you" (Jer. 1:8). After these words the Lord touches man's mouth and says: "Behold, I have put my words in your mouth" (Jer. 1:9). Have we not had the same experience? Does He not, when we take Holy Orders, place His words—the words of the Eucharistic consecration—in our mouth? Does He not seal our lips and man's whole being with the power of His grace?

With us also are the saints of the Church: the patron saints of your dioceses, the great ministers of your country, the famous women of charity, and above all Mary, the Mother of the Church.

When Luke the Evangelist describes the Lord's ascension to the disciples who were "persevering with one mind" in prayer, he specifically says: "with Mary the Mother of Jesus" (Acts 1:14). She, the Mother of the Lord, the Mother of all the faithful, the Mother, too, of priests, wants to be with us so that we can ever again be sent in the Holy Spirit into this world and to the people with their troubles.

A REWARD AWAITS YOU

9. Dear brothers, dear sons in the Lord! The lessons of this liturgy finally also tell us the reward that awaits shepherds who stay awake. The Apostle Peter speaks of the "never fading crown of glory" (1 Pt. 5:4).

But more impressive still are the words of Christ in the parable of the watchful servants: "Blessed are those servants whom the master finds awake when he comes; truly I say to you, he will gird himself and have them sit at table, and he will come and serve them. If he comes in the second watch, or in the third, and finds them so, blessed are those servants" (Lk. 12:37-38).

I will let these words stand as they are without any addition. But may I warmly commend them to your prayers and your contemplation. Amen.

Make Room for the Gifts of the Spirit: Power, Wisdom, Love

On November 17, 1980, the Holy Father met the members of the episcopal conference of Germany and delivered the following address.

Dear and venerated brothers in the episcopate!

1. Our memorable meeting today at the tomb of Saint Boniface is set against the background of the great and rich

history of the German people, which bears the decisive imprint of Christianity. Formed by so many forces, in the course of the centuries it has given numerous impulses of a religious, cultural and political character reaching far beyond its frontiers. I need only recall here the glorious name, pregnant with history, of the "Holy Roman Empire of the German Nation."

Your people, together with what is today the Netherlands, gave the Church seven Popes, about whom history informs us that they conscientiously carried out their service as Supreme Pastors of Christianity—even in the greatest external and internal agitations of the time. One of the main concerns common to nearly all of them during their pontificates, which were often too short, was the renewal of the Church. Special mention should be made of the zealous effort of Pope Hadrian VI for the maintenance and the re-establishment of the unity of Christians. Many of them made a personal visit as Pope to their German homeland and their former dioceses.

The interior renewal of religious and ecclesiastical life and the ecumenical effort for a rapprochement and understanding between separated Christians are the main concerns also of my apostolic journeys to the various local Churches and continents. They are also the main concerns in my pastoral visit to the Church of your country and at this meeting today. The spiritual renewal of the Church and the unity of Christians are the explicit charge of the Second Vatican Council, which is equally binding on the Pope, the bishops, the priests, and the faithful. To assume joint responsibility for these tasks is the urgent imperative of the hour. They are the great challenge and the duty, above all, of our collegial responsibility as pastors of the Church. The following considerations of mine also concern them and wish to be of value to them.

From the first hour of my pontificate I understood the office of Supreme Pastor as a service for the collegiality of the bishops who are united with Peter's Successor, and conversely I understood the *"collegialitas effectiva et affectiva"* of the bishops as an important help for my own service.

On this visit to your country, I am anxious, in the first place, to express my total closeness to you, my communion with you, and to strengthen it with my witness. And here my thoughts go back to September of 1978 when I stayed here with you, in the same area of Fulda, for a brotherly exchange between the episcopate of my country, Poland, and that of your country. I am happy to see the same faces again, while at the same time my thought and my prayer go to those whom the Lord has called to Himself in the meantime. Finally I wish to greet particularly those brothers who have since then entered the college of the successors of the apostles in your country.

COMMON WITNESS

2. *Have courage for common witness.*

"If we rightly call every man, and in particular every Christian, 'brother,' " as I wrote in my letter to all brother bishops in the world on Holy Thursday 1979, "this word assumes for us bishops and for our mutual relations a quite particular meaning: it is directly linked, in a way, with that brotherly community that united the Apostles round Christ."

I am happy and grateful that, in your conference, I have already on many occasions experienced this unity with Peter's Successors and this unanimity among you. I would like to strengthen you even more in this disposition. I say to you therefore: do not let yourselves be deceived by the often-heard opinion that a high proportion of unanimity within a conference of bishops is to the detriment of the liveliness and credibility of episcopal witness. The opposite is the case. Certainly everyone should introduce himself, in a brotherly atmosphere, without fear or reservations, and certainly everyone must contribute to build up with his contribution the unity of the body, which comprises members, services, and gifts of many kinds. But the fruitfulness of these services and gifts depends on their integration in the one life inspired by the one Spirit.

CONCERN FOR UNITY

3. *Be lovingly concerned with the unity of the presbyterate in every diocese.*

In the last few decades there have been heavy increases in what is expected and asked of priests. As a result of the decrease in the number of priests, a greater number of tasks falls upon them. The demands made on priests in their task of spiritual guidance are increased even more by the numerous professional and volunteer services of the laity in the care of souls. In a society surrounded by an ever-closer network of communications, an increasingly complex spiritual dialogue becomes necessary for priests. Many priests wear themselves out in work, but become solitary and lose their bearings. It is all the more important that the unity of the presbyterate should be lived and experienced. Support everything that strengthens priests to meet one another and to help one another to live the Word and spirit of the Lord.

Three things are particularly close to my heart:

1) The *seminaries.* They must be training-grounds of real priestly fellowship and friendship, as well as places of a clear and solid decision for life.

2) *Theology* must qualify for witness of faith and lead to a deepening of faith, so that priests will understand the problems of men, but also the answers of the Gospel and of the Church.

3) Priests must receive *help* in order to meet the high requirements of celibate life and dedication to Christ and to men, and to bear witness to them through priestly simplicity, poverty, and availability. Precisely spiritual communion can render valuable services here.

THAT ALL MAY BE ONE

4. *Take seriously the prayer of the high priest, Jesus Christ,* that all may be one, as an urgent task in order to overcome the division of Christians.

You live in the country in which the Reformation originated. Your ecclesiastical life and your social life are deeply marked by the scission of the Church, which has now lasted for over four and a half centuries. You must not resign yourselves to the fact that disciples of Christ do not give the testimony of unity before the world. Unshakable fidelity to truth, openness to others and readiness to listen to them, calm patience on the way, love and sensitivity, are necessary. Compromise does not count; what is important is only that unity which the Lord Himself founded: unity in truth and in love.

We often hear it said today that the ecumenical movement of the Churches is at a standstill, that after the spring of the changes brought by the Council, there has followed a period of coolness. In spite of many regrettable difficulties, I cannot agree with this judgment.

Unity, which comes from God, is given to us at the cross. We must not want to avoid the cross, passing to rapid attempts at harmonizing differences, excluding the question of truth. But neither must we abandon one another and go on our separate ways, because drawing closer calls for the patient and suffering love of Christ crucified. Let us not be diverted from the laborious way in order to remain where we are, or to choose ways that are apparently shorter and lead astray.

The ecumenical way, the effort for unity, must not be limited only to the Churches born of the Reformation —also in your country the dialogue and brotherly attitude toward other Churches and other ecclesial communities, for example, toward the Churches of Orthodoxy, are of the utmost importance. However, the memory of the *Confessio Augustana* published 450 years ago is a special appeal to the dialogue with Christianity that bears the stamp of the Reformation, and that has such a great part in the population and history of your country.

PROCLAIM THE WORD

5. *Gather the People of God, oppose false pluralism, strengthen real communion.*

I have already spoken of the high value of brotherly unity in the college of bishops and of the presbyterate. This unity, however, must be the soul by which there lives also the unity of the whole People of God in all communities. It is not a question at all of curbing or limiting the legitimate plurality of expression of spirituality, piety and theological schools. But all this must be an expression of the fullness, and not of the poverty, of faith.

The proclamation of the faith and also ecclesial life can, thank God, freely develop externally in your country. The dialogue to which you are called, however, is a demanding one. Men often find themselves spiritually in the situation of a great store in which all possible goods are praised and offered for customers to help themselves. Thus in the outlook on life of many people in your country, elements of Christian tradition are mingled with completely different conceptions. The external freedom of saying and thinking what one likes is often confused with the inner promptings of conviction; instead of a clear orientation, indifference towards many opinions and interpretations sets in.

What altogether are your tasks and your possibilities with regard to the situation indicated?

I would like to shout two words to you. First: proclaim the Word in all clarity, indifferent to applause or rejection! It is not we, after all, who determine the success or failure of the Gospel, but the Spirit of God. Believers and non-believers have the right to hear clearly the authentic message of the Church.

Second: proclaim the Word with all the love of the Good Shepherd who dedicates Himself, searches, understands. Listen to the questions raised by those who think they can no longer find any answer in Jesus Christ and in His Church. Believe firmly that Christ Jesus is united, so to speak, with every man, and that in Him every man can rediscover himself, his real human values and questions (cf. GS 22; RH 13).

I would like to recommend two groups particularly to your care as pastors: in the first place those who have drawn from the impulses of the Second Vatican Council the false conclusion that the dialogue upon which the Church has entered is incompatible with the clearly obligatory character of the Magisterium and of the norms of the Church, and with the authority of the hierarchical office, founded on Christ's mission to the Church. Show that the two go together: fidelity to the indispensable mission and closeness to man with his experiences and his problems.

The other group: those who, partly as a result of inappropriate or too hasty conclusions drawn from the Second Vatican Council, no longer feel at home in the Church of today, or even threaten to break away from her. Here it is a question of transmitting to these men with the utmost decision, but at the same time with the utmost prudence, that the Church of Vatican II, and that of Vatican I and of the Council of Trent and of the first Councils, is one and the same Church.

The importance of a genuine transmission of faith must not be underestimated. How grateful I am for everything that has been carried out in your country in the so-called community catechesis: believers who bear witness to faith, who transmit it to others!

The situation of faith indicated above is certainly a special challenge to priests. Will the whole heritage of faith as the Church presents it really be proclaimed everywhere in the course of a few years? Give encouragement for this; make it your responsibility. And be concerned, too, to the best of your ability, that religious instruction and catechesis will open the way to faith and life with the Church to those who often grew up in such a different background.

WITNESSING CHRISTIANITY
IN DAILY LIVING

6. *Make every effort in order that the unshakable criteria and the norms of Christian action may be expressed in the lives of believers in a way as clear as it is inviting.*

Between the habits of life of a secularized society and the requirements of the Gospel, there is a deep gulf. Many people wish to take part in ecclesial life, but they no longer find any relationship between the world in which they live and Christian principles. It is believed that the Church sticks firmly to her norms only out of obstinacy, and that this is in contradiction to that mercy of which Christ sets us the example in the Gospel. The hard demands of Jesus, His saying: "Go, and do not sin again" (Jn. 8:11), are ignored. People often fall back on personal conscience, but it is forgotten that this conscience is an eye that does not possess light by itself, but only when it looks at the real source of light.

Another thing: in the face of mechanization, functionalization and organization, there springs up precisely in the younger generation a deep mistrust of institutions, norms, and regulation. The Church with her hierarchical constitution, her dogmas and her norms, is contrasted with the spirit of Christ. But the spirit needs vessels which can preserve it and transmit it. Christ Himself is the origin of the Church's mission and authority, in which His promise is fulfilled: "Lo, I am with you always, to the close of the age" (Mt. 28:20).

Dear brothers, keep all needs and problems of men present in your heart, and in their midst proclaim firmly what Jesus demands, without leaving out anything.... Do this because you are concerned about man. Only the man who is capable of a complete and definitive decision, the man whose body and soul are in harmony, the man who is ready to use his whole strength for his salvation, is invulnerable against the secret decomposition of the fundamental substance of humanity.

So devote special attention to youth, among whom there can be seen such promising enthusiasm, but also such estrangement from the Church! Turn with particular care and cordiality to couples and families—the Synod of Bishops, which recently concluded in Rome, must not remain mere theory, but must be filled with life. The alienation of a large part of the working-class population from the Church; the distance between intellectuals and the Church; woman's need, in such changed conditions, to be accepted and feel completely fulfilled both on the Christian and on the human plane: these indications widen the field of our common effort, in order that men may believe tomorrow as well.

I am convinced that a new impetus of moral consciousness and Christian life is closely, in fact indissolubly, linked with one condition: the revival of personal confession. Make this a priority of your pastoral care!

ATTENTION TO SPIRITUAL VOCATIONS

7. *Turn your particular attention to the future of spiritual vocations and pastoral services.*

According to human reckoning, the number of priests who are available for service in the apostolate will be reduced by a good third within a decade. I share from the bottom of my heart the concern that this gives you. I am convinced with you that it is a good thing to stimulate with might and main the service of the permanent diaconate, and also the service of the laity, which is mainly volunteer service, but also professional, for the tasks of pastoral work. The service of priests, however, cannot be replaced by other services. Your tradition of the care of souls absolutely cannot be compared with the conditions of Africa or

Latin America. Yet this makes me think that I met far greater optimism there than in Western Europe, although the number of pastors available there is far less. I consider it one of the most important tasks to do everything possible, with the commitment of prayer and of spiritual testimony, so that God's call to the young to make themselves available for complete service of the Lord may become audible, and that premises in the family, in the community, and in youth associations may grow for this purpose. But panic at the difficult situation dims our view of what the Lord wants of us. The fact that sensitivity to the evangelical counsels and to priestly celibacy is decreasing considerably represents a state of spiritual emergency just as much as the shortage of priests. Certainly, the salvation of souls is the supreme law. But precisely this salvation of souls demands that we should stir up the communities themselves; that we should encourage every baptized and confirmed person to bear witness to faith; that we should stimulate spiritual vitality in our families, our groups, our communities and our movements. Then the Lord will be able to speak and call—and we will be able to hear.

I have also mentioned the great importance of the presbyterate round the bishop. Could not the spiritual service be perceived more effectively if the bond between priests were closer? I would like to mention here once more the great importance of the spiritual community of priests, which can free individuals from excessive demands and isolation. To the extent to which you commit yourselves unanimously and clearly for common testimony to the priesthood in celibacy and for a form of life based on the spirit of the evangelical counsels, the Lord will not be sparing of His gifts of grace.

CONCERN FOR UNIVERSAL HEART
AND VIEW

8. *Be concerned about a universal heart and a universal view for your faithful.*

Allow me to refer to my message for the Berlin Katholikentag: help to construct a universal "civilization of love!" I would like to call your attention in the first place to the dimension of the "universal." To be Christians and to be men today must be to be universal, to be "catholic." Join to the commitment of your availability for material aid also the commitment of your spiritual and religious forces for all, and be ready, too, to receive and learn! There is such humanity not utilized, such spiritual experience, such witness of constructive faith in the young Churches, that our Western countries, now weary, could draw new youth and new life from them.

We certainly cannot ignore a painful reality. In many parts of the world the Church is persecuted; many Christians, many people, are prevented from enjoying their full rights of freedom. Do not take the freedom in your society for granted, but as a commitment for others who do not have this freedom!

Your country is in Europe. I was able to collaborate repeatedly with many of you, when I was Archbishop of Krakow, to animate Europe, to anchor its unity to its spiritual and religious foundations. Just think, Europe can renew itself and unite only from those roots which brought Europe into existence! Think finally of this, precisely in your country: Europe embraces not only the north and the south but also the west and the east!

A piece of Europe, a piece of the world, becomes more and more present in your country through the many foreigners who are living and working among you. Here you have an urgent task, both on the ecclesial plane and on the social one. Think of Him who died for everyone and who made us all His brothers and sisters.

COMMITMENT TO HUMAN SOCIETY

9. *Commit yourselves for human rights and for the solid foundations of human society in your land.*

You live in a society in which a high degree of protection for freedom and human dignity is guaranteed. Be grateful for this, but do not allow arbitrary action to be propagated, in the name of freedom, which strikes at the inviolability of the life of every man, also of unborn life. Realize, too, the dignity and the right of marriage and the family! Only respect of inalienable, fundamental rights and values guarantees that freedom that does not lead to self-destruction! Think about this: The more law and morality differ, the more urgent is the juridical protection of fundamental moral convictions.

The Church in your country has an abundance of institutions for education and instruction, Caritas, and social service. Defend the ability of making your Christian contribution to the construction of society. Think also of this: Credible witness grows only from internal adherence to Jesus Christ and not from a mere external agreement with other forces of society.

A LIFE IN THE SPIRIT OF CHRIST

10. *Against excessive demands and consumerism propose the alternative of a life in the Spirit of Christ.*

On the one hand the desire for possessions and consumerism is growing, so that to have is considered far more than to be (cf. RH 16). On the other hand we are reaching the limit of economic and technical growth. Do we want to build a road towards the decline and ruin of life on our earth instead of towards progress? The example of Christians is necessary. In the hope of future goods, they do not cling to fleeting ones, and, therefore, develop a civilization of love. So stimulate the readiness, so indispensable to be a Christian, for sacrifice and renunciation, and let us also recognize the importance of the evangelical counsels for the whole of society!

11. "God did not give us a spirit of timidity but a spirit of power and love and self-control" (2 Tm. 1:7).

Dear and venerated brothers in the episcopal office, your task is a grave one. In order that the Apostles, whose successors we are, would be able to carry it out, the Lord gave them His Holy Spirit. Let us make room in us and among us for this Spirit. His characteristics are: power, wisdom, love. Power, unconcerned about approval or resistance, to let the Lord Himself speak and operate; power, the most interior measurement of which is the weakness of the cross. Wisdom, which looks with firmness at the truth of Jesus Christ, but also listens without prejudice to the problems and concerns of modern man. Finally, and above all, love, which risks everything, endures everything and hopes for everything; love, which creates unity, because it walks with Jesus Christ to the cross, unites heaven and earth and brings together all the separated. I promise you to bear your burden with you in a brotherly way and I implore from you unshakable unity, becoming deeper and deeper, in this Spirit. May Mary, Queen of the Apostles and Mother of the Church, be with us so that a new Pentecost may be prepared.

Undeniable Dialogue Between Theology and Magisterium

On November 18, 1980, the Holy Father met with German theologians in the Capuchin Convent of "Kloster San Konrad" in Altötting. The Pope delivered the following address.

Dear professors, dear brothers,

It is a special pleasure for me to meet you here this evening. It was my personal wish to see theologians of your country, for theological science is today especially one of the most important expressions and tasks of ecclesiastical life. I most cordially greet you, and in you all theologians. You are following a great tradition as manifest in the works of St. Albert the Great, Nikolaus von Kues, Möhler and Scheeben, Guardini and Przywara, to mention only a few. I name these distinguished theologians as representatives of many others who, both past and present, have enriched and are still enriching not only the Church in countries where German is spoken, but the theology and the life of the Church as a whole.

For this reason I wish to express my sincere thanks for this work to you and to all those you represent. Scientific study nearly always involves self-denial and quiet perseverance. This applies particularly to the task of providing reliable texts and exploring the sources of theology. Many patristic, medieval and modern text editions are the result of the selfless work of scholars from your country. The wider the range of theological knowledge, the more urgent the task of establishing a synthesis. In numerous glossaries, commentaries and handbooks, you have provided very helpful surveys on the state of developments in nearly all fields of study. Especially in the post-conciliar period such fundamental guidance is very important. These works inform us about the legacy of the past with the insight of the present. In the field of biblical interpretation, the cooperation among exegetes has been very gratifying. It has also given strong impulses for ecumenical work and will no doubt give more. May I request all of you to continue this well-founded theological research. In doing so, be very exact in your consideration of the problems and cares of the people. But do not let yourselves be led astray by chance and short-lived currents of human thought. Scientific and especially theological discernment calls for courage to venture forth and the patience of maturity. It has its own laws which it should not allow to be imposed upon from outside.

One reason why theological research is one of the real treasures of the Church in your country is no doubt the fact that the faculty of theology has a place in the state universities. The relationship between the freedom of scientific theology and its link with the Church, as embodied in the concordats, has time and again proved to be a successful model in spite of some conflicts. This relationship affords you the opportunity to study philosophy and theology in the context of, and in cooperation with, all the science faculties of a modern university. This situation has also enhanced the quality of the colleges of philosophy and theology of the dioceses and orders, of the comprehensive universities and teacher-training colleges, and of the ecclesiastical research institutes. Moreover, the publication of theological findings would not be possible without efficient Catholic publishing companies. My thanks go to all those who in their various ways help to foster the science of theology.

Those with exceptional intellectual gifts also have great responsibility, especially in the present situation which at times appears critical. I wish, therefore, to take this opportunity to draw your attention to three perspectives which I deem particularly important.

FOSTER ANEW THE UNDERSTANDING OF GOD

1. The complexity and specialization of today have produced an abundance of tasks and queries, methods and disciplines. They have produced valuable findings and new appraisals. But there is a danger of the sheer quantity in any one branch of learning blurring the meaning and purpose of theology from time to time. As God's tracks have in any case been largely covered up in this secularized world, the concentration on the divine Trinity as the origin and lasting foundation of our life and of the whole world is the foremost task of theology today. All the passion of theological perception must ultimately lead to God Himself. As late as during the Second Vatican Council it was still believed that the answer to the question of God's existence could be taken for granted. In the meantime, it has been seen that the very relationship between man and God has become shaky and needs to be strengthened. May

I therefore ask you to work with all your strength to foster anew the understanding of God, and here I would emphasize the Trinity of God and the concept of creation.

This concentration on God and the salvation He brings for mankind implies an inner system of theological truths. God the Father, Jesus Christ, and the Holy Spirit are the fulcrum of that system. The Scriptures, the Church and the sacraments remain the great historical institutions of the salvation of the world. But the "hierarchy of truths" demanded by the Second Vatican Council (Decree on Ecumenism, no. 11) does not imply a simple reduction of comprehensive Catholic faith to a few basic truths, as some people thought. The more deeply and the more radically we grasp the center of things, the more distinct and the more convincing are also the lines of communication from the divine center of things to those truths which appear to be on the periphery. The depth of that concentration also reveals itself in the fact that it extends to all branches of theology. The theologian's work in the service of teaching about God is, in the view of St. Thomas Aquinas, at the same time an act of love towards man (cf. *Summ. Theol.*, II-II, qq. 181, a. 3c; 182, a. 2c; I, q. 1, a. 7c). By making him as deeply and as abundantly aware as possible that *he* is the thou of all divine utterances and is the object of all divine action, it explains and illustrates to him his own ultimate and eternal dimension which transcends all finite limits.

2. Every theology is based on Holy Scripture. All theological traditions derive from Holy Scripture and lead back to it. Remain, therefore, faithful to the twofold task entailed in any interpretation of Scripture. Preserve the incomparable Gospel of God which was not made by man, and, at the same time, have the courage to carry it out again into the world in this purity. The study of the whole Scripture therefore remains, as the Constitution on Divine Revelation of the Second Vatican Council says, "the soul of theology" (no. 24). It nourishes and rejuvenates our theological searching ever anew. Let us live our lives from

the Scripture; then, whatever differences may remain, we shall still come closer to our separated brethren.

The Catholic theologian cannot build a bridge between the Scripture and the problems of the present without the mediation of Tradition. That Tradition is not a substitute for the Word of God in the Bible; rather, it testifies to it through the ages and new interpretations. Maintain your dialogue with the living Tradition of the Church. Learn from its treasures, many of which are still undiscovered. Show the people of the Church that in this process you do not rely on the relics of the past, but that our great legacy from the Apostles down to the present day is a huge reservoir from which to draw the answers to some of the questions as to the meaning of life today. We shall be better able to pass on the Word of God if we heed the Holy Scripture and its response in the living Tradition of the Church. We shall also become more critical of and sensitive to our own present. It is not the sole nor the ultimate measure of theological perception.

Explaining the great Tradition of our faith is not easy. To be able to open it up we need foreign languages, the knowledge of which is today unfortunately declining in many respects. It is essential not only to open up the sources historically, but to allow them to address us in our age. The Catholic Church, which embraces all ages of civilization, is convinced that every epoch has acquired some knowledge of the truth which is of value to us as well. Theology includes prophetic renewal from these sources, which at the same time imply an awakening and continuity. Have the courage to lead the young people, your students of philosophy and theology, to these treasures of our Faith.

FAITH AS THE BASIS

3. Theology is a science with all possibilities of human perception. It is free in the application of methods and analyses. Nevertheless, theologians must see where

they stand in relation to the faith of the Church. The credit for our faith goes not to ourselves; indeed, it is "built upon the foundation of the Apostles and prophets, Jesus Christ himself being the chief cornerstone" (Eph. 2:20). Theologians, too, must take faith as the basis. They can throw light on it and promote it, but they cannot produce it. They, too, have always stood on the shoulders of the fathers in the faith. They know that their specialized field does not consist of purely historical objects in an artificial test-tube, but that it is a question of the faith of the Church as experienced in life. The theologian, therefore, teaches not least in the name and on behalf of the religious community. He should and must make new proposals to contribute to the understanding of the faith, but they are only an offer to the whole Church. Much of what he says must be corrected and expanded in a fraternal dialogue until the Church as a whole can accept it. Theology is very much a selfless service for the community of the faithful. That is why objective disputation, fraternal dialogue, openness and the willingness to modify one's own views, are essential elements of it.

THE RIGHT TO KNOW

The believer has a right to know what he can rely on in practicing his faith. Theologians must show him the means of final support. For this reason in particular the Church has been blessed with the Spirit of truth. The sole object of teaching is to determine the truth of the Word of God, especially where there is a danger of distortion and misunderstanding. The infallibility of the Church's Magisterium must also be seen in this context. I should like to repeat what I wrote on May 15 in my letter to the members of the German Bishops' Conference: "The Church must...be very humble and certain that it remains within that very truth, that very doctrine of faith and morals, which it has received from Jesus Christ who has bestowed upon it in this field the gift of a special 'infallibility.' " It is true that infallibility is not of such central importance in the hierarchy of truths, but it is "to some extent the key to that certainty with which the faith becomes known and is preached, and also to the life and conduct of the faithful. For if one shakes or destroys that essential foundation, the most elementary truths of our faith also begin to disintegrate."

TWO DIFFERENT TASKS

Love for the physical Church, which also includes belief in the testimony of faith and the Magisterium of the Church, does not estrange the theologian from his work and does not deprive that work of any of its indispensable self-reliance. The Magisterium and theology have two different tasks to perform. That is why neither can be reduced to the other. Yet they serve the one whole. But precisely on account of this configuration they must remain in consultation with one another. In the years since the Council you have furnished many examples of good cooperation between theology and the Magisterium. Let us deepen this basis. And whenever conflicts arise, apply your common efforts in the spirit of the common faith, of the same hope, and of the love that forms the bond between all of them.

I wanted to meet you this evening in order to confirm you in your work so far and to encourage you to pursue further achievements. Do not forget your great mission for the Church of our time. Work with care and untiringly. And while being meticulous, let your research have not only reason but also feeling. It was St. Albert the Great in particular, the 700th anniversary of whose death brought me to Germany, who constantly pointed to the need to bring science and piety, intellectual judgment and the whole individual, into harmony. Be also models of practicing faith for the many students of theology in your country, precisely at this time. Be inventive in faith so that all of us together can bring Christ and His Church nearer again, with a new language, to the many people who no longer participate in the life of the Church. Never forget your responsibility for all members of the Church, and remember in particular the important task of teaching the faith which falls to missionaries all over the world.

Before I meet each one of you personally, please accept my fraternal greetings and God's blessing for all your colleagues, associates, and students. "The grace of our Lord Jesus Christ and the love of God and the fellowship of the Holy Spirit be with you all" (2 Cor. 13:13).

Message of Hope
for Growing Local Churches

The bishops of Thailand paid their ad limina Apostolorum *visit to the Pope on November 27, 1980. The Holy Father delivered the following address to them.*

Venerable and dear brother bishops from Thailand,

1. The most important aspect of our meeting today is the love that unites us in the name of Jesus Christ and in the service of His Gospel. This love is at the basis of our *collegialitas affectiva;* it is also this love which helps us to persevere in our task of fulfilling ever more perfectly the *collegialitas effectiva* to which the Lord is constantly calling us.

You have come also with the expression of the love that your people have for me as the Pastor and servant of the universal Church. I am deeply grateful, and on this occasion I offer to all of you the full measure of my own love in Christ Jesus our Lord.

It is indeed a pleasure for me to greet you today as the bishops of a great people with three centuries of Christian experience, in whose midst the word of God took root as in good soil (cf. Mt. 13:23); this same word of God continues to this day to be for you a source of strength and a cause of joy.

ONE FAMILY IN CHRIST

2. With particular satisfaction I have noted your commitment to the promotion of ecclesial unity. This commitment is demonstrated in your different activities and programs aimed at fostering the solidarity, collaboration and shared responsibility that should characterize all those who are one family in Christ, and are called to be His witnesses "to the ends of the earth" (Acts 1:8). Every effort to maintain and nourish Catholic unity is important above all because it is directed to the manifestation of the unity of the most Holy Trinity, which is the supreme revelation of God. As Christ's disciples we are called to be one even as He is one with His eternal Father. The credibility, moreover, of Christ's mission before the world is forever linked with the unity of His Church (cf. Jn. 17:21f.).

BUILDING COMMUNITIES

3. Your pastoral solicitude rightfully spurs you on to devote attention to the building up of various Christian communities, in which your people can find an effective support for their faith. These communities by their nature are based on the Word of God, which becomes the criterion for all the actions of redeemed humanity. Each community must be aware of a new birth, which, in the words of St. Peter, takes place "through the living and abiding Word of God" (1 Pt. 1:23). Each nucleus of God's people regenerated by water and the Holy Spirit is called to give glory, by the witness of good works, to the Father in heaven (cf. Mt. 5:17). Each community is called to be a community of prayer and thanksgiving; and each community of prayer and thanksgiving finds its complete fulfillment in the Eucharistic Sacrifice, to which all Christian living is oriented.

4. For this reason, everything you do as bishops to promote vocations to the priesthood is of vital importance for all your people. It is especially necessary that all the seminarians be trained in a deep understanding of

the nature of the Church, which is meant to spread the light of Christ and to be "a sign and instrument of intimate union with God and of the unity of the whole human race" (LG 1). Be assured of my special prayers for your national seminary, *Lux Mundi*, that it will always worthily fulfill its lofty mission of evangelization. It gives me, moreover, great joy to know that vocations both to the priesthood and to the religious life are increasing in your land. Indeed, for all of us this is a motive of thanksgiving and of praise. This fact summons us to accept the psalmist's invitation: "Sing to the Lord a new song, his praise in the assembly of the faithful" (Ps. 149:1).

LAY PARTICIPATION

5. My fraternal encouragement goes likewise in your endeavors to promote the participation of the laity in the Church's mission of salvation. I am confident that a realization by the laity of their distinctive and indispensable role will bear ever greater fruits in the years to come. At the same time may the laity be ever more aware of their sacramental configuration to Jesus Christ and of their personal vocation to holiness within the community of an evangelizing and catechizing Church. The whole Body of the universal Church is in solidarity with the Church in Thailand in the arduous tasks of bringing the Gospel into the lives of children, young people and adults. And the whole Church is at one with you as you proclaim for your people the aim of all Catholic education, which St. Paul succinctly summarizes as: *donec formetur Christus in vobis* (Gal. 4:19).

May the Lord sustain all the generous priests and men and women religious, both Thai and those who have come from abroad, who, together with their brothers and sisters in the laity, strive in times of joy and sorrow, hope and disappointment, to be faithful to the Gospel of the kingdom of God.

HELPING REFUGEES

6. Among the many good works of Christian witness and loving service that bring honor to the whole community of your people are those exercised for the benefit of the refugees, as well as for those persons whose lives are deeply touched by the refugee problem. The reward Christ promised for good deeds done to the hungry and the thirsty, to strangers and to all in need is nothing less than eternal life (cf. Mt. 25:31ff.).

May this assurance encourage you to continue to minister to those in need in this present hour, providing as much material and spiritual help as you can with the help offered by Catholics of the whole world through the various charitable organizations. I ask the Lord Jesus to show Himself once again in this generation, through your programs of pastoral assistance, to be the Good Shepherd of all humanity. Through the charitable activity of your people may Christ's Church be newly manifested as a symbol of hope and a sign of mercy. And may Mary, the Mother of mercy and of fair love, intercede for all who show mercy or receive mercy, for all who clothe themselves or are clothed with compassion and kindness (cf. Col. 3:12).

7. On this occasion I wish to express my best wishes for the authorities of your country and for all your non-Christian brethren. In particular, I send my respectful greetings to your Buddhist fellow citizens. The cordial relations that you endeavor to maintain with them are truly in conformity with the Second Vatican Council, which presents to us the Church's exhortation that her sons and daughters "prudently and lovingly, through dialogue and collaboration with the followers of other religions, and in witness of Christian faith and life, acknowledge, preserve and promote the spiritual and moral as well as social and cultural goods found among those people" (NA 2). This exhortation is indeed normative for the whole Church, but it has special meaning for the Church in Thailand, which

seeks to be faithful to Christ by being a herald of His Gospel and a servant of all His brothers and sisters.

8. Dear brothers, the advice given in the Letter to the Hebrews has a deep meaning for us in all our activities on behalf of the Gospel: "Let us not lose sight of Jesus who leads us in our faith and brings it to perfection" (Heb. 12:2). With all our might we believe in the power of the Paschal Mystery, in the saving grace of Christ, who is able to sustain His Church until He comes in glory to present us to His Father. In the love of Christ, I ask you to take this message of hope to all who make up your local Churches, "to all who love us in the faith" (Ti. 3:15).

Praised be Jesus Christ!

Effective Communion of Churches and Their Institutions

On November 28, 1980, the Holy Father received in audience the participants in the ninth session of the General Council of the Pontifical Commission for Latin America, led by the President, Cardinal Sebastiano Baggio. Pope John Paul II delivered the following address.

Your Eminence the President,
Your Eminences, Most Reverend Archbishops and Bishops,
Beloved brothers and sisters,

I am very happy to be able to have this meeting with you, in the framework of the ninth session of the General Council of the Pontifical Commission for Latin America, which brings you together in Rome. To the great satisfaction given me by the presence of so many and such elect persons, united by the same spirit of service to the Church, there is added, within myself, the firm conviction that you are also "united in the same mind and the same judgment" (cf. 1 Cor. 1:1) with regard to the task and methods of implementation in the specific ecclesial task that has been entrusted to you.

I wish, first and foremost, in union with you, to pay public tribute to my unforgettable predecessor, Pope Paul VI: His apostolic vision and talent gave life and impetus to this Council, for the purpose of emphasizing more the interest of the Catholic world in the Latin American Continent (cf. *Normas*, no. 1). To an equal extent his teachings and directives, always imbued with a manifest and constant evangelizing intention, have been outstanding guidelines in previous sessions of this same General Council. So let our admiration, our memory, and our thanks go to him.

The experience acquired by the various Institutional Commissions and the hierarchy's own pastoral intuition before the changing situations of society, which suggested the subjects of reflection and planning for these periodical meetings of the Council, followed the model of this evangelizing dimension laid down by Paul VI.

A summary reference to some of the questions tackled —such as the distribution of apostolic personnel, assistance for students and priests abroad, support of the clergy, etc.—clearly show a peculiar, zealous sensitivity, adapted to the needs, sometimes as vast as they are urgent, which are felt most deeply in the development of the life of the Church.

You are now preparing to take a step forward by dedicating your attention to the living forces of the apostolate, and among them to the lay volunteers sent to Latin America. For this reason, you have wished to cast a glance back at the work carried out in these years: a glance that is certainly indispensable to discover possible involuntary lacks or deficiencies in the application of the resolutions taken; but no less fundamental at the time of verifying the good results obtained and defining new aims to be attained. It is this serene attitude of mind, present in the course of this session, which urges me to say to you with St. Paul: "Let us hold true to what we have attained" (cf. Phil. 3:16).

In this connection, I am happy to emphasize an aspect which I consider vital and which you certainly feel stirring within you as an indispensable duty: to make effective the communion of the Churches and their institutions, of which you are worthy and qualified representatives. Fortunately your organism has a great many specialists and technicians, with direct knowledge of pastoral requirements. But this expertise cannot dim in any way—on the contrary, it must constitute the authentic overall witness—what has been the core and soul of your activities: to look for true "concord" between the particular Churches, that is, a *common heart*, a disposition that transcends mere sentiment to become a mutual presence and reciprocal service.

The Pope and the whole Church are grateful to you for that. Thanks to this inter-ecclesial presence, thanks also to your effort and collaboration with the Church in Latin America, the face of the latter is rejuvenated today: a face of Christian hope which looks at itself and is clearly reflected in the mirror of a humanity that has become ecclesial solidarity through the same communion in Christ.

May these words of mine be a testimony of gratitude to the episcopal conferences, the religious institutes, the organisms and persons who, with a spirit of genuine "concord" make their contribution, or even more, spend themselves—as leaven within the dough—for the good of the Church.

With my most cordial apostolic blessing.

The Proclamation of the Gospel Is Your Primary Task

On December 11, 1980, the Holy Father received in audience a group of priests from various dioceses in the U.S.A. who had been attending a theological course at the Casa Santa Maria. The group was led by Most Reverend Murphy, Rector of the North American College.

Dear brother priests,

1. I am happy to have this occasion to meet with you as you complete your course of continuing theological education at Casa Santa Maria, and as you prepare to return home. We know that, during these moments we spend together, *Jesus Christ is in our midst* because we are gathered in His holy name and in the fraternity of His priesthood.

By God's grace and with the encouragement of your bishops and religious superiors, you have had the wonderful opportunity for a prolonged reflection on theology and on Sacred Scripture. At the same time, I am sure that you have known the other advantages which the Second Vatican Council sees as linked with courses such as yours: a strengthening of the spiritual life and a beneficial exchange of apostolic experiences (cf. PO 19).

2. And now you are going back to your people, to all those communities in which you exercise your pastoral ministry. You are going back, please God, to proclaim with ever greater understanding and zeal the Good News of salvation, which was revealed by a merciful and loving Father, and which the Church, in fidelity to Christ, communicates from one generation to the next.

The proclamation of the Gospel is your primary task as co-workers with your bishops, and it reaches its fulfillment in the Eucharistic Sacrifice (PO 4, 13). It is the mission to which you were called; it is the reason for which you were ordained.

3. But to be totally effective as priests, *your whole life must be dedicated to the Word of God* and to Him

who is the Incarnate Word of the Father, Jesus Christ our Lord and Savior, our one High Priest.

The Word of God is the criterion for all our preaching. The power inherent in the Word of God is what we offer to our people, and it is this power that unites the faithful and builds them up in holiness and justice. The Word of God is a challenge to the People of God—and to the heart of each one of us—but it brings with it strength, immense strength; and when embraced, it produces joy and gladness. The Word of God which we are called to proclaim, and on which every community of faith is built, is the message of the cross. As we gather, day after day, week after week, to celebrate this mystery of faith, let us endeavor to present and explain its various aspects, which are so vital for the life of the Church: the healing and forgiveness, the suffering and deliverance, the victory and everlasting mercy held up to us by Christ. Like St. Paul, we may indeed be conscious of presenting ourselves "in weakness and fear and with much trepidation" and without "the persuasive force of 'wise' arguments," but with the Word of God we do possess always "the convincing power of the Spirit." And with St. Paul let us be always ready to speak truthfully to our people, saying: "Your faith rests not on the wisdom of men, but on the power of God" (1 Cor. 2:4-5).

4. May the lasting results of your course in Rome be *a renewed commitment to God's Word.* Continue, dear brothers, to study the Word of God, to meditate on it and to live it. Believe in God's word with all your hearts. Preach it, in union with the whole Church, in all its purity and integrity. And finally, surrender your own lives totally before its demands and inspirations.

And may Mary, spouse of the Holy Spirit and Mother of priests, sustain each of you in your ministry of the Word and in your priestly consecration to Jesus Christ, the Eternal Word, who "became flesh and made his dwelling among us" (Jn. 1:14).

The Church's Way for Building a More Just and Equitable World

On December 22, 1980, for the customary presentation of greetings for the upcoming Christmas holidays, the Holy Father received the Sacred College of Cardinals, the Pontifical Household, the Curia, and the Roman Prelature. At the beginning of the meeting, Cardinal Carlo Confalonieri, Dean of the Sacred College, delivered a devout address of homage to the Holy Father, to which John Paul II replied as follows.

Venerated members of the Sacred College, beloved brothers!

1. We meet in this Consistory Hall, in the unmistakable atmosphere of anticipation of the birth of Christ the Lord, for the presentation of greetings. These greetings are not only words: they express the reality lived by the *communio* of our souls, as well as of our physical energies, all extended in the one service of the Holy Church, all merged in the one love for Christ, whose birth we are awaiting.

I felt these souls vibrating in the expressions, always appropriate, kind and fervent, which the dear and venerated Cardinal Dean expressed here for you. I felt in them, in addition to the nobility of his spirit, well-known to everyone, also the sincerity of your sentiments at this unique moment of the liturgical year, in which we prepare to take into our arms, like the Blessed Virgin in Bethlehem, like Simeon in the temple, the Savior who comes. I thank Cardinal Confalonieri for all that, and, with him, all of you.

THE INCARNATION OF THE WORD

2. We are preparing to celebrate the birth in human flesh of the Word, the only-begotten Son of the Father, from the pure womb of the Blessed Virgin; it is the fulfillment of the expectations of centuries, which, in all the hap-

penings of the ancient covenant, as in the most secret aspirations of human hearts even outside Revelation, have turned their aspirations to this climax of the history of salvation: "Behold, I made him a witness to the peoples, a leader and commander for the peoples" (Is. 55:4). Christ is the one awaited by all peoples; He is God's answer to humanity. After the long period of "evangelical preparations" (Eusebius of Caesarea), here He comes from the Father's bosom. He comes to be a man, like us, to offer God the supreme act of worship and love which alone could reconcile Him with man; He comes to manifest the Father's condescension and "His own mercy" for man as we will say at the Christmas Masses: *"Apparuit benignitas et humanitas:* ...the goodness and loving kindness of God our Savior appeared" (Ti. 3:4); He comes to share the history, the life, the suffering, the poverty, the insecurity of man, so that man might reacquire familiarity with God, which he had lost through sin; He comes to elevate man to God, in a mystery of humiliation and of greatness at the same time, before which the human intellect is lost and can do nothing but worship and thank; He comes, in fact, to confer on man God's own greatness, His life, and to communicate His nature to man (cf. 2 Pt. 1:4): "He who is the real Son of God became the Son of man—St. John Chrysostom writes—in order to make men sons of God. When what is most sublime unites with what is most humble, the glory of the first is not diminished, while the humility of the other is exalted: this happened in Christ. He did not in fact diminish His nature with His own abasement, but He lifted us, who were sitting in ignominy and in darkness, to ineffable glory" *(Homily on John the Evangelist* I, 1; PG 59, 79). And with this extraordinary elevation of man, the incarnate Son of God brings peace, justice, freedom, truth, and love into the world.

PROCLAIMING THE CHRISTMAS MESSAGE

3. It is not a question of a commemoration, however pious and enchanting it may be; it is not a question of the

recalling of a myth. After two thousand years of Christianity, and almost at the threshold of the third millennium of our era, the Church reminds the world, firmly and joyfully, that this elevation is not just a theoretical enunciation, but it continues, it is in progress, and it is in our midst. The liturgy presents to us again, in the mysterious reality of the rite, the event that we are getting ready to relive; and the Church prolongs in time and in history the work of Christ; she makes His Incarnation present in the various historical contingencies of the *Kairos*, which she is called to live together with humanity, together with the peoples of the whole world. Immersed in it, the Church is the leaven of the world; she participates in the hopes, the conquests, as well as in the anxieties, the sorrows, the trepidations, the setbacks, the tragedies of man. I was thinking of this against the terrible background of the ruins of Campania and Basilicata, among the remains of the cataclysm which has just exterminated so many human lives and destroyed villages and houses, while I was speaking to those brothers and sisters and gazing into their sorrowful eyes, turned to me amid tears, but with so much faith.

The Church brings Christ into the midst of men: she wishes to communicate to them the life that appeared in the night of Christmas with the Word made flesh; she wishes to proclaim to them the hope of the future eon, which is already dawning in the present age; she wishes to spread, albeit among the sufferings of the world, that peace which was proclaimed by the angels in Bethlehem, and that approving love with which God has embraced us in giving us His Son: *"Gloria in excelsis Deo et in terra pax hominibus bonae voluntatis"* (Lk. 2:14).

This is the mission which the Church carries out *ad extra* in the close contacts she maintains with men, who are brothers.

In his first great encyclical, *Ecclesiam suam*, my Predecessor Paul VI of venerated memory highlighted her essential mission, speaking of "the relations that the Church must establish today with the world that surrounds her and in which she lives and works; a part of this world, as everyone knows, has profoundly come under the influence of Christianity and has absorbed it so deeply that very often it is not aware that it owes its best things to Christianity itself; but subsequently it has been separating itself and breaking away, in the last few centuries, from the Christian base of its civilization; and another, the greater part of this world, extends to the boundless horizons of the new peoples, as is said; but all together it is a world that offers the Church not one, but a hundred forms of possible contacts, some open and easy, others delicate and complicated, and today, unfortunately, very many that are hostile and obstinate toward friendly conversation" (August 6, 1964: *AAS* 56, 1964, pp. 612f.).

This contact of the Church with the world now forms the subject of this informal conversation of mine with you, leaving until next June, as is my usual intention, consideration of the *ad intra* life of the Church herself. This intention is particularly close to my heart every year: not to list dates and facts, but rather to pick out, in the concrete and sometimes tragic problems of humanity, the role that the Church is called to carry out in its midst, with serenity and frankness, with fortitude and with joy, in the spirit, precisely, of Christmas, which was the first fundamental event—to which reference must always be made—of God's dialogue with man.

CONTACTS
WITH THE WORLD

4. "The situation of the world today not only displays transformations that give grounds for hope in a better future for man on earth, but it also reveals a multitude of threats, far surpassing those known up till now. Without

ceasing to point out these threats on various occasions (as in addresses to UNO, to UNESCO, to FAO and elsewhere), the Church must at the same time examine them in the light of the truth received from God" (DM 2).

The Church is not uprooted from the world. Suffice it to think of the work that the local Churches are carrying out at every latitude, albeit in such differentiated historical, socio-political, economic and cultural conditions. In every country the Church meets a different face of humanity, in the fundamental unity of mankind. And here I wish to express my appreciation, my praise, my encouragement to the episcopates of the various nations, which are, in the context of their geographical and political surroundings, the force of cohesion and the tireless stimulus of all Catholic forms of life, through which the Church is publicly proclaimed "an ensign for the nations" (Is. 11:12), the sign of the eternal covenant between God and mankind.

And here I cannot fail to recall in the first place the episcopates I met this year during their *ad limina* visits, which brought me a living and concrete image of their countries: the bishops of Nicaragua, Japan, Malaysia, Singapore and Brunei, Indonesia, Vietnam and Brazil; Indian bishops of Malabar and Malankar rites; Chaldean bishops and those of the Greek Melkite rite; the bishops of Burma, Korea, Formosa, Bolivia and Thailand. Through those brothers in the episcopate I have truly come into contact with the various peoples of the world, and I have been able to make mine the experience of the pastors, who proclaim Christ sometimes in delicate situations, in full identification with the mystery of the cross.

But also all the other contacts that take place in the course of the year—from the great journeys, to the meetings with pilgrimages coming from everywhere, to familiar man-to-man relations with individual persons, with the parishes, with institutions of a civil, religious and cultural nature at all levels: they offer me, in that daily solicitude for all the Churches (cf. 2 Cor. 11:28) the possibility, one can say, of feeling the pulse of the world, with all its problems. The whole reality of man, the whole diversified and complex situation of the pluralistic society, nay more of whole nations, is thus present to the eyes of the Pope, who wants to be—though aware of his limited ability, but in the very humble and firm will to correspond to God's plan—not only the center of the unity of the Church, but also the reference point for the universal desire for brotherhood and international cooperation among the peoples, and to give constant proof of a firm will to meet the world.

This relationship with the world involves, therefore, the whole Church, and so also involves vital problems such as that of ecumenism—which I will consider expressly next June—because in this way too our brethren not yet fully united with us feel invited to take part in these contacts with which the Holy See tries to go towards the world to meet it and collaborate with it.

THE PASTORAL JOURNEYS— OPPORTUNITIES TO BUILD

5. And there rise before me, at this moment, the faces of the individual nations visited in the pastoral journeys that God has granted me to carry out this year, responding to the pressing invitations both of the episcopates and of the responsible authorities: six countries of Africa—Zaire, Congo Brazzaville, Kenya, Ghana, Upper Volta, Ivory Coast—immense Brazil, and, in Europe, France, Germany, and various Italian cities: each with its own history, its civilization, its culture, and its problems, also serious ones. I already spoke last June (*Insegnamenti*, III, 1, pp. 188?-1889) of the ecclesial meaning of these journeys, the possibilities they offer of meeting even brothers of other Churches, members of other religions, and also non-believers. Here I am anxious above all to point out that the high-level contacts that take place

on those occasions are as many firm points that the Church establishes in her way among men, taking advantage of the possibilities offered to her of having dealings with those responsible for the fate of peoples. I said in an interview to a Polish weekly, on my return from Brazil, that, "as I have often stressed also during meetings with the authorities, it is in the interest of those who wield power that the society should be a just one, so that, breaking with totalitarianism and realizing a real democracy, this society may become more and more just, in the wake of reasonable and provident social reforms. And by so doing it is possible to avoid revolts, acts of violence and bloodshed which cost so much human suffering" (to *Tygodnik Powszechny*; cf. *L'Osservatore Romano*, English Edition, August 25, 1980).

This possibility—a really extraordinary one which the Pope is offered, and which is prolonged in meetings with the high personalities and heads of state who come on an official visit to the Vatican—is by no means a negligible aspect of the mission of the Church; it is a very effective form of that collaboration which she wishes to offer to the responsible authorities for the construction of a more orderly and just world. In Kenya, speaking to the diplomatic corps accredited to that nation, I recalled precisely that "the state must reject anything unworthy of the freedom and of the human rights of its people, thus banishing all elements such as abuse of authority, corruption, domination of the weak, the denial to the people of their right to share in political life and decisions, tyranny or the use of violence and terrorism. Here again"—I went on—"I do not hesitate to refer to the truth about man. Without the acceptance of the truth about man, of his dignity and eternal destiny, there cannot exist among nations that fundamental trust which is one of the basic ingredients of all human achievement. Neither can the public function be seen for what it truly is: a service to the people, which finds its only justification in solicitude for the good of all" (6. V.: *Insegnamenti*, III, 1, p. 1191).

PRESENT IN THE SERVICE OF THE POOR

In this way the Church is present in the service of man, and above all in the service of the poor. "The Church would not be faithful to the Gospel if she were not close to the poor and if she did not defend their rights," I said in the above-mentioned interview. She contributes to the elevation of the less well-to-do strata, which are in the various nations very sad belts in which man, our brother, lives in sub-human conditions. She also contributes to the construction of today's society, which lives, sometimes in unconscious forms, on the great tradition inherited from the Gospel and to which it must continually appeal if it wants to safeguard its own identity and its own role: which is a role of life, animation, mutual respect, the proclamation of established values, never downtrodden or rejected. "The Church"—as I said at San Salvador da Bahia—"points out the way to construct society in human terms. Her task is to insert the leaven of the Gospel in all fields of human activity. It is in Christ that the Church is 'an expert in humanity' " (6. VII). Blessed be those who collaborate in this great undertaking, especially the missionaries, who always have the first place in my heart.

MEETING THE NATIONS

6. Therefore, in the various journeys—which, with God's help, and as I have announced, will soon resume in a worldwide range, touching other peoples of different and ancient civilizations—the Church, by means of her visible head, becomes concretely acquainted with the situations characteristic of the various nations, thus meeting the intense desire that springs up within those same nations.

In Africa I spoke to the various African ethnic groups and populations of the problems pressing upon their conscience, at the individual and collective level: possible use, in the framework of the specific characteristics of Catholicism, which is by definition "universal," of the specific elements of those particular cultures was encouraged; esteem for those special values that Africa has to offer the world was expressed; the necessity of safeguarding the spiritual heritage, the extraordinary richness of sensitivity to religious realities was affirmed, as well as the need to protect deeply rooted family traditions with all their African warmth and identity; attention was drawn once more to the tragedy of the areas suffering from drought, hunger, and illiteracy, which carries off populations and undermines their continuity, as I cried, with a lump in my throat, in my appeal for Sahel.

In Brazil the Church is in contact with a particular social situation which is waiting for vigilant attention and concrete measures on the part of the rulers; I cannot forget the meetings with the *favelados* of Rio de Janeiro, with the workers of São Paolo, with the farm workers in Recife, with the peoples of Amazonia. It was a unique opportunity to proclaim once more not only to those populations, but before the whole world, that "the Church, when she proclaims the Gospel, without abandoning her specific task of evangelization, tries to obtain that all aspects of social life in which injustice is manifested should undergo a transformation towards justice" (July 3, at São Paolo).

In France and in Germany the Church met nations of very ancient European civilization, with all the exalting riches of their cultural and artistic heritage, with the positive stimuli of their civilization that has contributed so much to the intellectual and spiritual development of humanity, but she also met models of behavior which have sometimes let themselves be conditioned by moral permissiveness and by the temptation of riches. The various aspects of those societies, in their essential elements, were considered in the unforgettable meetings which took place during those visits. It was a *tête-à-tête* of the Pope with the leaders of the great European civilization.

But a unique opportunity to recall old Europe to the genuine nature of its exquisitely spiritual origins was offered by the celebrations for the fifteenth centenary of the birth of St. Benedict, which enabled me to address the peoples that form this continent of ours, magnificent and yet contradictory in the intermingling of its opposite trends, so that its imminent process of unification might be facilitated. In my message to the Abbot of Montecassino (21. III), in the homily and the addresses delivered at Norcia (32. III), in the Apostolic Letter *Sanctorum altrix* to all the Benedictine religious communities (11. VII), in the pilgrimage to Montecassino (20. IX), and during the unforgettable and stupendously significant one to Subiaco, I was offered the happy opportunity to point out in St. Benedict the pioneer of a new civilization—the one that was to rise from the ruins of the ancient world to infuse new life in the peoples appearing in the limelight of history alongside the ones that had passed through the travail of decadence, indicating to both of them a simple and at the same time universal program of renewal and change. "In this way—so I was able to say at Norcia—St. Benedict became the Patron of Europe in the course of the centuries: long before he was proclaimed such by Pope Paul VI. He is the Patron of Europe in this age of ours. He is so not only in consideration of the new relevance of his figure as regards modern Europe.... One gets the impression of a prevalence of economy over morality, of temporal things over spiritual ones.... It is not possible to live for the future without realizing that the meaning of life is greater then temporality, that it is above the latter. If the societies and men of our continent have lost interest in this meaning, they must find it again...on the measure of Benedict" (*Insegnamenti*, III, 1, pp. 686f.).

Let us pray that Europe may have the wisdom and the far-sightedness to rediscover, in this rightful hierarchy of values, the only yardstick that is valid to promote its own progress in justice, truth and peace. It will find the Church always available in this service of man. And all the peoples of the world will always find her likewise available.

THE BLESSING OF PEACE

7. In this way the Church is aware of constructing peace. To remain faithful to the cause of peace is a primary duty of the Church, which is preparing to hear again, and will always preserve faithfully, the first message of peace, the one that rang out at Bethlehem over the cradle of the newborn Son of God. That calls for constant work, never satisfied even by flattering results because ever new problems arise to be solved; it calls for tireless vigilance, to prevent the symptoms of restlessness as they crop up, and to point out, with clarity and constancy, the ways to peace, which always has to be constructed anew, as happens, moreover, for all the most precious goods entrusted to man, which require a constant effort to be won and to be improved.

In this light, in addition to the journeys carried out, and the meetings with heads of state, there exists a closely-knit network of contacts at various ecclesial, civil and diplomatic levels, which the Holy See maintains with various and differentiated initiatives. I am happy here to recall the large number of ambassadors—among whom there are for the first time in history those of the People's Republic of the Congo, of Greece, and of Mali—whom I have had the pleasure of receiving, this year too, for the presentation of the Letters of Credence: "The composition of the diplomatic corps makes it possible to understand better, in a proper way, the important problem of the presence of the Church in the modern world," I said at the beginning of the year to those illustrious representatives of international society (*L'Osservatore Romano*, English Weekly Edition, Jan. 28, 1980); but it also makes it possible to collaborate in concord toward the great cause of peace in the world, in respect for the various "political systems and their temporal responsibilities" (cf. *ibid.*).

The 1981 Peace Day is drawing near. As you know, it has as its motto: "To serve peace, respect freedom." Paul VI's prophetic act in instituting the celebration at the dawn of the new year has proved to be of unequalled effectiveness in encouraging and stimulating the world to thoughts and works of peace. My message is now in your hands. But, during the whole course of the year, there are innumerable documents, audiences, and private contacts aimed at safeguarding the blessing of peace. The Holy See does not neglect any opportunity to stress the precious blessing of peace, to which the deepest human aspirations are addressed: I recall the two meetings, in February and in November, with the organism of the Curia which ideally nourishes the Church's action in favor of peace, that is, the Pontifical Commission *Iustitia et Pax*; the John XXIII Award for Peace, conferred on African catechists at Kumasi, on June 9; the message to the XI General Session of the United Nations, in August, and the one in preparation for the Madrid meeting on European security and cooperation, in November; the hope for growing peace among peoples, expressed from Munich on the point of leaving Germany. Thus the meetings, at a pastoral level, with pilgrimages from various nations of the world, in fact from whole continents, such as the one with the Africans of Rome, in February; the letters sent, on various occasions, to the bishops of Nicaragua (26. VI), El Salvador (20. X) and Guatemala (1. XI), because of the particular conditions of those tormented countries; those sent to the faithful of Mexico (28. I), Brazil (21. II), Hungary (6. IV), the United States of America (2. VI); the audiences to Brazilian members of Parliament (20. II), political personalities of Nicaragua (3. III); the meetings on cooperation between Europe and Latin America (20. VI), with the mayors of the most thickly populated cities in the world (4. IX), with eminent Swedish visitors (30. X), with the delegations of Argentina and Chile for the mediation happily started on the southern zone in the last few weeks. And I deeply desire to recall the appeal which I made to men of science whom I met at UNESCO and, through them, to those "of all countries and all continents," so that every effort may be made "to preserve the human family from the horrible prospect

of nuclear war.... Yes!"—I added—"World peace depends
on the primacy of the Spirit! Yes! The peaceful future
of mankind depends on love" *(Insegnamenti,* III, 1,
pp. 1654f.).

The steps that I have mentioned were all taken
together with men of good will, on the way to peace, to
help its consolidation, to appreciate its value more and
more, and to prepare its fruits, for the benefit of the whole
world.

SHADOWS ON WORLD PEACE

8. But in this overall review of the work carried out in
favor of world peace, there are not lacking, unfortunately,
as every year, sinister and deadly shadows which cause
apprehension in our hearts: the hearts of men, the hearts of
believers in Christ.

Is there not in the world, underground like the fiery
and destructive vein of a volcano, a constant threat to
peace? Are there not peoples who are suffering and dying
because of the terrible rivalries between one nation and
another, sometimes between opposing parties within the
same peoples? How could we fail to mention the conflict
between Iraq and Iran? The Afghan situation? The persistent tensions in Lebanon, the beloved nation always in my
mind, as I wished to emphasize several times this year,
both by writing to the Maronite Patriarch and by launch-
ing an appeal at the general audience on July 18, and also
by receiving qualified members of the National Assembly
(60. X)? How could I fail to think of beloved Ireland,
which is living hours of deep trepidation? But let us thank
the Lord that in these very days, in answer to appeals and
prayers from various parts of the world, the tensions seem
to have subsided. How could I fail to recall the grave acts
of violence which have caused bloodshed in some very
dear regions of Central America, and still continue to mow
down victims, the most eminent of whom was the late
Archbishop of San Salvador? I raised my supplication to

God for peace in that country on last April 2; but my heart weeps when news arrives of new acts of violence and killing.

Nor do I forget the tragedy—still alive, even if pushed in the background by other painful events to which, unfortunately, public opinion becomes accustomed—regarding refugees in Thailand and in some African countries, with immense human and social problems of justice and charity, of solicitude that cannot be postponed, which raise disquieting questions for the conscience of peoples.

I am close to all brothers and sisters who are suffering at this moment; just as I share deeply in the anxieties, travail, and hopes of my beloved homeland.

In particular, I renew my appeal to all the nations of the world—along the lines of the message sent on the occasion of the aforesaid meeting in Madrid on security and cooperation in Europe, at which a delegation of the Holy See was present—for respect, loyal and constructive, of religious freedom, to which all men have the right; as I recalled in the message sent to heads of state, signatories of the Helsinki Final Document, "this concrete freedom is based on man's very nature, the characteristic of which is to be free" (no. 2); and it must be safeguarded both as the foundation of the intrinsic dignity of the person and as the condition of an orderly and just civil society in which every citizen will be respected for what he "is," and not relegated to a second or third class because of the ideas that he is responsible and consistent enough to profess even in public life. In this field, the Church has laid down the principles of her behavior in the basic Declaration *Dignitatis humanae*, of the Second Vatican Council, and reference must always be made to it for a real and lasting spiritual peace within the nations.

VIOLENCE AND TERRORISM

9. Unfortunately, in some nations, such as Spain, Italy, Ireland, and elsewhere, there is still a very serious

danger of terrorism and violence, this real war waged against defenseless people and institutions, moved by obscure centers of power, which do not realize that the order which they hope to reach through violence cannot but call for further violence. "All who take the sword will perish by the sword," Jesus recalled at the moment when He was undergoing the most atrocious violence (Mt. 26:52). And an order that came into being on the ruins and killings of violence would be the peace of the cemetery, according to the well-known expression. No, that is not the way to build the new society, which must serve and elevate man! The Church does not fail to recommend the construction of a more just and healthy world by means of interior conversion and the radical renewal of morals. Once more, as at Drogheda, as at Turin, I beg the men of violence, who are also my brothers, to desist from their path of death; I call upon the young not to let themselves be swept away by the perverse ideology of destruction and hatred, but to collaborate with all generous forces existing in the various nations to construct a world "in the dimension of man": only in this way will it be possible to ensure a really positive future, in the impetus of industrious progress from which the humble, the excluded and the poor must benefit particularly.

And I again raise my thought, my prayer, for the many unknowing victims of terrorism, as I did with great sorrow last February, after the tragic end of the dear, good and unforgettable Professor Bachelet, and as I did in August at the barbarous slaughter in Bologna; and I renew my invitation, already addressed at the audience to the Committee and Provincial Council of Rome (6. II), and to Italian Catholic Jurists (6. XII), to defend the moral values denied by violence. I entrust this wish, which rises from the bottom of my heart, to the "Prince of Peace" (Is. 9:6), to Him who took upon Himself the condition of human nature in order to divinize it and make it participate in God's own greatness.

Our common prayer will rise in greater supplication on these days of Christmas to invoke comfort and serenity for so much suffering by persons, families and communities! We will not tire of praying for this; nor will we forget the hostages that are still deprived of freedom in various parts of the world, victims of political reprisals or of a wicked, cruel and unthinkable pecuniary speculation. I am close to them with prayer, on this Christmas that will be so sad for them; and I pray to the Lord for them all with tears in my eyes, asking those responsible to have pity: in God's name, in man's name.

THE WORKING WORLD AND INDIVIDUALS

10. The Church is not only concerned with the problems regarding continents and peoples; she turns to man in particular, who bears imprinted on him the creative image of God and who is redeemed by the Sacrifice of Christ. For the Church there does not exist a formless mass or nameless collectivity: she knows that every social and political reality is made up of individual persons, each with the problems inherent in his own identity, in work, profession, and family and social life, though in the diversity of geographical origins or of ideological positions. For this individual man the Church has her word to say. The Pope meets this man with simplicity and cordiality, with full "sympathy," that is, trying to share in his concrete situations of life, wherever they may take place and develop.

In the first place working man: there are printed in my heart the meetings, here in Rome and during the journeys, with marble quarrymen, miners, the workers in industry and farm laborers, with those who have emigrated to other nations and those of the various countries: they all bring forth from matter the means of subsistence for the whole of society, thus becoming collaborators of God, who needs man to continue to bring forth the immanent riches of His creation. Let workers of the whole world rest assured that the Church is close to them, esteems them and loves them for this irreplaceable contribution to which we are all indebted; it is a contribution made with the labor of a whole life and therefore incomparably higher and more sacred than the remuneration they receive, even if it were more just; let them rest assured that their work, as I said recently, "helps man to be more of a man, matures his personality, develops and raises his abilities, thus opening him to service, generosity and commitment for others; in a word, to love" (To the Christian Workers Movement, December 6).

Love! It is the great reality that must move society, today as yesterday, if society does not want to dry up completely in a dialectical opposition of exploitation and rebellion, in a pure and simple relationship of giving and having, in the selfishness of those who brush by one another without ever meeting, unless in mistrust and contempt. The secret of survival lies in love alone.

GUARDIANS OF HUMANITY'S HERITAGE

11. Then there is the man who makes his interior resources available also for the qualitative elevation of his brothers and sisters; this is the great world of culture, in its various facets which at the present time acquire extraordinary proportions in depth and in extension, due to the specializations in progress in all areas of intellectual life. The Church looks to this world with immense confidence, and she has dedicated particular attention to it this year, after the commitment solemnly made during the meeting of the Sacred College in November of last year, and on the occasion of the memorable session of the Pontifical Academy of Sciences during those same days.

I would like to mention one by one the audiences with people of study and culture, who have come one after another to this house in the course of the year that is about to end, bringing the echo and the fervor of their studies in all areas of knowledge: historians, economists, philosophers, scientists, jurists, Latinists, musicians. But time does not make it possible. However, three occasions particularly claim my attention: the visit to the United Nations Organization for Education, Science and Culture, in Paris on June 2; the meeting with men of culture in Rio de Janeiro on July 1; and the meetings both with scientists and students and with artists and journalists, at Cologne and Munich respectively on November 15 and 19, during the journey in Germany in the framework of the centenary commemorations of that great man of culture and piety, St. Albert the Great. Men of culture are the guardians of the most authentic heritage of humanity, and the architects of the future of nations: in their hands lies civilization, but there depends on them, too, God forbid, the barbarity of tomorrow: "Real culture is humanization, while non-culture and false cultures are dehumanizing. For this reason, man stakes his destiny on the choice of culture," I said at Rio de Janeiro. For this reason the Church expects so much from men of culture, on whom the future of humanity really depends in its deepest roots. It is also true, as I recalled at Munich, that "in the last few centuries, especially from 1800, the bond between the Church and culture, and therefore between the Church and art, has grown slack"; the reasons are multiple, owing to a mutual attitude of mistrust. But this state of affairs is no longer justified: "The Second Vatican Council has laid the foundations of a substantially new relationship between the Church and the world, between the Church and modern culture" (ibid.); and the moment has therefore come to proclaim again, as I humbly tried to do before the prestigious gathering of UNESCO, that "the fundamental link between the Gospel, that is, the message of Christ and the Church, and man in his very humanity…is in fact a creator of culture in its very foundation. To create culture, it is necessary to consider, to its last consequences and entirely, man as a particular and autonomous value, as the subject bearing the transcendency of the person. Man must be affirmed for himself, and not for any other motive or reason: solely for himself! What is more, man must be loved because he is man; love must be claimed for man by reason of the particular dignity he possesses" (*L'Osservatore Romano*, English Weekly Edition, June 23, 1980). Only the Church, which preserves in its entirety the Gospel of Christ, can safeguard man against all manipulations of other men: and in the re-found cooperation between Church and culture, in their respective and autonomous spheres of action, it is possible to look forward to that superior harmony which is a guarantee of peace, and as such is so greatly desired by men concerned about the fate of humanity.

A JOYFUL SOCIETY

12. The effort that the Church is making by building bridges to the various expressions of social life, in which individuals operate with the inexhaustible charge of their personal resources, has no other purpose than the building of a social life that is serene, constructive, peaceful and joyful: a society proportionate to man.

For this reason I have tried with every effort to establish relations with all leaders and architects of this society: with the educators of youth at school; with the men of the mass media, also bound, because of their very delicate function, to a precise ethics and a clear moral code; with the men of the social services most exposed to risk (I am thinking of the firemen, whom I meet every year); with the military and their officers of various ranks and specializations; with the railwaymen; with athletes engaged in various sporting activities. Following in the footsteps of my Predecessors—especially of the indefatigable teaching that Pius XII, in the most delicate phase of world reconstruction, did not spare any social category—I have reminded them all of the duty of contributing, each one according to his own abilities, their own qualification and responsibility, so that the world in which we live may bear more and more fully the trace of the original joy that God the Creator felt when, gazing on the grandeur of creation, He rejoiced in the deep heart of His trinitarian life: "And God saw that it was good" (cf. Gn. 1, *passim*);

"Behold, it was very good" (Gn. 1:31). May the man of today likewise know that "the joy of the Lord is our strength!" (cf. Neh. 8:10)

THE FAMILY TODAY

13. Man, beyond all intellectual or social activity, lofty though it may be, finds his full development, his complete fulfillment, his irreplaceable riches, in the family. Here man's destiny is really at stake, more than in any other field of his life. For this reason the Church continues to dedicate the warmest care and attention to the magnificent reality of the family. The memory of the days of the Fifth General Assembly of the Synod of Bishops, dedicated to the great problem—a vital one not only for the Church but also for the whole of mankind—is still vivid in our hearts as pastors. The problems dealt with by the bishops with lucid realism and fatherly solicitude were many, and the various episcopates expressed them, bringing the echo of the specific situations in the various parts of the world. In dealing with these problems, the Synod "moved along two main lines, as if on foundations"—I summed up at the conclusion of the assembly—"that is, faithfulness to God's plan regarding the family, and practical pastoral work characterized by merciful love and the respect due to men, considered in their completeness as regards their 'being' and their 'living' " (October 25). That is, the principles of matrimonial ethics, on which the institution of the family rests, were affirmed, according to the firm points laid down by Paul VI in his Encyclical *Humanae vitae*, and at the same time there were recalled, with the hearts of pastors and fathers, the difficulties, the anxieties, sometimes the tragedies of so many families who wish to preserve entirely their faithfulness to the Gospel and not to transgress the eternal norms of natural ethics, as well as the unchangeable law of God, inscribed in man's heart.

Today the family is touching perhaps the most acute point of an unprecedented crisis, matured with the uniting of the various permissive mentalities and theories which, in the name of an alleged autonomy of man, deny the mission entrusted to man himself by God the Creator, in the original plan of the communication of life (cf. Gn. 1:28): I have tried to illustrate this plan as completely as possible in the course of the whole year, already since the summer of 1979, precisely in view of the celebration of the Synod and in the framework of its doctrinal approach. God's law does not mortify, but exalts man, and calls him to extraordinary cooperation with Him in the mission and in the joy of responsible fatherhood and motherhood. In the face of contempt for the supreme value of life, which goes so far as to ratify the suppression of the human being in the mother's womb; in the face of the disintegration of family unity, the only guarantee for the complete formation of children and young people; in the face of the devaluation of clear and pure love, unbridled hedonism, the spread of pornography—it is necessary to recall emphatically the holiness of marriage, the value of the family, the inviolability of human life. I will never tire of carrying out this mission, which I believe cannot be deferred, taking advantage of journeys, meetings, audiences, messages to persons, institutions, associations, advisory bureaus which are concerned about the future of the family and dedicate study and action to it. Once more, with the words of the prayer dictated on the occasion of the Synod, I ask God that "love, strengthened by the grace of the sacrament of marriage, / may prove stronger than any weakness and any crisis through which our families sometimes pass. / ...By the intercession of the Holy Family of Nazareth, may the Church in the midst of all the nations of the earth / be able to carry out her mission successfully in the family and through the family."

RETURN TO THE SCHOOL OF CHRIST

14. I cannot conclude without at least a mention of the inexhaustible and promising charge of life and social

progress that the young are today for the Church and for the world. They are the first beneficiaries of the molding action of the family, which makes them jointly responsible; but they are also the first victims of disorders and imbalances, which undermine their lives today. I have spoken on other occasions of this matter, and let it suffice just to refer to it. Recalling that, in Africa and Brazil, I visited nations that are truly young because their populations are made up mainly of young people, I cannot but think of these men of the future, who will have in their hands the society of the year 2000. It is an immense human potential, which expects so much from us, from the whole of society: Christ looks to it with boundless love, with infinite confidence, looking them in the eye one by one, as He did with His Apostles, with children, with the rich young man of the Gospel.

Young people, I say to you, Christ is waiting for you with open arms: Christ is relying on you to build justice and peace, to spread love. As in Turin, I say again today: "You must return to the school of Christ...to rediscover the true, full, deep meaning of these words. The necessary support for these values lies only in possession of a sure and sincere faith, a faith that embraces God and man, man in God.... There is not a more adequate, a deeper dimension to give to this word 'man,' to this word 'love,' to this word 'freedom,' to these words 'peace' and 'justice': there is nothing else, there is only Christ" (Insegnamenti, III, 1, pp. 905f.).

Yes, beloved young people, whom I have met in every journey of mine—and how could I forget the characteristic meeting at Parc-des-Princes in Paris?—young people whom I have seen in all the latitudes of the world, in densely populated cities and in the countryside, in stadiums and in squares, at Masses in St. Peter's as in particular institutes such as that of Casal del Marmo; yes, university students, workers, athletes; yes, young people who have escaped from the tentacles of drugs: there is only

Christ, the Redeemer of man! Be convinced of this. And proclaim it in a loud voice around you.

JESUS—THE FATHER'S MERCY

15. Beloved brothers,

I have recalled what has been done in the relations of the Church with the world; but I am convinced that all the activities I have been able to carry out in the course of the year were possible, thanks precisely to the contribution of so many generous and silent forces, who sincerely love the Church; thanks to the help of Cardinals, bishops, priests, lay people engaged in the apostolate, organisms of various denominations, which offered me valuable support; and thanks to you, my first and irreplaceable collaborators of the Roman Curia, whom I feel are so close to me. To all I express my deep, sincere and heartfelt favor.

We are preparing to celebrate Christmas. We have seen taking shape before our eyes the multiple fields of man's life in the modern world, with its lights and its shadows, with its uncertainties and its hopes, with its dangers and its resources. The Savior is about to descend once again towards all these fields of human existence and activity in the modern world. The world is waiting for Him, even unconsciously; the world needs Him, who proclaims the Father's mercy, who is the Father's mercy. Despite external appearances, this world suffers from within: imbalances, discriminations, oppressions, natural calamities, indescribable hardships; dissatisfaction, fear, violence, death, and, above all, there is sin, the seed of disintegration and the source of deep unhappiness. Christ comes to save the world from sin and to offer it the extreme possibility of redemption. As I wrote in the Encyclical *Dives in misericordia*, which I entrusted to the meditation of the Church at the beginning of this Advent in preparation for Christmas—"By becoming the Incarnation of the love that is manifested with particular force with regard to the suffering, the unfortunate, and sinners,

He makes present and thus more fully reveals the Father, who is God 'rich in mercy.' At the same time, by becoming for people a model of merciful love for others, Christ proclaims by His actions even more than by His words that call to mercy which is one of the essential elements of the Gospel *ethos*" (no. 3).

Christmas is the sign of God's mercy, the appearing of His liberating love among men. The Church does not tire of repeating the proclamation, because she knows that the world needs this mercy, which does not debase man but gives him a new dignity, elevating him to the level of God. He humiliated Himself in Christ in order to bring man back to his lost greatness: *"Quia quomodo est Deus incommutabilis, fecit omnia per misericordiam, et dignatus est ipse Filius Dei mutabilem carnem suscipere, manens id quod Verbum Dei est, venire et subvenire homini:* As God is not changeable, and has done everything by means of His mercy, so the Son of God Himself deigned to assume a changeable flesh, remaining the Word of God; He deigned to come and help man" (S. Augustine, *Serm.* 6, 5; C.C.L., 41, *Sermones de Vetere Testamento*, ed. C. Lambot, Turnhout, 1961, p. 61).

Dignatus est venire et subvenire homini: This is Christmas for us. And this is what we try to do in the world, as members of that Church which recognizes that she was born, together with the birth of Christ, to help man to save himself; *subvenire homini.* This is our spur, beloved Brothers, our commitment, our effort; this is our one desire and the reward for which we strive with all our might, as long as the Lord gives breath and strength to us, to me and to all.

With my most affectionate apostolic blessing.

"You Must Be Men of Faith!"

On January 6, 1981, the Solemnity of the Epiphany of the Lord, the Holy Father ordained eleven new bishops. During the rite of ordination immediately after the Gospel, Pope John Paul II delivered the following homily.

1. "Arise, shine, / Jerusalem; / for your light has come, and the glory of the Lord has risen upon you" (Is. 60:1). With these words of the prophet Isaiah today's liturgy announces the celebration of a great feast: the Solemnity of the Epiphany of the Lord, which is the completion of the Christmas feast, of the birth of God.

The prophet's words are addressed to Jerusalem, to the city of the people of God—to the city of divine election. In this city the Epiphany was to reach its climax on the days of the Paschal Mystery of the Redeemer.

For the moment, however, the Redeemer is still a little baby. He lies in a poor cave near Bethlehem, and the cave is used as a place of refuge for animals. There He found His first shelter for Himself on this earth. There the love of His Mother and the solicitude of Joseph of Nazareth surrounded Him. And there, there took place also the beginning of the Epiphany: of that great light which was to penetrate hearts, guiding them along the way of faith in God, whom man can meet only on this way: living man meeting the living God.

Today on this way of faith we see the three new men who have come from the East, from outside Israel. They are wise and powerful men, who are led to Bethlehem by the star in the heavenly firmament and by the interior light of faith in the depths of their hearts.

A GUIDING LIGHT

2. On this day, such a solemn and eloquent one, you present yourselves here, venerated and dear sons, who by the act of ordination are to become our brothers in the episcopate, in the apostolic service of the Church.

I greet you cordially in this Basilica, upon which the light of the Messianic Jerusalem moved together with the person of the apostle Peter, who came here, guided by the Holy Spirit, according to the will of Christ.

Here, in this place, I meditate together with you on the words of today's liturgy, in which are manifested the light of the Epiphany and the mission born in the hearts of men from faith in Jesus Christ. May this light shine upon you particularly on this day—may it shine continually on the ways of your life and your ministry. May this light guide you—like the star of the Wise Men—and help you to guide others according to the substance of your vocation in the episcopate.

"The bishops"—the Second Vatican Council recalled —"in as much as they are the successors of the Apostles, receive from the Lord, to whom all power is given in heaven and on earth, the mission of teaching all peoples, and of preaching the Gospel to every creature, so that all men may attain to salvation through faith, Baptism and the observance of the commandments (cf. Mt. 28:18; Mk. 16:15-16; Acts 26:17f.). For the carrying out of this mission Christ promised the Holy Spirit to the Apostles and sent Him from heaven on the day of Pentecost, so that through His power they might be witnesses to Him in the remotest parts of the earth, before nations and peoples and kings (cf. Acts 1:8, 21ff.; 9:15). That office, however, which the Lord committed to the pastors of His people, is, in the strict sense of the term, a service, which is called very expressively in Sacred Scripture a *diakonia* or ministry (cf. Acts 1:17, 25; 21:19; Rom. 11:13; 1 Tm. 1:12)" (LG 24).

BE MEN OF FAITH

3. You must be, dear brothers, confessors of the Faith, witnesses to the Faith, teachers of the Faith. You must be men of faith. Look at this marvelous event, which today's Solemnity presents to the eyes of our soul.

One day, after the descent of the Holy Spirit, a great turning point took place in a community of the early Church. Paul of Tarsus became the protagonist of this turning point. Let us listen to how he speaks in today's liturgy: "The mystery was made known to me by revelation...how the Gentiles are fellow heirs, members of the same body, and partakers of the promise in Christ Jesus through the Gospel" (Eph. 3:3-6).

This mystery, on the strength of which Paul, and subsequently the other Apostles, brought the light of the Gospel outside the frontiers of the people of the old covenant, this mystery is still proclaimed today. Already at the moment of the Messiah's birth, three men who come from outside Israel are called with the light of the star and with the light of faith to His manger in Bethlehem, to a sharing in the promise that He has come to fulfill.

These three men speak of all those who are to follow the same Messianic light both from the East and from the West, from the North and from the South, to find again together "with Abraham, Isaac and Jacob" the promise of the living God.

This promise is fulfilled today before the eyes of the Wise Men, just as it was fulfilled in the night of the birth of God before the eyes of the shepherds, near Bethlehem.

Oh, how many things the words of the prophet, who summons Jerusalem, tell us today:

"Lift up your eyes round about, and see..., your heart shall thrill and rejoice" (Is. 60:4-5).

SERVING THE LIGHT

4. Dear sons and beloved brothers!

You must become the extraordinary witnesses of today's joy of the Jerusalem of the Lord. Your heart must thrill and rejoice before the Mystery you look at! Before the light that you must serve!

How great is the faith of the Wise Men! How sure they are of the light that the Spirit of the Lord has lit in their hearts! With what tenacity they follow it. With what consistency they seek the newborn Messiah. And when at last they have reached their goal, "...they rejoiced exceedingly with great joy; and going into the house they saw the child with Mary his mother, and they fell down and worshiped him. Then, opening their treasures, they offered him gifts, gold and frankincense and myrrh" (Mt. 2:10-11).

The light of faith enabled them to scrutinize all the unknown factors, the unknown ways, the unknown circumstances, as when they found themselves before the newborn Child—a human newborn Child, who did not have a roof over His head. They perceived the wretchedness of the place. What a contrast with their positions as educated and socially influential men. Yet "they fell down and worshiped Him" (cf. Mt. 2:11).

If this Child, Christ, had been able to speak then as He later spoke many times, He would have said to them: men, great is your faith! Words similar to those that once, later; the Canaanite woman listened to: "great is your faith" (cf. Mt. 15:28).

OFFER YOURSELF AS A GIFT

5. Dear brothers! In a moment you too will bow down deeply and fall down and, lying on the floor of this Basilica, you will prepare your hearts for the new coming of the Holy Spirit, to receive His divine gifts. They are the same gifts that illuminated and strengthened the Wise Men on the way to Bethlehem, at the meeting with the newborn child, and then on the way back and throughout their lives.

They responded to these divine gifts with gifts: gold, frankincense and myrrh, realities which have also a symbolic meaning. Following that meaning, offer your gifts today, offer yourselves as a gift, ready to offer throughout your lives love, prayer and suffering!

And then, rise up, walk along the way on which the Lord will lead you, guiding you along the ways of your mission and your ministry.

Rise up, strengthened in faith! As witnesses of Christ's ministry. As servants of the Gospel and dispensers of Christ's power. And walk in the light of the Epiphany, guiding others to faith and strengthening in faith all those you meet.

May the wisdom, the humility and the courage of the Wise Men from the East accompany you always.

Permanent Signs of God's Presence in Human History

On January 22, 1981, the Holy Father received a group of rectors of sanctuaries in France, Belgium and Portugal, gathered in Rome for a congress. John Paul II delivered the following address.

Dear Friends,

Welcoming you with particular joy this morning, I cannot help thinking of the crowds which, throughout the year, come to the sanctuaries whose care and promotion are your responsibility. That is why I attach to this brief meeting an importance which is added to the pleasure of personal contact with you. Allow me to greet especially your guide, the Bishop of Laval, so attentive to the influence of the sanctuary of Our Lady of Pontmain.

Your personal studies and your congresses of rectors have revealed to you that pilgrimages are a constant practice in the history of religions. Christianity has also adopted this custom, which is deeply rooted in the popular mentality and which answers a need to visit a religious place where the divine has been manifested. There would certainly be a very interesting history to write on Christian pilgrimages, from the very first ones which had as their goal Jerusalem and the holy places, to those of our times, whether they take place in Rome, Assisi, Lourdes, Fatima, Guadalupe, Czestochowa, Knock, Lisieux, Campostelle, Altötting or so many other places.

Rectors of the sanctuaries of France, like your colleagues in other nations, you are the heirs and the administrators of a considerable religious heritage, whose impact on the life of the Christian people and on many people who have remained at the frontiers of faith seems to be swinging upward today. You have a deep awareness of this. You can certainly bring many other people to share it. In these few moments, I would just like to strengthen your convictions on some essential points of your special ministry.

Always and everywhere, Christian sanctuaries have been, or have been intended to be, signs of God, of His entrance into human history. Each of them is a memorial of the Mystery of the Incarnation and of Redemption. Did not your poet Pegúy say, in his original style, that the Incarnation is the only interesting story that has ever happened? It is the history of God's love for every man and for the whole of mankind (cf. RH 13). And if numerous Romanesque, Gothic or modern sanctuaries have been dedicated to our Lady, it is because the humble Virgin of Nazareth gave birth, through the action of the Holy Spirit, to the Son of God Himself, the universal Savior, and because her role is always to present Christ "rich in mercy" to the generations that succeed one another.

EXPERIENCE GOD'S PRESENCE

In our age which knows in varying degrees the temptation of secularization, it is important that the high spiritual places, built in the course of the ages and often on the initiative of saints, should continue to speak to the mind and heart of men, believers or non-believers, who all feel the asphyxia of a society closed within itself and sometimes desperate. Is it a dream to long for the most frequented sanctuaries to become, or return to being, as many family houses, as it were, in which each of those who pass or who stay there will rediscover the meaning of their existence, a taste for life, having had there a certain experience of God's presence and love? The traditional vocation of every sanctuary, which still holds good today, is to be, as it were, a permanent antenna of the Good News of salvation.

One condition for the evangelical influence of sanctuaries is that they should be very welcoming. And in the first place very welcoming in themselves. Whatever their age or their style, their artistic riches or their simplicity, each of them must affirm its original personality, avoiding the incongruous accumulation of religious objects as well as their systematic rejection. Sanctuaries are made for God, but also for the people, who are entitled to respect for their own sensibility, even if their good taste needs to be patiently educated. The perfect order and real beauty of the most famous basilica or of a more modest chapel are already a catechesis, which helps to open the minds and hearts of pilgrims or, alas, to dampen their fervor. But if stones and objects have their language and their share of influence on beings, what are we to say of the pastoral teams dedicated to the animation of sanctuaries? Your role, my friends, may be a decisive one, taking into account the mystery of God's grace. Whether it is a question of welcoming organized groups whose coming is announced, or anonymous and isolated visitors, coming to beg for a grace or to express their thanks for one received; whether it is a question of facilitating the smooth running of the pilgrimages prepared by your confreres and their helpers, or to provide the services characteristic of worship in the sanctuary for which you are responsible, or to explain its history to visitors; whether it is a question of proposing a moment of prayer or accepting the dialogue requested by certain pilgrims—every member of the team must give proof of kindness and patience, competence, and insight, zeal and discretion, and above all humbly let his faith shine through; be a witness to the invisible. Your valuable ministry which is at stake, in a way, is the opening of souls to God, their conversion, and, for those who are just seeking, their first step towards the light and love of the Lord.

EFFORTS CONVERGE TO EVANGELIZE!

All these efforts to welcome and take care of children, students, people advanced in years, sick and handicapped people, very different socio-professional categories, fervent Christians and Christians in difficulty, must converge towards one purpose: to evangelize! My great and dear Predecessor Paul VI took care, in the Apostolic Exhortation *Evangelii nuntiandi*, to recall clearly and simply the essential content and the secondary elements of evangelization (cf. nos. 25-39). May every sanctuary continue to draw its guidelines from it! A Christocentric apostolate! Oh yes, help Christians to join Christ really, to unite with Him, to understand "the unceasing interplay of the Gospel and of man's concrete life, both personal and social" (EN 29). Help those with little faith to turn to Him who presented Himself as "the way, the truth and the life" (Jn. 14:6). Help pilgrims to integrate themselves better in the living Tradition of the Church, always made up of fidelity to the Faith and pastoral adaptation, from the time of the Acts of the Apostles to the Second Vatican Council. See even if it is possible to give, at least from time to time, spiritual and doctrinal lectures judiciously adapted to the various groups of pilgrims. Many important teachings of the Magisterium are practically unknown or only vaguely perceived.

Above all, let the whole life of sanctuaries foster as much as possible personal and community prayer, joy and meditation, listening to, and meditating on, the Word of God, truly worthy celebration of the Eucharist, and personal reception of the Sacrament of Reconciliation, brotherhood between persons who meet for the first time, the concern to help with their offerings poor regions and poor Churches, participation in the life of parishes and dioceses.

May the Virgin Mary, always honored in your sanctuaries which are dedicated to her, make your important pastoral work bear fruit, and may she help all pilgrims to enter the will of the Lord more! And I myself, in the very dear memory of the many pilgrimages I have had the privilege of carrying out or guiding, give you my affectionate blessing.

Safeguard the Values of Marriage

On January 24, 1981, the Holy Father received in audience the judges of the Sacred Roman Rota, at the beginning of the new judicial year. In reply to an address by Mons. Heinrich Ewers, Dean of the Sacred Roman Rota, John Paul II spoke as follows.

Very Reverend Dean,
Dear prelates and officials of the Sacred Roman Rota!

1. I am happy to meet you today, on the occasion of the opening of the new judicial year of your Court. I heartily thank the Dean for the noble words addressed to me and for the wise methodological resolutions formulated. I greet you all with fatherly affection, while I express my sincere appreciation for your work, so delicate and yet so necessary, which is an integral and qualified part of the pastoral office of the Church.

The specific competence of the Sacred Roman Rota with regard to matrimonial cases touches very closely the topical theme of the family, which has been the subject of study by the recent Synod of Bishops. Well, I now intend to speak to you about the juridical safeguarding of the family in the judicial activity of the ecclesiastical Courts.

MARRIAGE PROBLEMS

2. With a deep evangelical spirit the Second Vatican Ecumenical Council has accustomed us to look to man, in order to know him in all his problems and to help him to solve his existential problems by the light of the

truth revealed to us by Christ and with the grace that the divine mysteries of salvation offer us.

Among the problems that most affect man's heart today, and consequently the human environment, both family and social, in which he lives and works, the pre-eminent and indispensable one is that of conjugal love, which binds two human beings of different sex, making them a community of life and love, that is, uniting them in marriage.

Marriage gives rise to the family, "where"—Vatican II emphasizes—"different generations come together and help one another to grow wiser and harmonize the rights of individuals with other demands of social life"; and as such, "the family constitutes the basis of society" (GS 52). In fact, the Council adds, "the well-being of the individual person and of both human and Christian society is closely bound up with the healthy state of conjugal and family life" (ibid., 47). But with the Council itself we must recognize that "this happy picture of the dignity of these partnerships is not reflected everywhere, but is overshadowed by polygamy, the plague of divorce, so-called free love, and similar disfigurements; furthermore, married love is very often dishonored by selfishness, hedonism, and unlawful contraceptive practices" (ibid.).

Also owing to the serious difficulties that arise, sometimes with violence, from the deep changes in society today, the institution of marriage plainly shows its irreplaceable value, and the family still remains "a school for human enrichment" (ibid., 52).

In face of the grave evils which nearly everywhere today beset this great good which the family is, it has been suggested that there should be drafted a charter of the rights of the family, universally recognized, in order to ensure this institution just protection, in the interest also of the whole of society.

3. The Church on her part, and within the sphere of her competence, has always tried to protect the family also with appropriate legislation, as well as encouraging it and

helping it with various pastoral initiatives. I have already mentioned the recent Synod of Bishops. But it is well known that, right from the beginning of her Magisterium, the Church, encouraged by the Word of the Gospel (cf. Mt. 19:5; 5:32), has always taught and explicitly reiterated the precept of Jesus on the unity and indissolubility of marriage, without which it is never possible to have a secure, healthy family—a real vital cell of society. Contrary to the Greco-Roman and Judaic practice, which greatly facilitated divorce, the Apostle Paul already declared: "To the married I give charge, not I but the Lord, that the wife should not separate from her husband...and that the husband should not divorce his wife" (1 Cor. 7:10-11). There followed the preaching of the Fathers, who, before the spread of divorce, affirmed emphatically that marriage is, by divine will, indissoluble.

Respect, therefore, for the laws willed by God for the meeting between man and woman and for the continuation of their union was the new element that Christianity introduced into the institution of marriage. "The intimate partnership of life and the love which constitutes the married state"—Vatican II will subsequently say—"has been established by the Creator and endowed by Him with its own proper laws: it is rooted in the contract of its partners, that is, in their irrevocable personal consent. It is an institution confirmed by the divine law and receiving its stability, even in the eyes of society, from the human act by which the partners mutually surrender themselves to each other" (GS 48).

This doctrine immediately guided the apostolate, the behavior of Christian spouses, the ethics of marriage and its juridical discipline. And the catechetical and pastoral activity of the Church, supported and strengthened by the witness of Christian families, introduced changes even in Roman legislation, which, with Justinian, no longer admitted divorce *sine causa*, and gradually came to accept the Christian institution of marriage. It was a great achievement for society, since the Church, having restored dignity to woman and to marriage through the family, contributed to saving the best of Greco-Roman culture.

DANGER IN EASY DECLARATIONS OF NULLITY

4. In the present-day social framework, the original effort, doctrinal and pastoral, of conduct and praxis, as well as legislative and judicial, is again proposed to the Church today.

The good of the human person and of the family, in which the individual realizes a great part of his dignity, and the good of society itself, requires that the Church, today even more than in the recent past, surround the institution of marriage and the family with particular protection.

The pastoral effort, urged also by the recent Synod of Bishops, might turn out to be almost in vain if it were not accompanied by a corresponding legislative and judicial action. For the comfort of all pastors, we can say that the new codification of Canon Law is making provision with wise juridical norms to express what has emerged from the recent Ecumenical Council in favor of marriage and the family. The voice heard at the recent Synod of Bishops about the alarming increase of matrimonial cases in the ecclesiastical courts will certainly be evaluated during the revision of the Code of Canon Law. It is likewise certain that the pastors, also in response to the requests of the above-mentioned Synod, will be able, with increased pastoral commitment, to promote the adequate preparation of engaged couples for the celebration of marriage. The stability of the conjugal bond and the happy continuation of the family community depend, in fact, to a great extent on the way in which fiancés prepare for their marriage. But it is also true that the very preparation for marriage would be negatively influenced by the pronouncements or sentences of matrimonial nullity, if these were obtained too easily. If, among the evils of divorce, there is also that of making the celebration of marriage less serious and binding, to the extent that today it has lost due consideration among a good many young people, it is to be feared that also the sentences of the declaration of matrimonial nullity would lead to the same existential and psychological perspective, if they were multiplied as easy and hasty pronouncements. "Hence the ecclesiastical judge"—my venerated Predecessor Pius XII already admonished—"must not prove to be easy in declaring the nullity of marriage, but must rather endeavor first and foremost to bring it about that what has been contracted invalidly should be made valid, especially when the circumstances of the case make it particularly advisable." And in explanation of this admonishment he had first stated: "As for declarations of nullity of marriages, everyone knows that the Church is wary and averse to encouraging them. If, in fact, the tranquillity, stability and security of human dealings in general demand that contracts should not likely be proclaimed null, this applies even more to a contract of such importance as is marriage, whose firmness and stability are required by the common good of human society and by the private good of spouses and their offspring, and whose dignity as a sacrament forbids that what is sacred and sacramental should be easily exposed to the danger of profanation" (Address to the Sacred Roman Rota, October 3, 1941: *AAS* 1941, pp. 423-424). With its wise and prudent work of vigilance, the Supreme Court of the Apostolic Signatura is contributing in a praiseworthy way to warding off this danger. The judicial action of the Court of the Sacred Roman Rota seems to me likewise valid. The equally wise and responsible work of the lower courts must correspond to the vigilance of the Signatura and the sound jurisprudence of the Rota.

FULL CONFORMITY TO CHURCH DOCTRINE

5. No small contribution to the necessary protection of the family is made by the attention and prompt

availability of the diocesan and regional courts in following the directives of the Holy See, the constant jurisprudence of the Rota, and faithful application of the norms, both of substantial and of process law, already codified, without having recourse to presumed or probable innovations, to interpretations which do not objectively correspond to the canonical norm and which are not borne out by any qualified jurisprudence. Any innovation in law, whether substantial or regarding process law, which does not find verification in the jurisprudence or praxis of the courts and departments of the Holy See, is, in fact, rash. We must be convinced that a serene, attentive, well-pondered, complete and exhaustive examination of matrimonial cases calls for full conformity with the precise doctrine of the Church, Canon Law, and sound canonical jurisprudence, which has been developing above all through the contribution of the Sacred Roman Rota; all that must be considered, as Paul VI of venerated memory already said to you, a "wise means" and "a railroad track, as it were, whose central line of direction is precisely the pursuit of objective truth, and whose terminal point is the correct administration of justice" (Paul VI, January 28, 1978: *AAS* 1978, p. 182).

In this pursuit, all the ministers of the ecclesiastical tribunal—each one with due respect for his own role and that of others—must take into particular, constant and conscientious consideration, the formation of free and valid matrimonial consent, always combined with the concern, equally constant and conscientious, for protection of the sacrament of marriage. To the attainment of knowledge of the objective truth, that is, the existence of the matrimonial bond, validly contracted, or its non-existence, there contribute both attention to the problems of the person and attention to the laws on which, by divine or natural law, or the positive law of the Church, the valid celebration of marriage and its continuation depend. Canonical justice, which, according to the fine expression of St. Gregory the Great, we call more significantly sacerdotal justice, emerges from all the proofs of the process as a whole, evaluated conscientiously in the light of the doctrine and law of the Church, and with the support of the most qualified jurisprudence. The good of the family demands this, keeping in mind the fact that all protection of the legitimate family is always in favor of the person; while unilateral concern with the individual can lead to injury of the human person himself, in addition to harming marriage and the family, which are goods both of the person and of society. The provisions of the marriage code which is in force must be seen in this perspective.

HELP PEOPLE SEEK TRUTH

6. In the Synod's message to Christian families, stress is laid on the great good that the family, especially the Christian one, constitutes and realizes for the human person. The family "helps its members to become promoters of the history of salvation and at the same time living signs of the plan that God has for the world" (no. 8). Also judicial activity, being an activity of the Church, must keep in mind this reality—which is not only natural but also supernatural—of marriage and of the family which springs from marriage. Nature and grace reveal to us, though in different ways and to different degrees, a divine plan for marriage and the family, which must always be taken into consideration, protected and, according to the roles peculiar to each activity of the Church, promoted so that it may be accepted by human society as widely as possible.

The Church, therefore, also with her law and exercise of *potestas iudicialis*, can and must safeguard the values of marriage and the family, in order to promote man and emphasize his dignity.

The judicial action of the ecclesiastical matrimonial courts, like the legislative one, will have to help the human person in the search for objective truth and then to affirm this truth, so that the same person may be able to know, live, and carry out the loving plan that God has assigned to him.

The invitation that Vatican II addressed to all, particularly to "everyone who exercises an influence in the community and in social groups," responsibly involves, therefore, also the ministers of the ecclesiastical courts for matrimonial cases, so that they too, while serving truth and administering justice well, may devote themselves "to the welfare of marriage and the family" (GS 52).

7. Therefore I offer to you, Very Reverend Dean, to the prelate auditors and to the officials of the Sacred Roman Rota, my cordial wishes for serene and profitable work, carried out in the light of these considerations today.

And, while I am happy to renew the expression of my appreciation for the valuable and tireless activity of your Court, I willingly impart to you all the special apostolic blessing, invoking divine assistance for your delicate office and as a sign of my constant favor.

Strong in the Certainty that Comes from God

Continuing his visits to ecclesiastical institutes having their headquarters in Rome, the Holy Father went to the Pontifical International Missionary College, "St. Paul the Apostle," on January 24, 1981. The Pope presided over the celebration of Holy Mass in the chapel of the institute. During the Liturgy of the Word, he delivered the following homily.

Beloved priests!

1. It gives me great joy to meet you today in this College dedicated to St. Paul the Apostle, where you reside while you attend the University of "Propaganda Fide" to develop and complete your philosophical and theological studies and your pastoral preparation. In the visits that I am paying to the various institutes and universities of the city of Rome, I could not and should not miss, on the occasion, such a special one, of the feast of the College, this meeting with you, who come from all over the world

and bring here, to the center of Christianity, the characteristics and anxieties of your peoples and your cultures.

Accept, therefore, my cordial and affectionate greeting, which is addressed first of all to the Cardinal Prefect and to the Secretary of the Sacred Congregation for the Evangelization of Peoples, to the superiors and those in charge of the College, and then to each of you personally, including also all those who collaborate in various tasks for the smooth running of the house and of community life. It is a greeting that expresses satisfaction and appreciation for the goodwill you show in your commitment of study and *aggiornamento,* for a more effective ministry adapted to the needs of society, and for enlightened and concrete help for the ecclesial communities of your nations and your dioceses. And it is a greeting which expresses also my gratitude for your faithfulness to the Apostolic See and for the prayers you offer for me personally and for my universal mission.

STIMULUS TO HOLY PRIESTLY LIFE

2. I wish, however, that today's meeting round the altar, celebrating the Eucharistic Sacrifice, may become for you all also a stimulus to an increasingly holy priestly life and to a more and more responsible commitment in your studies and your ideals. And precisely the readings of the liturgy lend themselves to some reflections that are very important for this purpose.

In the first reading we heard what the Lord says through the prophet Isaiah: "For as the rain and the snow come down from heaven, and return not thither but water the earth, making it bring forth and sprout, giving seed to the sower and bread to the eater, so shall my word be that goes forth from my mouth; it shall not return to me empty, but it shall accomplish that which I purpose, and prosper in the thing for which I sent it" (Is. 55:10-11). These are very well-known words, which have given food for thought to the Fathers and Doctors of the Church, the saints and mystics of all ages, and which make an impression also on our minds, because they affirm the absolute power and efficacy of the revelation of God: no obstacle or human denial can stop it or extinguish it. We know that the "Word of God," in the fullness of time, became incarnate: "In the beginning was the Word, and the Word was with God, and the Word was God.... And the Word became flesh and dwelt among us" (Jn. 1:1, 14), and it has remained present in human history through the Church: "Lo, I am with you always, to the close of the age" (Mt. 28:20).

THE "WORD OF GOD" IS ALWAYS EFFECTIVE

The "Word of God" is always effective, because in the first place it puts human reason in a crisis: merely rational and temporal philosophies, purely humanistic and historicist interpretations, are thrown into confusion by the "Word of God," which replies with supreme certainty and clarity to the questions posed to man's heart, enlightens him about his true destiny, which is supernatural and eternal, and points out to him the moral conduct to practice, as the authentic way of serenity and hope. Not only does the "Word of God" give "the light" and "the way," it becomes a life of grace, participation in divine life itself, integration in the mysterious but real dynamism of the redemption of mankind. In fact, Jesus defined Himself as the life of souls, and the "light of the world": "I have come as light into the world, that whoever believes in me may not remain in darkness" (Jn. 12:46).

Strong in this certainty that comes from God, we must have the courage of His Word! No fear of truth: the "Word of God" is always efficacious, it is not inert, it is never disappointed! And so I say to you with St. Paul: "Walk as children of light" (Eph. 5:8). Certainly, the "Word of God" is disturbing, because the Lord says: "My thoughts are not your thoughts, neither are your ways my ways" (Is. 55:8); it causes a crisis, because it is demanding, it is as sharp as a two-edged sword and it is based not on persuasive speeches of human wisdom, but on the manifestation of the Spirit and His power (cf. 1 Cor. 2:4-5). "Let no one deceive himself," St. Paul wrote to the Corinthians. "If anyone among you thinks that he is wise in this age, let him become a fool that he may become wise. For the wisdom of this world is folly with God.... So let no one boast of men" (1 Cor. 3:18-19, 21). There is, in fact, a false wisdom that may tempt and give illusions, confusing people and making them become presumptuous. Commenting on the affirmation: "Let us offer to God acceptable worship, with reverence and awe; for our God is a consuming fire" (Heb. 12:28-29), Cardinal Newman, a lover of Saint Paul, said as follows: "Fear of God is the beginning of wisdom; until you see God as a consuming fire, and approach Him with reverence and holy awe, because you are sinners, you will not be able to say that you are even in sight of the narrow door.... Fear and love must go together; continue to fear, continue to love until the last day of your lives. This is certain; you must know, however, what it means to say: sow here below in tears if you want to reap in joy in the afterlife" *(Parochial and Plain Sermons,* Vol. I, Serm. XIV; cf. J. H. Newman, *La mente e il cuore di un grande,* Bari, 1962, p. 230).

YOU WILL BE A WITNESS

3. In the second reading, the famous episode of the conversion of St. Paul, which he himself narrated to the Jews of Jerusalem, is equally rich in teachings for your priestly life. On the way to Damascus, falling in the dust, St. Paul is blinded by the dazzling light of that Jesus whom he persecutes in the Christians; his immediate and decisive conversion follows, an evident miraculous work of the grace of God, because Paul was to be the first authoritative interpreter of the message of Christ, divinely inspired. The Divine Master orders him to get up and continue on his way; and from that moment, it can be said, St. Paul

becomes our teacher and guide in getting to know and love Christ.

But above all the words of the devout Ananias must interest us and make us meditate on them: "The God of our fathers appointed you to know his will, to see the Just One and to hear a voice from his mouth; for you will be a witness for him to all men of what you have seen and heard" (Acts 22:14-15). These words can also be applied to every priest, who is a minister of Christ. You too have been chosen, in fact appointed by the Almighty, to know the "Word of God," to meet Christ, to participate in His own divine powers, to proclaim Him and bear witness to Him before all men. Just as Paul, converted to the truth, threw himself with ardent fervor into his mission as an apostle and witness, and no difficulty could stop him, you too do the same. The world needs fervent and bold souls, humble in behavior, but firm in doctrine; generous in charity, but confident in proclamation; serene and courageous, like Paul, who, in the midst of difficulties and conflicts of every kind, overflows with joy in every tribulation, because for him, to live was Christ and to die was gain (cf. 2 Cor. 7:4; Phil. 1:21).

The Evangelist St. Mark reports the last words of Jesus, categorical and imperative ones: "Go into all the world and preach the gospel to the whole creation. He who believes and is baptized will be saved; but he who does not believe will be condemned" (Mk. 16:15-16). They mean that it is God's positive will that the Gospel message should be proclaimed to the whole world and that "God's Word" should be believed. To be a priest is certainly an immense and outstanding dignity, but it is also a great responsibility. Always be aware of your greatness and worthy of the confidence that God has placed in you!

Beloved in Christ, may you be enlightened in your studies and strengthened in your resolutions by the Blessed Virgin, to whom we pray in these days as "Mother of the Unity of the Church," and whom we always invoke as "the Seat of Wisdom," "the Cause of Our Joy."

Spirituality, Unity, Peace: Values To Be Defended and Lived in Depth

On January 26, 1981, the Holy Father received the Italian National Committee for the celebrations of the fifteenth centenary of the birth of St. Benedict. The Pope delivered the following address.

Venerated brothers, gentlemen,

It gives me great joy to receive in audience today you representatives of the National Committee for the celebrations of the fifteenth centenary of the birth of St. Benedict the Abbot and of his sister St. Scholastica, at the end of the jubilee year, during which you have been engaged in the noble task of ensuring the worthy celebration of this significant event.

I sincerely thank you for this visit: in particular, I express my deep gratitude to Mr. Rolando Picchioni, the President of the Committee, who, expressing also your sentiments, addressed such courteous words to me.

1. Your presence recalls to my mind and heart the devout assemblies of faith and prayer and the meetings with all those faithful, particularly the young, whom I was able to see during my pilgrimages to the places consecrated by the presence and the passing of the great Patriarch of the West: at Norcia, his birthplace; at Montecassino, the Motherhouse of Benedictine Monasticism; at Subiaco, where the saint spent most of his life as a hermit and monk.

Credit for the success of these events must be attributed to a very great extent also to the industrious work of your committee, which, coordinating the activities of the various departments of the government, of the national academies and qualified cultural centers, interested in the celebrations for various reasons, has made a considerable contribution for better knowledge of the spiritual and social message handed down to us by the saint. Within this framework falls the promotion of opportune and praise-worthy initiatives, such as the restoration of Benedictine monuments at Subiaco and Montecassino; the broadcasting, by the Italian Radio and Television Corporation, of suitable programs; the organization of meetings, lectures, debates and round tables at the scientific and popular level; a valuable issue of stamps, which honors Italian artistic and religious traditions. And all this thanks also to the good mediation of the media of social communication, carried out by the Ministry of Tourism and Entertainment, which is worthily represented here.

IRREPLACEABLE VALUES

2. But now that the Benedictine year has ended, I wish to express the hope that all these efforts, aimed essentially at the necessary Christian animation of society—a matter which haunted St. Benedict—will not end here, but that what you have done will stimulate you to ever new initiatives, aimed at illustrating Christian civilization. It is true that a special anniversary is now concluded, but the ideals it has recalled and proclaimed must last; they must be studied more deeply in all their aspects. This holds good all the more in that we live in an historical moment in which the necessity of a return to the irreplaceable values of spirituality, unity and peace is felt more urgently than ever: it is on these ideals that the whole admirable tissue of that golden booklet, which is the Rule of St. Benedict, is completely centered. For this reason he has a great deal to say and to give to modern men. In particular, the future of Europe will depend on how it will succeed in continuing to assimilate and internalize the Benedictine spirit, which once forged it and united it with the cross and the plough, and with the relative emblematic motto: *"Ora et labora."*

All that still remains fundamental for the construction of society. And it is an animating ferment also and above all in the present effort for the unification of Europe, so longed for today.

BENEDICT, CYRIL AND METHODIUS

3. You all know with what satisfaction the entry of Greece into the European Common Market was hailed: It is an important fact not only because of its economic and social aspects, but also for the religious and cultural ones, because Greek culture, alongside the Roman one, forms the other pillar of the European soul. In this connection, towards the end of the year of St. Benedict, whom we venerate as the patron saint of Europe, I wished to put at his side, as co-patrons of this ancient continent, St. Cyril and St. Methodius. Born at Salonika, "they highlight first the contribution of the ancient Greek culture and, subsequently, the significance of the influence of the Church of Constantinople and of the Eastern tradition, which is so deeply inscribed in the spirituality of so many peoples and nations in the Eastern part of the European continent" (EV 3). May the two brothers, Apostles of the Slav peoples, help us to understand the needs of the Slav nations, which form such a large part of Europe, and which also aspire to becoming full members of the concert of European families.

4. As for you, beloved brothers, I pray to the Lord that there may remain in your hearts satisfaction with the work carried out and awareness of the fruits it has yielded in the course of this year. May these benefits multiply and grow productively in this dear Christian Europe of ours.

This is the wish which, with great affection, I extend to each of you and your dear ones, and which, as a token of the most abundant heavenly rewards, I willingly confirm with my apostolic blessing.

Sacrament of Reconciliation Forms Christian Consciences

On January 30, 1981, the Holy Father received in audience the members of the Sacred Apostolic Penitentiary and of all the Colleges of Minor Penitentiary Fathers, ordinary and extraordinary, of the patriarchal basilicas of Rome, led by Cardinal Giuseppe Paupini. John Paul II delivered the following address.

Your Eminence,
Very Reverend Penitentiary Fathers!

I am particularly happy to receive together the Sacred Penitentiary and all the Colleges of Minor Penitentiary Fathers, ordinary and extraordinary, of the patriarchal basilicas of the city.

While I thank the Cardinal Major Penitentiary for the kind expressions with which he conveyed your sentiments, I willingly welcome you all to this house of the common Father, and I hope that this meeting of faith and mutual charity will be an efficacious hour of grace for all of us who are living it.

The satisfaction that this audience gives me is even greater because it takes place while the Encyclical *Dives in misericordia* is being read and studied in the Church: From various standpoints, which are complementary with one another, your office is dedicated to the exercise of the ministry of divine mercy. The Penitentiary, furthermore, has an extremely delicate and important role in helping the Pope in his office of the keys and in the power to loose and bind. In its sphere of competence it embraces the Church in all her catholicity, without limits arising from rites or territory. The Penitentiary Fathers, furthermore, because of their origin from the most varied countries in the world, the multiplicity of the languages in which they express themselves, and because in point of fact ecclesiastics and lay faithful of the whole world trustfully turn to them when they come *"videre Petrum"* (Gal. 1:18 Vulg.), represent in action the ministry of reconciliation which, by the power of the Holy Spirit, as at Pentecost, is exercised on *"viri religiosi ex omni natione, quae sub caelo est"* (Acts 2:5).

SOLVING DOUBTS

The Pope avails himself of the Sacred Penitentiary to meet problems and difficulties which the faithful feel and suffer in the depths of their consciences. This role is characteristic of the Sacred Penitentiary: While, in fact, other Departments of the Holy See, it is true, act in spiritual matters, but insofar as these are the object of the external forum, the Sacred Penitentiary touches those matters within the unique and mysterious relationship, worthy of the greatest reverence, that individual souls have with God, their Creator, Lord, Redeemer and Ultimate End. Hence the very deep and inviolate secrecy concerning the practices of the Court of the Sacred Penitentiary, whether it is a question of absolution from censures reserved to the Holy See, the solving of doubts of conscience, often tormenting, or fair and charitable settlements of obligations of religion or of justice.

And I am happy to recall how, apart from the grace of state with which the Lord helps anyone who carries out an institutional role in the Church, the Sacred Penitentiary enjoys, in this secret work of renewal and formation of consciences, the credit of over six centuries of refined experience and also of doctrinal contributions, which have come and still come to it from expert theologians and canonists.

MYSTERY OF INDIVIDUAL SOULS

Closely connected with this office is the other one entrusted to the Sacred Penitentiary, that is, to "moderate" the granting and the use of sacred indulgences in the whole Church. In this connection I wish to recall that love, understood supernaturally, for indulgences—connected as they are with the certainty of sin and of the Sacrament of Reconciliation, with faith in the hereafter, especially in purgatory, with the application of the merits of the Mystical Body, that is, with the Communion of Saints— bears the stamp of true Catholic Faith. I am glad to tell the Cardinal Major Penitentiary, the prelates and officials of the Sacred Penitentiary, that I have confidence in their work and that I am grateful to them for the help they give me in my apostolic ministry. I am happy to repeat for them the encouragement I have addressed on other occasions to the whole Roman Curia: above and beyond papers, let them continue to see souls, the mystery of individual souls, for whose salvation the Lord intends the mediation of other souls and of the whole Church in her hierarchical structure.

The Penitentiary Fathers of the patriarchal basilicas —as is known, the Franciscan Conventuals in St. Peter's, the Friars Minor in St. John Lateran, the Dominicans in St. Mary Major, the Benedictines in St. Paul, as ordinary Penitentiaries, and also, as extraordinary Penitentiaries, members of other well-deserving religious families in Saint Peter's, and those of the respective families of the Ordinaries in the three other basilicas—bear the *pondus diei et aestum* (cf. Mt. 20:12) of hearing sacramental confessions for long hours every day, and especially on feast days.

DEDICATE YOURSELVES
TO THE SACRAMENT OF PENANCE

With the very constitution of the Colleges of Penitentiaries and with the particular norms by which, at the cost of exempting them from the customary or *ex lege* practices of their respective religious families, it consecrates them to dedicating the whole of their ministry to confessions, the Holy See intends to show with these facts the extraordinary veneration with which it regards the use of the Sacrament of Penance, and in particular the form that must be its normal one, that is, that of auricular confession. And I still remember the joy and emotion I felt last Good Friday, when I came down to St. Peter's Basilica to share with you the high and humble and very precious ministry that you exercise in the Church.

I wish to say to the Penitentiary Fathers and also to all priests in the world: At the cost of any sacrifice, dedicate yourselves to the administration of the Sacrament of Reconciliation, and be certain that it forms Christian consciences, more and better than any human device, any psychological technique, any didactic and sociological method. In the sacrament of Penance, in fact, it is God, *"dives in misericordia,"* who is at work (cf. Eph 2:4). And keep in mind that the teaching of the Council of Trent about the necessity of the integral confession of mortal sins is still in force in the Church, and always will be (Sess. XIV, Cap. 5 and can. 7: D.S. 1679-1683; 1707). The norm taught by St. Paul and by the same Council of Trent, according to which the worthy reception of the Eucharist must be preceeded by the confession of sins when one is conscious of mortal sin, is and always will be in force in the Church (Sess. XIII, Cap. 7, and can. 11: D.S. 1647-1661).

Renewing this teaching and these recommendations, we certainly do not ignore that recently (cf. *AAS* 64 [1972] pp. 510-514) the Church has extended the use of general absolution, for serious pastoral reasons and under precise and indispensable norms, in order to facilitate the supreme good of grace for so many souls. But I wish to recall the scrupulous observance of the above-mentioned conditions and to stress that, in the case of mortal sin, even after general absolution, there exists the obligation of a specific sacramental confession of the sin, and to confirm that, in any case, the faithful have the right to their own private confession.

In this connection I wish to emphasize the fact that, rightly, modern society jealously watches over the inalienable rights of the person: how, then, precisely in that most mysterious and sacred sphere of the personality in which the relationship with God is lived, could one desire to deny the human person, the individual person of every faith, the right of a personal, unique conversation with God, by means of the consecrated ministry? Why would one desire to deprive the individual member of the faithful, who is precious *qua talis* before God, of the deep and extremely personal joy of this extraordinary fruit of grace?

A VALUABLE EXERCISE OF VIRTUE

I would like to add, furthermore, that the Sacrament of Penance, because of the wholesome exercise of humility and sincerity that it involves, the faith it professes *in actu exercito* in the mediation of the Church, the hope it includes, and the careful examination of conscience that it requires, is not only an instrument aimed at destroying sin—the negative phase—but also a valuable exercise of virtue, which is itself expiation, an irreplaceable school of spirituality, and a highly positive process of regeneration in souls of *vir perfectus in mensuram aetatis plenitudinis Christi* (cf. Eph 4:13). In this sense, confession, rightly administered, is already in itself a very high form of spiritual direction.

Precisely for these reasons the sphere of the use of the Sacrament of Reconciliation cannot be reduced to the mere hypothesis of grave sins: Apart from the considerations of a dogmatic character that could be made in this connection, we recall that confession periodically renewed, the so-called confession "of devotion," has always accompanied the ascent to holiness in the Church.

I am happy to conclude by reminding myself, you Penitentiary Fathers, and all priests, that the apostolate of confession already has its reward in itself: the consciousness of having restored divine grace to a soul cannot but fill a priest with unutterable joy. And it cannot but encourage him to the humblest hope that the Lord, at the end of his earthly day, will open to him the ways of life: *"Qui ad iustitiam erudierint multos, quasi stellae in perpetuas aeternitates"* (Dn. 12:13).

While I invoke on you personally, and on your delicate and meritorious ministry, the abundance of divine graces, I willingly impart to you the conciliatory apostolic blessing, the sign of my constant favor.

Ecclesial Union

A year after the conclusion of the work of the Particular Synod of the Bishops of the Netherlands, the Holy Father sent the following letter, dated February 2, 1981, to the Archbishop of Utrecht and to all the bishops of the dioceses of the Netherlands.

To His Eminence Johannes Cardinal Willebrands, Archbishop of Utrecht, and to the bishops of the other dioceses in the Netherlands,

The 31st of January marked the passing of a year since the conclusion of the work of the Particular Synod of Bishops of the ecclesiastical province of the Netherlands, which took place from January 17 to 31, 1980. They were days, dear brothers in the episcopate, in which, devoting ourselves "to the Apostles' teaching and fellowship, to the breaking of bread and the prayers" (Acts 2:42), we lived a deep experience of communion and collegial cooperation.

On the occasion of the first anniversary of the conclusion of our work, I feel the desire to write to you in order to go back to that special experience, which had as its purpose to consolidate and define more precisely the principles of communion, thanks to which the Church in your country—each of the diocesan Churches that the Holy Spirit has entrusted to your pastoral care—remains in the universal community of the Catholic Church. The same principles constitute, at the same time, the foundation of the internal communion of the Church on Dutch soil, of which you, as bishops, are the first servants.

At that time I had examined with joy the conclusions adopted by you in the Synod and, during the con-celebration in the Sistine Chapel at the conclusion of the Synod's work, I had confirmed them, giving thanks to Jesus Christ, in whose name and through whose power we all carry out our ministry.

IMPLEMENTING THE RESOLUTIONS

And now, to my satisfaction, in the course of the Synod Council's recent meeting, I was informed that the Synod's deliberations remain the essential foundation of your pastoral activity, which is engaged in a work of Church renewal according to the spirit of the Second Vatican Ecumenical Council and according to the principles that were elaborated there for the whole Church.

At the same meeting of the Synod Council there was expressed to me also your concern as pastors because of the various difficulties of a psychological and structural character which oppose a rapid and consistent implementation of the conclusions of the Synod.

Due to the special interest and affection with which I follow the life of the Church in your country, and looking only to its good, I cannot but share your concern. Allow me to tell you of my brotherly encouragement and to invite you to continue resolutely with the work begun.

The implementation of the resolutions of the Particular Synod, which are in conformity with the principles of the Second Vatican Council, is a fundamental condition, an indispensable objective basis for the building of communion both within the Church in Holland, and in the relations of your local community with the universal community of the Catholic Church; real communion, in fact, comprises both aspects.

This implementation is, at the same time, very important for the work of ecumenism, so relevant in your country. Ecumenical activity requires, in fact, that each of the Churches grows in faithfulness to its tradition in the field of doctrine, discipline and pastoral work, purifying and renewing itself in order to appear before Christ without stain (cf. UR 4 and 6).

There appears from these considerations our common duty of working perseveringly for the consistent implementation of the conclusions of the Particular Synod. The conclusions of the Particular Synod are binding on all of us in conscience, before God and before the Church: on you, who signed them, as pastors of your local Churches; on me, who approved them, as the first one responsible for the unity of the Catholic Church. The Synod was not only the meeting of different ways—as the original meaning of the word says—but itself became the way which we must travel together to the end. The present difficulties, some of which are certainly very serious, cannot frighten us; we cannot draw back before them. Like the Apostle, we must be able to say: "I endure everything for the sake of the elect, that they also may obtain the salvation which in Christ Jesus goes with eternal glory" (2 Tm. 2:10).

I think I am expressing your own thought, affirming that the work of implementation of the Synod conclusions must consist principally in promoting, in every suitable way, all that is positive—and there is certainly a great deal —in your Churches.

AUTHENTIC CHARISMS

Your episcopal ministry in favor of ecclesial communion must embrace all fields of the Church's life, as the list of the Synod resolutions taken a year ago sufficiently shows. It is necessary that, thanks to this ministry, room should be made for all the real gifts, that is, the authentic charisms that are found in the community of the People of God whom you serve. The deliberations of the Synod recalled the criteria by which it is necessary to let oneself be guided in the evaluation of the gifts and in their use for the common good.

a) In this way, therefore, alongside the contribution that can be made to the life of the Church by lay people, our brothers and sisters, there cannot be lacking that particular charism connected with the vocation to complete dedication to Christ in the ministerial priesthood, and also in religious life. A preeminent consideration, in fact, is due to it. The experience of the Church shows, from the most remote times, the great importance that this vocation has always had for the fruitful operation of the whole organism of the Body of Christ, and how indispensable it is. Therefore the Synod also recalled the principles by which we must let ourselves be guided in cultivating priestly and religious vocations and in preparing candidates for the exercise of priestly service, in the firm faith that God gives His Church vocations. Among the primary tasks of pastors of the Church is that of creating the institutes for specific training for the Catholic priesthood, as understood by the Second Vatican Ecumenical Council, in which young vocations can find clear reference points, that they may respond to the divine gift through an adequate spiritual and human maturation.

b) Due concern for this problem, so important for the regular community life of the People of God, certainly cannot lessen the attention that is due to the apostolate of the laity.

At the Particular Synod you had words of rightful recognition for the active and responsible participation of many lay people in your country in the life of the Church. Such participation was expressly encouraged by the Second Vatican Ecumenical Council, which recalled that lay people, men and women, are called to exercise "the apostolate, in all its many aspects both in the Church and in the world" (AA 9). The Council also indicated the more specific fields and proper forms according to which it must take place; and, with particular reference to "the harmony and apostolic cooperation" between clergy and laity, it stressed the necessity of "preserving the character specific to each" form of the apostolate, and that precisely "for promoting the spirit of unity" (ibid., 23).

In conformity with this teaching of the Council, as also with other of its significant enunciations, you found yourselves unanimous "in professing the essential distinction between the ministerial or sacramental priesthood, and the common priesthood of the baptized, and in wishing to watch over the practical consequences derived from it."

I am certain that there will be a new fervor of Catholic life if all care and attention is taken in promoting the apostolate of the laity, in the fields that belong to it and according to its own specific forms, without letting it become almost imperceptibly confused with the apostolate which is proper to the clergy.

The implementation of real communion involves precisely the authentic development of all charisms, so that, without confusion, all may carry out their service reciprocally for one another, contributing to the development of every vocation, in conformity with their own nature, as well as with the regular growth and spiritual enrichment of the whole community.

"STRENGTHENING BROTHERS"

Addressing my thought and my heart to you, dear brothers in the episcopate, and to your Churches, I cannot pass over in silence the great consolation that comes to me from knowing that there are many priests and lay people, men and women religious, whose lives aim at following Christ and who, united with Him, raise to the Father their incessant prayer and offer daily the spiritual sacrifice of their lives for the good of the Church. Before the Particular Synod, in my letter of January 6, 1980, I addressed the whole Catholic community of the Netherlands, asking for the spiritual help of prayer. I now renew this pressing appeal of mine, and I wish it to reach the individual families, the domestic Churches, the young—the hope of the Church and my own—the sick and all those to whom it is given to be more united with the cross of Christ in suffering. May their prayers and their sacrifices obtain that He who gave you the grace to begin the good work of the Synod may also enable you and your collaborators to carry out all the work that is still necessary.

Reading these words that I send to you in fulfillment of my office of "strengthening brothers" (cf. Lk. 22:32), be certain of my abiding sincere affection and of the ardent supplication that I address to Christ Jesus, the Lord of the Church, through the intercession of His and our Mother, that He Himself may assist you every day in your episcopal ministry, making you know His will and giving you the power to carry it out.

My affectionate fatherly greeting goes to the priests, your collaborators in the ministry, to men and women religious, to seminarians, and to all the faithful of your beloved country: "My love be with you all in Christ Jesus" (1 Cor. 16:24).

United with you in the one love for Christ and for the Church, I willingly send you the apostolic blessing.

The Church's Deepest Identity Is Found in Evangelization

On February 14, 1981, the Holy Father observed the feast of Sts. Cyril and Methodius with a concelebrated Mass in the Basilica of San Clemente, where St. Cyril was buried. Among the concelebrants were Cardinals Bertoli, Seper, Knox and Rubin, and several archbishops and bishops.

Pope John Paul II delivered the following homily.

Dear brothers and sisters,

1. I am particularly happy to be able to be present— together with numerous Cardinals and personalities, and with the faithful and religious of Slav origin resident in Rome—for this solemn Eucharistic Celebration in honor of the holy brothers Cyril and Methodius, in this basilica of San Clemente where the venerated remains of St. Cyril lie—a rightful and joyful celebration in honor of the two glorious saints whom, on last December 31st, in the

Apostolic Letter *Egregiae virtutis*, I proclaimed heavenly patrons of the whole of Europe, together with St. Benedict.

Last year, as you know, was the centenary of the publication of the Encyclical *Grande munus*, with which Leo XIII, after illustrating the many-sided personalities and intense apostolic action of the two saints, introduced their liturgical feast into the calendar of the Catholic Church. It was also the eleventh centenary of the Letter *Industriae tuae*, which my Predecessor, John VIII, in June of the year 880, had sent to Prince Svatopluk to recommend the use of the Slavonic language in the liturgy.

These important anniversaries, together with that of the fifteenth centenary of the birth of St. Benedict, impelled me to highlight, alongside the impressive evangelizing and civilizing work carried out by the Western Patriarch, the no less important and decisive task, from the ecclesial and historical point of view, accomplished by the two holy brothers, to whom the whole Church, Western and Eastern, owes a perennial debt of immense gratitude and filial acknowledgment.

SAINTS CYRIL AND METHODIUS

2. Today's Liturgy of the Word presented to us, in the first reading, the conclusion of the stage of the apostolic journey of Paul and Barnabas at Antioch of Pisidia. The two bold proclaimers of the Gospel, rejected by the Jews, declare frankly: "...Since you thrust it (the Word of God) from you..., behold, we turn to the Gentiles!" And Saint Luke comments: "And when the Gentiles heard this, they were glad and glorified the Word of God; and as many as were ordained to eternal life believed" (cf. Acts 13:46, 48).

Like Paul and Barnabas, Sts. Cyril and Methodius, brothers in blood, but even more in faith, were fearless followers of Christ and tireless preachers of the Word of God.

Natives of Thessalonica, the city where St. Paul carried out part of his apostolic activity and to whose first faithful he addressed two letters, the two brothers came into spiritual and cultural contact with the patriarchal Church of Constantinople, which then had a flourishing theological culture and missionary activity. They succeeded in combining the requirements and the commitments of the religious vocation with missionary service. The Khazars of Crimea were the first witnesses of their apostolic fervor; but their most important evangelizing work was the mission to Greater Moravia, undertaken after the prince of Moravia, Rastislaw, had presented a request to the Emperor and to the Church of Constantinople.

The apostolic and missionary work, so complex and varied, of Sts. Cyril and Methodius, considered from many standpoints eleven centuries later, is rich in extraordinary fruitfulness and also in exceptional theological, cultural and ecumenical importance. These are aspects that interest not only the history of the Church, but also the civil and political history of a part of the European continent.

The translation into the vernacular of the Sacred Books for liturgical and catechetical purposes made Sts. Cyril and Methodius not only the apostles of the Slav peoples but also the fathers of their culture. Their tireless missionary service carried out in union both with the Church of Constantinople, by which they had been sent, and with the Roman See of Peter, by which they were confirmed, manifests to us their indomitable love for the one, holy, and catholic Church, and is an incentive to us to live this unity fully.

Furthermore—as I stressed in my above-mentioned Apostolic Letter *Egregiae virtutis*—the two holy brothers highlighted in the first place the contribution of ancient Greek culture, and then the importance of the irradiation of the Church of Constantinople and of the Eastern tradition, which is so deeply inscribed in the spirituality and culture of so many peoples and nations of Eastern Europe.

REAL LABORERS IN GOD'S VINEYARD

3. At the tomb of St. Cyril—who concluded his earthly life in this city on February 14 of the year 869, at the age of 42, and recalling also his brother, St. Methodius, who was ordained archbishop by the Pope and sent to Moravia to go on with his valuable apostolic work, which he continued until his death on April 16 of the year 885 —we listened to the words that Jesus addressed to the seventy-two disciples before sending them two by two to preach the kingdom of God: "The harvest is plentiful, but the laborers are few; pray therefore the Lord of the harvest to send out laborers into his harvest" (Lk. 10:2).

Cyril and Methodius were two real "laborers" of God's harvest. And on this day of their feast, the Church, exalting their meritorious apostolic activity, is aware of needing even more today Christians capable of making their contribution of commitment, energies and enthusiasm for the proclamation of the message of salvation in Christ Jesus. But she is also aware of needing souls completely and exclusively consecrated to the preaching of the Gospel, to missionary action: she needs priests, men and women religious, and missionaries who, generously and joyfully renouncing their family, their country, and human affections, dedicate their whole life to working and suffering for the Gospel (cf. Mk. 8:35).

Before the historical importance of the evangelizing work carried out by the two holy brothers, the Church realizes even more deeply that evangelization is her own grace and vocation, her deepest identity. "She exists in order to evangelize," Paul VI wrote, "that is to say, in order to preach and teach, to be the channel of the gift of grace, to reconcile sinners with God, and to perpetuate Christ's sacrifice in the Mass, which is the memorial of His death and glorious resurrection" (EN 14).

For Sts. Cyril and Methodius that meant making the proclamation of the Gospel preeminent: a proclamation that did not mortify, destroy or eliminate, but integrated, elevated and exalted the authentic human and cultural values typical of the genius of the countries evangelized, contributing to an opening and a solidarity capable of overcoming antagonisms and of creating a common spiritual and cultural heritage, which laid solid foundations for justice and peace.

Reading in the ancient "Life" of St. Cyril in the Slavonic language some details of the last days of his earthly existence, we feel intense emotion, because we penetrate into the deepest dimension of his conscience and catch a glimpse of the great ideals for which the saint had lived, worked and suffered: "Lord, my God," he prayed, "keep your flock in the faith,...cause the number of your Church to grow, and gather all in unity. Make your people holy, harmonious in true faith and in right confession, and inspire the word of your doctrine in hearts."

PRAYER TO THE HOLY BROTHERS

4. As we prepare to celebrate the Eucharist, let us raise our humble and fervent prayer to the two holy brothers, Patrons of Europe, asking for their powerful intercession with the Holy Trinity:

O Sts. Cyril and Methodius, who brought the Faith with admirable dedication to peoples thirsty for truth and light, let the whole Church always proclaim the crucified and risen Christ, the Redeemer of man!

O Sts. Cyril and Methodius, who, in your hard and difficult missionary apostolate, always remained deeply bound to the Church of Constantinople and to the Roman See of Peter, bring it about that the two sister Churches, the Catholic Church and the Orthodox, having overcome the elements of division in charity and truth, may soon reach the full union desired!

O Sts. Cyril and Methodius, who, with the sincere spirit of brotherhood, approached different peoples to bring to all the message of universal love preached by Christ, bring it about that the peoples of the European continent, aware of their common Christian heritage, may live in mutual respect for just rights and in solidarity, and be peacemakers among all the nations of the world!

O Sts. Cyril and Methodius, who, driven by love for Christ, abandoned everything to serve the Gospel, protect the Church of God: me, Peter's Successor in the Roman See; the bishops, priests, men and women religious, men and women missionaries, fathers, mothers, young men, young women, children, the poor, the sick and the suffering; may each of us, in the place in which divine Providence has placed us, be a worthy "laborer" of the Lord's harvest!

Amen!

On Human Sexuality and Personhood

John Paul II sent the following message to the bishops taking part in the Dallas (U.S.A.) "Workshop on Human Sexuality and Personhood," published in the February 16, 1981, L'Osservatore Romano.

Dear brothers in our Lord Jesus Christ,

I am pleased to have this occasion to speak to you, a large number of my brother bishops of North America, who have gathered in Dallas for the Workshop on Human Sexuality and Personhood. Once again this year, aided by the generous assistance of the Knights of Columbus and urged on by your own pastoral zeal for proclaiming the Gospel of our Lord Jesus Christ, you have come together for the purpose of improving your understanding of important questions with which our episcopal ministry is vitally concerned at the end of the twentieth century.

You have wisely chosen to examine both the subject of human sexuality and the subject of personhood. This simultaneous treatment is not only praiseworthy, it is necessary. The subject of human sexuality cannot be brought into proper focus without reference to the human person. And likewise, if we were to study the human person without reference to sexuality, we would be overlooking a fundamental truth revealed to us in the book of Genesis—overlooking the fact that "God created them male and female" (Gn. 1:27).

The topic you have selected is of particular interest at this present moment in the Church's history. For this reason, I have spoken about certain aspects of it during my Wednesday audiences in Rome over the course of the past year and a half. And as you know, the recent Synod of Bishops also gave it considerable attention. Obviously, it is not possible for me today to speak exhaustively on the topic nor even to summarize what I have said previously. I would, however, like to indicate some important elements which should be included in pastoral and theological discussions dealing with this subject.

In his Encyclical *Humanae vitae*, Pope Paul VI underscored the importance of referring to the "total vision of man" (no. 7). I wish to draw attention to this emphasis of my Predecessor, for we live in an age in which, for a variety of reasons, this total vision can easily be dismissed or ignored. It can also be replaced by a number of partial viewpoints which, although they may be a faithful representation of one or another aspect of the complete truth, do not express a fully integrated vision of the human being.

In this light I am happy to note how your Workshop is seeking to bring together the latest insights of the medical and behavioral sciences with the truths of faith contained in the Sacred Scriptures and in the Church's tradition. You have rightly seen the need to incorporate into your deliberations both the truth of Revelation and the truth of human experience.

Human sexuality and personhood can be fully understood only when studied within the framework of the mystery of creation and the mystery of redemption. Following the example of Jesus (cf. Mt. 19:4), we need to look at what God the Creator intended *from the begin-*

ning. Thus in the Book of Genesis we read: "In the beginning...God created man in the image of himself, in the image of God he created him, male and female he created them" (Gn. 1:1, 17). Examining the plan of God as it existed *in the beginning* we discover the nuptial meaning of the body; we see that, in the mystery of creation, man and woman are *made to be a gift* to each other and for each other. In their very existence, as male and female, by their sexuality and freedom as persons, man and woman are capable of mirroring the creative activity of God. And in the mystery of redemption, through the grace won by the Savior on the cross, man and woman receive, not the power to return to the state of original innocence prior to the fall of Adam, but the strength to live, in Christ and through Christ, a *new ethos of redemptive love.*

An examination of moral norms and a quest for appropriate pastoral approaches to the various problems of human sexuality would be incomplete if reference were not made to the teaching of Christ found in the Sermon on the Mount, especially to the Lord's words: "You have heard that it was said, 'You shall not commit adultery.' But I say to you that everyone who looks at a woman lustfully has already committed adultery with her in his heart" (Mt. 5:27f.). As we examine this teaching, which reminds us of the importance of purity of heart, as well as the need for lifelong fidelity to one's spouse, we must continually recall that the words of our Savior are *not words of accusation or condemnation.* Rather they are words of invitation, words of truth spoken in love and compassion, words which lead men and women to the fullness of life and freedom. For they invite men and women to live in accordance with the truth of their own personhood and sexuality as revealed by God from the beginning. We, on our part, must help our people to see moral teaching on sexuality as part of the total *Christian ethos of redemption,* as part of their calling in Christ to "walk in newness of life" (Rom. 6:4). All pastoral charity that is authentic, all human compassion that is genuine, all fraternal support that is real, embraces and communicates the whole truth as revealed to us by the eternal Word and proclaimed by His Church.

My brother bishops: May God sustain the Pope John XXIII Medical-Moral Research and Educational Center in its important role of assisting the Magisterium of the Church. And may the Spirit of God be with you to direct your deliberations during these days. May you be renewed in your zealous pastoral service to humanity and in your desire to lead all men and women to the fullness of truth in our Lord Jesus Christ.

To Him, and to Him alone, we say with Peter: "You have the words of eternal life" (Jn. 6:68).

The Word of God, Unity and Holiness, Principal Aspects of Apostolate

On February 17, 1981, after his meeting with President Marcos in Malacañang, the Holy Father met the Episcopal Conference of the Philippines and the Asian bishops, to whom he spoke as follows.

Dear brothers in our Lord Jesus Christ,

1. Since my arrival on Philippine soil, I have already had the occasion to state that my first and principal reason for coming here is the beatification of Lorenzo Ruiz, whose martyrdom shows forth the holiness of the Church. At the same time I consider my pastoral visit a pilgrimage to the living shrine of the People of God in this land. And today, in you, the bishops, I greet every ecclesial community that makes up the Church in the Philippines.

My thoughts go likewise to the past generations who have received and passed on the Catholic faith. In the name of the universal Church I express praise and thanksgiving to God for this great gift that your people have received and preserved. I give thanks also for the special vocation that has been given to the Church in the Philippines. In coming to you it is my desire to fulfill my pastoral service to the faithful in your land and to all of you, their bishops. And so we gather together to re-present the scene of the Acts of the Apostles where Peter and the Eleven assemble to speak about Jesus and to reflect on the power of His Spirit. Just being with you is enough to draw strength and power from the One who is in our midst. And on my part I wish, in fidelity to Christ, to confirm you in the Faith that you hold and proclaim.

SHARING TWO TESTIMONIES WITH YOU

2. My coming is linked to the conviction that the Word of God is powerful and, when faithfully preached, is light and strength for our people. It is in truth the foundation of their faith. That is why we never cease to communicate to them the conviction of St. Paul: "Your faith rests not on the wisdom of men but on the power of God" (1 Cor. 2:5).

As pastors of God's people we have the role of announcing "God's design in its entirety" (Acts 20:27). Through the full proclamation of Christ and His Gospel a gentle but invincible force is unleashed in the world. In this regard let me share with you two testimonies of particular interest for you as bishops in the Philippines.

The first is that of Paul VI. It was the great testimony that he gave ten years ago in Quezon Circle. Speaking about Christ he said: "I feel the need to proclaim Him, I cannot keep silent. 'Woe to me if I do not preach the Gospel' (1 Cor. 9:16). I am sent by Him, by Christ Himself, to do this; I am an apostle, I am a witness.... I must bear witness to His name: Jesus is the Christ, the Son of the living God (cf. Mt. 16:16). He reveals the invisible God; He is the firstborn of all creation, the foundation of everything created. He is the Teacher of mankind, and its Redeemer.... Jesus Christ is our constant preaching; it is His name that we proclaim to the ends of the earth (cf. Rom. 10:18) and throughout all ages (cf. Rom. 9:5)" (November 29, 1970). This was his mission ten years ago, and some of you were present then, together with the late Cardinal Santos and with the other bishops of that time. And I am convinced that, sometime in the future, yet another Successor of Peter will gather with your successors in this same proclamation of the Faith.

The second testimony that I wish to recall with you is likewise a very special one. Certainly a number of you were present to hear John Paul I speak the following words to the Philippine bishops gathered in Rome for their *ad limina* visit: "On our part we hope to sustain you, support you, and encourage you in the great mission of the episcopate: to proclaim Jesus Christ and to evangelize His people.... A great challenge of our day is the full evangelization of all those who have been baptized. In this, the bishops of the Church have a prime responsibility. Our message must be a clear proclamation of salvation in Jesus Christ" (September 28, 1978). It was a memorable testimony for its contents and for the circumstances in which it was given. It was the last public act of John Paul I! It was the last hour of his public ministry. It was his legacy—and it was for you. And I wish to perpetuate his testimony and to make it my own today.

PROCLAIMING JESUS CHRIST

3. This proclamation of Jesus Christ and salvation in His name is the basis for all pastoral service. It is the content of all evangelization and catechesis. And it is a credit to you that you accomplish it in union with the Successor of Peter and with the whole Church. It must always be so. Your unity with the universal Church is the authentication of all your pastoral initiatives and the guarantee of their supernatural effectiveness. This unity was indeed the concern that motivated St. Paul to take counsel so that the course he was pursuing and had pursued "would not prove useless" (Gal. 2:2). I thank God today for your Catholic unity and the strength it gives you.

4. Fortified by the Word of Christ and strengthened in the unity of His Church, you are well able to pursue effectively your pastoral ministry in imitation of Jesus the Good Shepherd. The suggestion that St. Paul received in his consultation I would repeat today: "The only stipulation was that we should be mindful of the poor—the one thing that I was making every effort to do" (Gal. 2:10). And may this be the special mark of your ministry too: concern for the poor, for those who are materially or spiritually in need. Hence your pastoral love will embrace those in want, those afflicted, those in sin.

And let us remember always that the greatest good we can give them is the Word of God. This does not mean that we do not assist them in their physical needs, but it does mean that they need something more, and that we have something more to give: the Gospel of Jesus Christ. With great pastoral insight and evangelical love, John Paul I also expressed this thought succinctly on the day he died: "From the days of the Gospel, and in imitation of the Lord, who 'went about doing good' (Acts 10:38), the Church is irrevocably committed to contributing to the relief of physical misery and need. But her pastoral charity would be incomplete if she did not point out even 'higher needs.' In the Philippines Paul VI did precisely this. At a moment when he chose to speak about the poor, about justice and peace, about human rights, about economic and social liberation—at a moment when he also effectively committed the Church to the alleviation of misery—he did not and could not remain silent about the 'higher good,' the fullness of life in the kingdom of heaven."

LOVE AND GOOD EXAMPLE OF HOLINESS

5. Another aspect of your ministry is the fraternal interest that you have for your brother priests. They need to be convinced of your love; they need your example of holiness and they have to see you as their spiritual leaders, as heralds of the Gospel, so that they too can concentrate

all their energies on their proper priestly role in the building up of Christ's kingdom of justice and peace. In this regard it is important that the laity be given the full responsibility that is specifically theirs. Through their activity in the temporal order they have a special task to fulfill, in order to bring about the consecration of the world to God. It is a lofty task, and they need their bishops and priests to support them through spiritual leadership. At the same time it has to be apparent in the Body of Christ, where there is a diversity of functions, that the laity are worthy of trust, that they can accomplish what the Lord has assigned specifically to them. This will also make it possible for the clergy to pay full heed to the apostolic injunction to concentrate on "prayer and the ministry of the word" (Acts 6:4). The Spirit of God continues to confirm these priorities of the priestly ministry for each generation in the Church.

YOUR SPECIAL MISSIONARY VOCATION

6. In reflecting on the Church in the Philippines, the missionary aspect emerges in various ways. There is first of all your glorious missionary beginning, in which your ancestors embraced the message of salvation that was proclaimed to them. To reflect on this is to praise God in your history, in the generosity of the missionaries that continues into the present. To reflect on your missionary past is to be challenged to go forward with the same zeal. In order to understand your missionary destiny, it is enough to listen to the prophet Isaiah who urges you: "Look to the rock from which you were hewn" (Is. 51:1). There are indeed many places where the name of Jesus is not yet known and where His Gospel is yet to be proclaimed among you. It will be your zeal and that of your priests, together with the commitment of the whole ecclesial community, that will devise means to pursue initial evangelization and subsequent catechesis in the face of a harvest that is immense. At the same time you will hear other nations, especially your neighbors in Asia, calling to you: "Come

over...and help us" (Acts 16:9). There is no doubt about it: The Philippines have a special missionary vocation to proclaim the Good News, to carry the light of Christ to the nations. It must be accomplished with personal sacrifice, and in spite of limited resources, but God will not be wanting with His grace and He will supply your needs. Paul VI confirmed this missionary vocation of yours during his visit here, and repeatedly thereafter. From many points of view, dear brothers, you are truly called to be a missionary Church.

SENT OUT TO PREACH

7. As you endeavor to fulfill your pastoral charge, I know that you will recall the words with which the Gospel records the calling of the Apostles: "And he appointed Twelve to be with him and to be sent out to preach" (Mk. 3:14). The two aspects of the apostolic vocation may seem mutually exclusive, but it is not so. Jesus wants us both to stay with Him and to go out to preach. We are meant to be His companions and His friends, as well as His tireless apostles. In a word, we are called to holiness. There can be no successful episcopal ministry without holiness of life, because our ministry is modelled on that of the chief Pastor and the Bishop of our souls, Jesus Christ (cf. 1 Pt. 5:4; 2:25).

My dear brothers, in our intimate friendship with Jesus Christ we shall find strength for fraternal love, the power to touch hearts and to proclaim a convincing message. In the love of Jesus we shall discover the way to build community in Christ and to serve our people, giving them the Word of God. By sharing in the holiness of Jesus we shall exercise an authentic prophetic role: announcing holiness and courageously practicing it as an example to be followed in the ecclesial community. To be faithful to the tradition that is ours, let us remember the Apostle Peter exhorting us: "Be examples to the flock" (1 Pt. 5:3).

TRUST IN THE SPIRIT

8. To these important aspects of our pastoral ministry that I have mentioned—God's Word, unity and holiness—I would add a final word of fraternal exhortation, and it is this: Let us trust fully in the merits of our Lord Jesus Christ; let us trust in His power to renew, by the action of His Spirit, the face of the earth. Our mission and our destiny, linked with that of our people, are in the hands of God, who has given all power of redemption and sanctification to Jesus Christ. And it is Christ who tells us today that we are strong in Him and sustained by His promise: "I am with you always until the end of the world" (Mt. 28:20).

And finally, as bishops, we feel ourselves enveloped by the gentle and maternal love of Mary, Mother of Jesus and Queen of the Apostles. I am confident that by her intercession she will assist the Church in the Philippines—and you my brother bishops in particular—to proclaim Jesus Christ, the salvation of Asia and the eternal light of the world.

9. The joy of this meeting is increased by the presence of the other Asian bishops—all of you united in this common mission of proclaiming Jesus Christ.

We are rightly gratified by the awareness that exists in the Church today—thanks to the action of God's Spirit in our times—of the need to bring the Gospel to bear upon all cultures, to make it incarnate in the lives of all peoples, to present the Christian message in a way that is ever more effective. The goal is a noble one, a delicate one; it is a goal to which the Church is firmly committed. Indeed, on the opening day of the Second Vatican Council, John XXIII announced that the Council's principal aim was to ensure "that the sacred deposit of Christian doctrine should be more effectively guarded and taught" (October 11, 1962).

In all your efforts, my brother bishops, to pursue this aim throughout the postconciliar period, be assured of the support of the universal Church, which embraces every nation under heaven and yet proclaims the same Christ to every people and to every generation. Be mindful above all of the sovereign action of the Holy Spirit, who alone can stir up the new creation. For this reason Paul VI could declare that "techniques of evangelization are good, but even the most advanced ones could not replace the gentle action of the Spirit.... It must be said that the Holy Spirit is the principal agent of evangelization: it is He who impels each individual to proclaim the Gospel and it is He who in the depths of consciences causes the word of salvation to be accepted and understood" (EN 75).

It is to the Holy Spirit that we turn humbly to ask that our mission as evangelizers be fruitful for the kingdom of God and for the glory of the name of Jesus: *Veni Sancte Spiritus! Veni Sancte Spiritus!*

You Are Heirs of the Missionaries Who Evangelized These Islands

After the Mass at Quezon Memorial Circle, on February 19, 1981, the Pope left Manila for Cebu, a large city on the island of Mindanao, in the southern part of the Philippine Archipelago. The Pope's first meeting in Cebu was reserved for priests and seminarians who, together with the Archbishop, Cardinal Julio Rosales, gathered in the auditorium of the Sacred Heart School. After singing "Tu es Petrus," the group listened to the following discourse of the Holy Father.

Dear priests and seminarians,

I greet you in the name of Jesus! It is a joy for me to be with you, and through you to greet the priests of all the Philippines, and to bless and encourage the seminarians throughout this nation.

1. "How beautiful upon the mountains are the feet of him who brings glad tidings, announcing peace, bearing good news, announcing salvation, and saying to Zion, 'Your God is King!' " (Is. 52:7) These words of the prophet Isaiah readily come to mind when we recall the apostolic zeal of those missionary priests who over four centuries ago began to preach the Gospel of salvation to the people

of these islands. It was the mysterious working of God's grace which made their hearts anxious and set their feet in motion until peace and salvation had been announced in this land. Consider the Dominican priest Fray Domingo de Salazar. He left his native Spain to go first to Venezuela, then to Mexico, briefly to Florida, and finally to the Philippines. Here he became the first bishop in the Philippines—at Manila in 1578; here he preached the Good News not only to the people of these islands but also to his compatriots, in order to persuade them that the Lord's Gospel means justice and not slavery for the people they had come to colonize. It was Bishop Domingo de Salazar too, who, on his return to Spain, recommended the foundation of the ecclesiastical province of the Philippines.

HOMAGE TO MISSIONARIES

2. You are the heirs of the missionary task begun by Fray Domingo and the early evangelists of these islands: the Augustinian, Franciscan, Jesuit and Dominican priests whose evangelizing feet will forever be called beautiful. In paying homage to those missionaries and to all the other missionaries—to those of every generation in the Philippines, including the present generation—I praise the grace of God that sustained them in their zeal for His kingdom. In God's mysterious design you have been called by Christ to announce His glad tidings here in your own homeland. Together let us reflect upon this priestly task which is yours today, my brother priests, and for which, dear seminarians, you must diligently prepare yourselves.

3. It is faith in Jesus Christ, who is Lord forever, that is the response which God invites when He sends out His Word over the earth. It is faith at the heart of the priest's vocation that animates his ministry and grounds the witness of his life. In his Letter to the Romans, St. Paul says: "If you confess with your lips that Jesus is Lord, and believe in your heart that God raised him from the dead, you will be saved. Faith in the heart leads to justification,

confession on the lips to salvation. But how shall they call on him in whom they have not believed? And how can they believe unless they have heard of him? And how can they hear unless there is someone to preach? Scripture says, 'How beautiful are the feet of those who announce good news!'... Faith, then, comes through hearing, and what is heard is the word of Christ" (Rom. 10:9-17).

4. To preach the Word of God: this is the work of every generation. The "faith which comes through hearing" is a response invited by God Himself, a response which leads people to confess with their lips that Jesus is Lord and to become His disciples. The proclamation of the Word and the response of faith set up the initial encounter, the basic community of the Church. And it is for this encounter that the priestly apostle is "sent" to preach: *in persona Christi* he offers the Sacrifice of the Eucharist, which recapitulates the entire proclamation of the Word and in which Christ's own invitation to believe and to be built up into the Church is continually heard by His people. As the Vatican Council teaches: "Priests by sacred ordination and mission which they receive from the bishops are promoted to the service of Christ the Teacher, Priest and King. They share in His ministry, a ministry whereby the Church here on earth is unceasingly built up into the People of God, the Body of Christ and the Temple of the Holy Spirit" (PO 1).

SUMMONS TO RENEWAL

5. This Church is missionary by her very nature (cf. AG 2). All Christians who believe and are made one in Christ share in the missionary task of apostolic service to the world. But "hearing" the call to faith—the word of salvation—must be a constant summons to conversion and renewal within the Church herself, and it is to the Apostles and their successors in the episcopate, together with their priestly collaborators, that the Lord has entrusted the role of shepherding His missionary people. By God's own plan, the Church cannot exist without those apostolic men

"sent" to preach, to be within the Church herself a sacramental sign of the fundamental and perennial call to "believe in our hearts" that Jesus is Lord.

HE CAME TO SERVE

6. Today there are some who ignore or misunderstand this important dimension of the nature of the Church, and suggest that only by diminishing the importance of the priesthood can the laity be given their full place in the Church. Perhaps this is due to an overreaction to those priests who, through human frailty or spiritual blindness, have not taken to heart the profound lesson Jesus taught when He replied to the request of the mother of James and John: "You know how those who exercise authority among the Gentiles lord it over them; their great ones make their importance felt. It cannot be like that with you. Anyone who aspires to greatness must serve the rest, and whoever wants to rank first among you must serve the needs of all. Such is the case with the Son of Man who has come, not to be served by others, but to serve, to give his own life as a ransom for the many" (Mt. 20:25-28).

Nevertheless, an attitude which sees opposition or rivalry between the ministerial priesthood and the priesthood of the faithful fails to perceive the design of God in instituting the sacrament of Holy Orders within His Church. The Second Vatican Council's Constitution on the Church clearly teaches that "though they differ from one another in essence and not only in degree, the common priesthood of the faithful and the ministerial or hierarchical priesthood are nonetheless interrelated. Each of them in its own special way is a participation in the one priesthood of Christ" (LG 10). In the ministerial priesthood of Holy Orders, God has set within His Church a visible sign, by which the divine dialogue which He has initiated—the word of salvation inviting the response of faith—is sacramentally, and therefore efficaciously, represented. Priesthood is therefore a sacrament whose "celebration" affects the entire Church, and the whole Church—laity and clergy alike—must take care that its "celebration" is not diminished through misunderstanding or misplaced zeal for a multiplication of ministries intended as a substitution for the ministerial priesthood.

7. Jesus is Lord! This proclamation of the Word reaches its most perfect moment in the Eucharist: "The other sacraments, as well as every ministry of the Church and every work of the apostolate, are linked with the Holy Eucharist and are directed towards it.... Hence the Eucharist shows itself to be the source and summit of all evangelization" (PO 5). The celebration of the Eucharist is the heart of priestly ministry and of Christian life, because it is Christ's own service of self-sacrificing love. Through each Eucharist the Church herself is continually formed anew and given her definitive shape: Christ, through the ministry of His priests, calls all His disciples together, makes them one in His love, and sends them forth to be bearers of the unity and love of the Eucharistic Banquet as the pattern and model of all human community and service.

THE CHURCH NEEDS YOU

8. My brother priests, this missionary Church, this Eucharistic people, depends upon you for the authentic proclamation of the Good News. But if you are to be effective preachers of the Word, you must be men of deep faith who are hearers and doers of the Word as well. For with St. Paul we must always say: "It is not ourselves we preach but Christ Jesus as Lord, and ourselves as your servants for Jesus' sake" (2 Cor. 4:5). For this reason we must never cease examining carefully how we live our priestly lives, lest they become a countersign which disfigures the sacramental presence which the Lord intends us to be in and for His Church.

9. For this purpose I offer you today three brief reflections on living the priestly life according to the mind and heart of Christ.

In the first place, Jesus has called priests to a special intimacy with Himself. The very nature of our task requires it. If we are to preach Christ and not ourselves, we must know Him intimately in the Scriptures and in prayer. If we are to lead others to the encounter and response of faith, our own faith must itself be a witness. In the Holy Scriptures, God's Word is ever before us. Let us therefore make the Scriptures the nourishment of our daily prayer and the subject of our regular theological study. Only in this way can we possess the Word of God—and be possessed by the Word—in that intimacy reserved for those to whom Jesus said: "I call you friends" (Jn. 15:15).

The second consideration I wish to offer you concerns the unity of the priesthood. The Fathers of the Second Vatican Council reminded us that "all priests, together with bishops, so share in one and the same priesthood and ministry of Christ that the very unity of their consecration and mission requires their hierarchical communion with the order of bishops" (PO 7). This unity must take shape concretely in the realization that priests, diocesan and religious, form a single presbyterium around their bishop. The collegiality which describes the entire episcopal order's union of faith and sharing in responsibility with the Bishop of Rome is reflected by analogy in the unity of priests with their bishop and with each other in their common pastoral task. We must not underestimate the importance of this unity of our priesthood for the effective evangelization of the world. The sacramental sign of priesthood itself must not be fragmented or individualized: We constitute one priesthood—the priesthood of Christ —to which our harmony of life and apostolic service must testify. The fundamental oneness of the Eucharist offered by the Church requires that this unity be lived out as a visible, sacramental reality in the lives of priests. On the night before He died, Jesus invoked His heavenly Father: "I pray also for those who will believe in me through their word, that all may be one as you, Father, are in me, and I in you; I pray that they may be one in us, that the world may believe that you sent me" (Jn. 17:20-21). Our unity in the Lord, sacramentally visible at the center of the Church's own unity, is an indispensable condition for the effectiveness of everything we do: our preaching of the Faith, our service of the poor as a preferential option, our efforts at building basic Christian communities as vital units of God's kingdom, our work for promoting Christ's justice and His peace, all our varied parochial apostolates, every endeavor to furnish spiritual leadership to our people—all of this depends totally on our union with Jesus Christ and His Church.

In the third place I wish to reflect with you on the value of a life of authentic priestly celibacy. It is difficult to overestimate the profound witness to the Faith that a priest gives through celibacy. The priest announces the Good News of the kingdom as one unafraid to forego the special human joys of marriage and family life in order to bear witness to his "conviction about things we do not see" (cf. Heb. 11:1). The Church needs the witness of celibacy willingly embraced and joyfully lived by her priests for the sake of the kingdom. For celibacy is by no means marginal to priestly life; it gives testimony to a dimension of love patterned upon the love of Christ Himself. This love speaks clearly the language of all genuine love, the language of the gift of oneself for the sake of the beloved; and its perfect symbol is forever the cross of Jesus Christ!

The Gospel Must Be Shared

To the clergy, men and women religious and other members of the local Church, who had gathered in the cathedral in Agaña on February 22, 1981, the Pope gave the following address.

Dear brothers and sisters,

"We keep thanking God for all of you and we remember you in our prayers, for we constantly are mindful before our God and Father of the way you are proving your faith, and laboring in love, and showing constancy of hope in our Lord Jesus Christ" (1 Thes. 1:2-3).

1. I make my own these words of St. Paul, and I want them to express the sentiments of my heart as I give thanks to Almighty God for the witness of your faith. Gathered with you in this cathedral dedicated to the name of Mary, I am pleased to see many indications of how your faith in Jesus Christ has proved steadfast and true.

How can we fail to be grateful when we see how rapidly the Faith was accepted by the people of Guam? What tremendous love characterized the missionary men and women whose efforts so greatly enriched the life of the Church here. Their preaching and teaching did not have the force of mere human persuasion, but rather bore fruit through the power of the Holy Spirit.

And you who have gathered here today are heirs of this rich tradition, inheriting a living communion of faith, hope and love. Yet the bonds which join us together are constantly in need of being drawn closer, so that we may form a more perfect unity of fellowship and service.

"ONE LORD, ONE FAITH...."

2. For the Church in every age and in every place is called by Christ to make of many individuals a single people, united in "one Lord, one faith, one baptism" (Eph. 4:5). As one body, the Church must radiate the presence of her Lord to the world. Jesus Christ, therefore, is the reason

for everything the Church says and does! Jesus Christ is the focal point for that living communion which constitutes the Church!

3. It is good for us to return often to those sacred accounts of the Church's early life and to reflect on those elements which made up her ecclesial communion. In the Acts of the Apostles we read: "And they devoted themselves to the Apostles' teaching and fellowship, to the breaking of bread and the prayers" (Acts 2:42).

4. From the beginning, the Church recognized her duty to hand on what she had received from the Lord. The apostolic teaching enabled the disciples to be of "one heart and one mind" (Acts 4:32). Thus the early Christians confessed a common Faith before the world, and no authentic communion was possible where fidelity to the apostolic tradition was lacking.

Today no less than before, the Church is called to preserve the integrity of Christ's message. For His Word is not entrusted to her to do with as she pleases. Rather the Church is an instrument of evangelization, imparting Christ's message in its entirety, with the rich fullness of its content.

SERVICE TO THE WORD

5. At the same time, this Gospel message is not intended to be displayed as in a museum showcase, where it can only be studied or admired. No, it must be shared, passed on, so that others may hear it, accept it and be initiated into the community of the faithful. Service to the Word is the standard by which the apostolic Faith is known. It is a service that asks for nothing in return, save only the knowledge that Christ's love is made present in the world.

Within society there are many examples of love being so manipulated that some people suspect that a selfless love cannot exist. To these people we need to show again the spirit of detachment exemplified by the early Christians and recorded in the Acts of the Apostles: "No one said that any of the things which he possessed was his own, but they held everything in common" (Acts 4:32). Where such an attitude of generous self-giving is present, a true fellowship can flourish.

6. But where does the community receive the impulse for being a true communion? The Church finds this source in "the breaking of the bread." The Eucharist is "the summit toward which the activity of the Church is directed; at the same time it is the source from which all her power flows" (SC 10).

In the Eucharist, ecclesial communion is not only manifested but it is, in fact, brought about. "Because there is one bread, we who are many are one body, for we partake of the one bread" (1 Cor. 10:17).

It is essential, therefore, that our Eucharistic Communion, based on a common expression of faith, must never be the cause of dissension or of fragmentation in the community. Individual forms of expression must give way to building up the ecclesial communion of the entire Church.

NURTURED BY PRAYER

7. Lastly, the call of faith implies for each believer a continual call to holiness, nurtured by prayer. Left to his own devices, man does not possess the necessary strength to overcome the sin of the world. It is only the Holy Spirit who can ensure a true and lasting unity, since by His presence each member of the community is impelled towards more generous expressions of charity and mercy. Today the Church rejoices at the deep desire on the part of so many to know the Holy Spirit better through prayer. With all my heart I encourage this interest, and I pray that the Holy Spirit will instill into every sector of the Church a fervor of holiness that will prefer the love of God and the love of neighbor to every other consideration.

8. My brothers and sisters, let us love one another in Christ. Let the bonds of faith always be strengthened by

everything we do. Let our preaching and teaching be a clear reflection of the rich deposit of the Faith. Let us celebrate our fellowship with joyful hearts, and find in our Eucharistic Celebrations a greater realization of the unity which we share in faith. Let us be fervent in our life of prayer and implore the Holy Spirit to lead all bishops, priests, religious and laity in the paths of true holiness.

And finally, let us not fail to look to the example of Mary, whose faith was constant and persevering, and who is venerated in this place as Our Lady of Camarin. Let us entrust ourselves to her protection and invoke her powerful intercession: Holy Mary, Mother of God, pray for us sinners, now and at the hour of our death. Amen.

Eloquent Witnesses to Our God

In the Cathedral of Tokyo on February 23, 1981, where many members of the diocesan clergy and of male religious congregations were assembled, Pope John Paul gave the following discourse.

And now I wish to direct my thoughts to the religious brothers who strive for the high ideal of following Christ more closely in chastity, poverty and obedience. Later on I shall also have an opportunity to speak with the women religious of Japan.

Dear brothers, your union with Christ, which began in Baptism and which has been strengthened through your religious consecration, involves a special union with the Church. You share more fully in the mystery of her life and are more deeply committed to her mission in the world. Mindful of this ecclesial dimension of religious life, I repeat to you what I wrote in my first encyclical: "The Church's fundamental function in every age and particularly in ours is to direct man's gaze, to point the awareness and experience of the whole of humanity towards the mystery of God, to help people to be familiar with the profundity of the redemption taking place in Christ Jesus" (RH 10).

Your lives consecrated to Christ through the evangelical counsels are able to raise the minds and hearts of our generation to the One who is Holy, to the One who is the Maker and Savior of all. By being joyful messengers of the truth, generous servants of those in need, and men of prayer who are animated by a deep trust in the Lord, you lift the gaze of the men and women of our times. You raise their eyes in hope. You help them to see that it is indeed possible "to go upon the heights" (cf. Hb. 3:19), to enter into loving union and conversation with God.

PROCLAIM THE GOSPEL

I wish to say a special word to the priests who are present here, both religious and diocesan. The heart of the priestly ministry is to proclaim the Gospel of our Lord Jesus Christ, a proclamation which reaches its summit and goal in the celebration of the Eucharist. As you engage in this vital mission of the Church, I ask you to give particular attention to a point that I made in my recent encyclical: "The Church lives an authentic life when she professes and proclaims mercy—the most stupendous attribute of the Creator and of the Redeemer" (DM 13).

May your every word and deed be an eloquent witness to our God who is rich in mercy. May your sermons inspire hope in the mercy of the Redeemer. May the way you celebrate the sacrament of Penance help each person experience in a unique way the merciful love of God, which is more powerful than sin. And may your own personal kindness and pastoral love help everyone you meet to discover the merciful Father, who is always ready to forgive.

Also, my brother priests, may you always be united among yourselves and with your bishops. As Ignatius of Antioch wrote to Polycarp: "Let unity, the greatest of all goods, be your concern." Unity within the presbyterate is not something unimportant to our priestly life and service. In fact, it is an integral part of preaching the Gospel. And it symbolizes the very purpose of our ministry: to bring about union with the most Holy Trinity and to foster brotherhood among all peoples. Thus the same zeal which compels us to serve our people should also inspire us to be united among ourselves. Recall how Jesus' desire for unity prompted Him to pray at the Last Supper: "May they all be one. Father, may they be one in us, as you are in me and I am in you, so that the world may believe it was you who sent me" (Jn. 17:21).

"LOVE ONE ANOTHER..."

And so I exhort you in the words of St. Paul: "Love one another with the affection of brothers" (Rom. 12:10). Amidst all your pastoral duties may you still find opportunities to pray together, to offer hospitality to one another, to encourage one another in the work of the Lord. May you have a particular concern for those of your brothers who are lonely, sick or weighed down by the burdens of life. As "fellow workers in the truth" (cf. 3 Jn. 8), support your brother priests in the great task which is ours—the proclamation of the merciful love of God which has been made visible in Christ Jesus our Lord.

4. In expressing my love and esteem for all the priests and brothers present here, I wish to add a word of particular appreciation for the contribution of the missionaries to the Church in Japan. Through the generous labors of your predecessors the Church has been implanted in this land, and your own faithful ministry continues to be an effective service in the cause of the Gospel. Be assured that the whole Church greatly honors your missionary vocation and that of all your fellow missionaries throughout the world. On this day renew your confidence in Jesus Christ and your commitment to the glory of His holy name.

And to all assembled in this cathedral Church I say: "Grace to you and peace from God our Father and the Lord Jesus Christ" (1 Cor. 1:3).

Catechesis and Preparation for New Vocations

On February 23, 1981, the Holy Father met the bishops of Japan in the Apostolic Nunciature and addressed them as follows.

Dear brothers in Christ,

1. It gives me deep joy to come to your country on the occasion of the beatification of your Japanese martyrs. These holy martyrs take their place, alongside the many others that the Church already honors officially, to testify to the glorious Christian history of your people, in which the blood of martyrs has truly become the seed of Christians. I am looking forward to having the opportunity to honor these martyrs in a solemn way in Nagasaki. Meanwhile the important event of their beatification gives me this occasion to make a pastoral visit to the Church in Japan—the occasion to meet all categories of the faithful and the special joy of being with you, the pastors of the flock.

2. I have come here to offer you my fraternal support for your mission of proclaiming Jesus Christ to the *pusillus grex* of Japan and to anyone who may freely wish to listen to the Gospel message. I have come so that we may express together our unity in Christ and in His Church, that you may be reinforced in this unity, and that in the strength of this unity you may proceed with new vigor to face the challenges of your pastoral mission. When, as successors of the Apostles, as bishops of the Church of God and as servants of the Gospel, we listen attentively, we can hear the same cry that was addressed to the apostle Philip: "We wish to see Jesus" (Jn. 12:21). And today, does not this cry resound throughout the teeming metropolis of Tokyo and throughout all Japan? And is it not addressed in a particular way to you, the bishops of Japan?

FULL MATURITY IN CHRIST

3. Dear brothers, the Father wills to continue to manifest His beloved Son through our pastoral ministry. He wants to manifest Him as the loving and merciful Savior of the world, the Teacher of humanity, the perfect Son of man and the eternal Son of God. At the same time the Father wills that all people may have life in His Son, and through Him share in the life of the Most Holy Trinity. Our response to this plan of the Father is expressed in the programs of evangelization and catechesis, whereby we perseveringly proclaim Christ, and methodically endeavor to lead our people to the full appreciation of their Catholic Faith and to full maturity in Christ.

4. In order to show Christ to the world, in order to build up the community of the Church, we ourselves must be able to say with St. John: "Our fellowship is with the Father and with his Son Jesus Christ" (1 Jn. 1:3). This unity must be maintained in all its ecclesial dimensions, including communion with the universal Church. This unity requires from bishops the *collegialitas effectiva* and the *collegialitas affectiva* with the Successor of Peter and with all their brother bishops throughout the world. It likewise requires a special manifestation of unity among the bishops of each Episcopal Conference. This latter dimension is of particular importance for the effect that it has on all local apostolic endeavors. But above all, unity belongs to the mystery of the Church, and its value was deeply understood in the early Christian community, where the believers were "of one heart and soul" (Acts 4:32). From the beginning, the bishops of Christ's Church have held—and they still hold—special responsibility for the unity of the Church, with a serious obligation to be united among themselves. St. Paul's words of apostolic injunction have a personal meaning for every bishop and group of bishops: "I appeal to you, brethren, by the name of our Lord Jesus Christ, that all of you agree and that there be no dissensions among you, but that you be united in the same mind and the same judgment" (1 Cor. 1:10).

COLLABORATION IS NECESSARY

5. The expression of this close unity in fraternal collaboration is required for your pastoral programs. It is a condition for their successful coordination and for their effectiveness. In this way I urge you to do everything possible to find strength in unity, in order to promote common pastoral initiatives in evangelization and catechesis. Continue, dear brothers, in the same zeal that has already sustained hard work in the areas of the common translation of the Bible, the publication of the new Missal, the compilation of a new catechism and the translation of the documents of the Magisterium.

And there are many more pastoral issues that will require the full measure of your common commitment for the welfare of the Church in Japan. The fraternal collaboration of all the bishops among themselves in fulfilling the directives and genuine spirit of the Second Vatican Council, as well as the postconciliar norms issued by the Apostolic See, is indeed an act of pastoral love for the people.

CONTINUING CATECHESIS

6. Like the whole Church, you feel the urgent need for giving continuing catechesis to your people. I am sure that you will make every effort to see that no category of the faithful is neglected. In my Apostolic Exhortation on Catechesis, I spoke to all the bishops of the Church in the following terms: "I know that your ministry as bishops is growing daily more complex and overwhelming. A thousand duties call you.... But let the concern to foster active and effective catechesis yield to no other care whatever in any way. This concern will lead you to transmit personally to your faithful the doctrine of life. But it should also lead you to take on in your diocese, in accordance with the plans of the Episcopal Conference to which you belong, the chief management of catechesis, while at the same time surrounding yourselves with competent and trustworthy

assistants. Your principal role will be to bring about and maintain a real passion for catechesis, a passion embodied in a pertinent and effective organization.... You can be sure that if catechesis is done well in your local Churches, everything else will be easier to do. And needless to say, although your zeal must sometimes impose upon you the thankless task of denouncing deviations and correcting errors, it will much more often win for you the joy and consolation of seeing your Churches flourishing because catechesis is given in them as the Lord wishes" (CT 63).

One of the areas worthy of special pastoral zeal is the need to catechize the young people in preparation for marriage. This need is all the more pressing for those who will be endeavoring to live upright lives with marriage partners who do not have the same faith or the same religious convictions. Efforts made in this field can do much to foster the sanctity of marriage and the family. In all catechetical endeavors it will be necessary to proclaim clearly the teaching of Christ and His Church. Catechesis should never doubt the power of Christ's grace to lead the faithful to high degrees of Christian holiness.

ACCEPTANCE OF THE BEATITUDES

7. As bishops, we must be convinced of the need never to lower the standards of Christian living that we present to our people. Our pastoral responsibility urges us to propose a deep acceptance of the beatitudes, a radical commitment to evangelical values. Our people, redeemed and sanctified by the blood of the Savior, are capable of accepting the divine invitation that it falls on us to transmit. Over and over again Japanese Catholics have proved that they are able to maintain their cultural heritage, while making incarnate in it the original element of Christianity, that newness of life in Christ. They have shown an understanding of the doctrine of the cross and of the universal vocation to holiness. It is necessary to keep

alive the memory of your martyrs so that people will always know that it is their heritage to glory "in the cross of our Lord Jesus Christ" (Gal. 6:14).

THE APOSTOLATE OF VOCATIONS

8. Supremely worthy of intense united efforts on your part is the apostolate of vocations. By God's grace a high percentage of Catholic women have embraced the religious life. But the Gospel still has need of many witnesses. It is important that young people be given the opportunity to hear Christ's call. And many of the young people, once they have heard and seen Jesus, will want to follow Him. The promoting and obtaining of vocations by prayer and effort is followed by two other dynamic aspects: careful attention to the proper formation of those who have accepted God's call, and the rightful employment of priestly and religious talents. The major seminaries, in particular, should be the object of the bishops' deepest pastoral interest, so that the priorities of the priesthood will be appreciated long before ordination. For all of us—and it is worth repeating time and time again —the apostolic priorities of the priesthood are "prayer and the ministry of the word" (Acts 6:4). To sustain your priests in these activities is to promote Christ's plan for His Body, the Church. Of all the members of the flock, none have more right to your fraternal love than the priests and the missionaries who are your partners in the Gospel of salvation: your own diocesan priests and the missionaries who serve generously by your side. Your kindness, your interest, your personal concern for them as friends constitute a salutary example for them in their own relationship with the rest of God's people.

PENANCE AND EUCHARIST

9. In my first encyclical I devoted rather lengthy sections to two vital aspects of the Church's life: the sacraments of Penance and the Holy Eucharist. I have

repeatedly emphasized the great power of these sacraments in regard to Christian living. And today I would encourage you personally to do everything in your power to help the ecclesial community to appreciate fully the value of individual confession as a personal encounter with the merciful and loving Savior, and to be faithful to the directives of the Church in a matter of such importance. The norms of the Apostolic See in regard to the altogether exceptional use of general absolution also take into account "a right on Christ's part with regard to every human being redeemed by him" (RH 20).

EUCHARISTIC SACRIFICE

10. Your own ministry and that of your priests, as well as the whole activity of the universal Church, reaches its culmination in the Eucharistic Sacrifice. Here the proclamation of Jesus Christ is complete. Here evangelization finds its source and summit (cf. PO 5). Here our unity in Christ finds its fullest expression. With what joy I look forward to celebrating the Eucharist in your midst three times in the next three days, offering up to the Father, in union with Jesus Christ, all the hopes and aspirations, all the joys and sorrows of the Japanese people, praying "that the word of the Lord may speed on and triumph, as it did among you" (2 Thes. 3:1).

11. Let us continue then, dear brothers, despite obstacles and setbacks, despite human weakness, to offer the Gospel freely and in its entirety. It is our contribution in the face of the loneliness of the world; it is our answer to the selfishness of man, to the lack of meaning that many people find in life, to the temptation to escapism, to lethargy and discouragement. As ministers of Christ we offer His Word and the tender love of His Sacred Heart: It is our original and specific contribution to the dialogue of salvation, to the promotion of human dignity and to the final liberation of humanity.

In the name of Jesus let us go forth confidently, and in the name of Mary let us rejoice. St. Paul Miki and his companion martyrs understood the meaning of these names and their gentle power. And may this heritage long remain in Japan: to lead future generations to Jesus through Mary.

Dear brothers: thank you for your invitation to come to Japan. Thank you for your own fraternal support and for your partnership in the Gospel. "My love be with you all in Christ Jesus. Amen" (1 Cor. 16:24).

"You Are the Light of the World!"

In the cathedral of Nagasaki, one of the more Catholic communities of Japan (some 75,000), the Holy Father concelebrated holy Mass, on February 25, 1981. 15 deacons of Japan, Korea, Poland and the United States were ordained priests. After the Gospel the Holy Father delivered the following homily.

Dear brothers and sisters in Christ,

I thank God for letting me come here to Nagasaki, a city with a history that is marked by both glory and tragedy, and to address you who are the descendants and successors of those who won the glory and overcame the tragedy. I greet you with great affection, and with deep respect for the magnificent Catholic tradition of this local Church.

This is indeed a highpoint in my apostolic journey to Japan, for the Successor of Peter is ordaining priests at one of the most distant points from his See of Rome, and thus giving living testimony to the universality of his mission.

For the Pope this is a solemn and moving moment. But it is even more so for you, beloved sons, who are about to be sacramentally consecrated as "ministers of Christ Jesus to the Gentiles in the priestly service of the Gospel of God" (Rom. 15:16) and "stewards of the mysteries of God" (1 Cor. 4:1).

It is only in the course of many years of fidelity to the gift you are to receive today that you will gradually come to understand more and more this event and its wonder. Indeed, a whole life is not sufficient for full understanding of what it means to be a priest of Jesus Christ. We can here unveil only a few features of this mystery, with the help of the readings in this solemn liturgy.

"THE LORD HAS ANOINTED ME"

1. The first phrase that concerns you is the one which the prophet Isaiah uses to describe his vocation: "The Spirit of the Lord God is upon me, because the Lord has anointed me" (Is. 61:1).

These words apply to every priest. They apply to you. They mean that at the root of every priestly vocation there is not a personal human initiative with its unavoidable human limitations, but instead a mysterious initiative by God. The Letter to the Hebrews says of Christ's priesthood: "Christ did not exalt himself to be made a high priest, but was appointed by him who said to him, 'You are my son' " (Heb. 5:5). That is true not only of Christ Himself but also of all who share in His priesthood.

Every priest can say: "The Lord has anointed me." The Lord has anointed me, first of all, from all eternity, even before I came to be, when he called my name. "The Lord called me from the womb," says Isaiah, "from the body of my mother he named my name" (Is. 49:1). A complete understanding of a priestly vocation requires that we go back to this anointing of God's preferential love for a certain person even before his existence, and to the call that God addresses to him because of this love.

A priest can also say that the Lord has anointed him when, in childhood or youth, his heart responded to the Lord's call: "Follow me." It is not always easy to pinpoint this moment and identify the event through which the call came: the example of a priest or a friend? The discovery of a void that only complete service of God can fill? A desire to respond to material, moral or spiritual distress in a way that is fully effective? But whatever the circumstances, it is God who has called. Whether or not the priest can fix the day on which he staked his life by yielding to the Lord's influence—what the prophet Jeremiah calls the Lord's seduction (Jer. 20:7)—he should be aware that God has called him.

A PRIEST OF CHRIST FOREVER

Thirdly, a priest can say that the Lord has anointed him on the day of his ordination, the day he finally and forever becomes a priest of Jesus Christ. It is the day of literal anointing by the hands of a bishop. We priests should always keep that day in mind. Paul urged Timothy: "Rekindle the gift of God that is within you through the laying on of my hands" (2 Tm. 1:6). We should always remember our ordination, so as to rekindle constantly our first fervor and to draw strength from the memory, in order to live a life consistent with its profound significance. For today's anointing is for you, my beloved sons, the passing, the outward sign of a permanent mark on your personalities. It is the sacramental sign of a grace by which Christ the Priest consecrates you for a special mission at the service of His kingdom, making you priests of Jesus Christ forever.

"THE LIGHT OF THE WORLD"

2. What are you called to do as priests? Another passage in today's liturgy gives the answer: "You are the light of the world" (Mt. 5:14).

It is disconcerting for us, aware as we are of our littleness and sinfulness, to hear addressed to us the clear words: "You are the light of the world." The Apostles must have trembled at hearing them. So have thousands of people since then. And yet the Lord spoke those words to people whom He knew to be human, limited and sinful. For He also knew that they were to be light not by their own strength but by reflecting and communicating His light, for He said of Himself: "I am the light of the world" (Jn. 8:12; 9:5; cf. 1:5, 9; 3:19; 12:46).

Every priest finds that he can give light to people in darkness only to the extent that he himself has accepted the light of the Teacher, Jesus Christ. He is, however, wrapped in dangerous shadows and incapable of enlightening others when he departs from the one source of all true light. Therefore, beloved sons, you must always remain close to Christ the Priest by listening assiduously to His Word, by celebrating His mysteries in the Eucharist, and by intimate friendship with Him at all times. People will recognize your communion with Christ by your capacity to be true light for a world all too often in darkness.

LET CHRIST SHINE THROUGH YOU

3. But in the final analysis, it is not enough for a priest to reflect, more or less imperfectly, the light of Christ: he must eclipse himself and let Christ shine directly. "What we preach is not ourselves, but Jesus Christ as Lord.... For it is the God who said, 'Let light shine out of darkness,' who has shone in our hearts to give light of the knowledge of the glory of God in the face of Christ" (2 Cor. 4:5-6).

As priests, you will be ministers of the light shining from the face of Christ through faith. Your mission is, therefore, first and foremost, to provide that preaching from the hearing of which faith comes (cf. Rom. 10:17). The Second Vatican Council describes priests as "instructors in the faith" (PO 6). Your basic service is to proclaim to everyone Christ the Truth and the truths of Faith, to foster faith constantly, to strengthen it where it is weak and to defend it against every threat.

Needless to say, you will be better instructors in the Faith to the extent that you yourselves have a deep-rooted, mature, courageous and contagious faith. The Evangelists describe the years that Jesus spent in the company of the

Twelve as a process of fostering their faith: "Jesus... manifested his glory; and his disciples believed in him" (Jn. 2:11; cf. 11:15). You, like the Twelve, have spent years with Jesus before reaching this point. You must be disciples with a tried and mature faith, firmly anchored in the words of the Teacher and ready for combat. May you never cease to join in the humble and fervent prayer of the Apostles: "Increase our faith" (Lk. 17:5), and may you ever hear in reply what Christ said to Peter: "I have prayed for you that your faith may not fail" (Lk. 22:32). Thus you will be prepared for leading many others to the Faith.

There is a special obligation on each priest and on the presbyterium itself to promote vocations to the priesthood. In this regard prayer is essential; but it is also essential for young men to be supported by the example of holiness and joy that they see in their priests. For this reason Jesus Christ has truly given to the young priests this morning an important role to fulfill in influencing, by example, the hearts of the young.

CHURCH OF THE HOME

4. I would now say a few words to the families of the new priests, and to all the Christian families of Japan.

It is with deep emotion that I recall the meeting that took place here in Nagasaki between a recently arrived missionary and a group of people who, after making sure that he was a Catholic priest, told him: "We have been waiting for you for centuries." They had been without priests or churches or public worship for well over two hundred years. And yet, in spite of adverse circumstances, the Christian faith had not been extinguished; it had been handed down in the family from generation to generation. Thus the Christian family showed its immense importance for the vocation to being a Christian.

The Christian family is also supremely vital for vocations to the priesthood and the religious life. The majority of such vocations spring to life and develop in deeply

Christian families. That is why the Second Vatican Council called the family the first seminary (cf. OT 2). I am certain too that the numerous vocations within the "little flock" of the Catholic community in Japan are born and grow within families animated by a spirit of faith, charity and piety.

As I, the Successor of Peter, ordain new priests for your country, I exhort every Christian family in Japan to be truly a "church of the home": a place where God is given thanks and praise, a place where His Word is listened to and His law obeyed, a place where education is given for faith and where faith is fostered and strengthened, a place of fraternal charity and mutual service, a place of openness to others, especially the poor and the needy.

Be open to vocations from among you. Pray that, as a sign of His special love, the Lord will call one or more of your members to serve Him. Live your faith with the joy and fervor that encourage such vocations. Be generous when your son or daughter, your brother or sister, decides to follow Christ in this special way. Allow his or her vocation to grow and be strengthened. Give your full support to a choice freely made.

Let all of us who are gathered here continue now with faith and devotion this Eucharistic celebration of the Sacrifice of Christ the Priest. Recalling the Japanese priests, religious and lay people, who in this very area gave the supreme witness of their lives for love of Jesus Christ, let us pray for the Christian families of this country, that they may live their Christian vocation with intensity. We ask the Lord to grant that from among them there may come many priests, like those who are today beginning their priestly life and ministry, as well as many religious, for the glory of Jesus Christ and for the salvation of the world. Amen.

Teaching Religion and Catechesis— Distinct and Complementary Ministries

In the course of the work session with the Roman clergy, which took place on March 5, 1981, in the Clementine Hall of the Apostolic Palace, the Holy Father delivered the following address.

Venerated confreres!

1. Taking the floor after the various successive interventions in this Hall, which I have listened to with great interest, I express first of all my joy at this meeting, at which I have the privilege of receiving the priests of my diocese in their various orders and ranks. How could I fail to rejoice on seeing close to me, together with the dear and zealous Cardinal Vicar, the Vicegerent and the Auxiliary Bishops, such an elect array of pastors, who responsibly contribute to alleviating with their work the "burden of the day and the heat" of the apostolic labor entrusted to me by God in this beloved city of Rome, to which eyes turn from all over the world as the community "worthy of God, worthy of honor, worthy of blessing," because "it presides over the brotherhood of charity"? (Ignatius, *Ep. ad Romanos, Inscr.)*

Ours is a happy moment of spiritual intimacy, which calls to mind the early Christian community, which the Book of Acts describes as "one heart and mind" (Acts 4:32). The Lord is with us! We are assured of this by the promise He made in the Gospel to all those gathered in His name (cf. Mt 18:20). In Him I am happy to feel present here this morning, united by the common bond of a charity that has a brotherly depth and warmth, also those priests whom the commitments of their ministry have detained elsewhere. I want to embrace everyone, to thank everyone, to bless everyone.

OUR CATHOLIC SCHOOLS

2. The subject to which our attention has been called takes on a fundamental importance in the set of apostolic activities into which the pastoral plan of the diocese is divided; the religious formation of youth in schools is a delicate commitment in itself, which the present-day circumstances, both within scholastic structures and in the wider sphere of mentality and social morals, make extraordinarily difficult and, sometimes, even disagreeable and thankless. I wish to take advantage of this occasion to express, in the first place, my appreciation and esteem for all those who are spending their energies in this highly meritorious service: to them I affectionately address a special word of congratulations and exhortation, which I would like to be received as comfort and support in the difficulties of your daily labor.

My thought goes in the first place to Catholic schools, which are particularly numerous in our city. The qualified groups of men and women religious, who dedicate the best of themselves to educational work within these institutions, must be able to rely on the understanding and support of the whole ecclesial community. Their activity, in fact, daily reaches tens of thousands of boys and girls with whom they can establish a dialogue of formation which, starting from the many opportunities offered by the development of the various disciplines and availing itself of a certain life style nourished within the Institute, can exercise an educational influence that is particularly deep and lasting.

Every pastor of souls, therefore, cannot but look with favor and sympathy on the activity carried out by Catholic institutes operating within the diocese, and must offer them that collaboration that circumstances make, in turn, possible and opportune. At the same time those in charge of Catholic schools and members of the teaching staff must feel the commitment of taking an active place in the local Church, maintaining constant contacts with it at the places set up for this purpose, and directing the young towards the pastoral structures which, both on the diocesan and on the parish level, promote initiatives addressed to them. It is necessary to avoid forms of isolation which, turning the youth aside from participation in the life of the ecclesial community, would threaten to prejudice, once his studies are completed, perseverance in religious practice and perhaps even in the very choices of faith.

POSSIBILITIES OF APOSTOLIC ACTION

3. Then there is the "public" school. In this connection, I would like to say at once that the priest cannot underestimate the possibilities of apostolic action open to him in this field as well. I think, in fact, that it is right and proper not to waste any of the opportunities offered in this area by the juridical system in force. And this already at the level of the primary school, in which children are started along the way to an integrated knowledge of the rudiments of the various disciplines. How could one fail to see in this phase of scholastic apprenticeship an important premise for the subsequent developments of evangelization? Priests engaged in pastoral activity will do well, therefore, to make every effort to offer in this area, in the limits permitted, their whole collaboration, both in contacts with pupils, when they must integrate the religious instruction imparted by the teachers, and in constructive dialogue with the headmasters and teachers, and by means of any other initiative that may appear to be opportune.

Particular attention must be paid to the teaching of religion in junior and senior secondary schools. It is at this level, in fact, that the major difficulties and most frequent perplexities are encountered, but it is also in this area that the most stimulating perspectives open. Assuring you that the reflections set forth by those who have just spoken will not fail to be taken into due consideration, I am glad to take advantage of the occasion to recall some principles which should be kept in mind in this matter, and to indicate the consequent lines of action.

RELIGIOUS INSTRUCTION AND CATECHESIS

The fundamental principle that must guide commitment in this delicate area of the apostolate is that of the distinction and at the same time the complementary character of the teaching of religion and catechesis. In schools, in fact, the intended goal is the complete formation of the pupil. The teaching of religion will have to be characterized, therefore, in reference to the objectives and criteria peculiar to a modern scholastic structure. It will present itself, on the one hand, as the fulfillment of a right-duty of the human person, for whom the religious education of conscience constitutes a fundamental manifestation of freedom; on the other hand it will have to be seen as a service that society renders to Catholic pupils, who make up nearly all the students, and to their parents, who can logically be presumed to want for them an education inspired by their own religious principles. In this regard I wish to recall what I wrote in the Apostolic Exhortation *Catechesi tradendae:* "I express the fervent wish that, in response to a very clear right of the human person and of the family, and out of respect for everyone's religious freedom, all Catholic pupils may be enabled to advance in their spiritual formation with the aid of a religious instruction dependent on the Church, but which, according to the circumstances of different countries, can be offered either by the school or in the setting of the school" (no. 69).

Religious instruction imparted in schools, and catechesis, properly speaking, carried out within the parish, though distinct, must not be considered separate. There is, in fact, a deep connection between them: the subject addressed by educators is, in fact, the same in both cases, namely the pupil; and the objective content on which formation turns, though in different ways, in the teaching of religion and in catechesis, is also the same. Religious instruction can be considered either as a qualified premise for catechesis or as a further reflection on the contents of catechesis already acquired.

THE RELIGION TEACHER

4. A first conseqence of such an approach to the problem directly concerns the teacher of religion; he will have to become more and more deeply aware of his own identity as a committed Christian in the ecclesial community, feeling that it looks to him and follows him with demanding consideration in the serious task entrusted to him by the Church.

The carrying out of this delicate task calls for a specific professional preparation. The teacher of religion must, in fact, be in possession, on the one hand, of a systematic theological formation, which enables him to propose the contents of Faith competently, and, on the other hand, of that knowledge of human sciences, which is revealed as necessary to convey the contents themselves in a suitable and effective way.

A similar Christian and professional commitment—in order to be able to keep up with educational requirements, on the part of teachers of religion (from the nursery school to the senior secondary school)—calls for an effort of constant updating in content and method, and for the commitment of active participation in the life of the ecclesial community.

STUDENTS' INFLUENCE

5. I would like to reserve a word for the responsibility of Catholics as a whole in connection with the work of formation carried out by the school. It is clear that the impact of religious teaching is conditioned by the overall pedagogical context within which it takes place. Hence the importance of a respectful and active presence of Catholics in the various phases of formation through which the pupil goes: Catholic teachers in the first place will be able to make an important contribution with their specific professional character; then the action of parents will have to be stimulated and given new importance for the effective role of mediation and dialogue which they can carry out

between the civil community and the ecclesial one, particularly in the sphere of collegial organs; nor, finally, must the contribution of pupils be underestimated; their influence in the school will be manifested mainly through the testimony of study, listening and service.

The time of formation calls for particular attention and respect for the maturing personality of the young person. The commitment of individuals and the commitment organically planned by the ecclesial community will have to move in this direction, with the intention of promoting, in harmony with the specific characteristics of the school, the serene coexistence of human members different in mentality and culture, encouraging the establishment among them of that relationship based on an open and respectful dialogue, which alone can lead to a really civil society.

Among the many applications that such an orientation suggests, there is also the one that commits teachers of religion to feeling responsible for the proposal of the Christian message to *all* pupils, avoiding the temptation of confining their interest to those who consciously live a choice of faith and religious practice. To respect everyone, not to exclude anyone, to seek dialogue actively with every member of the school community, these are, in a word, the principles by which the teacher of religion must constantly be inspired.

6. These are, beloved sons, the thoughts I was anxious to communicate to you on such a complex and fundamental subject. I would like, before concluding, to urge the whole ecclesial community to bring its generous commitment to bear on the matter: what is at stake is the religious formation of those who will be responsible for the community of the future. All energies spent in this area must, therefore, be considered wisely spent.

There remains in any case and for everyone the difficulty of expressing divine things in human language, of giving our poor language that secret virtue which makes it persuasive and salutary, making it a sword that penetrates into the depths of the spirit: "For the word of God is alive and effective, more penetrating than any two-edged sword" (Heb. 4:12). This spiritual effectiveness depends, more than on human abilities and devices, on the transforming action of divine grace. And grace is gained by purification of the heart, achieved through prayer, penance, and the more disinterested and generous exercise of charity. Yesterday we began the Lenten season: this is the "acceptable time" in which each of us is called to start along the way of deeper experience of the strengthening presence of the Spirit of Christ.

My wish is that this Lent may be for everyone a time of interior renewal, in the joy of deeper contact with the fresh springs of grace. For this purpose I willingly impart to you my apostolic blessing, invoking every desired heavenly comfort.

Be Signs and Creators of Unity

After the visit to the steelworks and the meeting with the workers of Terni on March 19, 1981, the Holy Father went to the bishop's residence to meet the priests and religious of the Diocese of Terni and Narni. The Pope delivered the following address.

1. Even on such a busy day as this one, there could not fail to be a meeting with you, beloved priests and religious who, by virtue of the sacred ordination and mission received from the bishop, have been promoted to the "service of Christ the Teacher, Priest and King, and given a share in His ministry, through which the Church here on earth is being ceaselessly built up into the People of God, Christ's Body and the Temple of the Spirit" (PO 1).

I see with great pleasure that the venerated confreres of the Umbrian episcopate are also present. I address a particularly cordial greeting to them.

I wish to spend a few moments among you, dear priests, to tell you of my special affection, and so that you may feel increasingly strong and joyful in faith, which I hope will grow more and more in Christ, also because of this visit of mine (cf. Phil. 1:25-26).

STEWARDS OF THE MYSTERIES OF GOD

2. The reality so sublime that you bear within you—marked by a special character which configures you to Christ the Priest, in such a way that you are able to act in His name (cf. PO 2)—involves awareness of the greatness of the mission received and the necessity of becoming more and more worthy of it. It is necessary, in view of the Lord's gift, to have a clear and deep-rooted conviction about one's own being as a priest of Christ, steward and administrator of the mysteries of God, an instrument of salvation for men. These certainties of Faith make it impossible for us to have doubts about our own identity, to hesitate about the value of our life, to falter along the way undertaken.

I am here among you to strengthen and deepen these convictions, to make them invincible and constant, calling you to ever closer union with Christ, our reason for living and our strength.

Sometimes our harmony of faith with Jesus may weaken and fade, if His presence in us is dimmed by human tendencies and reasonings, which make us unable to reflect the whole magnificent light that He represents for us. "Every priest"—as I said to the ordinands at Nagasaki last February 25—"finds that he can give light to people in darkness only to the extent that he himself has accepted the light of the Teacher, Jesus Christ." We may sometimes speak of him influenced by premises and data of a sociological, political or psychological nature, instead of drawing the fundamental principles of our life from the Gospel, lived completely, joyfully, with that confidence and that immense hope that the cross of Christ contains.

SUPERNATURAL VALUES

3. You, dear priests, because of your very ministry, are obliged to live in the midst of men, to know your sheep

as good shepherds, and to try to lead back those who do not belong to this fold, so that they too may hear the voice of Christ (cf. PO 3). However, while you carry out this work of rapprochement, men must see in you credible witnesses of divine love and of a kingdom which, beginning here below, will be perfected in eternal life.

Also the particular socio-cultural reality of the Church that is in Terni, Narni and Amelia, a reality well-known to you in its aspirations and tensions, in its causes and in its orientations, and which sometimes seems to put serious obstacles in the way of the penetration of a Christian mentality, needs to find in you not social leaders or skillful administrators, but true spiritual guides who endeavor to direct and improve the hearts of the faithful so that, converted, they may live in love of God and their neighbor and commit themselves to the elevation and advancement of man. Let us not deceive ourselves that we are serving the Gospel if we yield to the temptation of "diluting" our charism in an exaggerated interest for temporal problems. Let us not forget that the priest must be a representative of supernatural values, a sign and creator of unity and brotherhood.

4. I would like to indicate to you another point for reflection. You are members of the presbyterium of a particular Church, whose center of unity is the bishop, towards whom every priest who aspires to real fruitfulness of ministry must have a convinced attitude of communion and obedience. "This priestly obedience"—the Council reminds us—"is based on that sharing of the episcopal ministry which is conferred on priests by the sacrament of Order and the canonical mission" (PO 7).

In pastoral activity, while taking into account the different local problems, let a spirit of understanding and cooperation reign between parochial initiatives and diocesan ones, which by their very nature are open to wider horizons and more general aspirations, such as the ones concerning the world of work, social communications, the school, culture, and presence in the civic field.

The union between the priests and the bishop is particularly necessary today, when the various apostolic initiatives often go beyond the limits of a parish or a diocese, and require that priests unite their forces with those of confreres, under the guidance of those who govern the Church.

GOD'S CONSECRATING LOVE

5. Beloved priests and religious, I would like to say so many other things to you and I would like to listen to the most personal anxieties of each of you, but I cannot prolong this meeting too much. I conclude by renewing my great confidence in you and by exhorting you to have confidence in Him who "determines the number of the stars, and gives to all of them their names" (Ps. 147[146]:4), and who called you by name, calling you from the womb (cf. Is. 49:1). Our confidence is based radically on this "preferential and consecrating love of God," which does not abandon, above all, those who, called to share in the priesthood of His Son, address Him confidently. Precisely for this reason, St. Paul reminds us that in all tribulations, "we are more than conquerors through him who loved us" (Rom. 8:37). I conclude with the exhortation of the author of the Letter to the Hebrews: "Do not throw away your confidence, which has a great reward. For you have need of endurance, so that you may do the will of God and receive what is promised" (Heb. 10:35-36).

Under the eyes of Mary, the Mother of priests and religious, so venerated at Terni as the Mother of Mercy, continue on your way with new enthusiasm, and may my apostolic blessing accompany you.

A Valid Instrument of Episcopal Collegiality

On March 21, 1981, the Holy Father took part in the final work session of the Council of the General Secretariat of the Synod of Bishops, which had come together for the first time since the Fifth General Assembly in October last year.

After listening to a brief report on the work, given by Paul Cardinal Zoungrana, the Holy Father gave the following address.

Dear brothers,

1. Before we bring this meeting to a close, we thank you all from the bottom of our heart for this opportunity you have given us of meeting you and speaking with you about that very important subject which was so thoroughly dealt with at the recent General Assembly of the Synod, namely, "the role of the Christian family in the modern world."

Indeed, we have repeatedly shown the great importance this question has in the world of our time, just as the Synod Fathers themselves did on that occasion. Moreover, this is confirmed by the fact that very many people throughout the world eagerly followed the work of the Synod also through the various channels of social communication and by the fact that the deliberations of the Synod were afterwards evaluated everywhere by experts.

In like manner in this meeting of yours you have examined more in depth the conclusions of that Synod so that you might be able to grasp the wealth of meaning they contain and at the same time to see how they can be introduced into the life of the Church. You now bring us the results of your consultations and we are very grateful to you for them. Likewise, as we have already mentioned in our address before the Angelus on December 28, we assure you that we will make use of them when we draw up a document on this matter.

PROPOSALS FOR THEME OF NEXT SYNOD

2. Moreover, taking advantage of this suitable occasion of your meeting, you have also considered the suggestions and proposals for the theme for the next synod, which have been sent in by the episcopal conferences, from the meeting of the bishops of the Eastern rite, from the departments of the Roman Curia and from the Union of Superiors General. We wish to thank very much all those who after mature deliberation have sent in these proposals to you, and we thank you yourselves for the shrewd judgment you have passed on them.

We have a high regard for the criteria you have followed in examining the various opinions about the theme for the next synod. For you adopted as your norms of assessment: first, the universality of the particular matter as it touches and affects the whole Church; secondly, its greater urgency; finally, its doctrinal and pastoral application and utility.

We shall give great thought, in turn, to what you have brought to our notice. Indeed, they will be most useful to us in finally deciding upon the theme to be dealt with in the next synod.

3. In itself it is already sufficiently clear and this recent Synod, on which you have worked up till now, convinces one what great importance and benefits this institution has for the life of the whole Church. It took its beginning from the provident plan of our Predecessor Paul VI, who welcomed and put into practice the wishes of the Vatican Council. Through it the bishops of the local Churches throughout the world bring to Peter the experiences and riches of the Christian life in their respective dioceses; and through it Peter also confirms his brothers in the Faith and truly and effectively safeguards the charity of the whole.

Hence the synod becomes a valid instrument of that collegiality which the Second Vatican Council has put in its true light. For, "just as by the Lord's will St. Peter and the other Apostles constituted one Apostolic College, so, in a similar way, the Roman Pontiff as the Successor of Peter, and the bishops as the successors of the Apostles are joined together" (LG 22).

Therefore desiring in the full discharge of our ministry to make use of the helps, the advice and the wishes of the whole of the Catholic episcopate, we are happy to think that we are complying with the will of our Predecessor Paul VI, who desired that by means of the synod of bishops, an opportunity should be given them "of sharing in a clearer and more effective way our care for the whole Church" (Motu Proprio *Apostolica sollicitudo*, *AAS*, 57, [1965], p. 776).

For we are in agreement with his opinion according to which if "what Christ entrusted to Peter for the good and service of the whole Church and after him passed it on to his lawful successors in this See of Rome, is useful for our primatial office, it equally refers to the office of the College of Bishops. For this reason the College of Bishops is associated in a certain way with the Roman Pontiff in the care of the universal Church" *(Insegnamenti di Paolo VI,* V, 1967, p. 468).

Therefore, while we greatly desire and earnestly pray that the synod of bishops may continue to do its work even better and more thoroughly, and that there may always be this reciprocal and helpful exchange between the principal See of the Church and the particular Churches, to each of you we willingly impart our heartfelt apostolic blessing.

With Prayer and Study, Bring Your Pastoral Sense to Maturity

On March 23, 1981, the Holy Father received in audience the students of the Pontifical Ecclesiastical Academy, which this year celebrates the 280th anniversary of its founding. John Paul II delivered the following address to the group of students, composed of thirty-one priests coming from many countries.

Beloved priests, students of the Pontifical Ecclesiastical Academy,

I gladly welcomed the request expressed to me by your dear president, Mons. Cesare Zacchi, for a meeting with you, at this moment which shortly follows the Spiritual Exercises you made at Assisi, and precedes the assignment of some of you to the service of the Pontifical Representations.

I would like to thank you, in the first place, for the good wishes you sent me from Assisi. Every signature that I saw in that letter now takes on the form of a face, to which I am happy to turn for a conversation which I would like to be simple but also significant.

The reference to St. Francis was prompted, I think, not by casual circumstances, but rather sprang from a deep intention and from the search for an inspiration for your vocation. St. Francis, in fact, is a shining example also for the ministry you are called to carry out and is an effective help to understand its real meaning and genuine spirit. His desire to be a man of the Gospel, his identification with Christ, his passionate love of the Church, without reservations or criticisms, in the witness of radical poverty, in meekness as a man of universal brotherhood and peace, are not these attitudes and values congenial with the nature and the task of the Pontifical Representative?

The Pontifical Ecclesiastical Academy, whose 280th anniversary falls this year, aims at forming you in this spirit. The Academy, which has a great tradition and has its qualified function as well today, has undergone in the course of the years, various updatings for the purpose of meeting the requirements of a suitable ecclesial service. More recently, it was renewed in the framework of the ecclesiology of the Second Vatican Council and of the new style of relations between the Apostolic See and the local Churches. The universality which is so well reflected by your origin, is accompanied by other fundamental characteristics that must distinguish the Ecclesiastical Academy. I would like to indicate some.

1) It must be first and foremost a place of spiritual development and a meeting-place of prayer. If the exercise of every priestly ministry demands a deep spiritual life, I would like to say that the mission you are called to fulfill involves such peculiar and sometimes difficult situations of life and action that, in the absence of a source of intense spirituality, you would run the risk of finding yourselves without inspiration or ideals. May the time that you spend in this institute, therefore, be a time of meditation and of depth; a time not of slackening of asceticism, but of persevering training in those virtues which will form tomorrow a solid and safe support for your mission.

2) The Pontifical Ecclesiastical Academy must furthermore be a place of assiduous cultural preparation, a center of study. Service of the Holy See, participating in the "sollicitudo omnium ecclesiarum," involves serious requirements today and demands qualifications that cannot be improvised.

I hope and trust that you will treasure this period, so precious for your formation, so that tomorrow you may be equal to the task entrusted to you. And I also hope that a serious commitment to study will accompany you all your lives.

3) In the third place, the Pontifical Ecclesiastical Academy must be a place in which the pastoral sense reaches maturity. Today extreme sensitivity is required of the Pontifical Representative in dealing with the pastors whom the Holy Spirit has placed at the head of the various local Churches, as well as a spirit prompt to grasp and

interpret pastoral situations and problems. This is a *forma mentis* that you must acquire and develop in order to become fit for the service of ecclesial communion between the local Churches and Peter's See.

I express hearty thanks to your president, who dedicates himself with enthusiasm and self-sacrifice to your formation, and I thank your teachers for the work they carry out. I hope that the students who are about to complete their studies will undertake their ministry with generous availability and serene confidence in the protection of the Blessed Virgin. And I willingly bless everyone in the name of the Lord.

The Importance of the Educational Apostolate

On March 26, 1981, the Holy Father received in audience the Cardinals and bishops participating in the Plenary Assembly of the Sacred Congregation for Catholic Education. After a short address of homage by the Prefect of the Sacred Congregation, Cardinal William Wakefield Baum, the Pope delivered the following address.

Revered brothers,

1. Addressing my cordial greeting to you, I wish in the first place to thank Cardinal Baum for the kind words he addressed to me, recalling moments spent together with you in past years. If I accepted promptly the invitation extended to me, it was also for the pleasure of seeing again known faces, and—as is obvious—out of concern to share the study of problems that are particularly urgent today.

Cardinal Baum, as Prefect of the Congregation, is directing this Assembly for the first time. While I renew to him my best wishes for fruitful work, I also wish to address a word of congratulations and gratitude to Cardinal Garrone, who presided over the Congregation in delicate moments for fourteen years.

The expression of my grateful appreciation is then extended to all members, Cardinals and bishops present, for the sacrifice and generosity with which they tackle the study of these questions which concern so closely the life of the Church. I also wish to thank the superiors and officials of the Congregation for the dedication which you show daily in carrying out your respective duties. My hearty thanks. It is not necessary for me to tell you how much I appreciate your collaboration, dear brothers and sons, how deep is my gratitude for your commitment.

CONGREGATION'S REPORTS

2. I have examined the four reports, now traditional for these meetings of yours. I appreciated the subjects proposed for study. As regards the seminaries, I am of the opinion that training in the use of the media of social communication deserves careful consideration, since the priests of today must confront these media, from which they can also draw benefits for their apostolate. The new document, moreover, fits well in the series of those already published by the Congregation on theology, philosophy, canon law, the liturgy and spirituality. I know that others will follow on the study of the Fathers, on the social doctrine of the Church, etc. While expressing my satisfaction, I hope that these initiatives may yield abundant fruit.

I also note with interest the ample documentation on what is being done for the preparation of future educators of the clergy. It is a field that can never be stressed enough, since the superiors and teachers of seminaries are the ones who really mold the future priests.

I would also like to emphasize the results of the inquiry with regard to adult vocations. This is a sector which seems to offer comforting prospects for the near future. Attentive as you are to grasping promptly the "signs of the times," you will not fail to address your solicitude also in this direction.

The short time available does not allow me to make a thorough study of the individual problems, although they interest me deeply, because each of them has its specific importance in the formation of that *homo Dei* whose characteristics I never tire of recalling in the numerous meetings I always seek to have with seminarians all over the world and with those who train them. Still I wish to repeat here also how much I have at heart that the Christian community should have holy and learned priests, inflamed with love for Christ, firm in Catholic doctrine, with a deep interior life, lovers of the Church, forming one heart and one soul with their bishop and the other priests, full of zeal for their brothers and sisters. All that is done to reach this aim cannot but have the blessing of the Lord and the most cordial encouragement on the part of His Vicar.

3. The questions that concern ecclesiastical universities and Catholic universities are also of fundamental interest for the life of the Church.

As regards the former, all that has to be done now is to carry out faithfully the norms of the Apostolic Constitution *Sapientia Christiana.* The document has been well received everywhere, even if, here and there, some objections have been raised, due to particular local and contingent situations. The Congregation will certainly be able to find a suitable solution for them.

I am particularly happy that a study of the Catholic universities is about to be carried out, to give them a "Magna Charta," in which their catholicity will be clearly defined, while their precise nature as real universities will be respected. It will not be an easy task; it deserves to be undertaken, however, in view of the importance that such a fundamental clarification takes on for all our centers of higher education. And the study should lead also to greater emphasis on the presence that the bishops must have in the life and work of our Catholic universities. In this way the indispensable collaboration, which must always exist between the Magisterium and science, will be further deepened.

THE ROLE OF LAY PEOPLE

4. As regards Catholic schools, I joyfully approve of the initiative which sets out to ensure the special Christian formation of the laity, who serve in the ranks of educators in our schools. The educational apostolate is congenial to them. The truly ecclesial testimony of lay people must have a particular importance among pupils, who, being mostly called to married life, will be able to see in their teachers models to be imitated unreservedly. It is to be hoped that the presence of excellent fathers and mothers of families among the teachers of Catholic schools will remove the cause for the complaints that are sometimes heard among parents, concerned because of certain questionable forms of expression on delicate subjects such as religion or sexual education.

CONGRESS FOR VOCATIONS

5. Finally, there is the area of vocations, which is a crucial point for the life of the Church today and tomorrow. The booklet on that subject bears witness to the hard work that is being carried out in this field in the whole Church. The "National Plans for the Promotion of Vocations," and the hundreds of "Diocesan Plans," that have arrived at the Congregation, offer well-grounded reasons to hope that the harvest will have sufficient laborers in the near future. The statistics reported in them are really consoling for some nations: We all hope that it will be possible to say the same for others before long.

The climax, and the starting-point for a new impetus, will be the forthcoming International Congress for Vocations, which will be celebrated here in Rome, in May. I myself will preside over the solemn opening concelebration, to stress the importance of that meeting, at which those most directly responsible in the dioceses for the promotion of vocations will make a deep study of the situation and will agree upon programmatic and operational lives for the future. My thanks and best wishes go straightaway to all those who are working hard for the success of the Congress.

Looking again at these individual aspects of your work, I cannot but thank the Lord, who shows me tangibly how much His grace is operating all over the world in your specific areas. In the course of my apostolic journeys, I have found everywhere seminarians full of enthusiasm, projected confidently towards the future. I have found university students committed in the name of Christ. I have met those engaged in educational activity, more and more aware of the ecclesial importance of their labors. It is these consoling visions that give us courage and make reecho in our mind the firm and encouraging reminder of the Lord: *"Ego sum...nolite timere."* May the Blessed Virgin, the Queen of the Apostles, accompany us all with her motherly protection.

In the Resurrection We Celebrate the Sacrament of the Priesthood

On April 24, 1981, in the Pauline Chapel, the Holy Father concelebrated Mass with eight Irish priests who were celebrating the silver jubilee of their priestly ordination. Among the jubilarians was Archbishop Thomas White, Apostolic Nuncio in Rwanda. Numerous deacons from various colleges also participated in the Mass, as did many relatives of the jubilarians. Pope John Paul delivered the following homily.

Dearly beloved in Christ,

1. After His resurrection, our Lord Jesus Christ returns to the company of His disciples. He is happy to be in their midst once again. He shows His deep personal interest in them; He calls them "friends" and eats with them. It is the third time, as St. John points out in this morning's Gospel, that He appears to His disciples. In so doing Jesus manifests the new life and power of His resurrection.

2. For us today it is important to note that the disciples to whom Jesus appeared—Peter and Thomas, Nathaniel, James and John—were now His priests; they were among those who had been with Him a short time before, at the Last Supper; they were among those who had heard Him say: "Do this in remembrance of me" (Lk. 22:19). By these words, according to the constant teaching of the Church and the solemn declaration of the Council of Trent, Jesus conferred the priesthood on His Apostles and ordained that they and their successors in the priesthood should offer the Sacrifice of His body and blood (cf. Sess. 22, cap. 1, can. 2).

HONORING THE PRIESTHOOD

3. This morning our celebration of the Lord's resurrection is linked with the celebration of the sacred priesthood. We honor this priesthood in the risen Lord, in Jesus Christ Himself. We honor it in Archbishop White and in the other members of his year, who are commemorating the twenty-fifth anniversary of their ordination. And thus we honor this priesthood of the New Testament as it has been transmitted through unbroken apostolic succession, and as it will be communicated in the near future to the new deacons here today—the sacrificial priesthood that will perpetuate the Paschal Mystery and fortify the Church until Christ comes again in glory to judge the living and the dead.

ANNOUNCING CHRIST RISEN

4. The priesthood that we are celebrating reenacts sacramentally in the Eucharist the death and glorification of the Lord. The Eucharist is the proclamation of Christ's resurrection in its highest form, just as it is the source and summit of all evangelization (PO 5). And all the efforts of those who share Christ's priesthood must be directed to announcing the mystery of the risen Savior.

Whether it seems expedient or not according to the standards of the world, the priesthood of the Catholic Church must incessantly proclaim the doctrine of the resurrection. In order to do this, it has been marvelously endowed with the power of the Holy Spirit. And through this power of the Holy Spirit, the proclamation of the resurrection has the same capacity today to elicit faith and to convert hearts as when it was made by the Apostles Peter and John. The name of the crucified and risen Jesus must be held up before the world. In the name of Jesus, the Church offers to all individuals and peoples an invincible hope—a hope that can overcome all sadness, take away all pessimism, conquer all sin and finally overcome death itself. The risen Christ gives hope to the world. In the name of Jesus there is the hope of salvation, resurrection and newness of life. Indeed, "of all the names in the world given to men this is the only one by which we can be saved" (Acts 4:12).

5. After having passed a number of years in the priestly ministry—a ministry exercised in different ways as the Church of God and His providence have disposed—there is not one of us concelebrating this Mass today who can imagine a joy in our priesthood greater than the joy of repeatedly proclaiming the Paschal Mystery in its sacramental reenactment in the Eucharistic Sacrifice.

Nowhere is Jesus Christ more strikingly the Lord of life than in the Eucharist, from which His saving and life-giving power goes forth over the earth. Through the Eucharist, the victory and triumph of Christ's resurrection are communicated to humanity craving for reconciliation, healing and life.

THE MASS IN YOUR LIVES

6. Dear jubilarians: The sacramental proclamation of Christ's Paschal Mystery does not make up the whole of your ministry in the Church, but it is certainly its most important aspect. The Mass is the center of your priestly

lives. It is the most dynamic and effective contribution you can make to the good of God's people: By dying, Jesus Himself has destroyed death and by rising He has restored His people to life. And this is communicated through the Eucharist, which is possible only through the priesthood.

These essential reflections do not minimize other aspects of your priestly ministry; they do not make you less available for the many services that God's people ask of you. But everything else takes its perspective from its relationship to the Eucharist and its relationship to the new life that Jesus gives through His resurrection for the glory of His Father.

And so, as you look back to the happy day of your ordination and recall your parents and families and all those who helped you to the priesthood, you must also look forward and think of all those who depend on you and who will be enabled, through your faithful ministry, "to walk in newness of life" (Rom. 6:4). For you, my brother priests, this is therefore a day for thanksgiving and for renewed fidelity. For you, dear deacons, this is an occasion that should elicit trust, generosity and prayer. And for the whole Church, represented here also by your families and friends, it is an hour of joy—a joy that we all share with Mary, the Queen of heaven, who rejoices in the Easter victory of her risen Son, our Lord and High Priest, Jesus Christ. Amen.

Making the Name of Jesus Known and Loved

On April 24, 1981, the Holy Father received in audience more than a hundred diocesan directors of the Society for the Propagation of the Faith who had come to Rome from the United States for their quinquennial meeting. Pope John Paul II delivered the following address.

My dear brothers and collaborators in the Gospel of Christ,

1. I extend a very cordial welcome to all of you, the diocesan directors of the Society for the Propagation of the Faith from the United States of America. I offer a particular greeting to the new National Director, Monsignor McCormack, and to his zealous predecessor, Archbishop O'Meara. I am happy that on this occasion you have chosen Rome for your quinquennial meeting. Your choice gives us the opportunity to gather together in the name of Christ; it likewise shows your determination to emphasize the ecclesial character of your work by integrating it within the universal mission of the Church. I am indeed grateful to you for the sentiments that motivate you in your ministry at the service of the Faith.

YOUR MISSIONARY WORK

2. At this time I wish to express my deep esteem for the special mission entrusted to you by your bishops. I thank you for the aid that you promote for local Churches throughout the world, and for what you do for your own dioceses. In a word, I thank you for your partnership in the Gospel, for your sustained efforts in making the name of Jesus ever better known and loved, at home and abroad.

3. Your activities are missionary, and they are directed first of all to the benefit of ecclesial communities in mission lands. In offering to young Churches the

solidarity of fraternal charity, you are performing a great and meritorious act. All the generous support that accompanies this solidarity is a faithful expression of the Gospel and is motivated by it. With your help, the work of Jesus goes on in the local Churches; Jesus remains with His people, "teaching...and preaching the gospel of the kingdom, and healing every disease and every infirmity" (Mt. 9:35). All the services made possible through your zealous collaboration are meant to be an expression of the Savior's love; they are intended to center attention on the Person and the Word of Jesus Christ, who alone adequately reveals God to man. But also because Christ alone can adequately reveal man to himself, everything you do to promote the proclamation of Christ's Word is a service that uplifts humanity itself, giving it a greater insight into its own nature and a greater awareness of its own dignity.

ASSISTING OTHERS

You are called to assist countless brothers and sisters throughout the world. What a great privilege it is to foster evangelization, promote catechesis and even facilitate the delicate aspect of the conversion of human hearts. This is how the Church understands the demands of the Gospel and how she asks for your collaboration, and you will never err in conceiving your missionary activity in this way.

4. But over and above the valued assistance you give to distant local Churches, you are in a position to make a stupendous contribution to your own people. As diocesan directors of the Society for the Propagation of the Faith working with your bishops in America, you can create a missionary mentality at home, enriching your own communities with that great truth so forcefully proclaimed by the Second Vatican Council: "The pilgrim Church is missionary by her very nature" (AG 2). By concentrating on this essential characteristic of the Church of Christ, and on the concrete consequences of this truth, you are offering

new horizons to the faithful, new challenges to their faith. And because we believe in the sovereign action of the Holy Spirit in the hearts of the faithful, we know that God's people respond generously to the lofty truth that they are called to live. And this great generosity of our people's faith and love is confirmed day after day by your pastoral experience and by mine.

In the very act of giving, your local Churches receive abundantly, just as Jesus predicted: "Give and it shall be given to you. Good measure pressed down, shaken together, running over..." (Lk. 6:38). Through a practical realization of the missionary nature of the universal Church, the local Churches themselves become truly strong and authentically post-conciliar. Being conscious of the need to adopt supernatural means to fulfill their missionary role, the local Churches become communities of prayer and intercession "that the word of the Lord may speed on and triumph..." (2 Thes. 3:1). Responding to grace, they open themselves to the immense needs of others, imposing on themselves a measure of restraint, frugality and sacrifice; above all, they become Churches on fire with the zeal of Christ the Head, who continues to exclaim in His members: "I must preach the Good News of the kingdom of God to the other cities also; for I was sent for this purpose" (Lk. 4:43).

MAINTAIN THE HIGH IDEALS
OF YOUR SPECIAL MISSION

5. It is my hope that you will always maintain those high ideals that correspond to your special mission in the Church. Having the personal conviction yourselves that you are working at something that is not peripheral but has lasting value and is essential to advancing the kingdom of God, try constantly to encourage your own fellow workers—those who work in your offices, as well as the great number of men, women and children in the parishes,

who have understood what Paul VI stated so succinctly: "Evangelizing is, in fact, the grace and vocation proper to the Church, her deepest identity" (EN 14).

Maintain, dear brother priests, with perseverance and deep joy, your missionary commitment to proclaiming, directly and indirectly, Jesus the risen Christ, the Son of the living God. And may Mary, Queen of the missions and Mother of priests, assist you by her prayers today and always.

INDEX

Daughters of St. Paul

IN MASSACHUSETTS
  50 St. Paul's Ave., Jamaica Plain, Boston, MA 02130;
    617-522-8911; 617-522-0875.
  172 Tremont Street, Boston, MA 02111; **617-426-5464;**
    617-426-4230.
IN NEW YORK
  78 Fort Place, Staten Island, NY 10301; **212-447-5071; 212-447-5086.**
  59 East 43rd Street, New York, NY 10017; **212-986-7580.**
  625 East 187th Street, Bronx, NY 10458; **212-584-0440.**
  525 Main Street, Buffalo, NY 14203; **716-847-6044.**
IN NEW JERSEY
  Hudson Mall — Route 440 and Communipaw Ave.,
  Jersey City, NJ 07304; **201-433-7740.**
IN CONNECTICUT
  202 Fairfield Ave., Bridgeport, CT 06604; **203-335-9913.**
IN OHIO
  2105 Ontario Street (at Prospect Ave.), Cleveland, OH 44115;
    216-621-9427.
  25 E. Eighth Street, Cincinnati, OH 45202; **513-721-4838;**
    513-421-5733.
IN PENNSYLVANIA
  1719 Chestnut Street, Philadelphia, PA 19103; **215-568-2638.**
IN VIRGINIA
  1025 King Street, Alexandria, VA 22314; **703-683-1741.**
IN FLORIDA
  2700 Biscayne Blvd., Miami, FL 33137; **305-573-1618.**
IN LOUISIANA
  4403 Veterans Memorial Blvd., Metairie, LA 70002; **504-887-7631;**
    504-887-0113.
  1800 South Acadian Thruway, P.O. Box 2028, Baton Rouge, LA 70821;
    504-343-4057; 504-381-9485.
IN MISSOURI
  1001 Pine Street (at North 10th), St. Louis, MO 63101; **314-621-0346;**
    314-231-1034.
IN ILLINOIS
  172 North Michigan Ave., Chicago, IL 60601; **312-346-4228;**
    312-346-3240.
IN TEXAS
  114 Main Plaza, San Antonio, TX 78205; **512-224-8101.**
IN CALIFORNIA
  1570 Fifth Ave., San Diego, CA 92101; **619-232-1442.**
  46 Geary Street, San Francisco, CA 94108; **415-781-5180.**
IN HAWAII
  1143 Bishop Street, Honolulu, HI 96813; **808-521-2731.**
IN ALASKA
  750 West 5th Ave., Anchorage, AK 99501; **907-272-8183.**

IN CANADA
  3022 Dufferin Street, Toronto 395, Ontario, Canada.

IN ENGLAND
  128, Notting Hill Gate, London W11 3QG, England.
  133 Corporation Street, Birmingham B4 6PH, England.
  5A-7 Royal Exchange Square, Glasgow G1 3AH, England.
  82 Bold Street, Liverpool L1 4HR, England.

IN AUSTRALIA
  58 Abbotsford Rd., Homebush, N.S.W., Sydney 2140, Australia.